Conservation and Development in Uganda

Uganda has extensive protected areas and iconic wildlife (including mountain gorillas), which exist within a complex social and political environment. In recent years Uganda has been seen as a test bed and model case study for numerous and varied approaches to address complex and connected conservation and development challenges. This volume reviews and assesses these initiatives, collecting new research and analyses both from emerging scholars and well-established academics in Uganda and around the globe. Approaches covered range from community-based conservation to the more recent proliferation of neoliberalised interventions based on markets and payments for ecosystem services.

Drawing on insights from political ecology, human geography, institutional economics, and environmental science, the authors explore the challenges of operationalising truly sustainable forms of development in a country whose recent history is characterised by a highly volatile governance and development context. They highlight the stakes for vulnerable human populations in relation to large and growing socioeconomic inequalities, as well as for Uganda's rich, unique, and globally significant biodiversity. They illustrate the conflicts that occur between competing claims of conservation, agriculture, tourism, and the energy and mining industries. Crucially, the book draws out lessons that can be learned from the Ugandan experience for conservation and development practitioners and scholars around the world.

Chris Sandbrook is Senior Lecturer in Geography and Director of the Masters in Conservation Leadership at the University of Cambridge, UK.

Connor Joseph Cavanagh is a Post-Doctoral Research Fellow in the Department of International Environment and Development Studies (Noragric), Norwegian University of Life Sciences.

David Mwesigye Tumusiime is Associate Professor, School of Forestry, Environmental and Geographical Sciences, Makerere University, Kampala, Uganda, and Director, Makerere University Biological Field Station, Uganda.

Earthscan Conservation and Development
Series Editor: W.M. (Bill) Adams, Moran Professor of
Conservation and Development, Department of Geography,
University of Cambridge, UK

This *Earthscan Conservation and Development* series includes a wide range of
inter-disciplinary approaches to conservation and development, integrating perspectives from both social and natural sciences. It includes textbooks, research
monographs and titles aimed at professionals, NGOs and policy-makers.

Conservation and Sustainable Development
Linking Practice and Policy in Eastern Africa
Edited by Jon Davies

Conservation and Environmental Management in Madagascar
Edited by Ivan R. Scales

Conservation and Development in Cambodia
Exploring Frontiers of Change in Nature, State and Society
Edited by Sarah Milne and Sanghamitra Mahanty

Just Conservation
Biodiversity, Well-being and Sustainability
Adrian Martin

Biodiversity Conservation in Southeast Asia
Challenges in a Changing Environment
Edited by Serge Morand, Claire Lajaunie and Rojchai Satrawaha

Conservation and Development in India
Reimagining Wilderness
Edited by Shonil Bhagwat

Conservation and Development in Uganda
*Edited by Chris Sandbrook, Connor Joseph Cavanagh and David
Mwesigye Tumusiime*

For more information about this series, please visit: www.routledge.com/
Earthscan-Conservation-and-Development/book-series/ECCAD

Conservation and Development in Uganda

Edited by Chris Sandbrook,
Connor Joseph Cavanagh and
David Mwesigye Tumusiime

Routledge
Taylor & Francis Group
LONDON AND NEW YORK

earthscan
from Routledge

First published 2018
by Routledge
2 Park Square, Milton Park, Abingdon, Oxon OX14 4RN

and by Routledge
52 Vanderbilt Avenue, New York, NY 10017, USA

First issued in paperback 2020

Routledge is an imprint of the Taylor & Francis Group, an informa business

British Library Cataloguing-in-Publication Data
A catalogue record for this book is available from the British Library

Library of Congress Cataloging-in-Publication Data
A catalog record has been requested for this book

ISBN 13: 978-0-367-58626-3 (pbk)
ISBN 13: 978-1-138-71092-4 (hbk)

Typeset in Sabon
by Swales & Willis Ltd, Exeter, Devon, UK

Contents

Acknowledgements   viii
List of contributors   x

PART I
Introduction   1

1 **Dynamics of uneven conservation and development
   in Uganda**   3
   CONNOR JOSEPH CAVANAGH, CHRIS SANDBROOK, AND
   DAVID MWESIGYE TUMUSIIME

2 **Histories and genealogies of Ugandan forest and wildlife
   conservation: the birth of the protected area estate**   16
   ABWOLI YABEZI BANANA, STEVE NSITA, AND ALLAN BOMUHANGI

3 **An overview of integrated conservation and development
   in Uganda**   45
   MEDARD TWINAMATSIKO, JULIA BAKER, PHIL FRANKS, MARK INFIELD,
   FANNY OLSTHOORN, AND DILYS ROE

PART II
**Celebrity sites and case studies of conservation,
development practice, and research**   59

4 **Bwindi Impenetrable National Park: a celebrity site for
   integrated conservation and development in Uganda**   61
   DAVID MWESIGYE TUMUSIIME, ROBERT BITARIHO, AND
   CHRIS SANDBROOK

5 Managing the contradictions: conservation, communitarian
   rhetoric, and conflict at Mount Elgon National Park   85
   DAVID HIMMELFARB AND CONNOR JOSEPH CAVANAGH

6 Budongo Forest: a paradigm shift in conservation?   104
   FRED BABWETEERA, CHRISTOPHER MAWA, CAROLINE ASIIMWE,
   ERIC OKWIR, GEOFFREY MUHANGUZI, JOHN PAUL OKIMAT, AND
   SARAH ROBINSON

PART III
Conservation and development approaches in policy
and practice   123

7 An environmental justice perspective on the state of
   Carbon Forestry in Uganda   125
   ADRIAN NEL, KRISTEN LYONS, JANET FISHER, AND
   DAVID MWAYAFU

8 Parks, people, and partnerships: experiments in the
   governance of nature-based tourism in Uganda   148
   WILBER M. AHEBWA, CHRIS SANDBROOK, AND AMOS OCHIENG

9 Cultural values and conservation: an innovative approach
   to community engagement   171
   MARK INFIELD AND ARTHUR MUGISHA

PART IV
Cross-sectoral dynamics and their links to conservation
and development   187

10 Conservation and agriculture: finding an optimal balance? 189
   KATY JEARY, MATT KANDEL, GIULIANO MARTINIELLO, AND
   RONALD TWONGYIRWE

11 Lost in the woods? A political economy of the 1998 forest
   sector reform in Uganda   206
   JON GEIR PETURSSON AND PAUL VEDELD

12 Dialectics of conservation, extractives, and Uganda's
   'land rush'   226
   PATRICK BYAKAGABA, BASHIR TWESIGYE, AND LESLIE
   E. RUYLE

PART V
Conclusion 247

13 **Conservation, development, and the politics of ecological knowledge in Uganda** 249
CONNOR JOSEPH CAVANAGH, CHRIS SANDBROOK, AND DAVID MWESIGYE TUMUSIIME

Index 265

Acknowledgements

This book has been many years in the making, and would not have been possible without the help and support of many people and organisations.

First, we thank those who have provided funding for the work that has gone into this book. Bringing decades of knowledge together into one volume for the benefit of Ugandan people and institutions was a central aim of this whole book project, and we are profoundly grateful for the funding that has assisted us in making progress towards this goal. The Cambridge Africa Partnership for Research Excellence (CAPREx), which is funded by the Carnegie Corporation of New York, the ALBORADA Trust and the Isaac Newton Trust, generously funded an authors' workshop in Kampala early in the project, which allowed us to bring together most of the Ugandan contributors to the book, along with a few others from further afield. This was immensely useful in setting the direction for the collection and ensuring that we had the right people involved and topics covered. They have also kindly agreed to fund a book launch event in Kampala. The Department of International Environment and Development Studies (Noragric) at the Norwegian University of Life Sciences (NMBU) generously provided funding to allow us to purchase a number of copies of the book for free distribution to key actors in Uganda. Also, NMBU provided an international leave mobility grant that allowed the second co-editor (Connor J. Cavanagh) to visit the Cambridge Conservation Initiative and Department of Geography, University of Cambridge, in 2016, which greatly facilitated collaboration at a crucial early stage of the writing process.

We thank all those who have contributed to the quality of the work contained within this volume. Tim Hardwick and Amy Johnston at Routledge were kind enough to accept our proposal, and have been helpful at every step of the process (including allowing us to miss a few deadlines). Bill Adams, as editor of the book series, provided excellent advice at the proposal stage. Ivan Scales, lead editor of a former book in the series, also provided very helpful advice on how to manage the editorial process. Abwoli Banana, Pål Vedeld, and Jon Geir Petursson provided sage advice at various critical junctures, drawing on their decades of academic and consultancy experience in Uganda and East Africa. Lisa Naughton provided some very useful ideas that we drew on in Chapters 1 and 13. In Uganda, Runyararo Jolyn Rukarwa provided valuable advice on how to handle the editorial process and gave useful views on the content of several of the book chapters. Mnason Tweheyo – Dean, School of Forestry, Environmental and Geographical Sciences at Makerere University – generously supported the printing of chapter drafts. We would particularly like to thank all the lead and co-authors of the chapters for their hard work. They are a wonderful group representing probably hundreds of years of relevant collective experience in Uganda, and we feel very lucky and proud to have brought their work together in this volume. Along the way we have chased some of them mercilessly, and we thank them for their patience and cooperation!

Finally, we would like to thank our close friends and family for putting up with all the field trips, phone calls and late nights that have gone into this book. We are immensely grateful, and hope the sacrifice has been worth it.

Contributors

Editor biographies

Connor Joseph Cavanagh is a Research Fellow in the Department of International Environment and Development Studies (Noragric), Norwegian University of Life Sciences, Norway. Connor's research and publications explore the political ecology of conservation and development interventions, with a focus on land and resource tenure conflicts and the institutional evolution of laws, regulations, and policies for governing both ecosystems and rural populations. Recent articles have appeared in *Environment and Planning D, Antipode*, the *Journal of Peasant Studies*, and *Geoforum*.

David Mwesigye Tumusiime is an Associate Professor of Environment and Natural Resources in the School of Forestry, Environmental and Geographical Sciences (SFEGS) of Makerere University, Uganda, and is the Director of Makerere University Biological Field Station. He has interdisciplinary training at both Masters and PhD levels from the Norwegian University of Life Sciences, Norway, and has extensive experience and interest in research on human dimensions of natural resource management drawing on perspectives from a variety of fields including sociology, economics, and political ecology. He has conducted research and provided graduate training on these dimensions for over ten years. He is a member of several academic, conservation, and community service boards in Uganda and the region. He is also a part-time farmer.

Chris Sandbrook is a Senior Lecturer in Geography at the University of Cambridge, UK, and Director of the MPhil in Conservation Leadership. He is a political ecologist with diverse research interests around a central theme of biodiversity conservation and its relationship with society. His research activities include: (i) investigating the relationship between conservation and development at the landscape scale in developing countries, (ii) investigating the role of values and evidence in shaping the decisions of conservationists and their organisations, and (iii) investigating the social and political implications of new technologies for conservation.

Chris carried out his PhD research at Bwindi Impenetrable National Park in Uganda in 2004 to 2005, and has continued to work in the country through various consultancy, PhD and collaborative projects ever since.

Author biographies

Wilber Ahebwa is an Associate Professor in the Department of Forestry, Biodiversity and Tourism, Makerere University, Uganda. He is the current Continental Coordinator of the Association of Leisure and Tourism Training Institutions (ATLAS) Africa. Dr Ahebwa is also the Coordinator of the East African Network for Sustainable Tourism (EANST). He holds a PhD in Tourism, Conservation and Development from Wageningen University, The Netherlands, an MSc in Tourism and Environment from Wageningen, a Bachelor degree in Tourism Management from Makerere University (Uganda), and he has completed a postdoctoral visit to the University of Cambridge, UK. His research interests fall in the following broader themes: Sustainable Tourism; Tourism, Conservation and Development; Entrepreneurship in Tourism; Tourism Business Management; as well as Tourism Planning and Policy Analysis. He has published widely and is a reviewer with a number of reputable international journals.

Caroline Asiimwe is a wildlife veterinarian at Budongo Conservation Field Station, Uganda, where she also serves as the conservation coordinator. Asiimwe has a Bachelors degree in Veterinary Medicine and a Masters degree in Public Health from Makerere University, Uganda. She is currently pursuing a Masters of Veterinary Science in Conservation Medicine with the University of Edinburgh, UK. Asiimwe believes that conservation challenges are complex and require holistic transdisciplinary approaches to monitor and combat them for the benefit of sustainable biodiversity conservation. With most conservation threats anthropogenic in origin, development of local people's livelihood could be looked at as a conservation strategy. Her motivation is to have a healthy planet.

Fred Babweteera is an Associate Professor at Makerere University, Uganda, and the Director of Budongo Conservation Field Station, Uganda. He holds a DPhil and an MSc (Distinction) Forest Science, Policy and Management, University of Oxford, UK. With over 20 years' experience in teaching biologists and managing multidisciplinary conservation programmes around the Budongo landscape, his work focuses on blending multidisciplinary research projects and conservation initiatives to generate pragmatic solutions to sustainable management of protected areas. He is a member of the Commonwealth Forestry Association and International Union of Forest Research Organisation Governing Councils. He is also a member of IUCN Species Survival Commission Primate Specialist Group and the *International Forestry Review Journal* Editorial Board.

Julia Baker has worked in Uganda since 2000, undertaking her PhD research on integrated conservation and development initiatives at Bwindi Impenetrable National Park. Julia was a co-author on the 'Mt Gorillas versus Development? Assessing 15 years of Integrated Conservation and Development at Bwindi' publication. She has also worked on a variety of research and ICD projects, including as Research Advisor to the International Institute of Environment and Development on their Darwin Initiative-funded project, which resulted in the Uganda Wildlife Authority agreeing to increase the amount of the mountain gorilla tourism levy that is shared with local communities.

Abwoli Yabezi Banana is a Professor of Forestry, School of Forestry, Environmental and Geographical Sciences, at Makerere University, Uganda. He holds a Bachelor's degree in Forestry from Makerere University (1977), a MSc degree in Wood Science and Technology from the University of California, Berkeley (1979) and a PhD degree in Forestry from the Australian National University (1985). He has taught Forestry at Makerere University for the last 40 years. He is a founding member of the International Forestry Resources research program (IFRI) established in 1993. As co-leader of the Uganda IFRI Collaborating Center, he established a forest monitoring programme aimed at understanding how forest governance arrangements and institutions shape forest outcomes and livelihoods of forest-adjacent communities in Eastern Africa.

Robert Bitariho is currently a director of the Institute of Tropical Forest Conservation, Mbarara University of Science and Technology, Uganda. His education, work and research experience has been majorly in the fields of environmental sciences, natural resource management and wildlife conservation. He holds a PhD degree in Environment and Natural Resource Management and is an Associate Professor of Mbarara University of Science and Technology. Robert has a wide experience in research on natural resource management spanning a period of over 18 years working in the Albertine rift region Protected Areas. He also lectures in Natural Resource Management and GIS at Mbarara University of Science and Technology.

Allan Bomuhangi holds a PhD in Environment and Natural Resources Management from Makerere University, Uganda (2018), an MSc in Agroforestry (2011) and a Bachelor's degree in Community Forestry (2007). He is currently consulting for the World Bank's Africa Gender Innovation Lab, where he provides technical support to the unit's impact evaluation studies in Uganda, Zambia, and Nigeria that seek to generate evidence on how to close the gender gap in productivity and assets. Prior to joining the World Bank, Allan taught at Makerere University as an adjunct faculty for five years. His research interests are in gender, land policy, forest governance and climate change adaptation.

Patrick Byakagaba holds a PhD in Forestry from Makerere University, Uganda. He acquired an MSc in Natural Resource Management and Sustainable Agriculture from the Norwegian University of Life Sciences, Norway, and a BSc in Forestry from Makerere University. He is currently a Lecturer at the Department of Environmental Management, Makerere University, where he teaches courses including environmental governance assessment and monitoring, natural resource policies, trade and environment, forestry and development and conflict resolution in natural resource management. His research focus is in ecological governance. He is a member of the Uganda Forest Governance Learning group and the Natural Resources Civil Society Organisation Network of Uganda. He has been on several working groups in national policy and planning processes in the environment and natural resources sub-sector in Uganda.

Janet Fisher is an environmental social scientist interested in the links between environmental change, environmental management and human development. She has two strands of research. The first uses ecosystem services concepts (that focus on the various benefits humans derive from nature) as a basis for interdisciplinary work with natural and social scientists to understand how the environment supports human well-being. In the second research strand, she is interested in understanding how the increasing use of ecosystem services concepts and associated policies, which are often market-based, are changing conservation practice.

Phil Franks is a Senior Researcher at the International Institute for Environment and Development, London, and an expert on the social dimension of natural resource management and conservation and related development efforts with more than 25 years' experience in Africa, Asia and Latin America supporting project design and implementation, and facilitating relevant action research and learning. He is currently working on the development of low-cost methods for assessing the social impacts and governance of protected areas, applying social equity principles to conservation, strengthening conservation–development linkages, and the better understanding and managing of the trade-offs between food production and the conservation of forests and woodlands in sub-Saharan Africa.

David Himmelfarb is an Instructor of Environmental Studies at Eckerd College in St Petersburg, Florida. He completed his PhD in Anthropology at the University of Georgia in 2012. He has been researching conservation-related conflict and the long-term socio-economic consequences of involuntary displacement on Mt Elgon, Uganda, since 2005. He has also carried out projects in Vietnam and the US South, exploring food insecurity, livelihoods, land rights, and perceptions of climate change. His present research focuses on how innovative economic, agricultural, and educational practices can contribute to a more socially just and environmentally sustainable world.

Mark Infield graduated with a degree in Zoology in 1980, and since then Mark has worked in nature conservation for NGOs and governments. Working mainly in the field, he developed an understanding of how communities effect and are affected by conservation and helped develop and implement innovations in the way protected area managers engage with communities. He has spent 20 years advising the Uganda Wildlife Authority on community conservation and cultural values approaches to protected areas.

Katy Jeary is currently completing her PhD in Geography at the University of Cambridge, UK, where her research investigates how land-use policies designed to minimise the trade-offs between biodiversity conservation and agricultural production affect food security and poverty in western Uganda. She previously worked at the policy and advocacy group Agriculture for Impact, a Bill and Melinda Gates Foundation initiative, researching and communicating strategies to improve small-holder agriculture as a means of tackling food insecurity in sub-Saharan Africa. She has an honours degree in Biology, a Master's degree in Environmental Technology, specialising in Ecological Management, and has spent time volunteering and working in conservation and agriculture in Namibia and East Africa.

Matt Kandel is a Visiting Scholar in the African Studies Center at Boston University, USA. From 2016–2018 he was a British Academy Newton International Fellow in Development Studies at SOAS, University of London, UK. His research focuses on land tenure, agrarian change, conflict, peacebuilding, and the impact of environmental change on rural livelihoods in Africa. He is particularly interested in how land – or, more specifically, access to and control over land – lies at the nexus of agrarian change and conflict in Africa. His work draws on the ethnographic research that he has conducted in northeastern Uganda since 2012 and has been published in journals such as *African Affairs, Journal of Peasant Studies*, and *Journal of Modern African Studies*. He has also written shorter articles on land-related issues in Africa for blogs such as *Africa Up Close*, published by the Africa Program at the Woodrow Wilson Center. His PhD in Anthropology was completed in 2014 at the City University of New York, USA.

Kristen Lyons is an Associate Professor in Environment and Development Sociology in the School of Social Science at the University of Queensland, Australia. With over 20 years' research, teaching and service experience, she is committed to delivering positive social change on national and international issues that sit at the intersection of sustainability and development. Kristen works in Africa, the Pacific and Australia, and her work is grounded in a rights-based approach.

Giuliano Martiniello is currently an Assistant Professor at the American University of Beirut, Lebanon. Giuliano obtained his PhD from the School of Politics and International Studies at the University of Leeds, UK, in 2011. He was a research fellow at the Makerere Institute of Social Research at Makerere University (2012–2015) and a post-doctoral research fellow at the School of Built Environment and Development Studies at the University of Kwazulu-Natal (2013–2014). He is broadly interested in the political economy, political sociology and political ecology of agrarian change and rural development in Africa. His articles have been published in internationally recognised journals such as *World Development, Journal of Peasant Studies, Third World Quarterly* and the *Review of African Political Economy*.

Christopher Mawa is an Assistant Lecturer in the Department of Extension and Innovation Studies, College of Agricultural and Environmental Sciences, Makerere University, Uganda. He holds a Double Master's of Science degree in Forestry from University of Joensuu (now University of Eastern Finland), Finland, and the University of Freiburg, Germany, and a Bachelor's degree in Community Forestry from Makerere University, Uganda. He is currently pursuing a PhD in Environment and Natural Resources at Makerere University. Christopher's expertise and research interests are in natural resource governance, rural livelihoods and agroforestry.

Arthur Mugisha, a forester by profession, has studied and worked in the field of natural resources management. He has a Master's degree in natural resources and environmental policy from London University College, UK, and a PhD in natural resources management from the University of Florida, Gainesville, USA. He has worked in government in the national parks service where he served as the Executive Director of Uganda Wildlife Authority, among other positions, and with international conservation organisations. He is a Director of AIMMGreen Ltd, a private consulting company on natural resources conservation and development. He serves on different governing boards of conservation organisations. He is an expert in policy formulation and community mobilisation.

Geoffrey Muhanguzi is Manager at Budongo Conservation Field Station, Uganda. He has over 15 years' practice and management experience in conservation of savanna and tropical forest landscapes having worked in areas around Lake Mburo national park, the Bwindi Mgahinga conservation area and Budongo forest reserve. Geoffrey has worked in the Budongo landscape for close to ten years and has successfully overseen projects on human–wildlife conflict management, advocacy for household livelihoods and conservation of natural habitats amidst a fast-growing population. He has a keen interest in sustainable natural resource management for communities that bear the costs of conservation around protected areas.

David Mwayafu holds an MSc Forestry and a BA Environment Management degree and has over ten years' experience. He has worked on various projects at the Uganda Coalition for Sustainable Development (UCSD). David is particularly interested in action research on issues of sustainable development that affect the rural livelihood and development, natural resources management, climate change adaptation and mitigation – especially REDD+ discourse and low carbon development pathways; strategic planning and projects/program development; and technical capacity building and training for skills and knowledge enhancement in sustainable development and natural resources management.

Adrian Nel is a senior lecturer in Geography at the College of Agriculture, Engineering and Science at the University of Kwazulu-Natal, South Africa. Prior to this he held a Visiting Scholar position with the Institute for Development Studies at the University of Sussex, UK, and a research associate position with the Institute for Development Studies at the National University of Science and Technology (NUST) in Bulawayo, Zimbabwe. Adrian researches and teaches in Political Ecology, focusing on contemporary human–environment relations in Southern and Eastern Africa.

Steve Nsita holds a Bachelor's degree in Forestry from Makerere University, Uganda, obtained in 1979. He worked in Uganda's Forestry Department for 25 years, Uganda National Forestry Authority for five years, and became a private consultant in 2008, specialising in forestry. During his professional work, Mr Nsita was mostly involved in responsible management of Uganda's natural forests, helping to improve management practices, developing guidelines for professional management of all types of forests in Uganda, and working with local communities. Over the span of his professional life, Mr Nsita has evaluated many forestry-related development projects in Uganda, and he has been involved in forestry research and training. This brought him face to face with policy development and forest governance assessment.

Amos Ochieng holds an MSc in Leisure, Tourism and Environment from Wageningen University, The Netherlands. He is currently an Assistant Lecturer in the Department of Forestry, Biodiversity and Tourism, Makerere University, Uganda. Amos is also currently finalising his PhD studies at the Cultural Geography and Forest and Nature Conservation Policy Groups at Wageningen University, The Netherlands. His current research focuses on the use of sport hunting to promote tourism, conservation and development.

John Paul Okimat is a Junior Research Fellow at Budongo Conservation Field Station, Uganda. His background is in forestry and his interests are mainly ecological aspects of forest ecosystems, feedbacks between conservation and social-ecological systems, and statistical and mechanistic modelling of ecological systems. He is currently undertaking a Master of Science in Tropical Forestry at the Institute of International Forestry and Forest Products, Dresden University of Technology, Germany.

Eric Okwir is a Junior Research Fellow at Budongo Conservation Field Station, Uganda. He is passionate about wildlife conservation and improving the livelihoods of marginalised communities bordering tropical forests. His work is driven by the belief that as people destroy nature, they destroy themselves. Recently, he has implemented livelihoods improvement projects and studied their impact in communities surrounding the Budongo forest reserve. His current research focusses on effectiveness and adoption of alternative crops as wildlife deterrents. Eric graduated from Makerere University, Uganda, with a Bachelor's degree in Wildlife Health and Management, where he is currently pursuing a Master of Science in Environment and Natural Resources. When not busy in the communities surrounding Budongo, Eric spends his time reading books and exploring his computer.

Fanny Olsthoorn is an ecologist with a passion for epidemiology. She completed her thesis for a MSc degree in Conservation Science in the rainforests of Bwindi national park, carrying out forest surveys and interviews on resource use in the park. Through this work, she discovered the multiple and intricate interdependencies between natural areas and the residents who lived in its surroundings, whether these are food, fuel, income or health. She is now further exploring human–nature interdependencies related to health as she is pursuing a PhD at the ETH Zurich with fieldwork in the Scottish Highlands, exploring the effect of woodland expansion plans on tick populations and Lyme disease risk.

Jon Geir Petursson is an Associate Professor (part time) in Environmental Governance at the Environment and Natural Resources Programme, Faculty of Social and Human Sciences, University of Iceland, doing research in social policy, institutional economics, livelihoods and environmental governance. Jon Geir has an interdisciplinary background with a PhD (NMBU Norway) in Environment and Development studies with a focus on institutional aspects of environmental and natural resources governance in Uganda, and degrees in Forestry (MSc, SLU Sweden) and Biology (BSc, UI Iceland). His work experience beyond academia is within government, consultancies and the NGO sector. He has extensive experience from Uganda since his first visit in 1994, including fieldwork, research, consultancies, student supervision, institutional collaboration and capacity-building programmes.

Sarah Robinson lives in Edinburgh, UK. After graduating with degrees in Zoology and Polar Studies from the University of Aberdeen, UK, and the University of Cambridge, UK, respectively, she initially worked as a zoologist for the British Antarctic Survey. Following this, Sarah joined the

Royal Zoological Society of Scotland (RZSS) where she worked for ten years on a variety of species conservation projects. This included supporting the Budongo Conservation Field Station for which she later became a member of the Board of Directors. She currently works for NASCO, an inter-governmental organisation established under the Convention for the Conservation of Salmon in the North Atlantic Ocean.

Dilys Roe is a principal researcher at the International Institute for Environment and Development (IIED), a sustainable development think-tank based in London. Dilys leads the IIED's work on biodiversity, which focuses on integrating social concerns into conservation policy and practice; supporting community-based approaches to biodiversity management; and mainstreaming biodiversity into development policy. She has written extensively on community-based natural resources management; "pro-poor" conservation; biodiversity conservation and poverty reduction; and, more recently, illegal wildlife trade. During her 20+ years at IIED, Dilys has also been seconded to the UK Department for International Development as a consultant biodiversity advisor. Dilys has a PhD in Biodiversity Management from the Durrell Institute for Conservation and Ecology, University of Kent, UK.

Leslie E. Ruyle is an ecologist working cross-disciplinarily to create innovative solutions for conservation, conflict, and development. She holds a PhD in Ecology from the University of Georgia, USA, has served as a Peace Corps Volunteer in Ghana, and managed university-based initiatives for NSF and USAID. She has experience in applied conservation and research at the Savannah River Ecology Laboratory, Smithsonian Tropical Research Institute, Panama, the Honduran Coral Reef Foundation, the Applied Biodiversity Science Program, Earthwatch, and at the Center on Conflict and Development. She is the Assistant Director at Scowcroft Institute of International Affairs in the Bush School of Government and Public Service at Texas A&M University, USA. She teaches courses on Natural Resource Policy; Gender, International Development, and Environmental Conflict; and a capstone course on development initiatives.

Bashir Twesigye is currently the Executive Director of the Civic Response on Environment and Development, Uganda. He is an Advocate of the High Court of Uganda. He holds a Bachelor's degree in Law from Makerere University, Uganda, and a Postgraduate Diploma in Legal Practice from the Law Development Center. He has over ten years' experience in research and advocacy in the environment and natural resources sector, including oil and minerals governance programmes. He is a member of professional bodies including the East African Law Society and the Uganda Law Society, where he contributes to the Land Law Cluster. He previously served on the National Land Policy Working Group – a task force that spearheaded the formulation of the National Land Policy for Uganda.

Medard Twinamatsiko is a Development Conservationist with 12 years of progressive research and academic engagement. He has a PhD in Policy Management and Natural Resource Governance. He is a Lecturer and Senior Researcher in the Department of Environment and Livelihood Support System at Mbarara University of Science and Technology, Uganda. His passion is in policy engagement and research uptake for Natural Resource Governance. He has done several research projects around protected areas in the Albertine rift and is recently participating in developing an equity framework in protected area management with colleagues in UK.

Ronald Twongyirwe is a senior lecturer at Mbarara University of Science and Technology, Uganda. He obtained his PhD from the University of Cambridge in 2015. He also possesses a couple of Masters degrees: an MPhil in Environmental Science, University of Cambridge, UK, and an MSc in Environment and Natural Resources, Makerere University, Uganda; and a BSc in Agriculture (Land Use and Management), Makerere University. His research interests lie in modelling socio-ecological systems; understanding complex (rural/urban) land use, vegetation and hydrological interactions; biodiversity conservation; emerging (debates on) climate change adaptation and mitigation strategies at both the local and international levels (e.g., REDD+); governance and environmental systems; soil and environmental science and policy.

Paul Vedeld is an institutional economist within agriculture, resource and development studies. He holds a Masters degree in Natural Resource Management and a PhD in Resource, Agriculture and Development Economics from UMB (now called the Norwegian University of Life Sciences (NMBU)), Norway. Apart from working at NMBU, he has been a Norwegian farm hand, a development worker in India and an advisor in the Norwegian parliament. He has been a local politician for 20 years. His main fields of interest are governance and policy analysis, biodiversity and climate change, livelihood and poverty studies, general development studies and theoretical issues around interdisciplinarity. Paul has extensive experience within the environmental and natural resources sector in Uganda.

Part I
Introduction

1 Dynamics of uneven conservation and development in Uganda

Connor Joseph Cavanagh, Chris Sandbrook, and David Mwesigye Tumusiime

Introduction

On the 15th of August 2006, former Executive Director of the Uganda Wildlife Authority (UWA) Moses Mapesa published an op-ed piece in one of Uganda's leading daily newspapers, the *New Vision*, entitled '[President] Museveni's defence of wildlife is good news'. Mapesa's article was intended to bolster public support for the country's forest and wildlife conservation agencies in the aftermath of a controversial eviction of refugee Basongora pastoralists from Queen Elizabeth National Park. In short, Mapesa's (2006, p. 2) argument in support of these and similar evictions was both straightforward and compelling. As he put it:

> To illustrate the importance of wildlife and its contribution to the national economy, I will use the gorilla, buffalo and elephant. Every individual gorilla in Bwindi Impenetrable National Park earns Uganda US $100,000 (sh180m) per year and creates employment for 30 people. Which individual Ugandan living near a National Park can raise that amount of money? Each buffalo contributes $20,000 (sh36m) and elephant $30,000 (sh54m). None of our indigenous livestock or even cross breeds livestock can contribute that much. A cow producing 20 litres of milk per day would yield at most only sh11m, all factors held constant.

Notably, Mapesa's position here was not merely that conservation must be pursued because of the intrinsic value of Uganda's storied flora and fauna, but rather because of their increasingly valuable contribution to national processes of economic growth and development. Associated evictions, then, were ostensibly not a matter of state prejudice against 'squatters' or 'encroachers' within protected areas, but simply rather a matter of prudence and concern for both sustainability and prosperity at the national scale.

From the perspective of contributions to state coffers and the gross domestic product, the logic of this position would to some perhaps seem beyond reproach. Today, Uganda reports a GDP per capita of approximately 615 US dollars, and nearly a quarter of the population lives below the 'poverty headcount ratio' of $1.90 per day (World Bank, 2018). Conversely, the tourism sector – which continues to be dominated by conservation-related wildlife ecotourism – contributes an estimated nine percent of Ugandan GDP (Kamukama, 2016), and is currently projected to grow at a rate of at least 7 percent per annum until 2027 (World Travel and Tourism Council, 2017). In this context, it seems unlikely that many evictees from the country's protected areas would have retained much hope of economically outperforming a buffalo – much less a mountain gorilla – had they remained in place.

The zoologist S.K. Eltringham (1994) once questioned whether wildlife might reasonably be expected to 'pay its own way' in the face of alternative – and potentially more lucrative – land uses. Although mountain gorillas might indeed contribute US $100,000 per year to Uganda's economy, many other forms of 'non-charismatic' flora and fauna in other parts of the country stand to 'earn' far less. Moreover, an equally pressing question today seems to be whether rural Ugandan *citizens* can 'pay their own way', or contribute sufficiently to national economic growth in order to avoid being displaced by either conservation or, similarly, more profitable forms of land and resource utilization.

In this sense, the contemporary geographies of conservation in Uganda – much like the geographies of 'development' more broadly (e.g., Smith, 1984) – are increasingly both uneven and dynamic, and it is both this unevenness and this dynamism that many of the contributions to the present volume address. Notably, these geographies of conservation are determined not only by the intrinsic value of diverse flora and fauna, but also by their variable economic appraisal and valuation in relation to a range of competing interests and land uses. These range from subsistence agriculture, foraging, and pastoralism, to artisanal or small-scale resource extraction, to lucrative oil and mineral developments. Hence, whilst thousands of rural Ugandans have faced eviction from various forest reserves and national parks over the last several decades (National Forestry Authority, 2011), conservationists themselves have also experienced a degree of relative 'displacement' in some instances. Here, notable cases include oil extraction within Murchison Falls National Park and Queen Elizabeth National Park (MacKenzie et al., 2017; Byakagaba et al., this volume, Chapter 12), as well as in other protected areas found within western Uganda's oil- and mineral-rich Albertine Graben (Wildlife Conservation Society, 2018). Consequently, one of the principal aims of this book is to explore and assess the implications, stakes, and consequences of such variable economic, political, and social (re)valuations for both conservation and development outcomes in the country.

Conservation and (sustainable) development: opportunities, challenges, and trade-offs

It is generally not disputed that conservation efforts of some kind are both warranted and urgently necessary in many of Uganda's rich and diverse ecosystems, notwithstanding important debates about the character, performance, and (in)justices of actual conservation practices in the country (e.g., Nel and Hill, 2013; Cavanagh and Benjaminsen, 2014; Lyons and Westoby, 2014). The territory now known as Uganda is effectively an intersection of several major African biomes, denoting that it hosts the wide array of flora and fauna associated with each of these.[1] Ugandan flora and fauna populate often-spectacular landscapes that range from the snow-capped Rwenzori mountains, to the vast Lake Victoria, to extinct volcanoes such as Mount Elgon or savannah and dryland ecosystems in the country's north. Consequently, recent estimates posit – to take just two examples – that approximately 7.5 percent of mammals and 10.2 percent of bird species currently recognized are present within Uganda, despite its relatively small size at only about 0.18 percent of the Earth's terrestrial and freshwater surface (USAID, 2006). The country is also home to 159 threatened species on the IUCN Red List, including '38 plants, 21 mammals, 18 birds, 6 amphibians, 54 fishes, 10 molluscs and 12 [. . .] other invertebrates' (Republic of Uganda, 2016, p. 14), as well as more than half of the world's remaining population of some 900 mountain gorillas or *Gorilla beringei beringei.*

In an effort to halt the loss of biodiversity and conserve existing species richness, large swathes of Uganda's terrestrial surface have been placed under the protection of two national conservation agencies – the Uganda Wildlife Authority (UWA) and the National Forestry Authority (NFA) – as well as a range of local government services (Banana et al., this volume, Chapter 2; Petursson and Vedeld, this volume, Chapter 11). The national parks, forest reserves, wildlife reserves, and other protected areas governed by these agencies number about 712, and at present encompass approximately 243,145 km² of land, or at least 16.1 percent of Uganda's surface area (UNEP-WCMC, 2018). These protected areas contain more than 30 percent of all forest in Uganda, including 1.9 million hectares of forests legally designated as the country's 'Permanent Forest Estate (PFE)'. The latter, moreover, is intended to be conserved 'in perpetuity' rather than harvested and regenerated (Ministry of Water and Environment, 2016).

Despite these measures, biodiversity continues to decline at an officially estimated rate of 10–11 percent per decade (Ministry of Water, Lands, and Environment, 2003), and deforestation processes appear to continue unabated in some parts of the country. For instance, Pomeroy et al. (2017) maintain that Uganda lost nearly half of its biodiversity value between 1975 and 1995. This is thought to largely be due to political instability and subsequent governance challenges associated with the authoritarian regimes of Presidents Idi Amin and Milton Obote, as well as the civil war that brought current President Yoweri Museveni to power in 1986 (Turyahabwe and Banana, 2008). Although the effectiveness of conservation governance has since improved in relative terms, the situation is highly variable across different regions of the country, where hotspots of deforestation and ecosystem degradation apparently remain intransigent. As Jeary et al.

(this volume, Chapter 10) note, this is not unrelated to the fact that agri-culture contributes nearly a quarter of GDP and almost 70 percent of employment in rural Ugandan households, denoting that there are nearly always potential trade-offs between conservation and agricultural land uses.

Recent efforts to conserve biodiversity in Uganda must still be understood in the context of the country's highly tumultuous governance and develop-ment history. This is marked by long periods of civil war and authoritarian rule (Kasozi, 1994); insurgencies by the Lord's Resistance Army in the north (Dunn, 2004) and the Allied Democratic Forces in the Rwenzori border-lands (Titeca and Vlassenroot, 2012); extra-territorial military engagements in South Sudan, Somalia, and the Democratic Republic of Congo (Clark, 2001; Fisher, 2012); and a domestic stance on democracy and human rights that has variously won Uganda's government both admiration and admoni-tion from Western countries and civil society organisations (e.g., Dicklitch and Lwanga, 2003; Boyd, 2013). The governance of many sectors, includ-ing conservation, is also influenced by ongoing processes of decentralisation across Uganda, which have seen the number of districts (the largest sub-national administrative unit) increase from only 16 in 1959 to more than 121 as of 2018 (Ministry of Local Government, 2018). Each of these dis-tricts understandably retains its own unique political *milieu*, with both local politicians and conservationists influenced to varying extents by the interests of local citizens, businesses, and civil society organisations.

Contemporary development policy also simultaneously promotes the growth of ecologically deleterious forms of extractive industry in Uganda and the rise of large-scale commercial agribusiness. However, prevailing environment and development policies continue to frame rural *communities* as perhaps the most pressing threat to both protected areas and ecosystems more generally. Such a conceptualisation owes much to neo-Malthusian concerns about population growth, and is both explicitly and implicitly enshrined at the highest levels of the country's economic and social devel-opment institutions. For instance, alongside neighbouring Kenya's national *Vision 2030* strategy and Rwanda's *Vision 2050* (see Mosley and Watson, 2016), Uganda's *Vision 2040* aspires to 'a transformed Ugandan society from a peasant to a modern and prosperous country', and one that enjoys 'sustain-able wealth, employment, and inclusive growth'. Here, growing populations of impoverished 'peasants' and other rural communities are associated with high levels of natural resource dependence, and such dependence is in turn associated with increased demand for or strain upon land and protected natural resources. As a recent assessment from the National Environmental Management Agency (2016, p. 57) succinctly puts it, the 'high population growth rate has increased demand for resources from the protected areas for agriculture leading to encroachment on tourism areas; increased illegal activities especially poaching; and increased human-wildlife interface lead-ing to conflicts'. In short, all of these factors are perceived as threatening to conservation efforts for both biophysical and economic reasons.

Conversely, efforts toward some iteration of sustainable development in the country are still urgently necessary. Indeed, the United Nations Development Programme's (2016) Human Development Index currently ranks Uganda in 163rd place out of 188 nations, denoting that the country is 'tied' in this assessment with Haiti, and is only one place above the war-stricken Republic of Sudan. Life expectancy at birth, although improving, is still only 59.2 years, and Ugandan children on average receive only 5.7 years of formal education (ibid). Similarly, the official deforestation rate is 1.8 percent per annum, again allegedly due primarily to a rapidly growing population, high rates of rural poverty, and widespread dependence upon natural resources for energy, building materials, and other basic needs (National Forestry Authority, 2011). In response, the Government of Uganda has now committed itself formally to a 'green growth' development strategy, one that aims to simultaneously 'deliver inclusive economic and social outcomes while protecting natural capital, addressing climate change, creating jobs and accelerating economic growth' (see Republic of Uganda, 2017, p. 8).

Key to this latter strategy is improving access to education and vocational training so as to diversify 'peasant' and other rural livelihoods into a range of professions that are not as closely tied to the exploitation of the natural resource base. Yet the construal of these livelihoods as at once both anti-modern and unsustainable links contemporary 'green' development policies with a long tradition of fundamentally colonial tropes and narratives (see also Adams, 2009). These often consist – as Benjamin Gardner (2017, p. 1) recently put it – of Westerners and other 'modern' elites ostensibly 'saving African wildlife [and flora] while also saving Africans from themselves'. The voices of ordinary Ugandans are indeed often conspicuously absent from most national plans and policies for protecting biodiversity, reversing deforestation, and facilitating 'green growth' in the country. The fact remains, however, that the agency of rural communities throughout East Africa has in practice often subverted the grand ambitions of colonial and post-colonial initiatives for conservation and economic development (Bunker, 1987; Feierman, 1990; MacKenzie, 1998; Anderson, 2002; Cavanagh and Benjaminsen, 2015). It is precisely this occasional incongruence between vision and execution – or between discourse and practice (Benjaminsen and Svarstad, 2010) – in conservation and development initiatives that many of the contributions to this volume examine in great detail.

The contribution of this book

As the discussion above makes clear, Uganda has an important story to tell about the often problematic intertwining of conservation and development agendas. Fortunately, many researchers have investigated aspects of this story and published their work in a wide range of both scholarly and more popular outlets. However, there has been a notable lack of any attempt to bring the different threads of Uganda's conservation and development story together in one place. Consequently, writings on environment and development in Uganda have occasionally spoken *past* rather than directly *to* the extant literature on the same geographical-empirical context, arguably limiting progress in the state of knowledge on these themes. In turn, this has somewhat impeded the emergence of a coherent knowledge base for use by practitioners and policymakers in government, multilateral organisations, and donor agencies.

This volume seeks to address this gap. In offering the first book-length treatment of conservation and development issues in Uganda, it seeks to achieve three main goals. First, the book collects together the work of a range of Ugandan and international scholars, from multiple disciplines, and creates a platform for their work to be considered as part of a common enterprise. Second, it offers a single reference point on conservation and development in Uganda, hopefully reducing the future risk of researchers missing the important work of those in whose footsteps they follow. Finally, by bringing many of the threads of the story together, it enables previously somewhat latent or implicit connections between conservation and development processes to be explicitly highlighted at multiple scales, allowing for an enhanced and enriched understanding of the co-evolution of conservation and development processes, as well as trade-offs between them.

Outline of the book

The book proceeds in five parts and 13 chapters, which introduce and analyse multiple sites across Uganda (Figure 1.1).

In the remainder of the introductory **Part I**, Banana et al. (Chapter 2) offer critical historical context to contemporary environment and development challenges in Uganda by outlining the evolution of institutions for forest and wildlife conservation in the country. In doing so, they focus on both continuities and discontinuities between the colonial (1896–1963), early post-colonial (1963–1986), and contemporary periods (1986–present) of conservation governance. Each of these periods has been marked by significant shifts in terms of the objectives, structure, and intended beneficiaries of conservation institutions. Yet, despite these fluctuations, the chapter draws particular attention to the ways in which monitoring and enforcement has constituted a recurring problem regardless of the specific set of institutions and policy objectives in place, and relates these challenges to the governance of Uganda's contemporary protected area estate.

Concluding **Part I**, Twinamatsiko et al. (Chapter 3) provide an overview of the crucial role of explicitly *integrated* conservation and development projects and policies in Uganda. Drawing on the authors' wealth of firsthand experience, the chapter reviews the history of such activities in Uganda from their earliest days, revealing how they were first developed and then spread around the country, and some of the successes and challenges associated

1. Murchison Falls National Park
2. Budongo Forest Reserve
3. Mount Elgon National Park
4. Rwenzori Mountains National Park
5. Kibale Forest National Park
6. Bwindi Impenetrable National Park
7. Lake Mburo National Park

Figure 1.1 A map of Uganda showing some of the key sites analysed by chapters in this book. These are Chapter 4 (site 6); Chapter 5 (3); Chapter 6 (2); Chapter 7 (3, 5); Chapter 8 (6, 4, 5, 7); Chapter 9 (4, 7); Chapter 10 (2); Chapter 11 (3, 4, 6); Chapter 12 (1). Several of these chapters also include material from other sites as well as cross-cutting issues, as do Chapters 2, 3, 11, and 13.

Source: kindly created with the assistance of the Department of Geography, University of Cambridge.

with their implementation. This provides the context for many of the chapters that follow, particularly those in Part III.

Part II, 'Celebrity sites and case studies of conservation, development practice, and research', explores the ways in which three sites within Uganda have risen to prominence within the international conservation and development sphere, being cited regularly as positive and negative examples of environmental management (or both). These sites have been exceptionally well studied, from a range of different epistemological perspectives, which allows for a rich understanding of how changing ideas about conservation and development have played out in practice.

Firstly, Tumusiime et al. (Chapter 4) examine how Bwindi Impenetrable National Park (BINP) became perhaps one of the most well-known and well-studied protected areas in Africa, and a laboratory for approaches that seek to integrate conservation and development. In part, this is due to the residence of approximately half of the world's remaining population of mountain gorillas (*Gorilla beringei beringei*) within the park (and the opportunities for ecotourism that this presents), in close proximity to a dense human population facing significant development challenges. Despite attaining the status of what we might term a 'celebrity site', researchers have occasionally reached vastly different – and sometimes even opposing – conclusions about the relationship between the park and neighbouring populations. Exploring such divergences and the both methodological and epistemological differences that underpin them, Tumusiime and colleagues review debates about conservation and development at BINP, extracting important lessons and insights.

Second, Himmelfarb and Cavanagh (Chapter 5) survey the trajectory of environmental protection on eastern Uganda's Mount Elgon from the British colonial era to the present, with a special focus on how conservation managers' ways of seeing and territorialising the landscape have been reflected in the often conflicted relationships between the protected area and local communities. Though Mount Elgon lies physically and politically on the margins of the Ugandan state, the shifting conservation policies enacted there provide insight into broader trends in the development and contestation of conservation in Uganda; the politics of colonial and post-colonial state-making; and the challenges of enacting effective and socially just conservation interventions. Indeed, the case of Mount Elgon illuminates quite clearly the ways in which the success of conservation institutions often depends upon their perceived legitimacy and resulting support from local populations.

Thirdly, Fred Babweteera et al. (Chapter 6) present a case study of Budongo Forest Reserve on the edge of the western Rift Valley, which is one of Uganda's largest reserves at approximately 825 km^2. Like many protected areas originally gazetted during the colonial period, Budongo also evinces a checkered history of use and protection, and uneven conflict and collaboration between communities and conservation authorities. This chapter reviews studies of efforts to ameliorate such conflicts, with a particular emphasis on recent initiatives to support alternative and forest-friendly livelihoods amongst the local population. Such initiatives are of particular importance for countering the prevalence of local and regional networks for illegally exploiting both forest and wildlife resources within the reserve.

Part III, 'Conservation and development approaches in policy and practice', examines the various conservation and development 'tools' that have been implemented in Uganda; several of which have subsequently been widely adopted around the world. These range from community-based conservation (CBC), to integrated conservation and development projects (ICDPs), to the more recent proliferation of neoliberalised conservation interventions based on the creation of new markets and payments for carbon sequestration or ecosystem services. In many cases the performance of these have been exceptionally well studied, providing a rich understanding of how particular approaches to conservation and development came to be adopted in Uganda, and how they have played out in practice.

First, Nel et al. (Chapter 7) analyse Uganda's experience with various modes of both carbon forestry and related payment for ecosystem service (PES) schemes. These include afforestation/reforestation projects associated with the Clean Development Mechanism (A/R CDM), voluntary carbon markets (VCM), and nascent Reducing Emissions from Deforestation and Degradation (REDD) schemes. In doing so, the chapter demonstrates how attention to notions of justice can contribute to a fuller understanding of the reactions of people to carbon forestry and other PES projects, as well as the pathways and ultimate outcomes of such interventions.

Second, Ahebwa et al. (Chapter 8) start by noting that – in recent years – the tourism sector has frequently contributed more than 9 percent of Uganda's GDP. Given its importance to the national economy, it is hardly surprising that tourism has played a crucial role in the story of efforts to integrate conservation and development goals in Uganda. They highlight the diverse range of partnership-based governance models that have been implemented in different sites, analysing how these have contributed to positive or negative outcomes for people and wildlife on the ground. They find surprising similarities across seemingly diverse governance models, and highlight the important role of the private sector in shaping outcomes.

Third, Infield and Mugisha (Chapter 9) report on the outcomes of a new 'cultural values' and rights-based approach to conservation and development that these co-authors have led in Uganda over the last several years. The chapter emphasises the need to harmonise conservation institutions with local cultural values, and highlights the resulting identification of synergies rather than trade-offs between the interests of conservationists and local communities. The benefits of adopting such an approach are illustrated with experiences and examples from several protected areas in Uganda that the authors have recently engaged with in their programme of work.

In the book's penultimate **Part IV**, 'Cross-sectoral dynamics and their links to conservation and development', the contributors examine the crucial role of major productive sectors of the Ugandan economy in shaping conservation and development policies and outcomes, whether directly or indirectly. These dynamics are crucial for understanding the fundamentally uneven nature of conservation and development processes in Uganda, which entail often rapidly shifting valuations of land and natural resources both for conservation as well as for alternative land uses.

First, Jeary et al. (Chapter 10) explore the interface between conservation and agriculture in Uganda, where farming accounts for an estimated

24 percent of Uganda's GDP, 48 percent of exports and 68 percent of household income. It is, however, a sector often at odds with the aims of conservation. Agriculture drives the conversion of land to farmland, fragmenting or isolating habitats and changing connectivity patterns, biotic and abiotic environments. Large-scale land acquisitions are also altering social patterns leading to unrest and, in some cases, displacement. Interventions intended to meet both agricultural development demands, driven by the country's increasing food needs, and to address a declining supply of natural resources, habitats, and wildlife, are few and far between. Where implemented, however, such programmes of work have had mixed success in terms of their long-term economic and social viability, sustainability, and real benefits for people and conservation. The implementation, beneficiaries, and outcomes of such interventions are discussed in order to draw lessons and provide future direction.

Second, Petursson and Vedeld (Chapter 11) draw on their own lengthy consultancy and academic research experience in Uganda to explore the troubled institutional history of the forestry sector. The authors illuminate how the development of state institutions for forest and wildlife conservation is influenced both by particular economic and political histories and through engagement with a range of bilateral donors and other transnational actors. Examining the nature of such influence, this chapter traces the emergence of Uganda's National Forestry Authority (NFA) from the late 1990s onward. In doing so, it notes the ways in which different transnational actors – especially American and European donors – influenced the character and mandate of the organisation, as well as its approach to the management of forest reserves on the ground. In particular, the chapter highlights the implications of this institutional pedigree for subsequent controversies related to informality and corruption, the outsourcing of forest conservation activities to non-state actors, and debates about illegitimate land acquisitions.

Lastly, Byakagaba et al. (Chapter 12) take a close look at the social and environmental implications of how, over the last decade, the Ugandan state has invested significant resources to secure its emergence as an oil-exporting country. To do so, it has engaged a range of multinational firms to pursue the exploration, appraisal, and extraction of oil resources, and especially so from the western or Albertine Rift Valley. In the process, however, these activities have brought certain companies and branches of the state into conflict with both conservation institutions and local communities, as such initiatives have sometimes occurred within or adjacent to ecologically sensitive protected areas. Accordingly, this chapter illustrates such controversies with a particular focus on Murchison Falls National Park in western Uganda, highlighting conflicts and contestations between communities, conservationists, state agencies, and oil industry firms within this process.

In a final concluding chapter, the three co-editors provide a brief summary and synthesis of the contributions to the volume. In doing so, we highlight points of recurring debate and contention throughout the chapters, as well as lessons that can potentially be drawn from these. Throughout, we focus on (i) the often 'experimental' or trial-and-error nature of many conservation and development interventions in Uganda over time, (ii) the politics of ecological knowledge evinced in often contending accounts of conservation and development outcomes, and (iii) the significance of cross-sectoral and transnational dynamics in shaping the latter. We conclude by pointing to emerging key questions and themes of increasing importance in conservation and development research. Most recently, this has been underscored by the tensions and opportunities presented by new imperatives to mainstream previous iterations of conservation and 'sustainable development' initiatives within a more holistic 'green growth' or 'green economy' paradigm, even as concerns about social and environmental (in)justices of older initiatives for many remain largely unresolved.

Note

1 It is also suggested that several of Uganda's forests have also been Pleistocene refugia (Hamilton, 1976; Linder, 2001).

References

Adams, W.M. (2009) *Green Development: environment and sustainability in a developing world*, third edition, Routledge, London, UK, and New York, NY, USA.

Anderson, D. (2002) *Eroding the Commons: the politics of ecology in Baringo, Kenya 1890–1963*, James Currey, Oxford, UK.

Benjaminsen, T.A. and Svarstad, H. (2010) 'The death of an elephant: conservation discourses versus practices in Africa', *Forum for Development Studies*, vol. 37, no. 3, pp. 385–408.

Boyd, L. (2013) 'The problem with freedom: homosexuality and human rights in Uganda', *Anthropological Quarterly*, vol. 86, no. 3, pp. 697–724.

Bunker, S.G. (1987) *Peasants Against the State: the politics of market control in Bugisu, Uganda, 1900–1983*, University of Illinois Press, Chicago, USA.

Cavanagh, C. and Benjaminsen, T.A. (2014) 'Virtual nature, violent accumulation: the 'spectacular failure' of carbon offsetting at a Ugandan National Park', *Geoforum*, vol. 56, pp. 55–65.

Cavanagh, C.J. and Benjaminsen, T.A. (2015) 'Guerrilla agriculture? A biopolitical guide to illicit cultivation within an IUCN Category II protected area', *Journal of Peasant Studies*, vol. 42, no. 3–4, pp. 725–745.

Clark, J.F. (2001) 'Explaining Ugandan intervention in Congo: evidence and interpretations', *The Journal of Modern African Studies*, vol. 39, no. 2, pp. 261–287.

Dicklitch, S. and Lwanga, D. (2003) 'The politics of being non-political: human rights organizations and the creation of a positive human rights culture in Uganda', *Human Rights Quarterly*, vol. 25, pp. 482–509.

Dunn, K.C. (2004) 'Uganda: The Lord's resistance army', *Review of African Political Economy*, vol. 31, no. 99, pp. 139–142.

Eltringham, S.K. (1994) 'Can wildlife pay its way?', *Oryx*, vol. 28, no. 3, pp. 163–168.

Feierman, S. (1990) *Peasant Intellectuals: anthropology and history in Tanzania*, University of Wisconsin Press, Madison, WI, USA.

Fisher, J. (2012) 'Managing donor perceptions: contextualizing Uganda's 2007 intervention in Somalia', *African Affairs*, vol. 111, no. 444, pp. 404–423.

Gardner, B. (2017) 'Elite discourses of conservation in Tanzania', *Social Semiotics*, vol. 27, no. 3, pp. 348–358.

Hamilton, A.C. (1976) 'The significance of patterns of distribution shown by forest plants and animals in tropical Africa for the reconstruction of the upper Pleistocene palaeoenvironments: a review', in E.M. van Zinderen-Bakker Sr (ed.), *Palaeoecology of Africa, The Surrounding Islands, and Antarctica*, Balkema, Cape Town, South Africa.

Kamukama, E. (2016) 'Tourism earns economy Shs 7.3b', *Daily Monitor*, 24 October, www.monitor.co.ug/Business/Tourism-earns-economy-Shs7-3b/688322-34269 38-8gtid1z/index.html, accessed 17 January 2018.

Kasozi, A.B.K. (1994) *The Social Origins of Violence in Uganda, 1964–1985*, McGill-Queens University Press, Montreal and Kingston, Canada.

Linder, H.P. (2001) 'Plant diversity and endemism in sub Saharan tropical Africa', *Journal of Biogeography*, vol. 28, no. 2, pp. 169–182.

Lyons, K. and Westoby, P. (2014) 'Carbon colonialism and the new land grab: plantation forestry in Uganda and its livelihood impacts', *Journal of Rural Studies*, vol. 36, pp. 13–21.

MacKenzie, C.A., Fuda, R.K., Ryan, S.J., and Hartter, J. (2017) 'Drilling through conservation policy: oil exploration in Murchison Falls Protected Area, Uganda', *Conservation and Society*, vol. 15, no. 3, pp. 322–333.

MacKenzie, F. (1998) *Land, Ecology, and Resistance in Kenya, 1880–1952*, Edinburgh University Press, Edinburgh, UK.

Mapesa, M. (2006) 'Museveni's defence of wildlife is good news', *New Vision*, 15 August, www.newvision.co.ug/new_vision/news/1142794/museveni-eur-defence-wildlife-news, accessed 10 January 2018.

Ministry of Local Government (2018) *Ministry of Local Government Fact Sheet*, www.molg.go.ug/sites/default/files/MoLG%20-%20%20Fact%20Sheet.pdf, accessed 18 January 2018.

Ministry of Water and Environment (2016) *State of Uganda's Forestry 2016*, Ministry of Water and Environment, Kampala, Uganda.

Ministry of Water, Lands, and Environment (MWLE) (2003) *National Biomass Study*, MWLE, Kampala, Uganda.

Mosley, J. and Watson, E. (2016) 'Frontier transformations: development visions, spaces and processes in Northern Kenya and Southern Ethiopia', *Journal of Eastern African Studies*, vol. 10, no. 3, pp. 452–475.

National Environmental Management Agency (2016) *National State of the Environment Report for Uganda*, National Environmental Management Agency, Kampala, Uganda.

National Forestry Authority (2011) *Assessment of Trends of Evictions from Protected Areas During the Period 2005–2010, and Their Implications for REDD+*, National Forestry Authority, Kampala, Uganda.

Nel, A. and Hill, D. (2013) 'Constructing walls of carbon – the complexities of community, carbon sequestration and protected areas in Uganda', *Journal of Contemporary African Studies*, vol. 31, no. 3, pp. 421–440.

Pomeroy, D., Tushabe, H., and Loh, J. (2017) *The State of Uganda's Biodiversity 2017*, National Biodiversity Data Bank, Makerere University, Kampala, Uganda.

Republic of Uganda (2016) *National Biodiversity Strategy and Action Plan II (2015–2025)*, National Environmental Management Agency, Kampala, Uganda.

Republic of Uganda (2017) *The Uganda Green Growth Development Strategy 2017/18–2030/31*, National Planning Authority, Kampala, Uganda.

Smith, N. (1984) *Uneven Development: Nature, Capital, and the Production of Space*, Blackwell, Oxford, UK.

Titeca, K. and Vlassenroot, K. (2012) 'Rebels without borders in the Rwenzori borderland? A biography of the Allied Democratic Forces', *Journal of Eastern African Studies*, vol. 6, no. 1, pp. 154–176.

Turyahabwe, N. and Banana, A.Y. (2008) 'An overview of history and development of forest policy and legislation in Uganda', *International Forestry Review*, vol. 10, no. 4, pp. 641–656.

United Nations Development Programme (2016) 'Human development index and its components', http://hdr.undp.org/en/composite/HDI, accessed 17 January 2018.

UN Environment Programme-World Conservation Monitoring Centre (2018) 'Uganda: protected areas coverage', www.protectedplanet.net/country/UG, accessed 18 January 2018.

US Agency for International Development (USAID) (2006) *Uganda Biodiversity and Tropical Forest Assessment*, USAID, Washington, DC, USA.

Wildlife Conservation Society (2018) 'The developing oil industry in Uganda', https://uganda.wcs.org/Initiatives/Oil-Development.aspx, accessed 18 January 2018.

World Bank (2018) 'Uganda: data', https://data.worldbank.org/country/uganda, accessed 10 January 2018.

World Travel and Tourism Council (2017) *Travel and Tourism Economic Impact 2017: Uganda*, World Travel and Tourism Council, London, UK.

2 Histories and genealogies of Ugandan forest and wildlife conservation

The birth of the protected area estate

Abwoli Yabezi Banana, Steve Nsita, and Allan Bomuhangi

Introduction

This chapter outlines the evolution of institutions for forest and wildlife conservation in Uganda, with a focus on both continuities and discontinuities between the colonial organization and growth phases (1896–1963), early post-colonial consolidation and collapse phases (1963–1986), and contemporary reorganization phase (1986–present). Each of these periods has been marked by significant shifts in terms of the objectives, structure, and intended beneficiaries of conservation institutions with markedly different outcomes for local people (including indigenous people, e.g., Benet, Ik and Batwa) and conservation. Yet, despite these fluctuations, this chapter draws particular attention to the ways in which protected areas were created and how boundary maintenance, monitoring, law enforcement and benefit sharing have constituted a recurring problem regardless of the specific set of institutions and policy objectives in place, and relates these challenges to the governance of Uganda's contemporary protected area estate.

The pre-colonial period

At the turn of the twentieth century, tropical moist forests were the most dominant vegetation type in central and western Uganda, whilst savannah woodlands were dominant in northern and eastern Uganda. Tree cover was estimated to be over 45% of the country (Webster and Osmaston, 2003). Despite the rich biodiversity and long history of sedentary settlement, cultivation and pastoralism, there has been very little historical account of how land/wildlife/forest resources were managed during the pre-colonial period in Uganda. Colonial administrators often downplayed the ability of indigenous peoples in Africa to manage their environment (Fairhead and Leach, 1996; Kjekshus, 1996; Reid, 2011) and often misread the extent of, and drivers of, deforestation and degradation. However, Uganda's oral history is rich with examples of indigenous knowledge used to manage land/wildlife/forest resources. For example, land ownership and use was administered by traditional chiefs and clan leaders on behalf of the communities (Gombya-Ssembajjwe et al., 2001), sacred groves with strict access and harvesting rules were set aside, possibly for 'conservation', in the various regions of Uganda (Gombya-Ssembajjwe, 1997), while wild animals were respected and were widely used as totems for the different clans and could therefore not be hunted for food (Roscoe, 2015). Specific tree species were extensively used for rituals and sacrifice and had rules for accessing them and fines for non-compliance, e.g., the Nakayima tree in Mubende District of Uganda (Okello, 2002). *Ficus natalensis* and *F. brachypoda* tree species were traditionally managed for bark cloth and boundary demarcation in Buganda (Vogt et al., 2006). Fires were routinely used to manage pastures and control pests and diseases for cattle and wildlife in general. There is no doubt that, at the turn of the twentieth century, various indigenous communities in Uganda had put in place land/wildlife/forest resources management strategies so that they could live in harmony with their environment as was the case in other communities in Eastern Africa.

Prior to the turn of the twentieth century, the priority of the British colonial administration was to bring large areas of present-day Uganda under their control as part of the Uganda Protectorate. However, during this period the British Colonial/Foreign offices were already concerned with the indiscriminate slaughter of the larger wild animals such as elephants and hippopotamus by European travelers in the East Africa Protectorate (Kenya) and Uganda Protectorate (Cioc, 2009). Orders-in-Council were issued beginning in 1896 pertaining to wildlife, land, and forest management in East Africa (Kamugisha, 1993). Hunting laws were introduced in British East Africa in 1897 and soon after to the Uganda Protectorate so that the "big game" would not disappear from the British Protectorate (Cioc, 2009). For example, in an attempt to control killing of young elephants, customs rules in both Kenya and Uganda authorised the confiscation of elephants' tusks that were less than five kilograms. An international hunting treaty, the 1900 London Convention, was negotiated with various colonial powers in the region and became the basis for the establishment of game reserves in sub-Saharan Africa (Cioc, 2009).

Given the high forestry and wildlife potential observed within the newly-formed Uganda Protectorate, the colonial government established the Scientific and Forestry Department in 1898, and renamed it the Forestry Department in 1917. The major objective of the department was to secure large areas of state-owned land (Crown land) under forest cover for forest preservation and management of both tropical and savannah woodlands and afforestation activities. A large area under forest cover was viewed by the colonial administrators as necessary in order to maintain favourable climatic conditions suitable for crop production, facilitate water catchment, control soil erosion in fragile ecosystems, and provide timber and fuelwood for industrial transformation or domestic use (Vogt et al., 2006).

Efforts to actively manage wildlife in the Uganda Protectorate started in 1923 following the establishment of the Elephant Control Department (Meredith, 2003), established to control the population of elephants and minimise damage to crops. The department was renamed the Uganda Game and Fisheries Department in 1924.

The evolution of institutions for forest and wildlife conservation in Uganda during the colonial period can be divided into three phases; the organisation, growth, and consolidation phases (Kambugu et al., 2013). These phases are briefly described below.

Organization phase: securing land for protected areas (1896–1930s)

The birth of the protected area estate in Uganda can be traced to the 1900 Buganda Agreement and the related agreements with the Kingdoms of Toro (1900) and Ankole (1901), and later the Crown Land Ordinance of 1903 (Nsita, 2014). The Buganda Agreement specifically emphasised that forests on Crown land were to be of continuity (one-half square mile or more in extent [Thomas and Spencer, 1938; Sangster 1950]). Where no private claim could be raised justifiably, these lands would then be reserved for government control and maintained as woodland in the general interests of the country (Uganda Protectorate, 1900 Buganda Agreement). Local resistance to the loss of rights to manage land in Buganda was muted because the chiefs and Kingdom officials (traditional leadership) were beneficiaries of the Buganda Agreement as they were allocated large expanses of land in perpetuity under the mailo land tenure system with rights to manage all the resources found on those lands (Nyende, 2011).

In other parts of Uganda, where no formal agreements existed, the colonial government under the Protectorate laws appropriated areas suitable for forest and wildlife conservation, allegedly 'after consultation' with local chiefs, as Crown land. Thus, the British Protectorate administration declared large areas of woodlands and tropical high forests in Uganda as Crown land – in other words, the colonial government nationalised most of the land. This policy took away ownership and management rights from the indigenous people and left them with 'privileges' of a subsistence nature.

During the early twentieth century, Uganda experienced epidemics of sleeping sickness, rinderpest and smallpox up until the mid-1930s. The areas where these epidemics occurred were depopulated as entire communities were evicted/transferred to other areas of Uganda not affected by these diseases. The disruption of social and economic activities allowed the population of wild animals to increase and vegetation to change significantly (Reid, 2011). The Protectorate administration declared some of these areas as game/forest reserves. Consequently, the displaced peoples (agricultural, pastoral and fishing communities) could not return to their ancestral lands following the eradication of the epidemics. The descendants of these people still lay claim to the ownership of these lands. The game reserves created following the epidemics include Lake George Game Reserve – present-day Queen Elizabeth National Park (1906) – Murchison Falls (1926) and

Toro game reserve (1932) – present-day Semuliki National Park. The forest reserves whose creation can be traced to the outbreak of sleeping sickness include Bukaleeba Forest Reserve in South Busoga, Busowe, Lutoboka and Bunjazi Forest Reserves in Sssese Islands. Thus the outbreak of epidemics also played a major role in the birth of the protected area estate in Uganda.

After securing land for the protected area estate, gazettement of the protected areas, production of forest policy, and boundary delineation and demarcation did not commence until the end of 1920s. There are several factors that explain the considerable delay in delineating boundaries of the protected areas and production of the necessary policies and laws.

First, Uganda's tropical moist forests and savannah woodlands are unique in the tropics since they are located between the lowland forests of the Congo and West and Central Africa and the woodland savannahs of Eastern Africa. Within the British administration, knowledge about the ecology and biodiversity of these forests and woodlands was limited, yet it was essential for preparation of the policies and management plans.

Second, the colonial government made a deliberate decision to delay boundary delineation and demarcation of the protected areas until mapping of private (mailo and freehold) land and public land were completed (Vogt et al., 2006). Survey and delineation of private land commenced in 1904 and was not completed until 1936. Boundary delineation of private (mailo and freehold) land was costly and took a long time to complete due to the limited number of cartographers, the tedious and inadequate surveying technologies available then, and the highly fragmented and irregularly shaped boundaries of private lands and forest patches earmarked for the establishment of the protected areas. For example, a 700 km² forest reserve in Buganda had a total boundary length of 1,432 km. A similarly sized forest reserve, but occurring in one block, would have a boundary of 105 km (Webster and Osmaston, 2003).

Third, there were limited numbers of staff in the colonial administration, and most of them were British expatriates with limited knowledge of tropical forestry and wildlife management. For most of the period between 1900 and the 1920s, the newly formed Scientific and Forestry Department employed only one or two expatriate staff (Webster and Osmaston, 2003). With limited staff and funding, no clear forest policy was developed. Harvesting of forest produce, mainly rubber and timber – mahogany (from Budongo), *Milicia excelsa* (from the grasslands of Busoga) and *Podocarpus spp* (from Sango Bay forests) – was the main forest management activity undertaken. Most of the timber was produced by pitsawying.

Growth phase: policy development, boundary demarcation, and delineation (1930–1950)

The growth phase started with approval of the first forest policy in Uganda in 1929. The 1929 Forest Policy led to an increase in funding and recruitment of more expatriate staff, including the appointments of a new Chief Conservator of Forestry, and of W. J. Eggeling, a forest ecologist. These two foresters are remembered for revitalising the Forestry Department. They were instrumental in initiating ecological research, gazettement and demarcation of reserve boundaries, formulation of policies and laws and preparation of forest management plans. Most of the large forests such as Mabira, Budongo, Sango Bay, Bwindi, Maramagombo, and Bugoma were demarcated during this period.

Early research efforts involved species identification, forest succession, regeneration, timber stock and growth rates (Esegu and Ndemere, 2002). Permanent sample plots were established throughout the major forest eco-systems to study forest ecology (Sheil et al., 2000). Silvicultural research included salvage felling, selective logging, clear felling and enrichment planting. This research provided useful information that led to the design of appropriate silvicultural systems for increasing regeneration in harvested forest reserves. The colonial Forest Department was concerned with the slow regeneration of valuable tree species such as *Podocarpus milanjianus, Entandrophragma spp., Khaya anthoceca, Alstonia spp., Lavoa trichiliodes* and many others. Wood properties of various valuable timber tree species were studied for promoting the wood industry that had started earlier in the organisation phase. Unfortunately, no research was conducted in the use of indigenous knowledge in the management of forestry resources.

Towards the end of this phase, and based on research findings, the 1929 Forest Policy was revised and a new one was gazetted in 1948. The new policy emphasised production forestry to meet the forest products needs of the people of Uganda and the establishment of an export trade. Thus the 1948 Forest Policy made the foundation for:

- completion of demarcation and delineation of forest reserves;
- preparation and enactment of the 1947 Forests Act to streamline the management of the forest sector, including harvesting regulations and trade;
- the first attempt to decentralise the management of forests to native (local governments) and local communities;
- capacity building of Ugandans at technical and professional levels in order to increase the workforce and to Africanise the forest service;
- expansion of the wood industry to meet the timber demand stimulated by the Second World War;
- the establishment of forest plantations to relieve pressure from the natural forests and to meet the predicted shortfall of log supply from the natural forests in the coming decades.

Outcomes for conservation for this period

Considerable advances were made in putting in place structures and institutions for forest management. First, extensive ecological studies had been completed and the relationship between harvest management and regeneration success had been established. In addition, inventory methods to assess growth rates and yield levels had been developed. Several books on tropical forestry ecology had been published, for example, *The Indigenous Trees of Uganda Protectorate* (Eggeling and Dale, 1951). Also, a new Forest Policy based on knowledge acquired from two decades of research had been put in place.

Second, during this period forest tenure regimes, under which forestry resources could be held and forest products accessed, were established. The 1947 Forests Act and the 1948 Forest Policy put in place the following forest and tree tenure regimes.

1   Central Forest Reserves (CFRs) under the control of the Chief Conservator of Forests.
2   Local Forest Reserves (LFRs) under the control of a local authority appointed by the Minister.
3   Village forests declared by a local authority on any lands occupied by a community within its jurisdiction. The forests were managed and controlled by bodies or persons appointed by the local authority.
4   Forests on open lands (public land) from where forest produce could be used under license issued by the Chief Conservator of Forests, or, where a local authority had been declared to have an adequate forest estate, the relevant local authority could issue the license.

In addition to defining the various forest tenure regimes, the Act defined rules and regulations for accessing forest products from forest reserves by local communities. For example, the Act provided forest use privileges for local people to harvest some forest produce for 'their own personal domestic use in reasonable quantities', but they could also get a license to harvest forest produce for other purposes.

It is important to emphasise the fact that the 1947 Forests Act and the 1948 Forest Policy weakened the customary tenure rights of the forest communities in contrast to the prevailing forms of pre-colonial customary rights. The Act and Policy provided privileges rather than rights to the local people. The issue of limited rights to forestry resources still persists today. The only legally recognised rights for local communities in the current Forest Act are the rights to collect dry wood, dry bamboo and water for personal domestic use (Naluwairo, 2015) as was the case in all previous Acts.

Furthermore, the 1947 Forest Act defined the role of the central and local governments in the management of forestry resources in order to legally implement the concept of Local Forest Reserves, introduced under the 1938 amendment of the Forests Ordinance and the Village Forest Reserves introduced in 1947. By the end of this phase, a total of 1,636,095 hectares of forests had been gazetted as CFRs and 162,000 hectares as LFRs. The total forest area under village forests and forests on open lands is not reported, possibly because most of the forests under these tenure regimes were not yet surveyed.

According to Vogt et al. (2006), very limited conflicts arose between the local communities, landlords and the Forest Department in Buganda Kingdom during the process of boundary demarcation and delineation. This was attributed to the way boundaries were established and maintained. For example, the boundaries of private land had already been mapped and separated from Crown land. As a result, establishment of forest reserve boundary points and markers were witnessed and agreed upon by neighbouring private (*mailo*) land owners, clan heads, local leaders, and administrators. Second, the chiefs and clan leaders who would have raised complaints to the colonial government had already been given many square miles of land for their use in perpetuity.

Although it was expensive, funds were available to the Forest Department to regularly re-open the boundaries using local labour. To ensure that the reserve boundaries were known and respected by everyone across subsequent generations, the Department planted *luwanyi* (*Dracaena sp.*) shrubs and *mutuba* (*Ficus natalensis*) and *F. brachypoda* tree species along the reserve boundaries, as was the practice of boundary delineation among the Baganda during the pre-colonial period (Mukwaya, 1953). In our view, it could be argued that most forest reserve boundaries in Buganda Kingdom were clearly defined and considered as legitimate by all stakeholders at the time of demarcation. This is in agreement with Ostrom's (1990) design principle characterising long-enduring common pool resources.

Outcomes for local people

The colonial government needed to keep large areas of land under forest cover in order to maintain favourable climatic conditions suitable for crop production, water catchment, and soil erosion control in fragile ecosystems. This provided a good base for the production of agricultural raw materials that were of interest to the colonial administration (Nyende, 2011). According to Nyende, natives were mobilised to produce agricultural products on their farms. The forest reserves were also to provide timber and fuelwood for the emerging middle class and for industrial transformation.

Often, boundary delineation and demarcation of both private and government forest and wildlife reserves in several countries led to violent displacement of small-holder farmers with culturally recognised user-access rights (Allen, 1992; Guha, 1985; Baland and Platteau, 1996). However, in Buganda, landlords with private *mailo* properties did not evict smallholders living on their properties as long as they paid *mvujjo* (tributes of produce) and *busulu* (labour) to the landlords. Similarly, demarcation and delineation of the protected areas by the colonial forest administration in Buganda and in other parts of the country did not lead to widespread displacement of communities. Crown land earmarked for the establishment of the protected area estate in 1900 was assumed to be devoid of people. A few smallholder farmers with justifiable claim on Crown land were allowed to stay on the land, forming enclaves of private land within the protected areas. Forest dwellers, such as the Ndorobo and Benet in Sebei sub-region on Mt Elgon and the Batwa in the Afromontane forest reserves in south-western Uganda, were allowed by the colonial Forest Department to continue residing in the forests according to their cultural norms, although as a privilege rather than as rights-bearing owners of land and forests.

However, the creation of forest and game reserves in areas formerly infested with tsetse flies and rinderpest led to permanent displacement of entire communities of smallholder farmers, pastoralists, and fishermen, and the loss of their culturally recognised user-access rights. Attempts by these communities to return to their ancestral lands were strongly resisted by the Protectorate administrators.

During the precolonial period, local communities derived their livelihood from forested land and savannah grasslands. They harvested forest foods, firewood, building materials and plant medicines. They hunted and grazed their livestock in the savannahs. These lands were also used for shifting cultivation and for other cultural and spiritual activities. Use and access rights were vested in clan heads, chiefs and traditional leaders. Therefore, scholars point out that demarcation and delineation of forest reserves effectively took away the rights of the indigenous people on their own land, and left them only with 'privileges' of a tenuous nature, which could be revoked at the Governor's pleasure (Nsita, 2014).

Other scholars, on the other hand, point out that, at the time of closure of the protected areas, there was a limited local market for forest produce since Uganda's population was still small. At the time, there were fewer than 2 million people and use of trees by local communities was confined to building poles, firewood and herbal medicines for subsistence use. Therefore, there were limited resource-use conflicts in the early 1930s. Most of these products could be obtained from private land and farmlands under fallow.

Consolidation phase: the birth of Local Forest Reserves, national parks, economic prosperity, and world prominence in forest management (1951–1963)

During this period, Uganda had a prosperous economy based on the export of coffee, cotton and copper. Although the colonial government was preparing the country for independence, most of the country was politically stable (except Buganda region). Thus the colonial government was keen to develop the country's infrastructure, transfer responsibilities to local governments, and build local administrative capacity. The country achieved independence in 1962 and, unlike neighbouring Kenya, transfer of power from the colonial administrators was smooth and peaceful.

Although the economy was based on agriculture and mining, forest management was given a high priority and was well funded. Most of the strategies and programmes specified in the 1948 Forest Policy were funded and implemented during this period. The most important activities undertaken included:

- strengthening of the native (local) governments to establish and manage local forest reserves;
- establishment of national parks;
- expanding technical and professional level training of Ugandans in order to Africanise the forest service following achievement of independence;
- expansion of wood industry to meet the expanding domestic timber demand and for export;
- the establishment of forest plantations to meet the predicted shortfall of log supply from the natural forests in the coming decades; and
- boundary demarcation and maintenance, monitoring and rule enforcement.

Decentralisation of the management of forests was vigorously pursued in the later years of colonial administration and there was a significant improvement in the participation of local governments in the management of forestry resources as well as other natural resources (Nyende, 2011). The 1947 Forest Ordinance was amended and entrusted to local governments with legislative authority over forests in their area of jurisdiction.

Local government forest services were established to manage the Local Forest Reserves and to establish pole, fuelwood and timber plantations. The policy put in place incentives to encourage the local governments to reserve adequate forest estate. For example, any local authority that met a set target of reserved local forest estate was declared by the Governor to have an adequate forest estate and was entitled to obtain revenue from forests on public land as well as from the Local Forest Reserves (Forest Department, 1951). This led to a substantial increase in revenue generated by the local governments. By 1956, the districts of Bunyoro, Buganda, Busoga, Bukedi, Acholi, Teso, and Ankole were declared to have adequate forest estates.

By the end of 1963, several districts, including Bunyoro, Kigezi, and Acholi, had gazetted their own forest rules after protracted negotiations with the central government (Nyende, 2011). This further consolidated the role of local governments in the management of forestry resources and strengthened the local forest services. Bunyoro, Toro, Buganda and many others established their own extensive pine and eucalypt plantations. However, there was resistance by some district councils to the establishment of CFRs and LFRs. For example, by the end of the colonial period, West Nile, Lango, and Karamoja districts were not yet declared as having adequate forest estate (Webster and Osmaston, 2003).

In 1952, the National Parks Ordinance was enacted and the game reserves established earlier in the colonial period were declared national parks.

The Queen Elizabeth and Murchison Falls were the first two national parks in the country. Part of Kalinzu Forest, Lake, Edward and George and the Kazinga channel were made part of Queen Elizabeth National Park. Kidepo game reserve was the third to be declared a national park just at the end of the colonial period in 1962. According to Webster and Osmaston (2003), the Forest Department welcomed the passing of the National Parks Ordinance and the declaration of the national parks.

Following the establishment of the protected areas, training of local staff (foresters and rangers) was given a high priority in the 1950s. Nyabyeya Forestry College, now located near Budongo Forest Reserve, was founded in 1948 to offer certificates and diplomas in forestry. The college was expanded several times between 1950 and 1965 and developed into an effective training college. Professional-level training of Ugandans, however, continued to be undertaken at universities abroad, especially in the United Kingdom.

In 1957, the Wildlife Conservation Society (MTWA, 2014), together with the Game and Fisheries Department, started undertaking biological surveys for developing a monitoring and research plan for the various national parks in the country. The WCS also supported capacity-building of protected area managers and researchers.

Following several studies on the demand for timber and other forest products, the colonial government concluded that it was not possible to meet the wood requirements in the foreseeable future from natural forests alone. An ambitious pine and cypress plantation establishment programme was initiated in the early 1950s. Extensive research and provenance testing was conducted by local governments' forest services and District Forest Officers. Technical notes describing the edaphic and climatic conditions of research sites, together with growth-rate data and the required silvicultural treatments for the various species and provenances, were produced (Stuart-Smith, 1967; Kriek, 1970).

By the early 1960s, more than 4,500 ha of pine, cypress and eucalyptus plantations had been established in the highlands of western Uganda and on the slopes of Mt Elgon by both local and central government forest services. Several savannah woodland forest reserves such as Katugo and Singo Hills in Central Uganda and Obera, Opiti and Opaka in Northern Uganda had been earmarked for softwood plantation establishment.

Fuel and pole plantations were also rapidly expanded in order to meet the increasing demand for fuelwood for curing tobacco and bricks. Attempts were also made to establish plantations of valuable indigenous timber species such as *muvule* (*Milicia excelsa*) but with limited success.

Boundary demarcation and surveying using aerial photography continued during this period. Aerial photography made mapping less costly and faster; as a result, most of the reserves were mapped by the early 1950s. However, reserve boundary maintenance continued to be expensive and yet it was a necessary activity to be undertaken because illegal harvesting and encroachment had become a major problem in many regions of the country, especially in Buganda.

Thus the cost of boundary maintenance consumed more than half of the annual budget for the Forestry Department (Webster and Osmaston, 2003).

To reduce the boundary maintenance costs the use of permanent boundary markers was recommended, and to curb illegal harvesting and encroachment forest patrol teams were formed, and footpaths to ease movement along reserve boundaries were established and maintained by the patrol teams. In mountainous areas of western Uganda, aeroplanes were regularly used to monitor encroachment. Thus, boundary maintenance, monitoring and rule enforcement, including eviction and prosecution, were given a high priority. Thousands of pounds were spent on these activities. However, Webster and Osmaston (2003) point out that the cost of monitoring and rule enforcement could have been low 'if local people understood the value of forests and if there was better cooperation with local chiefs'. The colonial forest officers were convinced that 'often local chiefs connived with illegal local people to encroach on forest reserve land' (ibid).

Outcomes for conservation for this period

The 1950s can be described as being the most productive period for the Forest Department. Despite the problem of boundary maintenance and rule enforcement, Uganda was a leader in research in tropical forestry ecology, including knowledge of species composition and succession, and in tropical forestry silviculture, including harvesting and management of tropical natural forests. Preparation of management plans for most of the forest reserves in the country and publication of journals and books on tropical forestry occurred in this period. These scholarly publications were widely used throughout the tropical countries of the Commonwealth.

With research in plantation establishment conducted in the 1950s and with availability of funds and staff, local governments established softwood and hardwood plantations in various parts of the country to complement the supply of fuelwood, poles and timber from natural forests. These forest plantations have been the source of timber for Uganda in the last two decades. With adequate staff, there was improved monitoring and rule enforcement in recently gazetted local natural forest reserves.

The 1948 Forest Policy extended the control of 'reserved tree species', such as muvule and mahogany growing on public and private land, by the Forest Department. According to this policy a farmer was obliged to pay a fee before harvesting of 'reserved tree species' growing on his/her land (MWLE, 2002). This caused a lot of resentment and confusion in the field and many farmers uprooted or killed these valuable timber trees, thereby reducing on-farm biodiversity.

Outcomes for local people

The concept of Local Forest Reserves managed by local governments was implemented during this phase. The two forest services – the central government represented by the District Forest Officers and the local government forest services – were fully functional and cooperating with each other. There was genuine devolution of power to local governments to make local forest rules, collect revenue from local forestry resources and to invest in the forest sector. This led to increased training and recruitment of staff (forest guards, rangers and foresters) from Nyabyeya Forestry College.

Following the end of the Second World War, there was an increased demand for timber and the sawmill industry expanded. Long-term concessions were extended to saw millers as an incentive to invest in modern machinery. Forest inventories to determine the volume of logs that could be extracted on a sustainable basis were conducted and harvesting regulations were put in place. A list of the more common Uganda timbers and their properties (Tack, 1969) and grading rules to improve trade and marketing were published. Plywood and particle board manufacturing were also started towards the end of this period. All this led to improved wood processing and increased job opportunities in the wood industry.

During this period, a significant amount of logs for wood production (about 45%) was procured from forests on private land (Webster and Osmaston, 2003), thereby providing an income to private forest owners, especially in Buganda. Unfortunately, harvesting regulations for private forests were not in place to guide private forest owners. This often resulted in over-harvesting of forests on private land. The lack of harvesting regulations for private forests still continues up to today and is partly the cause of rapid forest deforestation and degradation of forests on private land in the country.

Although the 1950s can be described as being the most productive period for the Forest Department, and for empowering district and local governments to manage forestry resources in their jurisdictions, there were very limited benefits accruing to local (forest-reserve-adjacent) communities. No village forests were declared by local authorities, although this was envisaged in the 1948 Forest Policy. Also, no forest-adjacent communities could engage in commercial harvesting of forest reserves since harvesting concessions were often issued to established wood processors.

Early post-colonial period (1962–1986): independence and eventual collapse

The early post-colonial period can be divided into two phases; the continuation of the consolidation period (1963–1971) and the collapse of the forest sector (1971–1986). The evolution of the forest sector during this period is briefly described below.

The continuation of the consolidation period (1963–1971)

Expatriate forest officers left the country on achievement of independence and were replaced by Ugandan professional foresters who were able to

continue the implementation of the 1948 Forest Policy. The 1962 independence constitution established the Uganda Land Commission (ULC) to
manage former Crown land, while forest reserves were put under the management of the Forest Department (Government of Uganda, 1964) instead
of being transferred to the local governments as had been agreed upon
during the negotiations for independence.

However, following the disagreements between the Uganda and Buganda
Governments in 1964, Uganda became a republic and management of forestry resources, including forests on public land and Local Forest Reserves,
were centralised and transferred to the Uganda Government Forest
Department. The 1964 Forests Act empowered the Commissioner for
Forests to manage all forest reserves and issue licenses for harvesting of forest produce on private and public lands. Local people could only freely take
forest products from forest reserves for domestic use. They had to obtain
a permit from the Forest Department if they wanted to trade in such products, even if the land on which the forests or forest resources were located
belonged to them.

With the exception of decentralisation of the sector to the local governments, all activities envisaged in the 1948 Forest Policy continued after
independence. Funds were obtained for maintenance and expansion of the
softwood plantations, silvicultural treatment of natural forests, preparation
of management plans, and research and training of staff at the forest college
continued. However, the highest priority was given to protection of the forest estate against encroachment since theft of forestland and forest produce
threatened the integrity of the forest estate.

In 1970 the forest policy was revised, and again the focus alternated
between conservation and utilisation and provided little guidance on principles and strategies for managing forests outside the FRs. Furthermore, the
policy did not clarify the roles of government, the private sector and rural
communities in forestry, and on linkages with other sectors and land uses.

The collapse of the forest sector: political, economic and social turmoil (1971–1986)

This period was dominated by the military government of Idi Amin
(1971–1979) and the civil war that ravaged the country between 1980 and
1985. During the military government, the Constitution was suspended,
the rule of law collapsed, and the country was ruled by decree. During
this period there was political, economic and social turmoil. Forest governance deteriorated as the rule of law broke down. Maintenance of
protected area boundaries was neglected and monitoring and enforcement of protected area rules and regulations was abandoned. This period
was also characterised by rapid population increase (total population
grew by about 33% during the period 1969 to 1980) (Kigenyi, 2006),
which further increased the pressure on the protected area network.

Following the collapse of the forest sector, the wood industries were accordingly also adversely affected (Carvalho and Eichinger, 2003). The sawmill industry had been dominated by Indian proprietors and they were expelled by Idi Amin in August 1972. Following their expulsion, the wood industries sector was nationalised under the Wood Industries Corporation (WICO), a government parastatal. Due to inexperience and political interference, WICO collapsed, and pitsawying by local people became the major mode of sawn timber production and has remained so up to today.

The softwood plantations that were established in the late 1950s and early 1960s were due for harvesting in this period. However, harvesting was delayed due to the collapse of the wood industries and also due to availability of hardwood logs poached from forest reserves and national parks. When forest reserves were completely exhausted of logs in the late 1980s, harvesting of the over-mature softwood and eucalyptus plantations commenced, again using two-man cross-cut saws and chainsaws.

One of the positive developments of the early 1970s was the establishment of the Department of Forestry at Makerere University to offer professional education and training. In addition, infrastructure at Nyabyeya Forestry College was greatly expanded and the college increased its intake of technical-level forestry trainees.

Outcomes for biodiversity

Gradually, all the good work that the colonial and the first post-colonial government had put in place collapsed. Limited scientific forest/national park management occurred during this period. Most silvicultural and ecological research programmes that were initiated in the 1940s were abandoned. Forest/national park managers were often corrupt and allowed, or were involved in, illegal harvesting and encroachment. Consequently, many forest reserves and national parks were converted into settlements and farmlands, leading to severe loss of biodiversity. The country's flagship timber species (mahoganies, muvule, Elgon olive, podocarpus and nkoba) were most affected.

Forest inventory, which was the basis for yield regulation, was no longer carried out and therefore no data on the status of biodiversity were gathered during this period. However, it can be said with certainty that indiscriminate clearance of forestland for human settlement, agriculture and un-regulated harvesting of trees for timber, firewood and charcoal, and controlled harvesting of game in national parks, destroyed important biodiversity habitats in the country.

Outcome for livelihoods

Following the collapse of the wood industries, forest-adjacent communities became involved in timber-harvesting operations using handsaws.

Again, one is tempted to say that the incursion of local communities into forest reserves enabled them to grow crops and produce timber that led to improved livelihoods, but the cost to biodiversity conservation and ecosystem stability was too high.

Although there are no employment records, one is tempted to think that the number of people employed as managers, rangers, forest/national park guards and casual labourers in the wood industries declined significantly. A large number of professionals in the forest sector and national parks left the country due to the prevailing difficult economic and political situation.

Reorganisation phase: contemporary dynamics and challenges (1986–present)

The National Resistance Movement led by President Yoweri Kaguta Museveni came into power in January 1986. The new government restored law and order in the country and prioritised the rehabilitation of Forest Reserves and national parks. The Forestry Rehabilitation Project funded through a consortium of agencies, including the World Bank, the European Union (EU), the governments of Denmark and Norway, UNDP, and CARE, was put in place in 1988. The European Union (EU) supported mainly natural forests and establishment of commercial timber plantations, while the Norwegian Agency for Development Cooperation (NORAD) mainly supported establishment of peri-urban plantations and GIS/remote sensing and technology transfer.

As part of the rehabilitation effort, a new forest policy that placed more emphasis on environmentally sound forest management approaches was formulated (Government of Uganda, 1988). New guidelines, almost similar to the forest management procedures that were implemented by the colonial administration during the growth period to facilitate responsible forest management and conservation, were put in place. These included, among others:

- timber inventories;
- management of buffer, production and nature conservation zones in natural forests;
- re-opening and/or re-demarcation of boundaries and eviction of encroachers;
- licensing for harvesting of forest produce;
- assessing forest degradation and the accompanying forest restoration actions;
- preparation of forest management plans and restoration of the ecosystems in fragile ecosystems;
- plantations planning and management;
- logging practices for natural forests;
- site species matching for tree growing;
- establishment and assessment of permanent sample plots.

The restoration of the biodiversity-rich and fragile ecosystems necessitated the elevation of selected forest reserves to national park conservation status. Despite resistance from the Forestry Department, six forest parks/forest reserves, namely Mt Elgon, Mgahinga, Bwindi, Rwenzori, Semuliki, and Kibale, were gazetted as national parks and their management transferred to Uganda National Parks in 1993 (Kamugisha and Cornelia, 1996). Because of this change in management status, more than 60% of the forest reserves area was taken out of timber production and other consumptive uses.

To ensure the sustainable management of wildlife conservation areas, and to coordinate the implementation of government policies in the field of wildlife management, a new Uganda Wildlife Act was enacted in 1996 and the Game and National Parks departments were replaced by a semi-autonomous Uganda Wildlife Authority.

The new constitutional order and forest governance reforms (1995–present)

A new Constitution was formulated in 1995 that empowered the central and local governments to 'hold in trust for the people and protect natural lakes, rivers, wetlands, forest reserves, game reserves, national parks and any land to be reserved for ecological and touristic purposes for the common good of all citizens' (Republic of Uganda, 2005). Under the new Constitution, the government decentralised the delivery of services, including the management of natural resources, to local governments. The National Environment Act 1995, the Local Government Act of 1997 (Government of Uganda, 1995, 1997), the Wildlife Act 1996, the Land Act 1998, and the National Forestry and Tree Planting Act 2003 operationalised these constitutional provisions.

The decentralisation of the management of forestry resources faced major challenges and took a long time to accomplish. For almost a decade, the management of forestry resources oscillated from local to central government (Turyahabye and Banana, 2008; Banana et al., 2007; Bazaara, 2006). Ribot et al. (2006) referred to this behaviour by central governments as 'centralization while decentralizing'. The cause of the 'oscillation' was because the local governments were deemed unable to manage the forestry resources due to lack of human and financial capacity (MWLE, 1999), but also because the centre did not want to let go of the authority of managing the forestry resources.

Following the review of the forest sector that started in 1999, a new Forest Policy (2001), the National Forest Plan (2002), and the National Forestry and Tree Planting Act (2003) were formulated (Government of Uganda, 2003). On the basis of these instruments, the century-old Forest Department was dissolved, leading to the creation of the semi-autonomous National Forest Authority, District Forestry Services (DFS) and the Forestry Inspection Division, later transformed into the Forestry Sector Support Department (FSSD). The FSSD was mandated to formulate policy and supervise all actors in the forestry sector in Uganda, including NFA and the District Forestry Services (DFS). It was finally decided that NFA would manage CFRs while local governments, through the DFS, would manage Local Forest Reserves (LFR) and supervise the activities of private forest owners. The local governments considered this to be unfair because local forest reserves were small in size (covering only 5,000 ha country wide) and degraded (Banana et al., 2007), with limited revenue accruing from them. Thus, with limited incentives to manage local forest reserves, the district councils did not prioritise the management of forestry resources and, as a result, these forest reserves continued to be degraded.

Initially, the NFA enjoyed high-level political support and had adequate resources, mainly from official development assistance, to support the management of CFRs. By now, timber plantations established in the early to mid-1970s were mature and pine timber was gaining popularity on the market, and so NFA was also generating its own revenues. On the other hand, funding and staff for the newly created DFS and the FSSD were inadequate and these two institutions could not perform their mandated tasks as expected. This situation persists to this day (2017).

Declaration of community forests and registration of private forests

According to the MWLE (2001), most of the deforestation and forest degradation (about 3.7% annually between 1990 and 2000) occurred on private and on customary lands, yet 70% of the country's forest cover occurred on these lands. In order to manage these resources, the new National Forestry and Tree Planting Act 2003 established and legally recognised ownership and management of natural forests on private, public and customary lands (Turyahabwe and Banana, 2008; and Banana et al., 2014). Guidelines were prepared by the Forest Sector Support Department (FSSD) to steer implementation. According to the guidelines, community forests can be established on:

- former public land held by the District Land Boards;
- land designated as 'fragile ecosystem' by NEMA;
- areas for community-managed plantations;
- woodland/pastoral areas that are communally used;
- customary land managed by traditional institutions.

Members of the local community can access the forest in line with procedures they have established. A legally constituted organization such as CBO or NGO controls access and use on behalf of the community and can legally exclude outsiders.

Local community responsibilities and rights to manage and withdraw forestry resources adjacent to their settlements under Collaborative Forest

Management (CFM) arrangements are negotiated with the NFA, DFS or the private forest owner (also known as responsible bodies), and rights are entrenched in a CFM agreement and CFM plan.

Under the guidelines, registered private forest owners are legally recognised as responsible bodies, and have a bundle of rights that includes rights to access, withdraw, manage, exclude, and alienate forest resources on their land and these rights are not extinguishable (Rights and Resources Initiative, 2012). These guidelines were developed after several years of piloting in several forests including Alimugonza, Ongo and Tengele forest patches near Budongo and Butto-Buvuma CFRs in the early 2000s (Gombya-Ssembajjwe and Banana, 2000).

However, it is important to point out that implementation of the above forest tenure reforms faced considerable institutional, economic and social challenges. The processes of registration, declaration of community forests and private natural forests, and negotiation of CFM arrangements, are lengthy, costly and require external assistance for capacity building and funding (Nsita et al., 2017).

The responsible government agencies were not adequately funded to implement these reforms and no institutional coordination mechanisms were put in place. In addition, there were limited benefits accruing to participating communities and households. Data from the FAO Forest Tenure Project shows that, by mid-2017, only 50 private forests covering an area of 593 hectares in four districts (Masindi, Bushenyi, Rubirizi, and Mitooma) were ready for registration by the District Land Board, while six Community Forests covering an area of 535 hectares in Lamwo and Masindi Districts were ready for declaration by the Minister (Langoya – pers. com). Similarly, the number of CFM agreements in operation are limited. By the end of 2015, only 49 CFM agreements had been signed between NFA and community groups, covering 63,700 hectares in 20 CFRs (Turyomurugyendo, 2016).

Establishment of commercial plantations under the Saw Log Production Grant Scheme (2004–to present)

In line with the privatisation policy of government, the new National Forestry and Tree Planting Act 2003 provided incentives for the private sector to invest in commercial timber plantation development. The Sawlog Production Grant Scheme (SPGS), a joint initiative between the Government of Uganda, the Government of Norway and the European Union, was initiated in 2004 to provide start-up capital, mainly to the private sector, but also to communities and public institutions to establish their own small-scale timber plantations/woodlots (MWLE, 2004). The scheme was designed to meet 50% of the costs of establishing and maintaining the sawlog plantations distributed over a period of three years. Under this scheme, the government leased forest reserve lands to investors at attractive rates for an initial period of 25 years, renewable to 50 years following good performance. The scheme also provided professional technical advice, training and research to support the growing of commercial timber plantations throughout Uganda.

Experimentation with payment for ecosystem services and efforts related to various types of carbon forestry

Following the Bali Climate Change Conference in 2007, Uganda started participating in the Reducing Emissions from Deforestation and Forest Degradation (REDD+) activities. The country benefited from the Forest Carbon Partnership Facility (FCPF) of the World Bank. Uganda's Readiness Preparation Proposal (R-PP) was approved by FCPF in 2012, paving the way for the start of implementing the REDD+ Readiness phase, which started in July 2013 (Ministry of Water and Environment, 2016). A secretariat was set up in the Ministry of Water and Environment (MWE) to coordinate these activities. In addition to support from the FCPF, Uganda also received funding from the Austrian Development Cooperation in 2013 and the UN REDD Programme starting in 2015.

In addition to government agencies, civil society organisations (CSOs) and private sector institutions are contributing towards REDD Readiness activities, including piloting carbon benefits for local communities through voluntary carbon markets, conducting studies, and building local community platforms, among others. Apart from carbon, other payments for ecosystem services have also been piloted but these have been limited in extent. For example, private forest owners in the Albertine Rift region of Uganda were organised into Private Forest Owners Associations and management plans were prepared so as to protect their private forests and to benefit from payment for ecosystem services (WWF, 2013).

Forestry research and capacity building to support forest management

The National Forestry Tree and Tree Planting Act 2003 stresses the importance of research in promoting sustainable forest management. A fully fledged research institute, the National Forestry Resources Research Institute (NaFORRI), was established as part of the National Agricultural Research Organisation (NARO) by an Act of Parliament in 2005. The Institute replaced the Research Section of the former Forest Department.

Research that has been undertaken at NaFORRI includes research on management of trees for optimal productivity, exploring impacts of investments in tree growing, tree pest and disease control, energy conservation, improved use of indigenous tree resources, quality agroforestry tree germplasm, improving forage production and utilisation, productivity of Uganda's dry lands for climate change and determining carbon sequestration capacities of pines and eucalypts. However, due to the limited number of scientists and lack of research funds, the institute is not able to conduct long-term ecological research (NaFORRI, 2017).

The School of Forestry, Environmental and Geographical Sciences at Makerere University also conducts a number of research projects. However, most of the projects are small in nature and do not holistically address issues affecting sustainable forest management in the country.

Forestry training at both professional and technical level continued to expand during this period. At Nyabyeya Forestry College, new certificate and diploma programmes in agroforestry, beekeeping, carpentry and biomass production were created and the old ones were revised. At Makerere University, new undergraduate and Masters degree programmes in Community Forestry and Forest Products Technology, and Conservation Forestry and Products Technology, were created. A curriculum review led to the re-introduction of the former Bsc degree programme in Forestry.

In addition to formal training, local and international NGOs have been building capacity and empowering communities to grow trees on their farms, and also building their capacity to lobby, advocate for, and negotiate CFM agreements (Banana et al., 2014). These skills are required by communities for reducing rural poverty and improving management of tree resources, thereby leading to improving the sustainability of forestry resources. Although funding by NGOs and CSOs is often short-lived, these organisations have been more successful in providing forestry advisory services than the government forest agencies such as the DFS and NFA. The NGOs and CSOs that have been involved in capacity building include VI Agroforestry, WWF, Nature Uganda, Jane Goodall Institute, CODECA, ECOTRUST, Prime West, IUCN and Tree Talk, among others.

Outcomes for biodiversity

Despite putting in place several initiatives to manage the forest estate on a sustainable basis, deforestation and forest degradation increased significantly during this period. Initially, the Forestry Rehabilitation Project (FRP) achieved a degree of success by systematic removal of encroachers, boundary opening and improved monitoring and rule enforcement (Nsita, 2010). Land titles issued in all protected areas were cancelled (National Forestry Authority, 2005).

Due to the improvement in forest management practices, the government initiated a process to certify several CFRs including Kalinzu, Budongo, Bugoma, Mabira, and Katugo through the Forest Stewardship Council (FSC) Certification Scheme. However, progress towards certification was delayed because Uganda started to develop its own FSC National Forest Stewardship Standard.

Unfortunately, the achievements gained through the FRP period were slowed down or reversed when funding from the EU came to an end in 1997. Worse still, the forestry sector reform process that started in 1997 and ended in 2003 created a vacuum during the transition from Forestry Department to NFA and DFS. There was a lot of uncertainty and low morale among forest managers at all levels of forest governance, resulting in mismanagement of forest resources due to limited funding and corruption. Consequently, illegal harvesting and encroachment of forest reserves became commonplace since there was limited monitoring and rule enforcement. Corruption among forestry staff became rampant.

The process of decentralisation and recentralisation also led to mismanagement of the forest resources and a decline in biodiversity. In addition, the phasing out of the Forest Department led to loss of institutional memory. Most of the new field staff employed by NFA had limited or no experience in forest management, further worsening illegal harvesting and encroachment. However, during the initial four years of NFA operation, there was political support and NFA had adequate resources, mainly from official development assistance to support the management of CFRs. Again, as we have seen, timber plantations established in the early 1960s and early 1970s were mature and pine timber was gaining popularity on the market, meaning that NFA was generating its own revenues. With these resources, NFA was able to evict the illegal encroachers. In 2004–2005, NFA evicted 180,000 encroachers living in 9,000 households and cultivating about 57,000 hectares (National Forestry Authority, 2005).

After five years of NFA operations, official development assistance to support the management of CFRs ended and political support declined. The NFA was then unable to fund most of the forest activities, including plantation development, forest restoration, boundary maintenance, monitoring, and rule enforcement, among others. Once again illegal activities began to escalate. In a bid to control the rate of deforestation, CFM was introduced in CFRs, However, this has not helped to stem the rate of deforestation as had been envisaged.

High rates of deforestation and degradation have also continued to occur in LFRs and in forests on public and private lands due to the non-functioning of the DFS. Thus, Uganda's forest cover, which was estimated to be 4.9 million hectares (24% of total land area) in 1990, had declined to 2.4 million hectares (about 12% of the total land area) by 2015 (MWE, 2016). Within a quarter of a century, Uganda had lost 50% of its forest cover.

However, during this period, the government was successful in stimulating the establishment of commercial timber plantations and woodlots by the private sector. By 2017, 63,568 ha of plantations have been established (NFA, 2017). Success was attributed to the performance-based nature of SPGS that provided safeguards against mismanagement and the scheme's autonomy provided flexibility to learn and adjust to new needs and demands. A new phase of SPGS has been funded by the EU, but it is under the stewardship of FAO. Within the next decade, these newly established plantations will be mature for harvesting and will contribute significantly to the revitalisation of the wood industries sector.

The prevailing peace and political stability experienced during this period has led to a steady improvement of the tourism industry, which brought in more funds for national park management. At the same time, UWA has been more successful in the management of the national parks, as compared with NFA and DFS. Consequently, the biodiversity in those forests that were turned into national parks has continued to improve and to bring in more tourists. Generally, UWA has been able to maintain the integrity of national parks with limited encroachment and illegal extraction except for Mt Elgon National Park, where boundary disputes and the conflicts between the indigenous peoples (the Benet) and park management continue to disrupt operations.

Outcomes for livelihoods

During the FRP period, communities were supported to grow trees on farms to provide fuelwood and poles. Forest-adjacent communities were also involved in the various forest rehabilitation activities such nursery establishment, boundary maintenance, enrichment planting and plantation establishment (especially peri-urban plantations). However, thousands of households who had encroached on CFRs and were evicted lost their livelihoods.

Harvesting and processing of forest produce continued during this period, using labour-intensive methods. Most of the harvesting operations were informal, but they provided employment for thousands of people. In a study conducted for the Forest Resources Management and Conservation Project, it was shown that 11–27% of household cash income of communities around FRs was derived from forestry (Bush et al., 2004). Later, Jagger (2008), using the same sites as Bush et al. (2004), concluded that the share of total annual household income from forests had increased by 4% since the sector reforms of 2000. The share of income from forests had declined by 10.7% for the poorest households and increased by 11.6% for the wealthiest households. This seems to suggest that the capacity to invest in timber harvesting has decreased for the poorest segment of society and increased for the wealthiest segment.

The elevation of the conservation status of forest reserves to national parks in 1993 led to loss of rights to harvest forestry resources from these areas by the local communities, leading to loss of livelihoods. Loss of community livelihoods created considerable conflicts between local people and park management. To minimise the level of conflicts, UWA introduced co-management approaches and benefit-sharing schemes with park-adjacent communities. In addition, the park authorities relaxed resource extraction rules and allowed the communities to harvest non-timber forest products for subsistence use. However, the people–wildlife conflict due to crop raiding by wild animals from the protected areas continue to be a major concern because it affects the livelihoods of adjacent communities.

Following the enactment of the National Forestry and Tree Planting Act of 2003, the private sector, including local communities, was able to access land in CFRs for tree growing under license. According to the NFA guidelines for allocation of land in CFRs, at least 5% of available land is reserved for allocation to local communities. On maturity, communities are able to harvest the crop for subsistence use or for sale to earn an income.

Under the CFM arrangement, the participating communities are able to co-manage the forest and they are able to extract resources as stipulated in the CFM agreements. With financial assistance from NGOs, CSOs, NFA, and FSSD, communities are supported to engage in alternative income-generating activities such as eco-tourism, beekeeping, tree growing on farms, improved agriculture and improved cook stoves. The contribution of these initiatives to household livelihoods have not yet been evaluated.

The SPGS project provides support to local communities that are organised into groups to grow trees for income generation. The project provides quality seedlings and training in tree management. With the prevailing high demand for timber, poles and fuelwood, local communities have been able to earn a living from tree growing.

The MWE in collaboration with CSOs have piloted payment for ecosystem services (PES) and carbon-benefits trading for local communities through voluntary carbon markets in the Albertine and Mt Elgon regions. Some farmers have received funds from this scheme. However, the protracted nature of the REDD+ preparation procedures have discouraged many communities and private forest owners from participating in PES and carbon-trading schemes. After a decade of experimentation, few communities have benefited from the PES scheme and consequently deforestation has continued. The Ministry of Water and Environment (MWE, 2017) attributes the continued deforestation and forest degradation mainly to expansion of commercial and subsistence agricultural activities into forest lands, unsustainable harvesting of tree products, mainly for charcoal, firewood, and timber, expansion of settlements, and uncontrolled wild fires.

The increasing deforestation in Uganda, as elsewhere in sub-Saharan Africa, suggests that traditional conservation measures, like routine patrols, are not sufficient to protect the forests in the long run. However, it is also not clear whether the current PES and REDD+ activities being piloted will achieve the desired end of achieving sustainable forest management. Additional conservation measures beyond the prevailing scenarios need to be crafted.

Boundary maintenance and law enforcement

The boundaries of the CFRs, which are of critical conservation importance, were re-opened mostly during the 1990s and the early 2000s. During the latter part of the 2000s, boundary re-opening was done mainly for CFRs where the boundaries were being disputed with the neighbours.

Boundary re-opening was followed by the planting of concrete pillars sunk into corner beacons made from earth or stones. For some of the stretches along farmlands, live markers were planted along the boundaries.

Biodiversity inventories were carried out in the early 1990s, resulting in the National Forestry Plan (Government of Uganda, 2002). One of the important aspects that came with the Master Plan was collaboration with adjacent communities in boundary planting. This was especially in areas where CFM arrangements had been negotiated and agreed. In these areas, each owner of land sharing a boundary with that of a CFR was allowed to plant their own trees in a strip of about 100 metres inside the CFR boundary. In exchange, the land owner was expected to guard the forest in their area against illegal activities.

Implementation of CFM had reduced the tensions between the NFA and the local communities wherever it was initiated, leading to a reduction of illegal activities. Consequently, there were definite signs that the natural forests were recovering (Nsita, 2010). When governance at the NFA went into a tailspin, and because the benefits to the CFM communities were less than expected, the rate of expansion of CFM reduced and the levels of illegal activities, even in areas where CFM had been in operation, started to increase again.

Conclusions

Forest management as we know it today was born during the colonial period. Protected areas were established with clear boundaries after consultation with traditional institutions, landlords and local communities. Appropriate policies, laws and management plans, informed by data and information obtained from extensive research conducted over two decades, were developed. This period was characterised by a strong economy and political stability. Thus, forest management activities were well funded by the colonial government when available. The attempt to decentralise forest management to local governments was largely successful as local governments were empowered to establish, manage, and directly benefit from local forest reserves.

It was envisaged that natural tropical forests would not be able to meet the demand for forest produce at the turn of the century, and, therefore, extensive softwood plantations were established in various parts of the country. From the perspective of the colonial state, there was no doubt that the outcomes of conservation for biodiversity and the livelihoods of local communities, including indigenous peoples, were perceived as generally positive. However, boundary maintenance, monitoring and law enforcement was a major challenge during this period.

The objectives, structure, and intended beneficiaries of conservation institutions were continued during the early post-colonial period (1962–1970). However, the major discontinuity that occurred during this period was the introduction of the Republican constitution in 1966, which abolished traditional kingdoms and led to the recentralisation of the management of local forestry reserves. The period between 1971 and 1986 was characterised by political, economic and social turmoil, leading to the collapse of the forest governance institutions that had been earlier established. The outcomes for biodiversity, the livelihood of local communities and the wood industry were catastrophic. Deforestation and forest degradation was rampant due to limited boundary maintenance, ineffective monitoring and rule enforcement.

During the contemporary period (1986–present) there have been significant shifts in terms of the objectives, structure and institutions. During this period, decentralisation, privatisation and community participation have been emphasised. Again, the outcomes for biodiversity, the livelihood of local communities and the wood industry are markedly different. The challenges of boundary maintenance, monitoring and forest rule enforcement are greater than ever before due to limited funding, corruption, conflicting government policies, political interference and other socio-economic factors. In conclusion, it can be stated that boundary maintenance, monitoring and law enforcement have constituted a recurring problem regardless of the specific set of institutions and policy objectives in place, and these challenges are related to the governance challenges of the country, especially concerning lacklustre accountability and transparency, and direct interference with law enforcement.

This chapter shows a forestry sector that has had a checkered history. There were periods of exemplary performance, but there were also periods of disastrous governance. In all those ups and downs, the forests have shown an impressive ability to bounce back after periods of bad management. This happened after the disastrous years of 1971–1986. Another disastrous period, starting in 2005 and continuing to the present, has again sent the natural forests into a tailspin, with unprecedented rates of deforestation, especially on private and public lands. Because of this, the nature of future forest management is set to take a turn that has not been known this far. Private forest plantations (mostly exotic pine and eucalyptus) are increasingly dominating the forestry sector. On the other hand, natural forests on public and private lands, and possibly even in protected areas, are on a trajectory that may lead to them being irrevocably lost. Even if rehabilitated in future, they may never be the same in terms of ecology and biodiversity as they were at the turn of the twentieth century when scientific forest management began.

References

Allen, R. (1992) *Enclosure and the Yeomen*, Oxford University Press, Oxford, UK.
Baland, J.M. and Platteau, J.P. (1996) *Halting Degradation of Natural Resources: is there a role for rural communities?* Food and Agriculture Organisation, Rome, Italy.

Banana, A.Y., Waiswa, D. and Buyinza, M. (2014) 'The impacts of decentralisation reforms on sustainable forest management in Central Uganda', *Forests Under Pressure: Local responses to global issues*, IUFRO World Series, Part ii, Chapter 22, p. 357.

Banana, A.Y., Vogt, N.D., Bahati, J., and Gombya-Ssembajjwe, W. (2007) 'Decentralized governance and ecological health: why local institutions fail to moderate deforestation in Mpigi district of Uganda', *Scientific Research and Essays*, vol. 2, no. 10, pp. 434–445.

Bazaara, N. (2006) 'Subjecting nature to central authority: the struggle over public goods in the formation of citizenship', *Africa Development*, vol. 31, no. 2, pp. 19–35.

Bush, G., Nampindo, S., Aguti, C., and Plumptre, A. (2004) *The Value of Uganda's Forests: a livelihoods and ecosystems approach*, Wildlife Conservation Society, Kampala, Uganda.

Carvalho, J. and Eichinger, F. (2003) *A Review of the Wood and Non Wood Product Markets in Uganda*, National Forestry Authority, Kampala, Uganda.

Cioc, M. (2009) *The Game of Conservation: international treaties to protect the world's migratory animals*, Ohio University Press, Athens, OH, USA.

Eggeling, W.J. (2002) *The Indigenous Trees of the Uganda Protectorate* (revised and enlarged by Ivan R. Dale), Government Printer, Entebbe, Uganda, and Crown Agents for the Colonies, London, UK, pp. xiii and 491.

Eggeling, W.J. and Dale, I.R. (1951) *The Indigenous Trees of the Uganda Protectorate*, Crown Agents for the Colonies, London, UK.

Esegu, J.F. and Ndemere, P. (2002) 'A century of forest management research in Uganda: 1898–1998', *Uganda Journal of Agricultural Sciences*, vol. 2, no. 2, pp. 7–11.

Fairhead, J. and Leach, M. (1996) *Misreading the African Landscape: society and ecology in a forest-savanna mosaic* (Vol. 90), Cambridge University Press, Cambridge, UK.

Forest Department (1951) *A History of the Uganda Forest Department 1898–1929*, Bulletin No. 3, D.L. Patel Press, Entebbe, Uganda.

Forestry Resources Management and Conservation Programme (2009) *Final Report for October 2006 to December 2008 Covered by Addendum No. 1 to Financing Agreement No. 6406/UG*, Forestry Resources Management and Conservation Programme, Kampala, Uganda.

Gombya-Ssembajjwe, W.S. (1997) *Indigenous Technical Knowledge and Forest Management: A Case Study of Sacred Groves (Traditional Forest Reserves), Mpigi District, Uganda*, Uganda IFRI Collaborating Research Center (UFRIC), Makerere University, Kampala, Uganda.

Gombya-Ssembajjwe, W.S., Abwoli, Y. and Bahati, J. (2001) *Case Study – Property Rights: access to land and forest resources in Uganda*, Oxford University Press, Oxford, UK.

Gombya-Ssembajjwe, W.S. and Banana, A.Y. (2000) 'Collaborative forest management in Uganda: the case of Butto-Buvuma Forest Reserve', in W.S. Gombya-Ssembajjwe and A.Y. Banana (eds) *Community-based Forest Resource Management in East Africa*, Makerere University Printery, Kampala, Uganda, pp. 25–33.

Government of Uganda (1964) *The 1964 Forest Act, Cap.246, Laws of Uganda*, Government Printer, Entebbe, Uganda.

Government of Uganda (1988) *The Uganda Forest Policy. Revised Forest Policy of the Republic of Uganda*, Government Printer, Entebbe, Uganda.

Government of Uganda (1995) *Local Government of Uganda*, Uganda Publishing and Printing Corporation, Entebbe, Uganda.

Government of Uganda (1997) *Local Government of Uganda*, Uganda Publishing and Printing Corporation, Entebbe, Uganda.

Government of Uganda (2002) *National Forestry Plan*. Uganda Publishing and Printing Corporation, Entebbe, Uganda.

Government of Uganda (2003) *The National Forestry and Tree Planting Act, Acts Supplement No. 5, The Uganda Gazette, No. 37 Vol XCVI*, Uganda Publishing and Printing Corporation, Entebbe, Uganda.

Guha, R. (1985) 'Scientific forestry and social change in Uttarakhand', *Economic and Political Weekly*, 1 November, pp. 1939–1952.

Jagger, P. (2008) *Forest Incomes after Uganda's Forest Sector Reform: are the rural poor gaining?* (No. 92), International Food Policy Research Institute, Washington, DC, USA.

John, C. and Franz, E. (2003) 'A review of the wood and wood products market in Uganda. Study report submitted to the Forestry Resources Management and Conservation Programme, Ministry of Water, Lands and Environment' (not published).

Kambugu, R.K., Banana, A.Y., Turyahabwe, N. and Okure, M. (2013) 'An institutional analysis of commodity chain evolution: a case study of sawn wood in Uganda', *International Forestry Review*, vol. 15, no. 4, pp. 489–498.

Kamugisha, J. R. (1993) *Management of Natural Resources and Environment in Uganda*, Regional Soil Conservation Unit, Swedish International Development Authority, Stockholm, Sweden.

Kamugisha, J.R. and Cornelia, S. (1996) 'Draft synthesis report: the consultative process for the promotion of natural forest and related land use programmes in Uganda in support of Inter-Governmental Panel on Forests (IPF) of the Commission for Sustainable Development (CSD) of the United Nations', Forest Department, Kampala, Uganda.

Kigenyi, F.W. (2006) 'Trends in forest ownership, forest resources tenure and institutional arrangements: are they contributing to better forest management and poverty reduction? A case study from Uganda', unpublished report, Food and Agriculture Organisation, Rome, Italy.

Kjekshus, H. (1996) *Ecology Control and Economic Development in East African History: the case of Tanganyika 1850–1950*, Ohio University Press, Athens, OH, USA.

Kriek, W. (1970) *Report to the Government of Uganda on Performance of Indigenous and Exotic Trees in Species Trials* (TA 2826), Food and Agriculture Organisation, Rome, Italy.

Meredith, M. (2003) *Elephant Destiny: biography of an endangered species in Africa*, PublicAffairs, New York, NY, USA.

Ministry of Tourism, Wildlife and Antiquities (MTWA) (2014) *Uganda Wildlife Policy 2014*, Ministry of Tourism, Wildlife and Antiquities, Kampala, Uganda.

Ministry of Water and Environment (MWE) (2016) *Forestry Sector Support Department, REDD+ Secretariat, 2016. Mid-term progress report for Uganda and request for additional funding from FCPF*, Ministry of Water and Environment, Kampala, Uganda.

Ministry of Water, Lands, and Environment (MWLE) (1999) *The Uganda Forest Policy: Draft for Consultation.* Uganda Forest Sector Co-ordination Secretariat, Ministry of Water, Lands, and Environment, Kampala, Uganda.

Ministry of Water, Lands, and Environment (MWLE) (2001) *The Uganda Forestry Policy 2001*, Ministry of Water, Lands and Environment, Kampala, Uganda.

Ministry of Water, Lands, and Environment (MWLE) (2002) *The National Forest Plan*, Ministry of Water, Lands, and Environment, Kampala, Uganda.

Ministry of Water, Lands, and Environment (MWLE) (2004) 'Guidelines for accessing grants under the Sawlog Production Grant Scheme', unpublished, Ministry of Water, Lands, and Environment, Kampala, Uganda.

Ministry of Water, Lands, and Environment (MWLE) (2014) *Enhancing Forest Tenure and Governance in Uganda, 2014–2016*, Ministry of Water, Lands, and Environment, Kampala, Uganda.

Ministry of Water, Lands, and Environment (2017) 'Proposed forest reference level for Uganda: preliminary document submitted to the United Nations Framework Convention on Climate Change (UNFCCC)', Ministry of Water, Lands, and Environment, Kampala, Uganda.

Mukwaya, A.B. (1953) *Land Tenure in Buganda: present day tendencies*, The Eagle Press, Kampala, Uganda.

Naluwairo, R. (2015) 'Strengthening tenure rights of Uganda's forest communities: a critical analysis of Uganda's forest legal and policy framework', report prepared for CIFOR, Bogor, Indonesia.

National Forestry Authority (2005) *Encroachment in Central Forest Reserves – tough challenges and hard choices*, National Forestry Authority, Kampala, Uganda.

National Forestry Authority (2017) *Land Cover Trends in Uganda 2017*, National Forestry Authority, Kampala, Uganda.

National Forestry Resources Research Institute (NaFORRI) (2017) *Annual Report 2015–2016*, National Forestry Resources Research Institute, Kampala, Uganda.

Nsita, S. (2010) *Forest Governance Reforms in Uganda*, proceedings of the workshop on forest governance in Uganda organized by the Ministry of Water and Environment and the World Bank, 15–16 June, Serena Hotel, Kampala, Uganda.

Nsita, S. (2014) *Overview of Forest Tenure, Forestry Research and Related Reforms in Uganda*, paper submitted to the Centre for International Forestry Research. Ministry of Water and Environment, Kampala, Uganda.

Nsita, S.A., Nakangu, B., Banana A.Y., Mshale, B., Mwangi, E., and Ojwang D. (2017) *Forest Tenure Reform Implementation in Uganda: current challenges and future opportunities*, CIFOR Infobrief No. 196, Bogor, Indonesia.

Nyende, J. (2011) 'Natural resources management in the Lake Victoria region of East Africa: a study in multi-level government', Doctoral dissertation, Cardiff University, Cardiff, UK.

Okello, B. (2002) *A History of East Africa*, Fountain, Kampala, Uganda.

Ostrom, E. (1990) *Governing the Commons*, Cambridge University Press, Cambridge, UK.

Reid, R. (2011) 'Past and presentism: the "precolonial" and the foreshortening of African history', *The Journal of African History*, vol. 52, no. 2, pp. 135–155.

Republic of Uganda (2003) *The National Forestry and Tree Planting Act of 2003*, Ministry of Justice and Constitutional Affairs, Kampala, Uganda.

Republic of Uganda (2005) *Constitution of the Republic of Uganda – Amended by the Constitution (Amendment) Act, Act 11/2005 and the Constitution (Amendment) (No.2) Act, 21/2005*, Ministry of Justice and Constitutional Affairs, Kampala, Uganda.

Ribot, J.C., Agrawal, A., and Larson, A.M. (2006) 'Recentralizing while decentralizing: how national governments re-appropriate forest resources', *World Development*, vol. 34, no. 11, pp. 1864–1886.

Rights and Resources Initiative (2012) *What Rights? A comparative analysis of developing countries' national legislation on community and indigenous peoples' forest tenure rights*, Rights and Resources Initiative, Washington, DC, USA.

Roscoe, J. (2015) *The Baganda: an account of their native customs and beliefs*, FB & C Limited, London, UK.

Sangster, R.G. (1950) *Working Plan for the South Mengo Forests, Uganda, for the period 1948–1957*, Government Printer, Entebbe, Uganda.

Sheil, D., Jennings, S., and Savill, P. (2000) 'Long-term permanent plot observations of vegetation dynamics in Budongo, a Ugandan rain forest', *Journal of Tropical Ecology*, vol. 16, no. 6, pp. 865–882.

Stuart-Smith, A.M. (1967) *Species and Provenance Trials*, Forest Department Technical Notes No.137/67, Uganda.

Tack, C.H. (1969) *Uganda Timbers: a list of the more common Uganda timbers and their properties*, Republic of Uganda, Forest Department, Uganda.

Thomas, H.B. and Spencer, A.E. (1938) *A History of Uganda Land and Surveys and of the Uganda Land and Survey Department*, Government Press, Entebbe, Uganda.

Turyahabwe, N. and Banana, A.Y. (2008) 'An overview of history and development of forest policy and legislation in Uganda', *International Forestry Review*, vol. 10, no. 4, pp. 641–656.

Turyomurugyendo, L. (2016) *The Extent and Effectiveness of Community Based Forestry in Uganda*, National Forestry Authority, Kampala, Uganda.

Vogt, N.D., Banana, A., Gombya-Ssembajjwe, W. and Bahati, J. (2006) 'Understanding the long-term stability of West Mengo forest reserve boundaries', *Ecology and Society*, vol. 11, no. 1, pp. 38–48.

Webster, G. and Osmaston, H. (2003) *A History of the Uganda Forest Department 1951–1965*, Commonwealth Secretariat, London, UK.

World Wide Fund for Nature (WWF) (2013) *Conserving Biodiversity in the Albertine Rift Forests. A project report*, World Wide Fund for Nature, Woking, UK.

3 An overview of integrated conservation and development in Uganda

Medard Twinamatsiko, Julia Baker, Phil Franks, Mark Infield, Fanny Olsthoorn, and Dilys Roe

Introduction

The term Integrated Conservation and Development (ICD), or more commonly Integrated Conservation and Development Projects (ICDPs), emerged in the late 1980s and early 1990s. The concept of ICD was intended to offer a more socially-acceptable alternative to the traditional "fines and fences" protectionist approach to conservation and protected area management (Hughes and Flintan, 2001). Initially, ICDPs mainly focused on protected area conservation. For example, Wells et al. (1992) suggested 'ICDPs aim to stabilise land use outside protected area boundaries and to increase local incomes in order to reduce pressure from further exploitation of natural resources in the protected area' (p. 3). Integrated Conservation and Development aims to provide services and employment to park-adjacent communities under the premise that when these communities become richer they are more likely to accept conservation policies and reduce their pressure on the environment (Wells et al., 1992). Similarly Brown and Wyckoff-Baird (1995) suggested that ICDPs are intended to 'enhance the conservation of biological diversity by focusing on the social and economic needs of people living in nearby communities' (p. 4). This creates a reconciliation of protected area management and the needs of local people.

The first generation of ICDPs of the late 1980s and early 1990s were mostly based on the assumption that providing communities that live adjacent to protected areas (PAs) with access to alternative types of resources and income sources generated from outside PAs (i.e., 'de-coupling' local livelihoods from park resources) would decrease the threats of unsustainable or illegal use of PA resources. From the early 1990s a number of ICDPs began to include measures to increase PA-related benefits to local communities (i.e., deliberately coupling local livelihoods to park resources), on the assumption that people would be more willing to support conservation because they could feel a direct benefit from doing so (Kremen et al., 1998; Baral et al., 2007). Franks and Blomley (2004) provides a summary of how new ICD approaches have been introduced over time, even as earlier approaches have continued to be implemented (Table 3.1).

Table 3.1 Different approaches to ICD in Uganda over time

Date	Approach
1985–*c*.1995	**Substitution and/or compensation:** Buffer zone communities offered livelihood alternatives to reduce pressure on natural resources and investment in infrastructure to generate support for conservation.
c.1995–*c*.2000	**Benefit sharing:** Benefit sharing mechanisms (e.g., for tourism revenues) introduced as means to add value to natural resources and give communities a 'stake' in conservation.
c.2000 onwards	**Power sharing:** Local communities empowered to have greater control/authority over natural resource management and the sharing of costs and benefits from conservation

Source: Franks and Blomley, 2004.

Even with the broad categories of ICD approaches described in Table 3.1, specific ICD interventions have taken a wide variety of forms over the years. This is reflected in the array of project strategies employing different levels of local participation, from passive benefit sharing to community-based management where management of resources is devolved to the local level (Johannesen and Skonhoft, 2004). Hughes and Flintan (2001) state that, 'Despite the diversity of terminology and variation in the scope of activities perceived to comprise of ICDPs, they have a number of common features;

- Biodiversity conservation is the primary goal
- There is a recognition that economic requirements of people who would otherwise threaten biodiversity need to be addressed
- The objective is to improve relationships between state managed PAs and their neighbours
- ICDPs do not necessarily seek to devolve control to local communities
- ICDPs usually receive funding from external sources and international conservation organisations and sometimes assistance from government
- The majority of ICDPs are externally motivated and initiated by conservation organisations or development agencies' (p. 5)

Robinson and Redford (2001), by contrast, see a clear divide in ICDP typologies, with some that emphasise conservation (conservation projects with development) while others have development as the primary goal (development projects with conservation). They note that conservation projects with development tend to focus on protected areas, with local people viewed as a threat that needs to be alleviated; while development projects with conservation focus on poverty alleviation, institution building, equity and social justice, but recognise the requirement that natural resources are managed sustainably and ecosystem services are maintained.

Others dispute this clear divide. Franks and Blomley (2004) concur that there are some ICDPs that genuinely seek to combine conservation and development with no hierarchy. They highlight CARE International's Development Through Conservation (DTC) project in Uganda, which, despite its name, had an equal emphasis on conservation and development. Sanjayan et al. (1997) state that [ICD] is not conservation through development, or conservation with development, or even conservation adjoined with development. It is the achievement of conservation goals and development needs together.

Further developing the debate over these issues, Adams et al. (2004) identify four possible articulations of the relationship between conservation and development. These are 'poverty and conservation are separate policy realms'; 'poverty is a critical constraint on conservation'; 'conservation should not compromise poverty reduction'; and 'poverty reduction depends on living resource conservation' (pp. 1147, 1148). The second through to the last of these formulations span a continuum from seeing development as a means to achieve conservation goals through to seeing conservation as a means to achieve conservation goals.

The rise in recognition of the importance of biodiversity-based ecosystem services over the last 20 years has done a lot to break down the perception of a dichotomous choice to be made between conservation and development goals. There has been growing recognition overtime that conservation in almost all cases serves multiple objectives, including what might be legitimately described as the conservation objectives of local people. The growing popularity of framing the benefits derived from nature as 'ecosystem services' by both conservationists and development practitioners has further helped to break down the apparent dichotomy. It is increasingly understood that development depends on the maintenance of ecosystems that supply goods and services on which economic development depends.

Early forms of ICD in Uganda

Uganda was an early pioneer of the ICD approach. Launched in 1987 by CARE International and the World Wide Fund for Nature (WWF), the Development Through Conservation project at Bwindi and Mgahinga Forest Reserves was an early initiative in the global context of ICD and can be considered as the start of ICD in Uganda. Both forests had been gazetted as forest reserves under the British colonial government in the 1930s, were subsequently jointly managed by the forest and game departments as both forest reserves and game sanctuaries, and then gazetted as national parks in 1991 (see Tumusiime et al., this volume, Chapter 4, for further details of ICD at Bwindi). Management of the forest reserves was not without local conflict – particularly with the indigenous Batwa people who were evicted from Bwindi in 1961 when it became a game sanctuary. Prior to gazettement as national parks, local people, while not allowed to live in the forest, had legal access to non-commercially valuable forest resources, such as firewood, medicinal plants and wild meat. However, there was also widespread illegal timber harvesting and mining, and growing concern for the future of the country's remaining population of mountain gorillas (*Gorilla beringei beringei*), especially given the Forest Department's limited capacity and mandate for wildlife conservation. Because of this concern, resource access for local people became progressively more and more restricted, resulting in worsening relationships between the forest authorities and surrounding communities and acts of protest such as fire setting.

Integrated Conservation and Development in Uganda emerged from the recognition that a more effective way to stop the destruction of natural resources would be to form an alliance between communities surrounding forested areas on the one hand, and conservation organisations and governments on the other (Wild and Mutebi, 1996; van der Duim et al., 2014). The expectation was that this integration would increase local engagement in conservation and yield support for conservation.

The earliest ICD activities of the DTC project were substitution initiatives, aimed at providing communities with on-farm alternatives to forest resources i.e., 'de-coupling' interventions (Franks and Blomley 2004; Blomley et al., 2010). The goal of the DTC project was to contribute to the conservation of Bwindi Impenetrable and Mgahinga forests and to improve natural resource-based economic security of 9,600 farm families in the surrounding farmland (Metcalfe, 1996). The programme started with a conservation education and woodlot project and expanded two years later, in 1989, with an agroforestry and agriculture project, both having the aim of reducing the dependence of people on forest resources by providing alternative sources of resources and income.

In 1989, similar ICD projects started in Kibale and Semuliki forest reserves, implemented by the Ministry of Water, Lands and Environment with funding from the Norwegian Government (Metcalfe, 1996). The first phase of this Kibale and Semuliki Conservation and Development Project (KSCDP) was geared towards the reduction of the negative impacts of local communities while strengthening the parks' managing capacity. Like the DTC project, it was a substitution or 'de-coupling' ICDP and included soil and water conservation techniques, improved crop husbandry, tree nurseries and crop diversification (Chege et al., 2002).

A substitution project was also implemented in Queen Elizabeth National Park in the early 1990s, to harmonise conflicting needs of the park and surrounding fishing communities. The goal was to relieve pressure on the park by increasing the on-farm supply of fuel for cooking and fish smoking through the planting of woodlots (CARE Denmark, 1993). Its results were mixed as the distribution of benefits was unequal – poorer households were unable to participate as they could not hire casual labour to invest in land clearance. Additionally, local people continued to access 'free' timber resources from the park for their subsistence needs, and used the woodlot programme to generate timber for sale at local markets (Blomley, 2000).

A particular challenge connected to the substitution strategy, especially the planting of indigenous trees on community land, was that it was seen as a systematic plan by park management to extend the protected areas. Given that some local residents were already resentful and unhappy with the parks, especially the recently gazetted ones, this led to considerable ill feeling. Conversely, park managers were resistant to the idea of planting the exotic tree species that were much preferred by communities, especially at the national parks boundaries. As a result, local leaders campaigned against the implementation strategy, which led to community resistance to the projects. For instance, at Bwindi, Mgahinga and Queen Elizabeth National Park, apart from production of bamboo for house construction, efforts to produce indigenous trees and other forest products on farm did not succeed. The only successful planting of eucalyptus trees by local people at the park boundaries was at Rwenzori National Park. The mixed experience of these early ICD projects stimulated experimentation and other types of approach began to evolve beyond simple substitution approaches.

The evolution of ICD in Uganda

In 1993 Bwindi pioneered the expansion of ICD from substitution interventions (meant to achieve de-coupling) to a 'multiple use programme' which allowed regulated harvesting of certain amounts of non-timber forest products, and then in 1996, in partnership with the International Gorilla Conservation Programme (IGCP), introduced a programme to share revenue from tourism taking place at the park. Both initiatives were designed to provide local people with benefits from the park (i.e., they were coupling interventions) in order to increase their willingness to support conservation (Blomley et al., 2010).

For the multiple use programme, the park authority – Uganda National Parks (now Uganda Wildlife Authority) – and DTC project staff worked with residents in three parishes surrounding Bwindi Forest to pilot the development of resource access agreements allowing registered resource users to enter the park in order to harvest medicinal plants, collect basketry materials and practice beekeeping (UWA, 2014). A more limited form of the multiple use programme was initiated in 1993 in Mgahinga, allowing harvesting of bamboo roots for on-farm planting and access to water sources within the park (Uganda National Parks, 1996). Access to other products was not permitted owing to the much smaller size of Mgahinga Park in relation to surrounding communities (Franks, pers. comm.). Later the scheme was rolled out further to Mount Elgon, Rwenzori Mountains and Kibale National Parks (Metcalfe, 1996). From 1992, the management of Lake Mburo National Park, working in collaboration with the African Wildlife Foundation, began negotiating access to park resources through specific agreements with communities including corridors to water sources for cattle during droughts, seasonal harvesting of catfish, and harvesting of medicinal plants and papyrus (Infield, pers. comm.). At the time of writing, many of the national parks in Uganda permit controlled use of certain non-timber products and, more recently, have begun providing access to certain cultural sites.

One limitation of the multiple use programme was the limited number of people that could be involved (specialised resource users) and the limited resources that could be utilised (Blomley et al., 2010). The tourism-revenue-sharing initiative was intended to help mitigate some of these limitations by delivering benefits to a wider range of local community members (MacKenzie, 2012). The underlying rationale of the programme was that provision of benefits to communities would offset the costs of living adjacent to the park – including from human–wildlife conflict as well as from restrictions on resource access – and improve community attitudes (Blomley et al., 2010). This in turn, it was assumed, would deter local people from engaging in activities that undermined conservation (Johannesen and Skonhoft, 2004). Additionally, it was assumed that, since the revenue-sharing scheme involved negotiations between the park authority, local government and communities, it would help improve park–people relationships (Manyindo and Makumbi, 2005).

The tourism-revenue-sharing programme started as a pilot in Bwindi and Mgahinga in 1994 whereby Uganda National Parks agreed to return 12% of the income generated through park entry fees to the local communities (Tumusiime and Vedeld, 2012). Initially, however, the scheme did not correlate directly to park income as this was returned to central government and used to contribute to the management needs of other national parks and game reserves (Adams and Infield, 1998). To expand the scope of community support linked to the parks, the Mgahinga and Bwindi Impenetrable Forest Conservation Trust was established in 1995 with support from the World Bank and USAID.

The revenue-sharing scheme initiated in Bwindi was formalised in 1996 in the Wildlife Statute (section 70 c) and updated in the Wildlife Policy (2000), which required 20% of park entry fees to be redistributed to park-adjacent communities (Chege et al., 2002; Manyindo and Makumbi, 2005; MacKenzie, 2012). Similar initiatives by the International Union for Conservation Network (IUCN) were piloted at Mount Elgon National Park. In exchange, communities that benefited were expected to help in case of park emergencies like fires, to refrain from and to report illegal activities, and to participate in management, conservation and community education activities (Moghari, 2009).

Following its piloting at Bwindi and Mgahinga, the revenue-sharing scheme has been rolled out to other national parks including Murchison Falls, Queen Elizabeth, Lake Mburo and Mount Elgon (Manyindo and Makumbi, 2005). The manner in which the revenue is actually shared has taken different forms at different times and in different places. In some cases the funds have been used to pay for traditional resource substitution projects such as on-farm planting and agricultural improvements (Tumusiime and Vedeld, 2012). Earlier schemes had a stronger focus on funding community infrastructure projects such as schools and roads and then later shifted to funding household-level projects such as livestock rearing or beekeeping (Manyindo and Makumbi, 2005). Some commentators argue that the rationale for this shift was that public infrastructure and services should be funded by government agencies rather than by conservation or tourism (MacKenzie, 2012). An example of this is Bwindi, where 80% of revenue was spent on community development projects between 1996 and 2009 but, after that, more emphasis was put on household-level projects like goat rearing, potato growing and tree planting (Tumusiime and Vedeld, 2012). This change in strategy was partially a response to pressure from UWA's donors who still firmly believed in the substitution approach (Twinamatsiko, 2015). A recent review of the 20 years of experience of revenue sharing at Bwindi reveals that revenue sharing delivers conservation impact through multiple pathways, the least significant of which is the substitution pathway (Franks and Twinamatsiko, 2017). The study goes on to predict that conservation impact could be increased by placing more emphasis on mitigation of human–wildlife conflict and, under this overall strategy, empowering the frontline communities most affected by human–wildlife conflict to decide for themselves what would be the most relevant projects.

A further evolution in Ugandan ICD was the Collaborative Resource Management (CRM) programme, which intended to embed multiple-use agreements and revenue sharing within a broader co-management (now called shared governance) approach. In the Ugandan context, CRM meant that the Uganda Wildlife Authority would share benefits and responsibility to sustainably manage natural resources, and give communities some real influence over at least some aspects of PA decision-making (Chege et al., 2002). At Bwindi and Mgahinga, given the concerns over mountain gorilla conservation and the importance of income from gorilla tourism in subsidising the costs of other less 'profitable' national parks (Adams and Infield, 1998, 2003), there was, in reality, no sharing of management rights and responsibilities with communities. Collaborative Resource Management was also introduced in the later phases of the Kibale and Semuliki Conservation and Development project, which continued throughout the 1990s and which gave communities real influence over certain management decisions (Chege et al., 2002; MacKenzie, 2012). Similarly, in Lake Mburo National Park, a Community Conservation programme provided training and representation of local communities in management meetings and built capacity of park staff to engage in positive and proactive ways with communities, allowing a shift toward more conciliatory approaches to park management (Infield and Namara, 2001; Infield and Mugisha, this volume, Chapter 9).

In terms of the institutional arrangements that underpin CRM, the key platform at park level for community participation in decision-making was the Park Management Advisory Committee (PMAC), which was first established in 1994 and then evolved in the mid-1990s into the Community–Park Institution (CPI). Many parks established these in the 1990s and they had a leading role in implementation of the revenue-sharing scheme. Both local residents and some park management officials looked at CPI as a strategy to promote collaborative park management and increase community involvement in Protected Areas management. Community–Park Institutions were finally institutionalised by the Uganda Wildlife Policy of September 2000, which was reviewed in 2004 (CARE, 2006; Namara, 2006). The Community–Park Institution was mandated to do the following:

- To act as a forum for mobilising local communities to participate in various community conservation issues.
- To channel and voice community concerns and thus provide an avenue for Protected Area Managers to seek active involvement in natural resource management.

Central to the role of CPI as an institution of collaborative management was governance of the revenue-sharing scheme. This included deciding how the funds would be allocated to different communities around the PA and different types of project, and monitoring the performance of the scheme to promote accountability of UWA and local government for proper management of the scheme. The CPIs were looked at by park stakeholders as the facilitators for collaborative management or shared governance. Despite these good intentions, a review of the composition, legitimacy, functionality and relevance of CPIs conducted by independent consultants in 2010 recommended disbandment of CPI. The CPIs were viewed by many as political structures that no longer commanded the respect of some key stakeholders and that competed with elected Local Councils (LC), which included members responsible for the environment. Having one community councillor for every local government unit (parish), the CPI committees were often very large. These councillors had not been elected based on their knowledge and skills for the job and certainly not based on their ability to steer implementation of projects. The evaluation report asserted that CPI should be a project management organ rather than a political organ and that it should function with efficiency and effectiveness. The report recommended CPI disbandment and proposed that, for revenue sharing, UWA deal directly with the mainstream institutions of local government (UWA, 2012). This decision is consistent with the argument of leading natural resource governance scholar Jesse Ribot, who holds that working through local government is a better long-term solution than creating specific new resource governance institutions (Ribot, 2010). The reluctance of UWA to delegate real decision-making authority to the CPI was also a factor in its demise.

The termination of CPI and its replacement by local government was effectively the end of the collaborative resource management programme that had been started by NGOs. The UWA remains committed to active engagement with local communities but when and how communities might influence PA management is determined by UWA. In other words, after a brief experiment with co-management/shared governance, the governance type of national parks in Uganda has reverted to governance by government with some community consultation at the discretion of UWA (Franks, pers. comm.). It is worth noting, however, that the original PMAC, and the CPI that followed, were largely ineffective at representing community interests to the park authorities. The PMAC/CPI members tended to adopt the interests of the parks, often becoming, in effect, proxy park staff, carrying park positions and messages to the communities rather than vice versa (Biira, pers. comm.).

Effectiveness of ICD in Uganda

Many of Uganda's ICD initiatives have improved park–community relations (Infield and Adams 1999; Infield and Namara, 2001; Twinamatsiko et al., 2014; Twinamatsiko, 2015), but it remains unclear whether they have achieved conservation objectives, namely to reduce illegal activities (Blomley et al., 2010). One of the key reasons for this are the fundamentally flawed assumptions that underlie how de-coupling interventions (alternative livelihood and substitution projects) will generate sufficient behaviour change to bring about conservation impact (Blomley et al., 2010). In addition, there are several other factors, particularly those associated with the lack of equity on how benefits and costs are distributed (Franks et al., 2018).

At Bwindi, recent research has pointed to a lack of equity in benefit sharing as a key motivator for continued illegal behaviour (Twinamatsiko et al., 2014; Franks and Twinamatsiko, 2017). In particular, ICD initiatives have often failed to benefit those who suffered the greatest cost of conservation such as the communities closest to national park boundaries who suffer more crop raiding and other forms of human–wildlife conflict. Notably, the practice of revenue sharing does not appear to be well aligned with the current UWA policy that clearly indicates that it should prioritise the mitigation of human–wildlife conflict (MacKenzie, 2012; Harrison et al., 2015). Indeed, few ICD projects have been specifically targeted at those who bear the greater costs of conservation (Tumusiime and Sjaastad, 2014; Twinamatsiko et al., 2014; Twinamatsiko et al., 2015).

Linked to this is the problem of elite capture. Not only have ICD projects often failed to effectively target those who bear the costs of conservation, they have also tended to benefit wealthier households more than poorer ones and, in some cases, there is evidence of political interference in the allocation of benefits (Tumusiime and Vedeld, 2012; Twinamatsiko et al., 2014). The funds from revenue sharing, for example, are not disbursed directly to communities by UWA but via several layers of local government, providing multiple opportunities for funds to be diverted away from uses that would benefit communities and deliver conservation outcomes, to uses of interest to local government or even individuals. A recent review of the scheme at Bwindi highlighted that it is 'hampered by corruption and inequity leading to worsening economic inequality and resentment' (Franks and Twinamatsiko, 2017: p. 14).

A further issue is the sustainability of ICD initiatives. Where these are donor-funded initiatives, the short time frame of project interventions can be problematic. For example, local government did not adopt the interventions put into place by CARE International through the DTC project and so, when the CARE project ended and CARE left, the ICD initiatives ceased to have any support. Even if there is no reliance on donor funding, financial support for ICD can be unreliable. In Uganda, the availability of funds for revenue sharing is dependent on the success of the national parks in attracting tourists. However, tourism is notably unpredictable and subject to influence by external events including, recently, the global economic downturn. Indeed, owing to the sometimes low figures of revenue set aside for sharing with the communities, the UWA usually does not share revenues every year, but uses the gap years to accumulate sizeable amounts. As Tumusiime and Vedeld (2012) note, such a practice means the flow of benefits is unpredictable, which damages the reputation of the scheme and consequently its anticipated benefits.

Conclusions

Uganda has been a pioneer of approaches to integrating conservation and development over three decades, during which there has been considerable evolution in practice. Further details of several of these approaches can be found in Part III of this volume. In most of Uganda's PAs, and particularly Bwindi and Lake Mburo, conflicts between park and people have reduced because of ICD interventions during this period (Infield and Adams, 1999; Baker, 2004; Blomley et al., 2010; Bitariho, 2013; Twinamatsiko et al., 2014; Infield and Namara, 2001). However, this headline outcome does not reveal the full picture of the ICD experience.

Substitution/decoupling interventions have proved largely ineffective in terms of conservation (Blomley et al., 2010). A number of reviews of ICD interventions have pointed to the need for a stronger base in collaborative or co-management (MacKenzie, 2012), and for local communities to be considered as partners rather than a threat to conservation (Infield and Namara, 2001). As Brown and Wyckoff-Baird (1995) described,

> Perhaps the most important lesson learned in development over the last 20 years is that the failure to equitably involve projected beneficiaries as partners in all phases of project implementation, from design through evaluation, has consistently led to disappointing project results.
>
> (p. xiv)

In practice, this means maximising local responsibility and authority (Brown and Wyckoff-Baird, 1995). Over 20 years later, this lesson still remains valid in Uganda today.

While ICD interventions in Uganda have undoubtedly made a significant contribution to people–park relations and the livelihoods of local people, they have generally not led to more equitable sharing of the benefits and costs of conservation. The ICDPs have also failed to achieve the greater equity in governance that is increasingly emphasised in conservation policy at all levels, both as an ethical issue and as a means to more effective conservation (Franks et al., 2018). As a result, while Uganda was an early leader in the integration of conservation and development, it has now fallen behind what is currently regarded as best practice. To return to the forefront, a further round of innovation in conservation and development policy and practice will be required.

References

Adams, W.M., Aveling, R., Brockington, D., Dickson, B., Elliott, J., Hutton, J., Roe, D., Vira, B., and William Wolmer, W. (2004) 'Biodiversity conservation and the eradication of poverty', *Science*, vol. 306, no. 5699, pp. 1146–1149.

Adams, W.M. and Infield, M. (1998) *Community Conservation at Mgahinga Gorilla National Park*. Community conservation research in Africa, principles and comparative practice, Working Paper No. 10. Institute for Development Policy and Management, University of Manchester, Manchester, UK.

Adams, W.M. and Infield, M. (2003) 'Who is on the gorillas payroll? Claims on tourist revenue from a Ugandan national park', *World Development*, vol. 31, no. 1, pp. 177–190.

Baker, J. (2004) 'Evaluating conservation policy: integrated conservation and development at Bwindi Impenetrable National Park', PhD thesis, University of Kent at Canterbury, UK.

Baker, J. (2015) *Fairer, better. A guide to more effective Integrated Conservation and Development in Uganda*, International Institute for Environment and Development, London, UK.

Baral, N., Stern, M.J. and Heinen, J.T. (2007) 'Integrated conservation and development project life cycles in the Annapurna Conservation Area, Nepal: is development overpowering conservation?', *Biodiversity and Conservation*, vol. 16, no. 1, pp. 2903–2917.

Bitariho, R. (2013) 'Socio-economic and ecological implications of local people's use of Bwindi Forest in South Western Uganda', PhD thesis, Mbarara University of Science and Technology at Mbarara, Uganda.

Blomley, T. (2000) *Woodlots, Woodfuel and Wildlife: Lessons from Queen Elizabeth National Park, Uganda*, International Institute for Environment and Development, London, UK.

Blomley, T., Namara, A., McNeilage, A., Franks, P., Rainer, H., Donaldson, A., Malpas, R., Olupot, W., Baker, J., Sandbrook, C., Bitariho, R. and Infield, M. (2010) *Development and Gorillas? Assessing the effectiveness of fifteen years of integrated conservation and development in South Western Uganda*. Natural resources. Issue 23. International Institute of Environment and Development, London, UK.

Brown, M. and Wyckoff-Baird, B. (1995) *Designing Integrated Conservation and Development Projects*, Revised Edition, Corporate Press, Washington, DC, USA.

CARE (2006) 'CARE's Work: Project Information: Development Through Conservation, Uganda', www.care.org/careswork/projects/UGA030.asp, accessed 23 August 2006.

CARE Denmark (1993) *Appraisal Report and Project Proposal: Queen Elizabeth National Park Conservation Project*, CARE, Uganda.

Chege, F., Onyango, G., Drazu, C. and Mwandha, S. (2002) 'Kibale and Semuliki Conservation and Development Project, end of Phase III/end-of-project evaluation'. *Unpublished report*, available at: www.iucn.org/downloads/kscdp_final.pdf.

Cicin-Sain, B. and Knecht, R.W. (1998) *Integrated Coastal and Ocean Management, Concepts and Practice*, Island Press, Washington, DC, USA.

Franks, P. and Blomley, T. (2004) 'Fitting ICD into a project framework: a CARE perspective', in T.O. McShane and M.P. Wells, (eds) *Getting Biodiversity Projects to Work: towards better conservation and development*, Columbia University Press, New York, NY, USA, pp. 79–97.

Franks, P., Booker, F. and Roe, D. (2018) *Understanding and Assessing Equity in Protected Area Conservation: a matter of governance, rights, social impacts and human wellbeing*, IIED Issue Paper. International Institute for Environment and Development, London, UK.

Franks, P. and Twinamatsiko, M. (2017) *Lessons Learnt From 20 Years of Revenue Sharing at Bwindi Impenetrable National Park, Uganda*, IIED Research Report, International Institute for Environment and Development, London, UK.

Harrison, M., Dilys, R., Baker, J., Mwedde, G., Travers, H., Plumptre, A., Rwetsiba, A. and Milner-Gulland, E.J. (2015) *Wildlife Crime: a review of the evidence on drivers and impacts in Uganda*, International Institute for Environment and Development, London, UK.

Hughes, R. and Flintan F. (2001) *Integrating Conservation and Development Experience: a review and bibiliography of the ICDP literature*, International Institute for Environment and Development, London, UK.

Infield, M. and Adams, W.M. (1999) 'Institutional sustainability and community conservation: a case study from Uganda', *Journal of International Development*, vol. 11, no. 1, pp. 305–315.

Infield, M. and Namara, A. (2001) 'Community attitudes and behaviour towards conservation: an assessment of a community conservation programme around Lake Mburo National Park, Uganda', *Oryx*, vol. 35, no. 1, pp. 48–60.

Johannesen, A.B. and Skonhoft, A. (2004) 'Tourism, poaching and wildlife conservation: what can integrated conservation and development projects accomplish?', *Resource and Energy Economics*, vol. 27, pp. 208–226.

Kremen, C., Raymond, I. and Lance, K. (1998) 'An interdisciplinary tool for monitoring conservation impacts in Madagascar', *Conservation Biology*, vol. 12, no. 1, pp. 549–563.

Lele, S., Wilshusen, P., Brockington, D., Seidler, R. and Bawa, K. (2010) 'Beyond exclusion: alternative approaches to biodiversity conservation in the developing tropics', *Environmental Sustainability*, vol. 2, no. 1, pp. 94–100.

MacKenzie, C.A. (2012) 'Trenches like fences make good neighbours: revenue sharing around Kibale National Park, Uganda', *Journal for Nature Conservation*, vol. 20, no. 2, pp. 92–100.

Manyindo, J. and Makumbi, I. (2005) 'A review of revenue sharing around the Queen Elizabeth Protected Area', *Wildlife Series*, vol. 4, pp. 1–8.

Martin, A., Gross-Camp, N., Kebede, B., McGuire, S. and Munyarukaza, J. (2014) 'Whose environmental justice? Exploring local and global perspectives in payments for ecosystem services scheme in Rwanda', *Geoforum*, vol. 54, no. 1, pp. 167–177.

Metcalfe, S. (1996) CARE *"Development Through Conservation" Project, Final Evaluation, Main Report*, CARE, Kampala, Uganda.

Moghari, N.M. (2009) 'A survey of Queen Elizabeth National Park (QENP) communities' attitudes toward human–lion conflict and lion conservation', unpublished doctoral dissertation, George Mason University, Fairfax, VA, USA.

Namara, A. (2006) 'From paternalism to real partnership with local communities? Experiences from Bwindi Impenetrable National Park, Uganda', *Africa Development*, vol. 31, no. 2, pp. 39–68.

Ochieng, A. (2011) 'Linking tourism, conservation and livelihoods: an analysis of sport hunting around Lake Mburo National Park, Uganda', MSc dissertation, Wageningen University, Wageningen, Netherlands.

Oldekop, J.A., Bebbington, A.J., Brockington, D. and Preziosi, R.F. (2010) 'Understanding the lessons and limitations of conservation and development | Entendiendo las lecciones y limitaciones de la conservación y el desarrollo', *Conservation Biology*, vol. 24, no. 2, pp. 1–9.

Ribot, J. (2010) 'Forestry and democratic decentralisation in Sub-Saharan Africa: a rough review', In L. German et al. (eds) *Governing Africa's Forests in a Globalised World*, Routledge, London, UK.

Robinson, J.G. and Redford, K.H. (2001) *Jack of All Trades, Master of None: inherent contradictions within ICDPs*, Columbia University Press, New York, NY, USA.

Sanjayan, M.A., Shen, S. and Malcolm, J. (1997) *Experiences with Integrated-Conservation Development Projects in Asia*, Washington, DC, USA.

Schreckenberg, K., Franks, P. and Martin, A. et al. (2016) 'Unpacking equity for protected area conservation', *Parks*, vol. 22, no. 2, pp. 11–26.

Tumusiime, D.M. and Sjaastad, E. (2014). 'Conservation and development: justice, inequality, and attitudes around Bwindi Impenetrable National Park', *Journal of Development Studies*, vol. 50, no. 2, pp. 204–225.

Tumusiime, D.M. and Vedeld, P. (2012) 'False promise or false premise? Using tourism revenue sharing to promote conservation and poverty reduction in Uganda', *Conservation and Society*, vol. 10, no. 1, pp. 15–28.

Twinamatsiko, M. (2015) 'Linking conservation to the implementation of revenue sharing policy and livelihood improvement of people bordering Bwindi Impenetrable National Park', PhD thesis, Mbarara University of Science and Technology at Mbarara, Uganda.

Twinamatsiko, M., Baker, J., Harrison, M., Shirkhorshidi, M., Bitariho, R., Wieland, M., Asuma, S., Franks, P. and Roe, D. (2014) *Linking Conservation, Equity and Poverty Alleviation: understanding profiles and motivations of resource users and local perceptions of governance at Bwindi Impenetrable National Park, Uganda*, International Institute for Environment and Development, London, UK.

Twinamatsiko, M., Kagoro-Rugunda, G., Basheka, B. and De Herdt, T. (2015) 'Can governance in revenue sharing be a pathway for a win-win situation between people's livelihood improvement and conservation?' *Journal for Social Sciences Research*, vol. 8, no. 1, pp. 1437–1453.

Uganda National Parks (1996) *Mgahinga National Park Management Plan 1996–2000*, Uganda National Parks, Kampala, Uganda.

Uganda Wildlife Authority (UWA) (2000) *The Uganda Wildlife Law*, Ministry of Tourism, Trade and Industry, Kampala, Uganda.

Uganda Wildlife Authority (UWA) (2012) *Revenue Sharing Policy Review*, Final Draft of the Main Report, Uganda Wildlife Authority, Kampala, Uganda.

Uganda Wildlife Authority (UWA) (2014) *Bwindi Impenetrable National Park General Management Plan 2014–2024*, Uganda Wildlife Authority, Kampala, Uganda.

van der Duim, R., Ampumuza, C. and Ahebwa, W.M. (2014) 'Gorilla tourism in Bwindi Impenetrable National Park, Uganda: an actor-network perspective', *Society and Natural Resources*, vol. 27, no. 1, pp. 588–601.

Wells, M., Brandon, K. and Hannah, L.J. (1992) *People and Parks: linking protected area management with local communities*, World Bank, Washington, DC, USA.

Wild, R.G. and Mutebi, J. (1996) *Conservation Through Community Use of Plant Resources: establishing collaborative management at Bwindi Impenetrable and Mgahinga Gorilla National Parks, Uganda*, People and Plants Working Paper, UNESCO, Paris, France, available at: http://unesdoc.unesco.org/images/0011/001117/111731e.pdf.

Part II
Celebrity sites and case studies of conservation, development practice, and research

4 Bwindi Impenetrable National Park

A celebrity site for integrated conservation and development in Uganda

David Mwesigye Tumusiime, Robert Bitariho, and Chris Sandbrook

Introduction

Since it was gazetted in 1991, Bwindi Impenetrable National Park has been the site of extraordinary attention. Home to an iconic population of mountain gorillas within a small patch of forest that is surrounded by a densely populated region with high levels of poverty, it has attracted an army of conservationists, development agencies, documentary film makers, celebrities, human rights activists, missionaries, and thousands of international tourists. Bwindi has been the site of multiple interventions, carried out by various combinations of these actors, often with combined conservation and development objectives. Many of these were cutting edge when first applied at Bwindi, making the site a test case for conservation tools that were subsequently adopted around the world. At the same time, Bwindi has attracted a multitude of researchers, from various disciplines, who have come to explore issues ranging from mountain gorilla ecology to the politics of NGO activities. Bwindi is also the poster child of Ugandan conservation, endlessly featured in glossy magazine articles and Sunday supplements around the world, allowing it to hold the attention of millions of people who will never visit the site, but nonetheless feel that they have a stake in its future. Meanwhile, local people, and local wildlife, have had to find ways to adapt to life in something of a goldfish bowl (or Petri dish), constantly observed, manipulated or studied by the latest external project. In short, Bwindi is something of a 'celebrity site' for conservation and development.

In this chapter we explore the multiple dimensions of Bwindi's celebrity, and ask what we can learn from a single case study that has been the focus of such attention (and at what cost to other sites). We begin with a brief history of the park and its people, to set the scene. We then consider Bwindi as a *laboratory* for integrated conservation and development interventions; what has been tried, by whom, and with what effects? We then turn to Bwindi as a *site of contestation*, considering the politics of conservation and development, and the history of conflict between these issues that has characterised the region. Finally, we examine Bwindi as a *storyline*, through a comparison

of the contrasting narratives that have emerged from researchers and practitioners with different perspectives on the same topics, and how these have
been used to portray Bwindi to diverse external audiences. The chapter ends
with some conclusions, focusing on wider lessons for Uganda and beyond
that can be learned from the Bwindi case study.

A history of Bwindi Impenetrable Forest and its use by humans

The first human settlements in southwest Uganda forests may have coincided
with the migrations of the Bantu-speaking people from the southern and
central parts of Africa into East Africa between 1000–1800 AD (Huffman
1970). Batwa initially inhabited the forests in southwestern Uganda up until
the mid-16th century when Bakiga and Bafumbira-Bahutu joined following wars in northern Rwanda (Kingdon 1990; Lewis 2000; Marchant et al.
2000). The Batwa, Bakiga/Bafumbira-Hutu and Batutsi clans lived together,
albeit in a precarious harmony, due to their complimentary livelihoods as
hunter-gatherers, agriculturists and pastoralists respectively. There were
low levels of subsistence hunter-gatherer activities in the forest, mainly by
the Batwa (Lewis 2000; Marchant et al. 1995).

The earliest forest clearances in southwestern Uganda date back approximately 2200 years before present (BP), probably caused by low level
human impacts of agriculture by the ancestors of today's Bakiga/Bafumbira
(Marchant et al. 1995). This coincided with the iron-smelting technology
developed between 2500 to 2000 years BP and taken up by the Bakiga and
Bafumbira-Hutu agriculturalists (Phillipson 1986; Marchant et al. 2000).
Population increase in and around Bwindi forest due to the influx of Bantu-
speaking people into the region increased clearing of forests for agriculture
and use of the forest for grazing domestic animals. The Bakiga/Bafumbira
were free nomadic cultivators who practiced shifting cultivation of slash-
and-burn in the high altitude forests of southwestern Uganda (Kingdon
1990; Edel 1957). This practice eventually led to encroachment on the
Batwa forest territories as the Bakiga/Bafumbira populations increased. The
forests started becoming patchy and started decreasing, resulting in conflicts of the agriculturalists with the Batwa forest hunter-gatherers (Kingdon
1990; Edel 1957).

Prior to the gazettement of Bwindi forest (in 1932) by the British colonial
regime, the forest was mainly used for commercial exploitation of timber by
European missionaries and colonial administrators (for constructing churches,
hotels and government buildings) and hunting of fauna for trophies and
meat. The local people were engaged in artisanal mining for gold and other
minerals, hunting by mainly the Batwa, and extraction of plants for building poles, firewood, medicinal use and basketry weaving purposes. When
combined, all these activities increased forest cover loss with some reduced
populations of fauna and increased forest patchiness (Marchant et al. 2000).

Unfortunately, no record exists of any pre-colonial resource management institutions. In 1932 the British colonial government enacted legislation for the gazettement of Bwindi Impenetrable Forest Reserve under the district administration. The aim was to stop encroachment by agriculturalists and regulate timber exploitation (Leggat and Osmaston 1961; Butynski 1984; Kingdon 1990; Lewis 2000). Other activities, such as gold mining, hunting and extraction of plant resources, remained unregulated and the commercial exploitation of the forest for timber continued. As a result, there was continued increase in forest cover loss, and increased loss of some fauna species including a reduction in the population of mountain gorillas (Wild 2001; Leggat and Osmaston 1961).

In 1964, the Game Act established the Bwindi Impenetrable Game Reserve and put restrictions on hunting, mainly to protect the endangered mountain gorillas (Butynski 1984). Hunting by the local people (both Batwa and Bakiga), but also the hunting of fauna for trophies, continued illegally as there was low manpower to patrol the entire forest, and this was exacerbated by a breakdown of institutions during the period of civil wars (1971–1984), including Idi Amin's dictatorship. Thus, there was continued loss of forest cover and of some fauna species (e.g. leopards, buffaloes, giant forest hogs, and mountain gorillas) (Butynski 1984; Wild 2001). Although the Batwa were not evicted from using the forest, the gazettement of Bwindi as a forest and later game reserve limited their use of the forest. Restrictions on hunting and forest climber (lianas) collection led to Batwa becoming dependent on Bakiga/Bafumbira agriculturalists for food and other resources. The Bakiga/Bafumbira were principally agriculturalists that used the Bwindi forest to supplement their livelihoods, unlike the Batwa who entirely depended on the forest. This was the beginning of the complex relationships between resident human groups that are still manifested in the present day.

In August 1991 the Bwindi Impenetrable Forest became gazetted as Bwindi Impenetrable National Park in order to strengthen the efforts of protecting the mountain gorillas and their habitat. This led to restrictions on all forms of human activities within the forest, including settlement. The national park recruited and employed paramilitary rangers to patrol the forest and enforce regulations, but poaching and pitsawing still continued on a large scale as the rangers could not patrol the entire Bwindi park area to look for such activities. In the early 1990s, after Bwindi was gazettted a national park, several conflicts between park managers and the local people arose that led to about 5% of the Bwindi forest being set on fire (ITFC 1999). Furthermore, park rangers were occasionally harassed by the local people who were protesting the creation of the national park (Cunningham 2001; Wild 2001; Bitariho et al. 2006; Bitariho et al. 2016). At this time, and up to the present day, Bwindi has faced a wide range of conservation threats and issues, summarised in Table 4.1.

Table 4.1 Conservation issues and impacts at Bwindi Forest from 1991 to the present day

Period/era	Key conservation issues	Impact	References
After gazettement of Bwindi forest as a national park in 1991	• Strengthened efforts of protecting the mountain gorilla and its habitat. • No commercial or subsistence extraction of forest resources (no timber cutting, no hunting, etc. were allowed). • Increased paramilitary ranger forces to patrol the forest. • Traditional forest users denied access to the forest.	• Conflicts between park managers and the local people. • Numerous fires deliberately set in the forest by the local people, burning up to 5% of the forest. • Park staff increasingly harassed by the local people and vice versa. • Loss of some fauna and flora from forest fires and deliberate killing of fauna by the local people.	Cunningham 2001; Wild 2001
Period between 1994 and 1999	• The introduction of a new park management strategy, the Integrated Conservation and Development Programmes in Bwindi (including multiple use, tourism, revenue sharing), all focused on the involvement of local people in park management.	• Reduced conflicts between park management and the local people, reduced forest fires caused by arsonists, reduced poaching and better protection of fauna in Bwindi.	Cunningham 2001; Blomley et al. 2010; Bitariho et al. 2006

Period between 2000 to present	A section of local people around Bwindi (the marginalised frontline poor people) increasingly developing negative attitudes towards park management. • Increased human population around Bwindi coupled with increased poverty and crop raiding issues with wild animals from Bwindi forest. • Increased demand for forest resources. • Inequity issues in access to park resources (revenue sharing, resource use and tourism). • Marginalisation of minority groups in access to park resources (Batwa and women). • Lack of access to park resources by the poorest people around Bwindi. • Increased demand for Bwindi resources (revenues, forest climbers for basketry, food and water). • Crop loss from crop raiding wild animals leading to poverty and famine of the frontline park-adjacent local people. • No reduction in poaching and other illegal access to forest resources (fish, firewood and water, etc.).	Davey et al. 2001; Bitariho et al. 2006; Namara 2006; Bitariho et al. 2016; Tumusiime and Vedeld 2015; Tumusiime and Vedeld 2012; Tumusiime and Sjaastad 2014; Twinamatsiko et al. 2014
Current and emerging issues	• The tarmacking of the Ruhija-Buhoma road through Bwindi Park. • More tourism infrastructure developments around Bwindi (lodges and shops). • Feared impacts on biodiversity, particularly the gorillas. • Increased access to Bwindi by outside communities could create negative social impacts on the local people (tourism associated negative impacts such as prostitution, and local cultural erosion).	Barr et al. 2015

Bwindi as a laboratory for integrated conservation and development

With the park management conflicts experienced in Bwindi, donor and development agencies influenced the Uganda National Parks (now Uganda Wildlife Authority (UWA)) to change its paramilitary approach strategy to one that focused on the involvement of local people in park management (see Table 4.1). In 1993, the Bwindi park management adopted a set of new park management strategies to this end. The strategies were: law enforcement, multiple use, tourism development, revenue sharing, agricultural interventions and on-farm substitution of wild plants. Later on, the problem animal management programme to mitigate the impacts of crop raiding animals was also introduced as another park management programme. All these park management programmes were aimed at involving the local people in park management so they could appreciate its benefits (Table 4.1). The programmes were intended to work in tandem with each other for better park management results.

Like interventions elsewhere in Uganda (see Twinamatsiko et al., this volume, Chapter 3), conservation and development interventions at Bwindi have drawn on a variety of different theories of change regarding how desirable outcomes might be achieved. Blomley et al. (2010) provide a useful typology for these interventions, which defines them according to whether or not they were 'coupled' with park natural resources, and whether they promoted financial or natural resource-based strategies (Table 4.2). The diversity of interventions that have been attempted across these categories has contributed to Bwindi's status as a laboratory for integrated conservation and development.

By 2003, when they were emphasised by the World Parks Congress in Durban, strategies similar to those applied in Bwindi in the early 1990s had become mainstream practice in conservation. However, when they were launched in Bwindi they were cutting edge (see Twinamatsiko et al., this volume, Chapter 3). Indeed, Bwindi is arguably one of the earliest sites anywhere in the world to experience such a wide range of integrated conservation and development interventions.

Table 4.2 A typology of ICD strategies implemented at Bwindi (after Blomley et al. (2010))

	Park resource-dependent 'coupling' strategies	Park resource-independent 'decoupling strategies'
Financial resource-dependent strategies	• Tourism • Revenue sharing • Conservation Trust Fund	• Agriculture development
Natural resource-dependent strategies	• Access to forest resources (multiple use)	• Resource substitution

In addition, the interventions at Bwindi have been intensively studied by a wide range of different researchers, making it possible to consider their impacts in some detail. In Table 4.3 we provide a summary of the key characteristics of each of these interventions, including timing, actors involved, funding, intended outcomes, the theory of change by which the desired outcomes were expected to occur, and information on their outcomes for conservation and development. For reasons of space and to avoid excessive replication of the Blomley et al. (2010) review, we provide only a summary of the large number of studies that have been conducted on the impact of these various interventions.

Although strict and militaristic approaches to management of protected areas (PAs) can in practice suppress local dissent (Brockington 2004) and 'local support is not necessarily essential for conservation' (Holmes 2013, p. 72), calls for the participation of local residents in conservation activities remain standard practice at many protected areas (Cunningham 2001; Hutton et al. 2005; Adams and Hutton 2007). At Bwindi, this has been approached through the promotion of Integrated Conservation and Development Programs (ICDPs), as described above. On the side of conservation, a lot of success has been registered. As an indicator example, there was an estimated increase of about 7% in the total population size of the area's flagship species (the mountain gorilla) between 1997 and 2002 and 12% between 1997 and 2006 (Guschanskia et al. 2009; McNeilage et al. 2006; Olupot et al. 2009) gradually ranging over larger areas (Blomley et al. 2010). In comparison, nearly all other African great ape sites have been experiencing sharp declines (Caldecott and Miles 2005). Bwindi is therefore a successful case of in situ conservation (Laudati 2010). On the side of people, mixed outcomes have been registered. Some local people have benefited with improved livelihoods, but others have been left out and have suffered costs (Blomley et al. 2010; Sandbrook and Adams 2012).

It is difficult to attribute overall outcomes to particular ICDP interventions at Bwindi (Tumusiime and Sjaastad 2014), particularly because so many have been tried in the same place and at the same time, making it very difficult to untangle the web of potentially causal linkages between them. This reflects the fact that, despite all the research attention that Bwindi has received, interventions attempted there over the years were never designed with the intention of contributing to wider understanding of 'what works'. Rather, they were implemented, often simultaneously, in the hope of addressing serious and urgent conservation and development challenges. Somewhat ironically, this means that although Bwindi has been celebrated as a testing ground for various approaches, it has not in practice produced the kind of results of wider significance that one might expect from a laboratory of integrated conservation and development.

Table 4.3 Summary of the key characteristics of the conservation and/or development interventions implemented at Bwindi

Name	Timing	Actors	Funding	Strategies used	Theory of Change	Blomley et al classification	Actual Conservation outcomes	Actual Development outcomes	Key references
Law enforcement by park rangers and military	1932–present, with increased military presence since 1999 when several international tourists were murdered.	Uganda Wildlife Authority (and earlier park/reserve management); Uganda People's Defence Force (UPDF).	Government of Uganda with donor support (e.g., WWF 1986–1997; USAID 1999–2006; IGCP 1996–present; WCS 2014–present).	Ranger patrols, Management Information System (MIST), Spatial Management and Reporting Tool (SMART).	Risk of detection and punishment will reduce illegal activities leading to improved conservation outcomes; military presence will ensure safety of tourists, leading to greater tourism revenues for conservation and development goals.	Not applicable	Reduced poaching and killing of gorillas and other large mammals. Increase in animal and plant populations.	Reduced access to forest resources by the local people (firewood, medicinal, basketry plants, building materials etc.). Negative attitudes towards park management as a result of reduced access to park resources.	Harrison et al. 2015; Baker et al. 2011; McNeilage et al. 2006; Guschanskia et al. 2009; Bitariho et al. 2016; Olupot et al. 2009; Blomley et al. 2010
Multiple Use Programme	1994–present	Uganda Wildlife Authority with support from CARE (1993–1997). ITFC 1999 to present.	UWA, BMCT, USAID, MacArthur Foundation	People allowed to collect non-timber products from 20% of park area.	Benefits from the park will improve livelihoods of local people and motivate them to report illegal activity.	Natural resource-dependent and 'coupled' to park resources.	Minimal impact on local people's role in park management. Park neighbours still carry out illegal harvesting.	Minimal. Few people participate and resource use agreements hardly cover high value resources.	Bitariho 2013; Bitariho et al. 2016; Bensted-Smith et al. 1995; Bitariho et al. 2006; Wild and Mutebi 1996.
Tourism	1993–present. (For visitor numbers each year see Figure 4.1.)	Uganda Wildlife Authority, UPDF, various NGOs (IGCP, ITFC).	UWA, USAID, AWF	Development of tourism facilities, habituation of mountain gorillas, creation of wildlife trails in the forest, allocation of 20% of park entrance fees for sharing between park-adjacent communities.	Income generated from tourism will support local development and fund conservation activities. Local benefits will create motivation for conservation.	Financial resource-dependent and 'coupled' to park resources.	Significant funding that supports park conservation activities. However, from the desire to increase this revenue base, more gorilla groups have been periodically habituated, which increases risks, e.g., of disease transmission across the human–wildlife interface.	Significant benefits but spatially restricted and access limited mostly to well educated men. Some costs to non-participants like higher food prices.	Archabald and Naughton-Treves 2001; Ahebwa et al. 2012a; Tumusiime and Vedeld 2012; Tumusiime and Sjaastad 2014; Tumusiime and Sjaastad 2014; Twinamatsiko et al. 2014; Sandbrook and Adams 2012; Sandbrook 2010; Laudati 2010.

Intervention	Timing	Organisations	Funding	Activity	Assumption	Financial coupling	Impact on attitudes	Impact/effectiveness	References
Revenue sharing	Early 1990s. Formalised with Act in 1996.	UWA, local government, CARE, IGCP, ITFC, IIED local institutions (PMAC, CPI).	A % share of tourism revenues.	Distribution of tourism revenues for community development projects around park borders.	By receiving a financial benefit from tourism, local people will benefit and be motivated to support conservation.	Financial resource-dependent and 'coupled' to park resources.	Some impact on local attitudes towards conservation, but also some concern about how it has been administered.	Impact reduced by 1996 Act, which lowered revenue to be shared at Bwindi. Some success but beset by corruption, funds not reaching targets, delays, lack of targeting to those suffering problems.	Archabald and Naughton-Treves 2001; Ahebwa et al. 2012a; Tumusiime and Vedeld 2012; Tumusiime and Sjaastad 2014; Twinamatsiko et al. 2014; Twinamatsiko et al. 2015.
Problem animal management programme	Various programmes tried at different times (2001).	UWA, IGCP, local people particularly through the Human Gorilla Response Teams (HuGO), ITFC.	USAID, BMCT, UWA, GVTC.	Mauritius thorn hedge, tea growing as buffer crop, guarding, scare shooting, chilli peppers, chasing gorillas from crop fields back into the park.	Strategies will reduce impact of wildlife damage and thereby benefiting livelihoods and increasing tolerance for conservation.	Not Applicable	Reduced risk of disease transmissions between wildlife (gorillas) and humans. Reduced risk of death/harm to wildlife and humans.	Some success with Mauritius thorn and Nkuringo buffer zone (using multiple methods). Depends on good maintenance. No compensation is a point of conflict.	Andama 2009; Akampurira et al. 2015; Masiga et al. 2011.
Agricultural extension	1988–2002	CARE Development Through Conservation.	USAID	Provision of improved crop varieties, improved crop management and soil conservation measures.	If people earn income from other sources, they will no longer need to take resources from the park.	Financial resource-dependent and 'decoupled' from park resources.	Positive impact on conservation attitudes, despite being decoupled. Likely down to NGO education activities.	Widespread benefits at individual level meeting priority needs. Food security Firewood from woodlots and agroforestry.	Wild (2001) Blomley et al. (2010)

(continued)

Table 4.3 (continued)

Name	Timing	Actors	Funding	Strategies used	Theory of Change	Blomley et al classification	Actual Conservation outcomes	Actual Development outcomes	Key references
On-farm substitution	1988–2002	CARE Development Through Conservation	USAID	Provisions of tree seedlings to provide timber, stakes, firewood, etc.	If people have access to natural resources on-farm, they will no longer need to take resources from the park.	Natural resource-dependent and 'decoupled' from park resources.	Despite over 1m seedlings distributed, very few woodlots remain around Bwindi. National Park still used for wood.	Tree planting positively received and meets some subsistence and income needs.	Wild 2001; Blomley et al. 2010.
Local institution development	1999–2004	CARE DTC	CARE DTC	Establishment of Forest Resource User Committees, Parish Production and Environmental Committees, Community Protected Area Institutions.	Decentralised decision making will deliver better outcomes for local people and conservation.	Not Applicable		Many local institutions wound up when DTC finished. Shift by UWA to support local government instead. This was unpopular with local people.	Namara 2006; Bitariho 2013.

Bwindi as a site of contestation: struggles between conservation and development

We now turn to Bwindi as a site of contestation, considering the politics of conservation and development, and the history of conflict between these issues that has characterised the region. The struggle over interests within local conservation arenas is a common feature around the world, and Bwindi is no exception. The struggles first began at the time when the area was first reserved a Crown Forest in 1932 to protect and preserve the mountain gorilla (UWA 2001), and have continued to the present day. Important recent struggles include those over: (i) the balance between conservation and development; (ii) control of access to permits to view gorillas; (iii) leakage of tourism revenues outside the locality and the governance issues surrounding the distribution of tourism revenues that remain; and (iv) security issues owing to the location of the park by a national border.

The intricate balance between conservation and development

Although with varied motivations, all conservation actors seem to agree on the need to maintain a good balance between conservation and development, particularly for the local communities. However, a lacuna is how to achieve this in practice as pursuit of both tends to require trade-offs as opposed to synergies (McShane et al. 2010). Imbalances in the pursuit of both persist at Bwindi and there are some growing concerns. This is exemplified by the struggle over the number of gorilla groups to habituate.

Habituation of the mountain gorilla is a fairly lengthy process that takes two to three years. The process is about familiarising gorillas to human beings so that the gorillas are able to go on with their day-to-day activities in their natural environment even in the presence of humans. According to UWA regulations, each successfully habituated group can be tracked by a maximum of eight adult humans on any given day. The cap on permissible numbers is intended to limit the exposure of gorillas to humans (Homsy 1999). Each foreign tourist paid $600 in 2017 amounting to $4,800 per group per day. Thus, the more gorilla groups habituated, the more revenues that can be earned. Habituation was initiated in 1991 for the Mubare gorilla group in Buhoma area. The process was a success and tourists tracked the group for the first time in 1993. Since then, ten other gorilla families have been habituated for tourism. The increase in the number of habituated gorilla groups has resulted in a dramatic increase in annual tourist numbers from a paltry 1,300 in 1993 to 20,000 in some recent years (Figure 4.1). Gorilla tourism in Bwindi contributes over 50% of UWA's total income or 9.2% ($1.2 billion) of the country's GDP (Tumusiime and Vedeld, 2012).

In the early days of the tourism programme at Bwindi it was frequently argued that gorilla tourism was for conservation. Habituation was seen as a necessity to enable tourism to generate much needed revenues for conservation and for national and local development, therefore justifying any

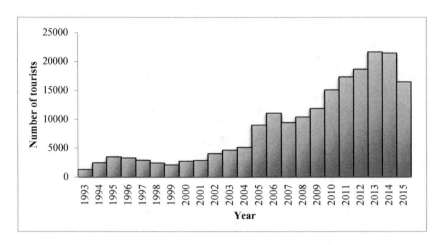

Figure 4.1 Tourist numbers received in Bwindi the past two decades. (Data source: Bwindi Park Management 2016.)

potential loss of 'wildness' implied by the habituation process. However, as the number of groups habituated has increased, the conservation rationale has become less clear, and some have argued that conservation is now for tourism, rather than vice versa. From a conservation point of view, negative aspects of habituation for gorillas include impact on behavioural responses, risks of disease transmission and possible impacts on reproductive success of habituated individuals. There is also an argument that at least some gorillas should be left unhabituated and 'truly' wild.

Habituation can also be detrimental to local livelihoods. Habituated gorillas get used to humans and tend to spend increasingly more time in human-dominated landscapes. This increases incidence and intensity of human–wildlife conflicts, particularly crop raiding. Crop raiding is reportedly on the increase in the area adjacent to Bwindi, partly because the habituated gorillas are increasingly spending significant amounts of foraging time on community land (Goldsmith 2005).

Arguments over habituation pitch gorilla researchers and conservationists, on the one hand, against tourism operators, Uganda Wildlife Authority and the government on the other, with moderating NGOs caught in between. At present those arguing for increased habituation, with the additional revenue it brings, seem to be winning the day.

Control of access to permits to view gorillas

Gorilla tracking permits are high value commodities and the key to the gorilla tourism market. When permits are scarce, tour operators holding them are able to sell not just the permit to a potential tourist but a whole package, which might include a multi-stop itinerary all around the country. The buying and selling of permits has therefore been a site of contestation for many years. In the early days of gorilla tracking, unsold or returned permits could be bought at the park gate, resulting in large numbers of backpackers waiting in the area, with considerable benefits for the local economy. However, there were accusations of corrupt double-selling of permits, and all permit sales were moved to the UWA head office in Kampala.

More recently, when gorilla tracking was first opened in Nkuringo on the south side of Bwindi, the Clouds Lodge was given exclusive access to all the permits for the new site. This was justified as a means to ensure that the lodge got enough business to be profitable for its community beneficiaries, but created a storm of protest from tour operators and local government that ended up going all the way to the national level (Ahebwa et al. 2012b; see Ahebwa et al., this volume, Chapter 8, for further details).

Finally, on 1 January 2014, UWA embarked on a project for online sale of permits to view gorillas, purportedly to improve the marketing since the sale would be open to everybody. The online platform was meant to replace the old procedure where registered tour companies had preferential access to the permits on behalf of their clients. It was considered to also potentially increase the sale of permits from the traditional 80%. However, the project was resisted by the tour operators, under their umbrella body Association of Uganda Tour Operators (AUTO), for its perceived potential to kill the tour operator business as the clients and foreign travel companies would obtain the permits directly online. Further, it was suggested this would, in effect, reduce tourist visits to other Ugandan National Parks that were being marketed by the tour operators when selling the much treasured experiences of gorilla viewing. The antagonistic views between UWA and AUTO resulted in an impasse, only settled by the adoption of the recommendation of a committee of inquiry set up by the Ministry of Tourism to look into the matter. The committee recommended that local tour operators have all rights concerning viewing, selling and obtaining gorilla permits belonging to the tour operators. Thus they are the only ones able to see the availability of gorilla permits online.

The struggle over permits is unusual in that both parties emerged as winners. The Uganda Wildlife Authority was able to show online the available gorilla trekking permits, which improved visibility. However, by managing to block possibilities for online sale of the permits and ensuring that they are viewed by only locally registered operators, AUTO emerged as winners with their business protected.

Governing the distribution of tourism revenues

Governance of tourism revenues at local sites remains a contested issue for a variety of reasons, but the primary reasons are the leakage of these revenues on one hand and, on the other, the irregularities in the administration of the local share. Sandbrook (2010) found out that over 75% of the tourism revenues leaked out of the Bwindi area, even when not considering revenues from gorilla permits. Leakages can be due to structural issues whereby some necessary goods and services must by default be procured from outside the Bwindi area. Importantly, Sandbrook (2010) also found that the 25% of retained revenue in the Bwindi area was still considerably more than the combined value of all other sources of external revenue to the area (such as government employee salaries and sale of goods to non-local markets).

Gorilla permit revenues also create a significant source of leakage, as most of the funds are retained by UWA for their national budget. A small percentage of funds are distributed to local communities around Bwindi, but this has been a source of considerable conflict over the years (see Twinamatsiko et al., this volume, Chapter 3). The genesis of the problems with the percentage allocation can be traced to the passing of the 1996 Uganda Wildlife Statute (Blomley 2003; Tumusiime and Vedeld 2012). Prior to this, parks were obliged to allocate to local communities 12% of their total revenue. In 1996 the Statute changed this to 20% of park gate fees. Whereas this resulted in a net increase in the amounts allocated to communities at most of the parks running mass tourism, for Bwindi this meant a dramatic decrease in the local people's share. The current price of a gorilla viewing permit is $600 per person per day and of this only $40 is park entrance. Under the pre-1996 agreement, 12% of $600 (or $72) would be set aside for community sharing. In accordance with the post-1996 legislation, only 20% of $40 (or $8) was put into the scheme. This is only 1.3% of the receipt for a gorilla permit ($600). Earlier efforts to revert to the pre-1996 arrangement were not supported by both top management and the board of trustees of the UWA given that the agency has other substantial costs to meet (Adams and Infield 2003). The total annual allocation has gradually improved with increases in the number of habituated gorilla groups, fees charged per tourist, and following the introduction of the Gorilla Levy fund in 2006, which collects $10 from each gorilla permit for eventual redistribution among communities. However, dissatisfaction continues amongst the local people.

Further, distribution of the allocated revenues is also problematic. A key issue relates to the gap years when no distributions are made as the funds are accumulated to sizeable amounts that can create an impact when shared. For example, in the 11 years between 1996 and 2009, the revenues were shared only four times (in 1996, 2002, 2006 and 2007; Tumusiime and Vedeld 2012). Such a practice means the local government and people cannot predict and plan for the flow of benefits. Even then, when the allocation is finally done, its distribution is through a local government structure that is largely non-accountable to the local communities, resulting in multiple forms of local governance failure including the capture of benefits by the local elites, favouritism, and limited involvement of local people in deciding on both the magnitude and nature of benefits. These failures ultimately diminish trust in the system. Thus, as Tumusiime and Vedeld (2012) conclude, for the tourism revenue sharing scheme to deliver on the twin objective of local development and conservation it will have to be scaled up in magnitude, be secured by legitimate and competent institutions that are accountable to the local people and adequately involve them when decisions are made regarding how to distribute the revenues.

Security issues

In April 1999 there was an attack by rebels who crossed from the DRC and killed seven tourists and park personnel. Following the incident, tourist arrivals declined dramatically, prompting the government of Uganda to increase military presence in the area to secure the property and lives of tourists and park personnel. Since then, armed guards can be seen patrolling the area day and night and accompany tourists on any UWA-sanctioned activity, be it a trek into the forest to see the gorillas or into the community to consume local culture along the popular community walks (Laudati 2010). Following the improved security, tourist arrivals (and thus revenues) have increased steadily, as discussed above. The local people also seem to perceive some benefits from the military presence. In a study by Tumusiime and Sjaastad (2014), over 60% of the local people acknowledged the military presence to have increased security in the area. There are, however, also some negative consequences of the military presence in the area, especially emanating from improper behaviour and conduct of the armed personnel who are reported to beat local people, steal or inadequately compensate local properties, and also compromised sexual relations with local females through rape, sexual assault (both of which are associated with increased spread of HIV/AIDS), and abandonment of wives following military transfers (Sandbrook 2006; Laudati 2010). No detailed study has been conducted on the impact of military deployment in the area, and this would be a valuable contribution. Nonetheless, it seems that viability of the all too important tourism will depend on the presence of the military for as long as the adjacent national border remains insecure.

Social relations between Bakiga and Batwa

Bwindi is surrounded by local people of varied ethnic groups. The majority are Bantu, with 90% of the population Bakiga and 9.5% Bafumbira. The remaining 0.5% of the population are Batwa, Bahunde, Bahororo, and immigrants from Rwanda, DR Congo, and other areas of Uganda (Plumptre et al. 2004).

The Ugandan group of Batwa are part of a larger group that lived across the Great Lakes region for centuries, almost exclusively in and around the region's most dense rain forests, living a traditional nomadic lifestyle of hunting and gathering. The forest resources were their sole source of livelihood. Around BINP also lives a sedentary group of people, the Bakiga, who have principally lived as cultivators but with an occasional dependence on the park's resources such as medicinal plants.

Bwindi forest became a forest reserve in 1932 but the Batwa continued to live within the forest and, together with their Bakiga neighbours, continued to depend on the forest's resources even after the official eviction in the 1960s, until 1991 when the area was gazetted a national park and stronger efforts were invested in evicting local people, riding on the momentum generated as similar evictions were undertaken in the other five Ugandan Forest Reserves (Rwenzori, Mt Elgon, Mgahinga, Semuliki, and Kibale) that attained National Park status over the same period (1991–1993). Following the strict evictions at Bwindi, the Batwa in the area were forced to permanently abandon any remaining forest-based and nomadic elements of their livelihood activities, and were forced to settle permanently among their sedentary Bakiga neighbours.

The creation of the national park fundamentally altered the nature of the relationship between the two groups. The Batwa became share croppers and labourers, often exchanging labour for food, and slowly transitioned to a sedentary life and market economy. As Kingdon (1990) noted, the nature of the relations between the Batwa and Bakiga changed considerably following local conservation efforts, even well before the national park was established. It varies between places, but ranges from ambivalence, tolerance, and friendly paternalism, to, in other instances, outright hostility. In particular, friendly paternalism is premised on the need by Bakiga to exploit Batwa casual labour in different agricultural activities including land tilling and guarding crops against wildlife damage. The labour is paid for in cash, but more frequently in kind including provision of food. On the other hand, hostility which sometimes gets expressed in aggressive behaviours, may be historically linked to clan wars of the last decades of the 19th century, but more recently as a response to unequal exchanges from the exploitative tendencies and economic domination of the Bakiga. There also is a certain degree of social barrier between the two groups. Intermarriages are rare, and one explanation for those casual sexual relations that do exist is that some Bakiga men believe that intercourse with Batwa women is a curative remedy for back ache (D. Tumusiime, pers. comm.).

As the foregoing section shows, conservation is an inherently political process involving multiple actors with varied and often conflicting interests. As the Bwindi case demonstrates, actors wield different powers and thus different abilities to promote and protect their own interests. It is thus often power relations, rather than any technical analysis of the 'best' solution, that determines the outcome in conflict situations.

Bwindi as a storyline: the various narratives deployed to describe ICD at Bwindi

Emerging from the complex web of conflicts and practices at Bwindi described in the previous section are a series of clear and elegant storylines, or narratives, within which the complexities are rendered silent. A narrative is (as Benjaminsen and Svarstad paraphrase Roe 1991, 1995, 1999) a story told by actors, with a beginning, middle and end, or, when cast in the form of an argument, constitutes beliefs of what will happen if particular premises are present. In the case of Bwindi, at least three narratives have been produced about the relationship between conservation and development following the declaration of the National Park. Two are discursive narratives promoted by external actors; a win–win narrative and a critical counter-narrative. The third is a narrative of ambivalence told by local people.

The win–win narrative about Bwindi holds that the conservation efforts have benefited both conservation and the local people. Claims of local people as winners from conservation practice are based on the numerous efforts and approaches undertaken by UWA and its partners to (i) ameliorate local conservation costs (e.g., through management of human wildlife conflicts) and (ii) generate conservation benefits locally. For example, a World Wildlife Fund (WWF) report cited by Tumusiime and Svarstad (2011) presents Bwindi as one of six examples from Africa, Asia, and Latin America to demonstrate 'that species conservation and poverty reduction can be delivered together' (p. 9).

Contrary to the win–win narrative, the critical narrative is sceptical of the outcomes for the local people. For example Laudati (2010) describes the situation for local communities adjacent to Bwindi as one of 'inequality, exploitation, vulnerability, and insecurity' (p. 727) emanating from a combination of low levels of revenues allocated to local people, low park-related employment, and the negative cultural influence of the tourism business amidst increasing human–wildlife conflicts. The situation of the Batwa has also been used variously to support a critical narrative (see Kidd 2008).

On the other hand, the local people's ambivalence narrative described by Tumusiime and Svarstad (2011) significantly deviates from both narratives. According to it, local people largely share negative views on low levels of economic benefits from employment and sharing of tourism revenues, and are critical of uncompensated costs of wildlife damage, limited access to natural resources, and limited to no influence in decision-making. With these, the local people's narrative significantly deviates from the win–win and is in line with the critical narrative, but crucially deviates from the latter by wanting Bwindi to remain a national park with its tourism-related opportunities as this brings local hope for the future. This also deviates from the claims in the win–win narrative that the present situation is satisfactory for the local communities.

Stepping back, one may wonder how one location can produce such different narratives, and how the narratives it does produce are so stable and consistent. Tumusiime and Svarstad (2011) compare claims in the narratives with empirical knowledge from realist research conducted in the area. The realist studies justify disappointments with the present situation including with regard to economic benefits (Hatfield 2005; Tumusiime and Vedeld

2015; Adams and Infield 2003; Sandbrook and Adams 2012; Sandbrook 2010), disappointment with uncompensated and increasing costs of crop raiding (Baker 2005; Baker 2004; Goldsmith 2005; Tumusiime and Vedeld 2015), restricted access to natural resources of the park (Blomley and Namara 2003; Worah et al. 2000), and a lack of influence on decision-making (Namara 2006; Atuhaire 2009). Thus, the main elements of the ambivalence narrative seem to provide a sound presentation of the situation.

In contrast, the win–win narrative and the critical narrative are not well supported by evidence of what is happening on the ground. These narratives are probably better understood in terms of what the actors promoting them wish to achieve through their deployment. The win–win narrative is largely promoted by NGOs and the UWA, both of which have a vested interest in being seen to succeed and in keeping complexity and conflict out of the public eye. In a sense they are selling a storyline for funding and support, and the quality of the story (and associated images) may matter more for this end than its basis in reality (Igoe 2017; Lund et al. 2017). On the other hand, the critical narrative is mainly promoted by critical social scientists who have a vested interest in identifying conflict and complexity and in critiquing prevailing conservation and development practice, as this is what helps to achieve publication and promotion (Redford 2011). Bwindi provides a classic example of how widely circulated narratives can become detached from the reality they purport to describe, and a cautionary lesson for those who take such narratives at face value.

Conclusions

As this chapter has shown, Bwindi Impenetrable National Park is a celebrity site for conservation and development within Uganda. It has been a laboratory for conservation and development, testing innovative approaches and providing (mixed) evidence as to their effectiveness. It is a site of contestation, bringing together numerous actors with different priorities and resources to influence events. And it is represented through multiple storylines, each of which provides a different version of events, themselves tailored to suit the different interests of those promoting them. What then can be learned from Bwindi for sites elsewhere in Uganda and the wider world? We identify five key messages.

First, Bwindi has attracted a huge amount of attention, helping to put Uganda and its conservation and development activities on the global map. This has been tremendously important in various ways, as this chapter has shown. Nonetheless, this does leave open the question of whether Bwindi's success has been boon or curse to other sites in the country. For example, it seems quite possible that the overwhelming focus on gorillas in tourism marketing for Uganda has undermined other forms of tourism in the country, particularly considering the limited number of gorilla permits that are ever available. Equally, Bwindi has acted like a vortex for researchers and NGOs, perhaps leaving other areas of the country understudied and lacking in support from outside agencies, despite being just as deserving as the Bwindi area.

Second, it is clear that money is not the (only) solution to conservation and development challenges. The incredible success of gorilla tourism has pumped millions of dollars into Uganda Wildlife Authority and the local (and national) economy. This has had undoubted positive impacts, but it has not been able to resolve longstanding injustices in relations with local communities, or a host of other arenas of contestation identified above. In fact, in some cases it has made them worse. Many of the problems facing Bwindi relate to governance and institutions, and cannot be solved by money alone.

Third, it is important not to jump too quickly to conclusions about the effectiveness and wider implications of conservation and development interventions. Several of the interventions that have taken place at Bwindi are perhaps best understood as pilots or trials of approaches that have subsequently become widespread. They haven't always gone well, and have been rightly scrutinised and critiqued. However, over time their performance has improved somewhat, at least for some beneficiaries. For example, the Clouds Lodge in Nkuringo had a very difficult start, with conflicts over permits and ownership of the lodge as described above. However, now that it has been operational for ten years things seem to have settled down, and the lodge is providing a steady stream of revenue to the local community as had been planned (Ahebwa et al. 2012b).

Fourth, many of the interventions at Bwindi have been designed and delivered by external actors that are not accountable to local people. International NGOs have their donors and members elsewhere, tour companies and lodges tend to be owned outside the area (Sandbrook 2010), and Uganda Wildlife Authority is answerable to central government. This has created the sense that much of what has happened at Bwindi has been done 'to' the local community rather than 'with' it. In this sense, Bwindi perhaps lags behind more recent developments in conservation and development thinking that have tended to emphasise full participation in decision making as the ideal target for achieving socially just forms of conservation (e.g., Ribot 2010).

Finally, Bwindi demonstrates the importance of taking narratives with a pinch of salt, whether presented by NGOs, the private sector or academics. The frequency of contradictions between these narratives demonstrates that it is simply not possible for everything that is said about Bwindi to be true. Each actor puts forward a version of events that is aligned to their particular way of understanding, constructing and interpreting reality, and that suits their particular agenda. This is not to say that all accounts of Bwindi are deliberately misleading. Rather, it should act as a reminder of the importance of interpreting narratives critically, paying attention to the source material on which narratives are based and the positionality of actors deploying them.

References

Adams, W.M. and Hutton, J. (2007) 'People, parks and poverty: political ecology and biodiversity conservation', *Conservation and Society*, vol. 5, no. 2, pp. 147–183.

Adams, W.M. and Infield, M. (2003) 'Who is on the Gorilla's payroll: claims on tourist revenue from a Ugandan National Park', *World Development*, vol. 31, no. 1, pp. 177–190.

Ahebwa, W.M., Van der Duim, R. and Sandbrook, C.G. (2012a) 'Tourism revenue sharing policy at Bwindi Impenetrable National Park, Uganda: a policy arrangements approach', *Journal of Sustainable Tourism*, vol. 20, no. 3, pp. 377–394.

Ahebwa, W.M., Van der Duim, R. and Sandbrook, C.G. (2012b) 'Private–community partnerships: investigating a new approach to conservation and development in Uganda', *Conservation and Society*, vol. 10, no. 4, pp. 305–317.

Akampurira, E., Bitariho, R. and Mugerwa, B. (2015) *An Assessment of the Effectiveness of Nkuringo Buffer Zone in Mitigating Crop Raiding Incidences around Bwindi Impenetrable National Park, S.W. Uganda*, ITFC, Ruhija-Kabale, Uganda.

Andama, E. (2009) *Community Based Human Wildlife Conflict Management. The Case of Nkuringo Buffer Zone Bwindi Impenetrable National Park, Uganda*, ITFC, Ruhija-Kabale, Uganda.

Archabald, K. and Naughton-Treves, L. (2001) 'Tourism revenue-sharing around national parks in Western Uganda: early efforts to identify and reward local communities', *Environmental Conservation*, vol. 28, no. 2, pp. 135–149.

Atuhaire, H. (2009) *Involvement and Participation. Practices and perceptions in collaborative resource management: the case of Bwindi National Park, Uganda*, University of Oslo, Norway.

Baker, J. (2004) 'Evaluating conservation policy: integrated conservation and development in Bwindi Impenetrable National Park, Uganda', PhD thesis, University of Kent, Canterbury, UK.

Baker, J. (2005) *Mountain Gorillas: crop raiding and conflict at BINP, Uganda*, Durrell Institute of Conservation and Ecology, University of Kent, Canterbury, Kent, UK.

Baker, J., Milner-Gulland, E.J. and Leader-Williams, N. (2011) 'Park gazettement and integrated conservation and development as factors in community conflict at Bwindi Impenetrable Forest, Uganda', *Conservation Biology*, vol. 26, no. 1, pp. 160–170.

Barr, R. et al. (2015) *Pave the Impenetrable? An economic analysis of potential Ikumba-Ruhija road alternatives in and around Uganda's Bwindi Impenetrable National Park*, Conservation Strategy Fund, Technical Series No. 35, Arcata, CA, USA.

Benjaminsen, T.A. and Svarstad, H. (2008) 'Understanding traditionalist opposition to modernization: narrative production in a Norwegian mountain conflict', *Geografiska Annaler Series B Human Geography*, vol. 90, no. 1, pp. 49–62.

Bensted-Smith, R. et al. (1995) *Review of the Multiple Use (Resource Sharing) Programme on Bwindi Impenetrable National Park*, CARE-International-DTC, Kampala, Uganda.

Bitariho, R. (2013) *Socio-Economic and Conservation Implications of Local People's Use of Bwindi Forest in South West Uganda*, Mbarara University of Science and Technology, Mbarara, Uganda.

Bitariho, R. et al. (2006) 'Plant harvest impacts and sustainability in Bwindi Impenetrable National Park, S.W. Uganda', *African Journal of Ecology*, vol. 44, no. 1, pp. 14–21.

Bitariho, R., Sheil, D. and Eilu, G. (2016) 'Tangible benefits or token gestures: does Bwindi Impenetrable National Park's long established multiple use programme benefit the poor?', *Forests, Trees and Livelihoods*, vol. 25, no. 1, pp. 16–32.

Blomley, T. (2003) 'Natural resource conflict management: the case of Bwindi Impenetrable and Mgahinga Gorilla National Parks, southwestern Uganda', in A. P. Castro and E. Nielsen (eds) *Natural Resource Conflict Management Case Studies: an analysis of power, participation and protected areas*, FAO, Rome, Italy.

Blomley, T. et al. (2010) *Development and Gorillas? Assessing fifteen years of integrated conservation and development in south-western Uganda*, IIED, London, UK.

Blomley, T. and Namara, A. (2003) 'Devolving rights or shedding responsibilities?— Community Conservation in Uganda over the last decade', *Policy Matters*, vol. 12, pp. 283–289.

Brockington, D. (2004) 'Community conservation, inequality and injustice: myths of power in protected area management', *Conservation and Society*, vol. 2, no. 2, pp. 411–432.

Butynski, T.M. (1984) *Ecological Survey of Impenetrable (Bwindi) Forest, Uganda, and Recommendations for its Conservation and Management*, New York Zoological Society, New York, USA.

Caldecott, J. and Miles, L. (2005) *World Atlas of Great Apes and their Conservation*, University of California Press, University of California, Berkeley, USA.

Cunningham, B. (2001) *Applied Ethnobotany, People, Wild Plant Use and Conservation*, Earthscan, London, UK.

Davey, C., Peters, C. and Byarugaba, D. (2001) *Participatory Review of the Multiple Use Programme, Bwindi Impenetrable National Park and Mgahinga Gorilla National Park*, Kampala, Uganda.

Edel, M.M. (1957) *The Chiga of Western Uganda*, Oxford University Press, Oxford, UK.

Goldsmith, M. (2005) 'Impacts of habituation for ecotourism on the gorillas of Nkuringo', *Gorilla Journal*, vol. 30, pp. 11–14.

Guschanskia, K. et al. (2009) 'Counting elusive animals: comparing field and genetic census of the entire mountain gorilla population of Bwindi Impenetrable National Park, Uganda', *Biological Conservation*, vol. 144, no. 2, pp. 290–308.

Harrison, M. et al. (2015) 'Profiling unauthorized natural resource users for better targeting of conservation interventions', *Conservation Biology*, vol. 29, no. 6, pp. 1636–1646.

Hatfield, R. (2005) *The Economic Value of Bwindi and Virunga Gorilla Mountain Forests*, African Wildlife Foundation (AWF), Nairobi, Kenya.

Holmes, G. (2013) 'Exploring the relationship between local support and the success of Protected Areas', *Conservation and Society*, vol. 11, no. 1, pp. 72–82.

Homsy, J. (1999) *Ape Tourism and Human Diseases: How Close Should We Get?* Kampala, Uganda.

Huffman, T.N. (1970) 'The early Iron Age and the spread of the Bantu', *The South African Archaeological Bulletin*, vol. 25, no. 97, pp. 3–21.

Hutton, J., Adams, W.M. and Murombedzi, J.C. (2005) 'Back to the barriers? Changing narratives in biodiversity biodiversity', *Forum for Development Studies*, vol. 32, no. 2, pp. 341–370.

Igoe, J. (2017) *The Nature of Spectacle. On Images, Money, and Conserving Capitalism*, University of Arizona Press, Tucson, Arizona, USA.

Institute of Tropical Forest Conservation (ITFC) (1999) *The Potential Supply of Weaving and Medicinal Plant Resources in the Proposed Kifunjo/Masya Multiple-Use Zone of Bwindi Impenetrable National Park, S.W. Uganda*, Ruhija, Kabale, Uganda.

Kidd, C. (2008) 'Development discourse and the Batwa of South West Uganda', PhD thesis, University of Glasgow, UK.

Kingdon, E. (1990) 'Caught between two worlds: moral problems relating to conservation in south-west Uganda', *International Journal of Moral and Social Studies*, vol. 5, no. 3, pp. 235–249.

Laudati, A. (2010) 'Ecotourism: the modern predator? Implications of gorilla tourism on local livelihoods in Bwindi Impenetrable National Park, Uganda', *Environment and Planning D: Society and Space*, vol. 28, no. 4, pp. 726–743.

Leggat, G.T. and Osmaston, H.A. (1961) 'Working plan for the Impenetrable Forest Reserve, Kigezi District, western Province', unpublished report to the Uganda Government, Uganda Forest Department, Entebbe, Uganda.

Lewis, J. (2000) *The Batwa Pygmies of the Great Lakes Region*, Minority Rights Group International, London, UK.

Lund, J.F. et al. (2017) 'Promising change, delivering continuity: REDD+ as a conservation fad', *World Development*, vol. 89, pp. 124–139.

Marchant, R., Taylor, D. and Hamilton, A. (1995) 'Late Pleistocene and Holocene history at Mubwindi swamp, southwest Uganda', *Quaternary Research*, vol. 47, no. 3, pp. 316–328.

Marchant, R., Taylor, D. and Hamilton, A. (2000) 'Late Holocene fluctuations in the composition of montane forest in the Rukiga highland, Central Africa: a regional reconstruction', in G. Bailey, R. Charles and N. Winder (eds) *Human Ecodynamics*, Oxbow Books, Cambridge, UK.

Masiga, M., Byamukama, B. and Akampulira, E. (2011) 'A review of sustainable financing and implementation of problem animal management interventions in Bwindi Mgahinga Conservation Area, Kabale, Uganda', unpublished technical report for CARE Uganda, Kampala, Uganda.

McNeilage, A. et al. (2006) 'Census of the mountain gorilla *Gorilla beringei beringei* population in Bwindi Impenetrable National Park, Uganda', *Oryx*, vol. 40, no. 4, pp. 419–427.

McShane, T.O. et al. (2010) 'Hard choices: making trade-offs between biodiversity conservation and human well-being', *Biological Conservation*, vol. 144, no. 3, pp. 966–972.

Namara, A. (2006) 'From paternalism to real partnership with local communities? Experiences from Bwindi impenetrable national park (Uganda)', *Africa Development*, vol. 31, no. 2, pp. 39–68.

Olupot, W., Barigyira, R. and Chapman, C.A. (2009) 'The status of anthropogenic threat at the people–park interface of Bwindi Impenetrable National Park, Uganda', *Environmental Conservation*, vol. 36, no. 1, pp. 1–10.

Phillipson, D.W. (1986) 'African pre-history: life in the Lake Victoria basin', *Nature*, vol. 320, no. 6058, pp. 110–111.

Plumptre, A.J. et al. (2004) *The Socio-economic Status of People Living Near Protected Areas in the Central Albertine Rift*, Albertine Rift Technical Reports Series. 4. IGCP, WCS and CARE, Uganda.

Redford, K. (2011) 'Misreading the conservation landscape', *Oryx*, vol. 45, no. 3, pp. 324–330.

Ribot, J. (2010) 'Forestry and democratic decentralisation in Sub-Saharan Africa: a rough review', in L. German et al. (eds) *Governing Africa's Forests in a Globalized World*, Earthscan, London, UK, p. 31.

Roe, E.M. (1991) 'Development narratives, or making the best of blueprint development', *World Development*, vol. 19, no. 4, pp. 287–300.

Roe, E.M. (1995) 'Except-Africa: postscript to a special section on development narratives', *World Development*, vol. 23, no. 6, pp. 1065–1069.

Roe, E.M. (1999) *Except-Africa, Remaking Development, Rethinking Power.* Transaction, New Brunswick, NJ, USA.

Sandbrook, C.G. (2006) 'Tourism, conservation and livelihoods: the impacts of gorilla tracking at Bwindi Impenetrable National Park, Uganda', PhD thesis, University College London, London, UK.

Sandbrook, C.G. (2010) 'Putting leakage in its place: the significance of retained tourism revenue in the local context in rural Uganda', *Journal of International Development*, vol. 22, no. 1, pp. 124–136.

Sandbrook, C.G. and Adams, W.M. (2012) 'Accessing the impenetrable: the nature and distribution of tourism benefits at a Ugandan National Park', *Society & Natural Resources*, vol. 25, no. 9, pp. 915–932.

Tumusiime, D.M. and Svarstad, H. (2011) 'A local counter-narrative on the conservation of mountain gorillas', *Forum for Development Studies*, vol. 38, no. 3, pp. 239–265.

Tumusiime, D.M. and Sjaastad, E. (2014) 'Conservation and development: justice, inequality, and attitudes around Bwindi Impenetrable National Park', *Journal of Development Studies*, vol. 50, no. 2, pp. 204–225.

Tumusiime, D.M. and Vedeld, P. (2012) 'False promise or false premise? Using tourism revenue sharing to promote conservation and poverty reduction in Uganda', *Conservation and Society*, vol. 10, no. 1, pp. 15–28.

Tumusiime, D.M. and Vedeld, P. (2015) 'Can biodiversity conservation benefit local people? Costs and benefits at a strict protected area in Uganda', *Journal of Sustainable Forestry*, vol. 34, no. 8, pp. 761–786.

Twinamatsiko, M. et al. (2014) '*Linking Protected Area Conservation with Poverty Alleviation in Uganda: Integrated Conservation and Development at Bwindi Impenetrable National Park*', research report, International Institute for Environment and Development, London, UK.

Twinamatsiko, M. et al. (2015) 'Can governance in revenue sharing be a pathway for a win-win situation between people's livelihood improvement and conservation?', *Journal of Social Science Research*, vol. 8, no. 1, pp. 1–19.

Uganda Wildlife Authority (UWA) (2001) *Bwindi Mgahinga Conservation Area General Management Plan (July 2001–June 2011)*, Uganda Wildlife Authority, Kampala, Uganda.

Wild, R.G. (2001) *Plants from the Park: Establishing Community Harvesting of Plants as a Conservation Tool at Bwindi Impenetrable and Mgahinga National Parks, Uganda*, University of Cape Town, Cape Town, South Africa.

Wild, R.G. and Mutebi, J. (1996) *Conservation Through Community Use of Plant Resources: Establishing Collaborative Management at Bwindi Impenetrable and Mgahinga Gorilla National Parks, Uganda*, UNESCO, Paris, France.

Worah, S., Moyini, Y. and Ssuna, J. (2000) *Report on the Participatory Review of CARE's Development through Conservation Project*, CARE, Kampala, Uganda.

5   Managing the contradictions

Conservation, communitarian rhetoric, and conflict at Mount Elgon National Park

David Himmelfarb and Connor Joseph Cavanagh

Introduction[1]

Over the past century, the socio-political context of natural resource use and conservation in Uganda has undergone tremendous upheaval and change (Turyahabwe and Banana, 2008). So too have prevailing forms of conservation policy, which have gradually evinced greater concern with what one might term the 'communitarian rhetoric' of local participation, co-management, and collaborative approaches to conservation governance. Yet, the institutional structure of many protected areas and official management *practices* have remained remarkably consistent over time (Petursson and Vedeld, 2015, 2017). At Mount Elgon in southeastern Uganda, for instance, the protectionist model – wherein a centralised state agency oversees resource access and control in a bounded and surveyed 'natural' domain – has formed the enduring institutional foundation of a succession of protected areas. These have ranged from the colonial declaration of a forest reserve in 1929, to subsequent iterations of a forest reserve, to a contemporary national park that formally embraces various types of 'collaborative' and 'community-based' approaches to conservation (e.g., Gosamalang et al., 2008).

Straddling the Uganda–Kenya frontier, the geographic position of Mount Elgon on the border of the colonial and, later, independent nation-state has introduced a unique politics of management for conservation agencies, development organisations, local administrators, and the central government (Scott, 1998; Petursson et al., 2011; Sassen et al., 2013).[2] In this context, the (colonial) state's efforts to annex and establish control over the mountain's forests and grasslands have been inextricable from controlling, administering, and disciplining the bodies and economic activities of the people who have relied on those resources for centuries. Importantly, the contested nature of these strategies for social, economic, and ecological control have frequently provoked considerable local resistance (Norgrove, 2002; Norgrove and Hulme, 2006; Cavanagh and Benjaminsen, 2015). At times, such resistance has been expressed in ways that have threatened the very ability of certain conservation activities to effectively proceed

(Cavanagh and Benjaminsen, 2014; Fisher et al., 2018). At issue, then, is not only conservation governance and its implications for local economic activities, but also more fundamental concerns about colonial legacies of land expropriation and the very nature of the rights and protections that citizens of the contemporary state of Uganda can expect to enjoy (Cavanagh and Himmelfarb, 2015).

In many ways, then, the task of governing both ecosystems and economic development on Mount Elgon has been the task of managing a variety of tensions or even outright contradictions. Not least, the latter arise from the simultaneous imperative to uphold strict conservation and boundary enforcement goals; to discipline or suppress local dissent emerging in response to the latter; and – nonetheless – to express concern for the rights, prosperity, and wellbeing of local communities. In such a context, one can perhaps also sympathise quite readily with the occasional reluctance of local residents to enthusiastically embrace each new conservation buzzword or 'approach'. Viewed over the course of nearly a century, such policy formulations have changed remarkably little in practice for the nature of the hardships and resource access restrictions faced by the average park-adjacent resident (e.g., Nakakaawa et al., 2015; Vedeld et al., 2016; Petursson and Vedeld, 2017).

Examining the implications of such tensions, contradictions, and contestations, this chapter traces the trajectory of simultaneous economic development and environmental protection on Mount Elgon from the British colonial era to the present. In doing so, the chapter proceeds in four sections. First, we provide a brief introduction to both the physical geography and ethnographic context of Ugandan Mount Elgon, illuminating the region's significance and appeal to both conservationists and local inhabitants. Second, we examine the coevolution or simultaneous development of both colonial conservation and colonial economic policy in the region, the legacies of which continue to impinge upon the contemporary nature of conservation governance. Third, we note how the *de jure* expropriation of land and forests as state property during the colonial era has enabled widespread *physical* evictions for conservation after independence, and laid the institutional foundation of the land and boundary conflicts that continue to date. Fourth, we examine the diverse policies and conservation 'tools' that have been introduced in this context of unresolved conflict, from carbon offset forestry, to collaborative resource management agreements, to more recent experimentation with payments for avoided deforestation in the form of community revolving funds (Cavanagh and Freeman, 2017). In light of these experiences, we conclude with a discussion of the ways in which the pursuit of effective conservation at Mount Elgon appears to depend upon the frank acknowledgement and negotiation of appropriate means of redress for past and present environmental injustices. If conservation at Mount Elgon is to be sustainable, in other words, it will likely also need to be just.

Physical geography, conservation values, and ethnographic context

A review of the physical geography and ecological characteristics of Mount Elgon quickly illuminates why the mountain is of such significance to both the livelihoods of local communities and the priorities of conservationists. A broad shield of a mountain, Mount Elgon is now more than 80 km in diameter (Bussmann, 2006), and features an 8 km-wide caldera at its centre: one of the largest intact calderas in the world (King et al., 1972). Rising to an altitude of 4,321 m – and 3,000 m above the surrounding plains – the mountain sits astride the contemporary Kenya/Uganda border, 100 km northeast of Lake Victoria. Rainfall varies across the mountain, with rains heaviest to the western summit (2,000–4,000 mm/year) and lightest to the northern plains (approximately 625 mm/year) (McMaster, 1962; National Environmental Management Authority, n.d.). Importantly, Mount Elgon thus serves as a regionally significant water catchment area, providing drinking and irrigation water for thousands of people in both Kenya and Uganda (Vedeld et al., 2016). Simultaneously, however, heavy rains on southern and western portions of the mountain in particular have also resulted in periodic landslides – sometimes with disastrous consequences for local communities and livelihoods (e.g., Mugagga et al., 2012).

Mount Elgon's fertile soils are composed of volcanic ash and soda-rich agglomerates (Langlands, 1974). These support widespread agricultural cultivation up to 2,200–2,500 m and a mosaic of forest and grassland habitats above the cultivation zone. The mountain is one of the so-called Afro-alpine 'sky islands', solitary mountains on which plant communities have evolved in relative isolation from other montane environments, thus supporting high levels of species endemism especially in the grasslands, heath and moorlands (Bussmann, 2006). Some researchers have suggested that Mount Elgon features more extensive grassland areas outside its caldera than other East African mountains because of its long history of anthropogenic intervention through livestock grazing and burning (Reed and Clokie, 2000). Observed fauna include elephants, buffalo, antelope and duiker, leopards, hyenas, black-and-white colobus and blue monkeys, and at least 144 bird species (Scott, 1998). Though the ecosystems of Mount Elgon do not support the degree of species biodiversity found in Uganda's western forests, the density of endemic plant species and the mountain's role in regional water catchment have made Mount Elgon an important focus for conservation activities (Reed and Clokie, 2000).

Humans have made their lives and livelihoods on Mount Elgon's varied terrain, from the semi-arid plains to the caldera, for at least 400 years and likely much longer (Goldschmidt, 1967). The Ugandan side of Mount Elgon is occupied primarily by two ethnic groups, Bantu-speaking Bagisu agriculturalists (2014 population, 1,646,904) to the south and Nilotic-speaking Sabiny (historically known as Sebei) agro-pastoralists (2014 population,

273,839) to the north (Uganda Bureau of Statistics, 2014). While it is not known when exactly people began making their homes on Mount Elgon, Goldschmidt (1967) estimates that, by the eighteenth century, Kalenjin-speakers occupied the entire mountain. Bagisu agriculturalists appear to have moved to the south side of the mountain early in the nineteenth century, using their superior military might to push Sabiny residents northward (Bunker, 1987). Further, Goldschmidt (1967: 37) observes that the balance of cultivation, pastoralism and foraging generally varied across three physiographic zones (distinguished primarily by altitude and rainfall): i) the plains from the foot of the mountain to the grassy areas that extend to 1,220 m, where residents practiced limited cultivation and transhumant pastoralism; ii) the fertile central escarpment between 1,220 m and 2,130 m, where the population was the largest and livelihoods emphasised intensive cultivation; and iii) the highlands above 2,130 m, where residents practiced a mixture of foraging and pastoralism.

Pre-colonial societies both on Mount Elgon and elsewhere in Uganda certainly practiced 'conservation' in a general sense, understood as the formulation and enforcement of institutions related to the sustainable use of land, wildlife, and natural resources (Scott, 1998: pp. 14–17, see also Turyahabwe and Banana, 2008). On Mount Elgon, land and forests were typically seen as common property rather than as an open-access resource stock, and institutions governing wildlife, timber, and non-timber resource harvesting amongst both the Bagisu and Sabiny were managed via systems of customary law and authority (Goldschmidt, 1967; see also Heald, 1999). In addition to their economic value as natural resource stocks, forests were also valued in relation to cultural rites that reinforced a perceived connection with the ancestors and their practices (Norgrove, 2002), including 'twin ceremonies', circumcision ceremonies, burial ceremonies, and for the harvest and administration of medicinal herbs. As a result, one could argue that pre-colonial human societies on Mount Elgon practiced forms of conservation that implicitly evinced an appreciation of the nonhuman world similar to what Morton (2007) terms 'ecology without nature' (see also Cavanagh and Benjaminsen, 2015). That is to say, ecosystems were intuitively valued for practical, economic, and cultural reasons, but not in a way that fostered a categorical – or even ontological – distinction between one domain of 'nature' and another of 'society'. Efforts to impose such a distinction in the colonial era and enforce it both institutionally and materially – violently, even – would prefigure many of the conflicts in the region that continue to date.

The political ecology of colonial conservation and development

In contrast with pre-colonial systems of resource management, early colonial conservation efforts on the Ugandan side of Mount Elgon were linked to – and co-evolved with – a much broader set of political and economic concerns. These included the facilitation of capitalist economic development generally, as well as more specific issues related to timber demand and the sustainability of water resources for cash crop production on the mountain's slopes (Bunker, 1987; Webster and Osmaston, 2003). Especially prior to the Second World War, British economic policy in eastern Africa emphasised the necessity for each colony or protectorate to recoup the costs of its own administration (Low, 2009; Cavanagh and Himmelfarb, 2015). In the Ugandan case, this was to be accomplished primarily via the extraction of taxes, livestock, and cash crops from African households rather than the facilitation of European settlement, and especially so near market centres accessible to the newly constructed Uganda Railway (Parker, 1952). In particular, Bugisu – the well-watered and populous region that sprawled from the southwestern slopes of Mount Elgon – was a major centre of cash crop production, especially coffee (Bunker, 1987; see also Twaddle, 1993).

As both the coffee industry and broader peasant economy in Bugisu burgeoned, colonial administrators turned their attention to the forests and grasslands on the upper regions of the mountain, whose water catchment functions were crucial for supporting the region's coffee industry. In 1928, one year before the formal declaration of a forest reserve on Mount Elgon (Petursson and Vedeld, 2015), coffee production in Bugisu accounted for 13% of all native lands dedicated to the crop (Wrigley, 1959, p. 42). By 1958, farmers in the region produced at least two thirds of Uganda's Arabica harvest. In tandem with the emergence of this export-oriented coffee sector, the Forest Department began establishing control of Mount Elgon's forests in the late 1920s (Webster, 1954), and eventually demarcated a 690 km² Crown Forest Reserve in 1938 that encompassed all lands from the caldera down to the lower margins of the forest belt (Cavanagh and Himmelfarb, 2015; see also Scott, 1998; Norgrove, 2002).

Initially, conservation officials tolerated some resource use by forest-adjacent communities, and generally ignored those primarily foraging and pastoralist groups – often referred to as 'Dorobo' (see Cavanagh, 2017) – who had historically made their homes and livelihoods within the Mount Elgon Forest Reserve. Hence, while the establishment of the Mount Elgon Forest Reserve may have at first had a modest *economic* impact on forest-adjacent communities – who may have continued to graze their animals and harvest certain forest resources in many cases – it was significant in dispossessing the historical residents of Mount Elgon of their underlying property rights to land and resources. Crucially, it is this form of *de jure* dispossession via the imposition of a foreign legal system of state property rights that would enable the physical dispossession and evictions that would later follow.

Coercion, evictions, and the transition to independence

In subsequent decades, the legal status of the protected area on Mount Elgon changed from Crown Forest to Central Forest Reserve in 1948 and to a Demarcated Protection Reserve in 1951 (Petursson and Vedeld, 2015; see also Table 5.1). Gradually, the attitude of the Forest Department toward in-Reserve residents shifted away from general disinterest toward progressively stricter protectionism and draconian enforcement (Gosamalang et al., 2008). Independence itself in 1962 had little immediate effect on this trajectory of changing conservation values on Mount Elgon, reflecting the resilience of conservation institutions to processes of decolonisation throughout Britain's African colonies more generally (Adams and Mulligan, 2003). Forest Department officials emphasised continuity between colonial and post-colonial forest policy, retaining several of the same expatriate staff and making no major changes in their overall programme of activities, which was geared toward reducing local pressure on protected resources (Forest Department, 1961; Webster and Osmaston, 2003).

Opposition toward human settlement in the Mount Elgon Forest Reserve grew in response to a perception that upland communities were

Table 5.1 Chronology of salient conservation and development institutions at Mount Elgon, Uganda

Year	Institution	Local characteristics	References
Pre-1894	Historically evolving customary systems for the regulation of land and natural resource use.	Hunting, resource extraction, and agricultural extensification into forests managed via clan, lineage, or other customary laws and authorities.	Goldschmidt (1967, 1989); Bunker (1987); Heald (1998, 1999); Scott (1998).
1894–	Uganda Protectorate.	British Protectorate declared over the Buganda Kingdom. Gradually expands outwards to include the whole of Mount Elgon through a series of treaties that grant the Crown ownership rights to certain lands, forests, and other natural resources. Protectorate boundary adjusted in 1902 to bisect Mount Elgon between the Uganda Protectorate and the East Africa Protectorate (later Kenya Colony).	Johnston (1902); Twaddle (1993); Low (2009).
1900–	Hut taxes, poll taxes, and coffee production.	Hut and poll taxes begin to be enforced. Multiple revolts against taxation suppressed with military force. Mount Elgon residents encouraged to cultivate coffee as a means to raise finances for paying colonial taxes.	Bunker (1987); Himmelfarb (2012); Sassen et al. (2013); Cavanagh and Himmelfarb (2015).

1929–	Mount Elgon Forest Reserve and Forest Policy of 1929.	Mount Elgon Forest Reserve declared in 1929. Limited conservation activities on the ground, surveying not fully completed. Forest Department initiatives hampered by the Great Depression. Nonetheless, first colonial forest policy of 1929 stresses the need to expand the forest estate and Forest Department activities for both economic and preservationist reasons.	Scott (1998); Webster and Osmaston (2003); Turyahabwe and Banana (2008); Petursson and Vedeld (2015).
1938–	Mount Elgon Crown Forest Reserve.	Mount Elgon Crown Forest Reserve designated under Legal Notice No. 100 of 1938. Forest intended primarily for preservation rather than plantation harvesting. Entire boundary surveyed and demarcated.	Webster (1954)
1948–	Mount Elgon Central Forest Reserve.	Mount Elgon Central Forest Reserve designated under Legal Notice No. 41 of 1948. Forest still owned by the Crown and intended for preservation. Multiple boundary disputes and occasional evictions of 'encroachers'.	Webster (1954); Webster and Osmaston (2003).
1951–	Mount Elgon Demarcated Protection Reserve.	Formal status changes to Mount Elgon Demarcated Protection Reserve following efforts to re-survey the forest boundary. Mounting conflicts between communities and conservationists, as well as between Bagisu and Sebei/ Sabiny communities adjacent to the reserve.	Synott (1968); Scott (1998).
1975–	Land Reform Decree and Double Production Policy.	Idi Amin's Land Reform Decree in 1975 and Double Production Policy often interpreted as encouraging farmers to encroach upon protected forests at Mount Elgon or elsewhere and covert these to agricultural production.	Webster and Osmaston (2003); Turyahabwe and Banana (2008); Cavanagh and Benjaminsen (2015).

(continued)

Table 5.1 (continued)

Year	Institution	Local characteristics	References
1983–	Benet Resettlement Area.	Benet Resettlement Area created on 6,000 hectares of park-adjacent land to resettle evicted members of the Benet community. Resettlement exercise fraught with allegations of corruption and mismanagement.	Himmelfarb (2006, 2012); Bintoora and Matanda (2017).
1988–	Forest Policy of 1988.	First Forest Policy of President Yoweri Museveni's National Resistance Movement (NRM) government emphasises the need to balance economic and preservationist objectives in the forest estate.	Turyahabwe and Banana (2008).
1991–	Mount Elgon Forest Park.	Multiple use and zoning system devised to alleviate boundary conflicts.	Scott (1998); Norgrove (2002).
1993–	Mount Elgon National Park.	Transition to national park supported by bilateral and multilateral donors. Accompanied by extensive evictions of communities found to reside within the re-demarcated park boundary. Experimentation with carbon-offset forestry begins. Increased implementation of CRMAs and other community-based conservation mechanisms.	Scott (1998); Norgrove (2002); Norgrove and Hulme (2006); Cavanagh and Benjaminsen (2014).
2004–	Mount Elgon Regional Ecosystem Conservation Programme.	Supported by NORAD and IUCN, the East African Community's Lake Victoria Basin Commission and its MERECP programme aim to harmonise conservation governance activities between protected areas on both Ugandan and Kenyan Mount Elgon. Ushers in new benefit-sharing mechanisms, such as the use of Community Revolving Funds and payments for avoided deforestation.	Mwayafu and Kimbowa (2011); Nakakaawa et al. (2015); Cavanagh and Freeman (2017).

adopting extensive agriculture to an unprecedented extent in the 1950s and 1960s. In practice, however, this process of livelihoods change was also compounded by the political and economic directives of both the late colonial and the independent Ugandan state. Whereas the introduction and encouragement of commercial agriculture by the colonial regime had generally provided more economic incentives for agrarian extensification into forests than ever before (e.g., Mamdani, 1987), such processes were also affected greatly by the dynamics of specific government regimes after independence. For example, President Idi Amin's 1975 Land Reform Decree and 'double production' policy encouraged rural populations to encroach upon protected areas and convert them to agricultural use in many cases (Webster and Osmaston, 2003, p. 167). Likewise, under Milton Obote's second regime, forest conservation officials appear to have sold counterfeit titles to land within both the Mount Elgon forest reserve and other protected areas to local farmers, many of whom believed these to be legitimate (Norgrove and Hulme, 2006; Cavanagh and Benjaminsen, 2015). In aggregate, these processes led to the quasi-legal encroachment and deforestation of approximately 25,000 hectares of the forest reserve (White, 2002).

Official efforts to drive out the reserve's human inhabitants were redoubled at the outset of the 1980s, culminating in a three-month-long resettlement exercise in 1983 (Scott, 1998). In one of the most controversial aspects of this process, a committee of local administrative officials, Forest Department staff, and chiefs allocated plots of land to 2,872 households on an estimated 6,000 ha between the Kere and Kaptokwoi rivers, which became known as the Benet Resettlement Area (Himmelfarb, 2012). However, displaced people from the plains and lower escarpment – as well as a loosely-defined group of 'needy' people – were included in the resettlement exercise and comprised two-thirds of the allocations (Luzinda, 2008). By 31 May 1983, the allocation committee concluded the resettlement amidst allegations of unfair distribution and misappropriation. Even for Adonia Bintoora and Richard Matanda – Mount Elgon warden and community conservation warden, respectively – 'the resettlement exercise was mismanaged and as a result, many people were either not properly resettled or totally ignored' (Bintoora and Matanda, 2017, p. 1).

Consequently, this and similar resettlement exercises brought about two major changes. First, they effectively cleared out the majority of human occupants from within the protected area, thus ending centuries of continuous human habitation. Second, for the populations from the plains and uplands, they reoriented livelihoods away from mobile pastoralism and foraging toward agricultural cultivation fixed on nucleated, individually-held plots of land. As we will see, the unresolved nature of local grievances related to, first, the *de jure* expropriation of customary property rights by the colonial administration, and, second, the apparently mismanaged removal of communities from within the forest reserve after independence would continue to pose significant challenges for subsequent conservation efforts on Mount Elgon.

Boundary conflicts and the transnationalisation of conservation governance

A new era of contestation, conflict, and land tenure insecurity on Mount Elgon emerged with the transition of the protected area from Forest Park to National Park in 1992–1993 at the urging of USAID, IUCN, and Norad (Norgrove, 2002; Scott, 1998; Gosamalang et al., 2008). The change in status marked a dramatic increase in the involvement of foreign donors, who introduced a variety of different goals, objectives, policy concepts, and conditionalities. Hence, unlike the period of political instability during the Amin and Obote regimes, Mount Elgon's new managers had an unprecedented reserve of donor-provided resources with which to enforce regulations (Chhetri et al., 2003). Violent conflicts arose as 'law enforcement rangers' began to impound cattle found in and around the park's new boundaries and to levy severe fines against anyone collecting forest products. Addressing informally 'sanctioned' settlements and forest clearance along the edges of the protected area – a practice that had become widespread during the relative management vacuum of the 1970s and 1980s – emerged as a central policy mandate of the newly created National Park (Norgrove and Hulme, 2006).

Toward this end, USAID's $33 million 'Action Program for the Environment' (APE) was instrumental in enabling this recentralisation of state control over protected areas. As an American regional advisor for USAID's conservation efforts in East Africa in the early 1990s put it, recalling the pressure USAID exerted upon the Ugandan government to expand the area under strict protection: 'We said to them, "we won't give you money if you don't create parks"' (pers. comm., 2011). This reestablishment of control over – and, in some cases, expansion of – the national protected area estate resulted in large-scale evictions from forest reserves and national parks across the country, an outcome that was ultimately sanctioned at least implicitly by both USAID and other donors (e.g., Aluma et al., 1989; NFA, 2011).

In this context, the IUCN also initiated the Mount Elgon Conservation and Development Project (MECDP) with support from Norad in 1987. Early phases of the project centred on strengthening government control over the protected area and re-establishing the 1963 boundary (Scott, 1998). However, as MECDP-associated staff White and Hinchley (2001, p. 13) would later observe – and although IUCN initially considered these evictions to be 'partially successful' – it rapidly also became clear that they had 'led to conflict with surrounding communities dependent on the forest for basic needs such as firewood, food, and medicinal plants'. Partially in response to these conflicts, IUCN began piloting 'collaborative resource management agreements' (CRMAs) between UWA and local communities, which allowed the latter to access forest products in quantities that were deemed to be sustainable. As documented by subsequent analyses, however, these agreements were not universalised to all park-adjacent communities, and in practice appear to have been used as a 'reward' for those communities who have avoided conflict with conservation authorities, rather than as a means of ameliorating existing conflicts in highly contested portions of the national park (e.g., Nakakaawa et al., 2015; Vedeld et al., 2016).

The territorial goals of securing the park boundary and reclaiming 'encroached' land were further motivated by a 1992 agreement between conservation authorities and a Dutch NGO – known as the Forests Absorbing Carbon-dioxide Emissions (FACE) Foundation – to plant 25,000 ha of trees in deforested areas along the margins of the national park. In exchange for financing these reforestation activities, FACE acquired the right to market the carbon stored within the newly established plantations over voluntary markets. An implicit condition of this arrangement, however, was that any communities remaining within the 25,000 hectares of 'degraded' lands would have to be removed (Cavanagh and Benjaminsen, 2014). Controversially, these same 25,000 hectares comprised lands that were most affected by the formerly government-sanctioned 'encroachment' of local communities under the Amin and Obote regimes. As White (2002, p. 2), the former IUCN Chief Technical Advisor for the Mount Elgon region, observed, '[t]he evictions typically were rigorously enforced and carried out without prior consultations with local people. They often involved destruction of crops, confiscation of livestock, burning of houses, beatings, etc.'. Understandably, such violence generally fostered a highly tense and adversarial relationship between conservation authorities and local communities affected by the eviction process. The paradox of the rise of an era of 'community conservation' at Mount Elgon, in other words, is that it was coupled with a considerable degree of violence and alleged human rights abuses (e.g., Hurinet, 2011; see also Nel and Hill, 2013; Cavanagh and Benjaminsen, 2015).

With the transition to national park status, conservation authorities on Mount Elgon also once again turned their attention to boundary surveying and demarcation. Accordingly, the park boundary was officially measured and (re)demarcated several times between 1993 and 2008. When these surveying exercises were carried out, however, numerous boundary discrepancies were uncovered. Some of these were quite substantial; according to one UWA report, for instance, discrepancies between previously-demarcated and *de jure* park boundaries were found to range between '0 km–1 km' in size, with the areas in between frequently being quite densely populated (UWA, 2011, p. 5). For instance, the Benet Resettlement Area, which was planned to be no larger than 6,000 ha, was found to be more than 7,500 ha (Himmelfarb, 2012). Although conservation and local government authorities had previously allocated land to households throughout this same 7,500 ha area, which the households subsequently cleared and planted, 1,500 ha from the resettlement area was subsequently reclassified as within the national park. Overnight, approximately 6,000 people who had invested great effort and resources clearing and planting the 'illegitimate' 1,500 ha were told the land no longer belonged to them, and they would have to relocate once more – this time without an allocation of land for their resettlement (see Himmelfarb, 2006, 2012; Bintoora and Matanda, 2017).

In various locations around the protected area, villagers and their local government representatives vehemently protested these newly demarcated boundaries. In the case of the Benet community, local leaders eventually secured a Parliamentary order calling on UWA not to forcibly relocate any residents until the dispute could be resolved (Okwaare and Hargreaves, 2009). Hoping to force a definitive resolution to land tenure insecurity in their resettlement area, community leaders joined with ActionAid and the Uganda Land Alliance to pursue litigation against the Ugandan government in 2003. Likewise, three separate groups of farmers in Bagisu-majority districts also filed lawsuits to contest their eviction from territories that had been reclassified as within the national park following boundary demarcation exercises (Cavanagh and Benjaminsen, 2015). In the former case, the Benet lawsuit culminated in a 2005 'consent judgment' at the High Court in Mbale, which recognised the community as the 'historical and indigenous' inhabitants of forests on Mount Elgon, as well as the legitimacy of Benet land claims in disputed sections of the resettlement area. Though lauded by the African Commission on Human and Peoples' Rights (ACHPR and IWGIA, 2009, p. 55), UWA and the central government have failed to recognise the court's ruling in practice more than ten years after the consent judgment. Similarly, lawsuits elsewhere around the protected area have either been dismissed, or have yet to be resolved, and in some cases after more than a decade of expensive litigation. Notwithstanding UWA's refusal to recognise the land rights claims of local communities, however, the agency has implemented a variety of 'community based' strategies, as we explore below.

Carbon forestry, co-management, and communitarian rhetoric

Since the early 1990s, management plans for Mount Elgon have incorporated a variety of 'community-based' conservation and revenue-sharing initiatives (Petursson and Vedeld, 2015; Vedeld et al., 2016). Whereas the latter revenue-sharing arrangements are required by conservation legislation in Uganda (the 2000 Uganda Wildlife Act and subsequent provisions), the former mechanisms follow the precedent set by IUCN's piloting of collaborative resource management agreements (CRMAs). In addition to CRMAs, these include boundary management agreements, beekeeping agreements, agro-forestry or *taungya* reforestation projects within park boundaries, employment opportunities, and tourism revenue-sharing arrangements (Norgrove, 2002; Nakakaawa et al., 2015; Vedeld et al., 2016). Employment opportunities with the UWA-FACE carbon forestry project and payments for avoided deforestation via community revolving funds from the more recent Mount Elgon Regional Ecosystem Conservation Programme (MERECP) have also been widely advertised as a means of jointly pursuing conservation and development objectives (Mwayafu and Kimbowa, 2011; Cavanagh and Freeman, 2017). Due to unresolved boundary disputes, however, communities in open conflict with UWA in most cases have not qualified for participation in these schemes.

Numerous evaluations of the socioeconomic impacts of these mechanisms at Mount Elgon have now been undertaken. For instance, Nakakaawa et al. (2015) estimate that communities participating in CRMA arrangements can – in certain best-case instances – earn household incomes that are between 26–28% above the local average, depending on the livelihood activities sanctioned under specific CRMAs. However, these authors note that the overall impact of these agreements is limited by their relatively small scale of deployment to date, and UWA's tendency to withhold such agreements from communities who do not enjoy amicable relationships with park management. The aversion to negotiating such agreements more widely is especially fraught given that similar levels of environmental dependence and 'park environmental income' (PEI) are found around the park (e.g., Nakakaawa et al., 2015, p. 10). That is to say, many communities appear to have been left out of the CRMA process despite a degree of reliance on protected resources that is just as pressing as that found in communities selected for participation.

Likewise, in an assessment of wider costs and benefits of conservation governance at Mount Elgon, Vedeld et al. (2016) find that benefits from CRMAs, revenue sharing, the MERECP's community revolving funds, and other such mechanisms amount to only approximately 1.2% of household income on average. By contrast, the costs of park-adjacent residency – due to crop and livestock raiding, exclusion from resource access, and evictions or other conflicts with park authorities – were found to constitute approximately 20.5% of total household incomes. Even in cases where benefits are in fact received at the household level, moreover, these authors found that these remained 'unevenly distributed and instrumentally used to reward compliance with park regulations', and that they did 'not necessarily accrue to those incurring costs due to eviction and exclusion, crop raiding, resource access restrictions and conflicts' (Vedeld et al., 2016, p. 183).

Putting the scale of benefit-sharing mechanisms into wider regional context, Cavanagh (2015) further substantiates that the distribution of revenue-sharing disbursements and resource-access agreements is highly spatially uneven. Local administrative units that also host park entrances have disproportionately benefitted from these mechanisms, whereas districts with high levels of conflict have been comparatively marginalised. For instance, at the time of Cavanagh's (2015) study, Manafwa district – the location of two farmers' groups suing UWA – had received only 7.7% of redistributed revenue over the preceding nine years, despite hosting nearly a quarter of the park-adjacent population, and 12% of the park-community boundary. Further, the amount of revenue actually redistributed to the district was approximately $3,027.31 – amounting to only $0.0085 per district resident over a nine-year period. In contrast to the regular and substantial costs of park-adjacent residency, this amount is meagre indeed.

As such, the simultaneous embrace of these seemingly contradictory goals of *both* strict boundary protection and economic development via 'benefit' sharing from conservation is the result of a complex institutional politics. On one hand, both local and national politicians frequently attempt to solicit community support at Mount Elgon by either encouraging further encroachment into the park, or by promising to support those communities who have elected to press claims to land rights in disputed portions of the protected area. In such a context, support for 'encroachment' will likely remain a mainstay of electoral politics at multiple scales, whether promulgated by an incumbent official or the opposition. President Yoweri Museveni himself has occasionally pursued such a strategy, most notably perhaps in a series of speeches delivered in the region in 2010 (Edyegu and Watala, 2010), only to change tack and order further evictions after his re-election.

On the other hand, however, state agencies such as UWA and NFA have been under increasing pressure to maximise rents and incomes received from donors, investors, and ecotourism operations, thereby reducing the financial burden of conservation for the central government (Nel, 2015; Petursson and Vedeld, this volume, Chapter 11). Given such incentives, there is little to gain from entertaining the land rights claims of local communities, which might either diminish the receipt of the aforementioned rents or impede their transfer entirely. Yet, in the context of prevailing donor norms and conditionalities, human rights standards and responsibilities cannot simply be overtly dismissed. The result to date has been substantial economic incentives for the often violent removal and exclusion of communities residing in contested areas of the national park, coupled with strong rhetoric about – but often financially insignificant performance of – mechanisms related to revenue and benefit sharing. As we discuss in conclusion, however, it remains to be seen whether or not these contradictions between official rhetoric and the consequences of actual management practices will become increasingly untenable.

Conclusion

In a speech to community leaders in Kapchorwa in 2002, the Former Chief Warden of Mount Elgon National Park – James Okonya – framed the predicament facing conservationists at Mount Elgon as follows:

There is a lot of pressure that this land be changed into gardens, but the Government has resisted and will continue to resist because your lives depend on it. This is an area of interest to you and the rest of the world.

(cited in *New Vision*, 2002)

Highly conscious of its national and international image, UWA has to date pursued a strictly protectionist approach on the ground, albeit one often carefully embedded in the language of rights, livelihoods, and the mutual pursuit of conservation and development goals. As at certain other protected areas throughout Uganda and eastern Africa, successive attempts to introduce the 'communitarian rhetoric' of participation and collaboration has often been contradictorily shot through with violence, coercion, and the destruction of both lives and livelihoods (e.g., Hurinet, 2011). As a result, one can certainly appreciate that local residents have often been less than enthusiastic about the introduction of new conservation buzzwords and 'approaches', particularly in instances where the adoption of such concepts has repeatedly been perceived to change little on the ground. In the most heated cases, aggrieved local communities have actually deployed a range of resistance strategies in response to prevailing or evolving forms of conservation governance, ranging from litigation in Ugandan courts, to the violent confrontation of conservation staff, to more subtle means of informally maintaining access to contested land and resources (Norgrove and Hulme, 2006; Cavanagh and Benjaminsen, 2015).

At present, the conservation status quo on Mount Elgon appears to be invested in the 'management' and attempted suppression of these contradictions, rather than their resolution in the form of the substantive redress of local grievances. However, whether or not state agencies can simply suppress such opposition indefinitely remains an empirically open question. In an era of both global and regional environmental change, what is certain is that the stakes of effective conservation management at Mount Elgon are increasingly high: not simply for the preservation of the mountain's significant flora and fauna, but also for the sustenance of growing rural communities both adjacent to the national park and throughout the region. Virtually no one residing on the slopes of Mount Elgon opposes the principle of conservation *as such* – indeed, many residents echo James Okonya's statement above that their 'lives depend on it'. The question is not whether, but rather how conservation might proceed in ways that ameliorate rather than exacerbate long histories of social and environmental injustice. Unresolved to date, this remains one of the most pressing and empirically open questions facing conservation agencies, institutions, and researchers in the twenty-first century.

Notes

1 This chapter is based on ethnographic and mixed-methods research conducted by Himmelfarb (14 months between 2005 and 2010) and Cavanagh (14 months

between 2009 and 2011), as well as on document analyses and a review of the secondary literature on conservation and development at Mount Elgon.
2 Following the declaration of British control over the Uganda Protectorate in 1894, the whole of Mount Elgon was initially located in Uganda. However, the border was readjusted in 1902, which denoted that the mountain was thereafter bisected by the political boundary between the Uganda Protectorate and the East Africa Protectorate (Kenya Colony and Protectorate after 1920). See, for instance, Khadiagala (2010).

References

Adams, W.M. and Mulligan, M. (2003) 'Introduction', in W.M. Adams and M. Mulligan (eds), *Decolonizing Nature: strategies for conservation in a post-colonial era*. Routledge/Earthscan, London, UK, pp. 1–15.

African Court of Human and Peoples Rights (ACHPR) and International Working Group on Indigenous Affairs (IWGIA) (2009) *Report of the African Commission's Working Group on Indigenous Populations/Communities: Research and Information Visit to the Republic of Uganda 14–17, 24–29 July 2006*. Eks-Skolens Trykkeri, Copenhagen, Denmark.

Aluma, J. and Drennon, C., Emmanuel, K., Kigula, J., Lawry, S., Muwanga-Zake, E.S.K., et al. (1989) *Settlement in Forest Reserves, Game Reserves, and National Parks in Uganda*. Makerere Institute of Social Research, Makerere University, Kampala, Uganda, and Land Tenure Centre, University of Wisconsin, Madison, WI, USA.

Bintoora, A.K.K. and Matanda, R.G. (2017) 'Governance of forests: assessment of the resettlement of Benet/Ndorobos issues in the management of Mount Elgon National Park, Uganda', *Asian Journal of Environment & Ecology*, vol. 5, no. 2, pp. 1–18.

Blomley, T. (2003) 'Natural resource conflict management: the case of Bwindi Impenetrable and Mgahinga Gorilla National Parks, southwestern Uganda', in A. P. Castro and E. Nielsen (eds) *Natural Resource Conflict Management Case Studies: an analysis of power, participation and protected areas*. FAO, Rome, Italy.

Bunker, S. (1987) *Peasants Against the State: The politics of market control in Bugisu, Uganda, 1900–1983*. University of Chicago Press, Chicago, IL, USA.

Bussmann, R.V. (2006) 'Vegetation zonation and nomenclature of African Mountains: an overview', *Lyonia*, vol. 11, no. 1, pp. 41–66.

Cavanagh, C.J. (2015) *Protected Area Governance, Carbon Offset Forestry, and Environmental (In)Justice at Mount Elgon, Uganda*. Report prepared for the EU Research Council Project 'I-REDD', DEV Reports and Policy Paper Series, University of East Anglia, Norwich, UK.

Cavanagh, C.J. (2017) 'Anthropos into humanitas: civilizing violence, scientific forestry, and the "Dorobo question" in eastern Africa', *Environment and Planning D: Society and Space*, vol. 35, no. 4, pp. 694–713.

Cavanagh, C.J. and Benjaminsen, T.A. (2014) 'Virtual nature, violent accumulation: the 'spectacular failure' of carbon offsetting at a Ugandan National Park', *Geoforum*, vol 56, pp. 55–65.

Cavanagh, C.J. and Benjaminsen, T.A. (2015) 'Guerrilla agriculture? A biopolitical guide to illicit cultivation within an IUCN Category II protected area', *Journal of Peasant Studies*, vol. 42, no. 3–4, pp. 725–745.

Cavanagh, C.J. and Freeman, O. (2017) 'Paying for carbon at Mount Elgon: two contrasting approaches at a transboundary park in East Africa', in S. Namirembe, B. Leimona, M. van Noordwijk and P. Minang (eds), *Co-Investment in Ecosystem Services: global lessons from payment and incentive schemes*. World Agroforestry Centre (ICRAF), Nairobi, Kenya.

Cavanagh, C.J. and Himmelfarb, D. (2015) '"Much in Blood and Money"': necropolitical ecology on the margins of the Uganda Protectorate', *Antipode*, vol. 47, no. 1, pp. 55–73.

Chhetri, P., Mugisha, A. and White, S. (2003) 'Community resources use in Kibale and Mt. Elgon National Parks, Uganda', *Parks*, vol. 13, pp. 28–49.

Edyegu, D. and Watala, P. (2010) 'Museveni directs on Busoga, Elgon reserves', *New Vision* (24 October), http://allafrica.com/stories/201010250296.html, accessed 11 June 2012.

Fisher, J.A., Cavanagh, C.J., Sikor, T. and Mwayafu, D.M. (2018) 'Linking notions of justice and project outcomes in carbon offset forestry projects: insights from a comparative study in Uganda', *Land Use Policy*, vol. 73, pp. 259–268.

Forest Department (FD) (1961) *The Forests and the Forest Administration of Uganda*, Forest Department and the Government Printer, Kampala, Uganda.

Goldschmidt, W. (1967) *Sebei Law*, University of California Press, Berkeley, CA, USA.

Goldschmidt, W. (1989) *The Sebei: a study in adaptation*, Holt, Rinehart, and Winston, New York, NY, USA.

Gosamalang, D., Vedeld, P. and Gombya-Ssembajjwe, W. (2008) *From Forest Reserve to National Park: change in legal status and impacts on livelihoods and biodiversity resources, Mt. Elgon, Uganda*, Noragric Working Paper No. 44, Norwegian University of Life Sciences, Ås, Norway.

Heald, S. (1998) *Controlling Anger: the sociology of Gisu violence*, Ohio University Press, Athens, OH, USA.

Heald, S. (1999) *Manhood and Morality: sex, violence, and ritual in Gisu society*, Routledge, New York, NY, USA and London, UK.

Himmelfarb, D. (2006) *Moving People, Moving Boundaries: the socio-economic effects of protectionist conservation, involuntary resettlement and tenure insecurity on the edge of Mt. Elgon National Park, Uganda*, Agroforestry in Landscape Mosaics Working Paper Series. World Agroforestry Centre, Tropical Resources Institute of Yale University, New Haven, CT, USA, and The University of Georgia, Nairobi, Kenya.

Himmelfarb, D. (2012) 'In the aftermath of displacement: a political ecology of dispossession, transformation, and conflict on Mt. Elgon, Uganda', PhD thesis, University of Georgia, Nairobi, Kenya.

Human Rights Network (Hurinet) Uganda (2011) *Resource Based Conflicts and Human Rights Violations in Uganda: a case study of selected protected areas*. Hurinet-Uganda/Diakonia-Sweden, Kampala, Uganda.

Johnston, H.H. (1902) *The Uganda Protectorate*. Hutchinson & Co., London, UK.

Khadiagala, G.M. (2010) 'Boundaries in eastern Africa', *Journal of Eastern African Studies*, vol. 4, no. 2, pp. 266–278.

King, B.C., le Bas, M.J. and Sutherland, D.S. (1972) 'The history of the alkaline volcanoes and intrusive complexes of Eastern Uganda and Western Kenya', *Journal of the Geological Society*, vol. 128, no. 2, pp. 173–205.

Langlands, B.W. (1974) *Soil Productivity and Land Availability Studies for Uganda*. Makerere University, Kampala, Uganda.

Low, D.A. (2009) *Fabrication of Empire: the British and the Uganda kingdoms, 1890–1902*. Cambridge University Press, Cambridge, UK.

Luzinda, H. (2008) 'Mobile boundary and mobile people: involuntary resettlement of the Benet People in Mt. Elgon National Park, Uganda', MSc thesis, Norwegian University of Life Sciences, Ås, Norway.

Mamdani, M. (1987) 'Extreme but not exceptional: towards an analysis of the agrarian question in Uganda', *The Journal of Peasant Studies*, vol. 14, no. 2, pp. 191–225.

McMaster, D.N. (1962) *A Subsistence Crop Geography of Uganda*. Geographical Publications, Berkhamsted, UK.

Morton, T. (2007) *Ecology Without Nature*, Harvard University Press, Cambridge, MA, USA.

Mugagga, F., Kakembo, V. and Buyinza, M. (2012) 'A characterisation of the physical properties of soil and the implications for landslide occurrence on the slopes of Mount Elgon, Eastern Uganda', *Natural Hazards*, vol. 60, no. 3, pp. 1113–1131.

Mwayafu, D. and Kimbowa, R. (2011) *Issues and Options for Benefit Sharing in REDD+ in East Africa: a case study of Mount Elgon Regional Conservation Programme*, REDDnet/Overseas Development Institute, London, UK.

Nakakaawa, C., Moll, R., Vedeld, P., Sjaastad, E. and Cavanagh, C.J. (2015) 'Collaborative resource management and rural livelihoods around protected areas: a case study of Mount Elgon National Park, Uganda', *Forest Policy and Economics*, vol. 57, pp. 1–11.

National Environment Management Authority (NEMA) (n.d.) *Kapchorwa District Environment Profile*, NEMA, Kampala, Uganda.

National Forestry Authority (NFA) (2011) *Assessment of Trends of Evictions From Protected Areas During the Period 2005–2010 and their Implications for REDD+*, NFA, Kampala, Uganda.

Nel, A. (2015) 'The neoliberalisation of forestry governance, market environmentalism and re-territorialisation in Uganda', *Third World Quarterly*, vol. 36, no. 12, pp. 2294–2315.

Nel, A. and Hill, D. (2013) 'Constructing walls of carbon: the complexities of community, carbon sequestration and protected areas in Uganda', *Journal of Contemporary African Studies*, vol. 31, no. 3, pp. 421–440.

New Vision (2002) 'Sabiny Press for Mt Elgon Park Land', *New Vision* (17 June), www.newvision.co.ug/D/8/17/23042, accessed 5 June 2012.

Norgrove, L. (2002) 'Parking resistance and resisting the park: the theory and practice of national park management, a case study of Mount Elgon National Park, Uganda', PhD thesis, University of Manchester, Manchester, UK.

Norgrove, L. and Hulme, D. (2006) 'Confronting conservation at Mount Elgon, Uganda', *Development and Change*, vol. 37, no. 5, pp. 1093–1116.

Okwaare, S. and Hargreaves, S. (2009) *Mountains of Trouble: the Benet community of Uganda*, ActionAid Critical Stories of Change Series. ActionAid, Kampala, Uganda.

Parker, G.G. (1952) 'British policy and native agriculture in Kenya and Uganda', *Agricultural History*, vol. 26, no. 4, pp. 125–131.

Petursson, J.G. and Vedeld, P. (2015) 'The "nine lives" of protected areas: a historical-institutional analysis from the transboundary Mt Elgon, Uganda and Kenya', *Land Use Policy*, vol. 42, pp. 251–263.

Petursson, J.G. and Vedeld, P. (2017) 'Rhetoric and reality in protected area governance: institutional change under different conservation discourses in Mount Elgon National Park, Uganda', *Ecological Economics*, vol. 131, pp. 166–177.

Petursson, J.G., Vedeld, P. and Kaboggoza, J. (2011) 'Transboundary biodiversity management: institutions, local stakeholders, and protected areas: a case study from Mt. Elgon, Uganda and Kenya', *Society & Natural Resources*, vol. 24, no. 12, pp. 1304–1321.

Reed, M.S. and Clokie, M.R. (2000) 'Effects of grazing and cultivation on forest plant communities in Mount Elgon National Park, Uganda', *African Journal of Ecology*, vol. 38, no. 2, pp. 154–162.

Sassen, M., Sheil, D., Giller, K.E. and ter Braak, C.J. (2013) 'Complex contexts and dynamic drivers: understanding four decades of forest loss and recovery in an East African protected area', *Biological Conservation*, vol. 159, pp. 257–268.

Scott, P. (1998) *From Conflict to Collaboration: people and forests at Mount Elgon, Uganda*, IUCN, Gland, Switzerland and Cambridge, UK.

Synott, T.J. (1968) *Working Plan for Mount Elgon Central Forest Reserve (1968–1978)*. Uganda Forest Department, Entebbe, Uganda.

Turyahabwe, N. and Banana, A.Y. (2008) 'An overview of history and development of forest policy and legislation in Uganda', *International Forestry Review*, vol. 10, no. 4, pp. 641–656.

Twaddle, M. (1993) *Kakungulu & the Creation of Uganda 1868–1928*. James Currey, Oxford, UK.

Uganda Bureau of Statistics (UBOS) (2014) *National Population and Housing Census*. Uganda Bureau of Statistics, Kampala, Uganda.

Uganda Wildlife Authority (UWA) (2011) *UWA-FACE Progressive Forest Restoration Report*, Uganda Wildlife Authority, Kampala, Uganda.

Vedeld, P., Cavanagh, C., Petursson, J.G., Nakakaawa, C., Moll, R. and Sjaastad, E. (2016) 'The political economy of conservation at Mount Elgon, Uganda: between local deprivation, regional sustainability, and global public goods', *Conservation and Society*, vol. 14, no. 3, p. 183.

Webster, G. (1954) *Working Plan for Mount Elgon Forest Reserve*, Government printer, Entebbe, Uganda.

Webster, G. and Osmaston, H. (2003) *A History of the Uganda Forest Department, 1951–1965*, Commonwealth Secretariat, London, UK.

White, S. (2002) 'People-park conflicts in Mt. Elgon: the role of collaborative management in conflict resolution', paper presented to the National Conference on Mountains and Highlands in Uganda, 3–4 October, Makerere University, Kampala, Uganda.

White, S. and Hinchley, D. (2001) 'Managing Mt. Elgon', *Arborvitae* (October), p. 13.

Wrigley, C.C. (1959) *Crops and Wealth in Uganda: a short agrarian history*, East African Institute of Social Research, Kampala, Uganda.

6 Budongo Forest

A paradigm shift in conservation?

Fred Babweteera, Christopher Mawa,
Caroline Asiimwe, Eric Okwir, Geoffrey
Muhanguzi, John Paul Okimat, and
Sarah Robinson

Introduction

This chapter highlights the historical trends of conservation initiatives in Budongo Forest with particular emphasis on political and socio-economic drivers at local, national and international levels. The first section of the chapter provides a description of the forest in terms of its biophysical characteristics, management history and socio-cultural and economic changes that have taken place around the forest over time. This is followed by a review of the current challenges that face the various development and conservation initiatives in the area. The third section provides a description of the conservation and development projects and programmes that have resulted in the forest's status quo. The fourth section sheds light on the role of the different actors, their power relations and how these have shaped the conservation and development outcomes in and around the forest. The last section highlights policy recommendations to improve conservation and development in the area in future.

Overview of Budongo Forest Reserve

Budongo Forest Reserve is a medium altitude, moist semi-deciduous forest forming the northernmost arc of the Albertine Rift forests in western Uganda (31°22'–31°46'E and 1°37'–2°03'N). It is a prime forest reserve among 506 forest reserves managed by the National Forestry Authority (NFA), a government agency. It covers an area of 853 km² and was gazetted in the early 1930s, although selective timber extraction by the Forest Department started as early as 1910 (Eggeling, 1947). Initial logging regimes targeted all old timber trees over 1.3 m dbh (diameter at breast height) followed by the felling of those above 85 cm dbh 80 years later (Dawkins, 1958; Philip, 1965). Enrichment planting with high-value mahogany timber trees (*Khaya anthotheca* and *Entandrophragma* spp.) was carried out between the 1940s and 1950s but was later abandoned after it was realised that natural regeneration in logged areas was equally good (Babweteera et al., 2012). However, during the 1950s and

1960s, arboricide treatments were carried out on 'weed species' (trees that had no market value) (Plumptre and Reynolds, 1994). This was aimed at eliminating the 'weed species' and opening up the canopy to encourage regeneration of the mahoganies. These treatments were stopped in the 1970s when more tree species became marketable. Due to political instability in Uganda in the 1970s and 1980s, most logging companies closed down (Babweteera et al., 2012) and, at present, there is no operational sawmill in the Forest Reserve. However, most sawmill concessions were gradually transferred to pitsawing groups and, as a result, all the timber produced at present is by pitsawing, some of which is illegal. Budongo Forest has been the prime source of the most valuable timber (*Khaya* and *Entandrophragma* spp.) in Uganda.

Budongo Forest is contiguous with Murchison Falls National Park and Bugungu Game Reserve to the north and west respectively. Consequently, there are limited human settlements to the north and west of the forest. The communities settled to the east and south of the forest are economically poor and vulnerable with an average of $0.8/capita/day (BCFS, 2016). The population is ethnically diverse as a result of waves of migrations into the area in search of employment opportunities and/or fleeing civil unrest in neighbouring districts and the Democratic Republic of Congo. The Banyoro who are traditionally the indigenous inhabitants of this area often allowed incomers to occupy land close to the forest edge, forming a buffer between Banyoro cultivated lands and wildlife known to reside in the forest (Beattie, 1960). Although subsistence farming has defined the agricultural landscape over the years, the emergence of a commercial sugarcane out-growers scheme by Kinyara Sugar Works has become a major economic activity. This scheme provides opportunities for the rural poor to grow sugarcane on their farms and sell to the factory.

Conservation and development challenges

Although the boundaries of the forested landscape of Budongo have not changed much, the area faces many challenges that, if left unaddressed, could undo the forest's much celebrated historical stability. The forest's major conservation and development challenges can be broadly categorised under five themes: unsustainable resource harvesting, land-use change, human-wildlife conflicts, ineffective law enforcement and policy discord.

Unsustainable resource harvesting

In order to ease management of the forested area, Budongo Forest Reserve is divided into eight forest blocks (GoU, 2011). The blocks have been further sub-divided into compartments that fall under the four main management regimes: production, buffer, recreation and strict nature reserve areas (Howard, 1991). The National Forestry Authority issues licenses to individuals, companies or groups of people for selective timber extraction in specified production zones in accordance with the management plan for these zones. All extractive activities are strictly prohibited in the nature reserve.

Selective timber harvesting was carried out in most compartments during the 20th century to supply valuable timber to both local and distant communities. To date, the forest continues to experience harvesting pressure, not from the National Forestry Authority but from pitsawyers who engage in illegal timber harvesting (Plumptre, 1996). Recently, it has also been an important source of fuelwood and construction poles for the various institutions such as Kabalye Police Training School as well as semi-urban communities around Kinyara Sugar Works. Although the forest's Management Plan (GoU, 2011)bans timber harvesting in the strict nature reserve, Budongo Conservation Field Station (BCFS) research teams have recorded evidence of timber harvesting that is undetected by the NFA patrol teams, probably because of their limited human resource. Selective harvesting (both legal and illegal) of timber trees mainly targets high value timber species such as mahoganies and, recently, *Cordia millenii*, which is used for making fishing canoes. The unsustainable harvesting of the species to feed the boat-making industry around Lake Albert to the west of Budongo Forest, coupled with the tree's low regeneration potential, is slowly driving it to extinction (Babweteera, 2009; Tanna, 2012). Such unregulated harvesting of trees for timber, fuelwood and building poles is likely to affect the forest's regeneration and ecosystem stability (BCFS, 2010). For example, the regeneration and recruitment of *Cordia millenii* in Budongo Forest has been hampered by ineffective dispersal and the inherent inability of the species to establish under closed canopy (Babweteera, 2009; Mwavu and Witkowski, 2009).

Land use change

Widespread clearance and fragmentation of forests on private land around Budongo is recent, having gained momentum in the 1990s and which continues to the present day (see Jeary et al., this volume, Chapter 10). Factors contributing to these land-cover changes are complex and should be viewed in the context of the national development agenda as articulated in the country's National Development Plans (NDPs). For example, NDPII (2015/16–2019/20) through the Plan for Modernisation of Agriculture (PMA) focuses on the modernisation and transformation of subsistence agriculture into commercial agriculture (GoU, 2015). This national drive to promote commercial agriculture gives fresh impetus to commercial farming at the expense of forests. The presence of the sugar industry around Budongo Forest has resulted in conversion of private forests and bushland, viewed to be of less monetary value, to sugarcane estates that generate quick cash returns. For instance, between 1988 and 2002, the area under sugarcane increased more than 17-fold: from 6.9 km² to 127 km² (690 ha to 12,729 ha), with a corresponding loss of 47 km² (4,680 ha) of forest (Mwavu and Witkowski, 2008). Most of the forest loss appears to be affecting non-gazetted forests on private land. Budongo Forest now remains an island amidst agricultural fields, unlike in the past where the surrounding landscape had a substantial number of private forest fragments. The local communities around the forest now rely on it as the sole source for domestic supplies of fuelwood, building poles and non-timber forest products. There is a growing belief that even if NFA enhances its effectiveness in protecting the reserve, the increasing population remains a threat to protecting the reserve and its biological resources. Moreover, there is no substantial forest restoration or tree planting programme visible around Budongo Forest that would cushion the existing forest cover in the face of growing population and harvesting pressure.

Human–wildlife conflicts

Studies among farmers living around the southern edge of the Budongo Forest reveal that large vertebrates, particularly baboons, are a major threat to their livelihood (Hill, 2000). In a survey in the adjacent villages, Webber (2006)noted that over 80% of farms were reported to have been raided by large vertebrates. Human–wildlife conflicts have been exacerbated by increased habitat fragmentation fuelled by agricultural expansions (McLennan, 2008) and human population densities. Among the direct impacts of this habitat loss has been wildlife community isolation and depletion of natural food sources. Indeed, long-term tree fruiting data in Budongo Forest Reserve indicates that, over the last 25 years, the proportion of fruiting trees (> 10 cm dbh) has declined from 17% to less than 2% (Babweteeraet al., 2012). This trend is likely to have profound effects on the dynamics of the forest in relation to its regeneration potential, primate foraging, as well as increased cases of human–wildlife conflict due to reduced in-forest food availability for the wildlife.

Ineffective law enforcement

Whereas there are various policies intended to support conservation, there are challenges in enforcement as a result of inadequate funding, limited human resource and conflict of interest among the lower tiers of local governments. In some cases, district local governments expect to get revenues from forest reserves and tree products in order to fund their budgets. This has compelled the relevant departments to focus on revenue collection at the expense of sustainable forest resource management. Furthermore, there have been reports of local leaders and forest managers engaging in illegal resource harvesting (Muhereza, 2005). Although some culprits may claim ignorance of the law on forest protection, there is a general belief that underfunding of the sector, including delays in salary remittances to staff who are meant to be custodians of the forest resources, fuels the illegal activities. In some cases, funding to complement the work of the statutory organisations has come from development partners in the form of short-term projects but this is unsustainable and insufficient to tackle the ever-growing challenges.

Policy discord

Uganda has various policies intended to complement each other on conservation. However, there have been points of weakness in governance, especially the insufficient integration of policies in related sectors such as forestry and agriculture (Jagger, 2010). In addition, the creation of multiple statutory bodies housed in different departments has created weaknesses in coordination and law enforcement. The National Forestry Authority is mandated to manage central forest reserves whereas the District Forestry Services (local government) is mandated to oversee sustainable management of local forest reserves and forests on private land (GoU, 2003; Petursson and Vedeld, this volume, Chapter 11). Both institutions are underfunded and rely on revenues from the forest estates in their realm to fund their activities. However, the recent resurgence of the drive by the Ministry of Water and Environment to operationalise the National Tree Fund casts hope for the underfunded sector. The Fund was established under Section 40 of the country's National Forestry and Tree Planting Act in 2003 as one of the avenues to ensure predictable and sustainable funding of the forestry sector. The monies of the Fund are sourced from loans, grants, gifts, donations and appropriations by the Parliament of Uganda (GoU, 2003) and are specifically meant to promote tree planting and growing, including those without direct commercial value.

Additionally, there is often confusion over the mandate of the Uganda Wildlife Authority that manages wildlife resources in the country, some of which are in natural forest reserves. As a result, there has been laxity in some departments as to who is responsible for managing particular resources. For instance, when there are conservation issues relating to wild fauna in Budongo Forest, the National Forestry Authority usually refers the matter to Uganda Wildlife Authority even though the wild fauna is in a forest reserve under NFA's mandate.

Conservation and development interventions

For most of the 20th century, management of Budongo Forest focused on timber production with few conservation and development interventions. The first conservation and development initiative in Budongo was piloted in the early 1990s through an ecotourism and conservation project that attempted to involve local people in the management of forest reserves and to create opportunities for local communities to benefit from the forests (Langoya and Long, 1998). Furthermore, the establishment of Budongo Forest Project, now Budongo Conservation Field Station (BCFS), in the early 1990s (Reynolds, 2005) catalysed conservation and development initiatives around Budongo. The field station, which has been at the heart of most conservation and development programmes in and around Budongo, is a nexus of research and conservation initiatives aimed at improving forest-edge community livelihoods and sustainable forest management. In the following section we describe four major conservation and development initiatives in and around Budongo Forest that stand out: (i) the Alternative Livelihoods Scheme under BCFS; (ii) Collaborative Forest Management under NFA; (iii) Ecotourism Development under NFA; and (iv) Mitigating human–wildlife conflicts under BCFS and Masindi District Local Government.

Alternative Livelihoods Scheme

The BCFS implements conservation and development initiatives largely through projects that focus on promotion of alternative sustainable livelihoods. These projects have been jointly implemented in partnership with other non-government organisations (NGOs), government agencies, and local communities. Such initiatives seek to benefit conservation of biodiversity and improve community livelihoods. For example, all beneficiaries of the scheme were required to have functional latrines (sanitation conditioning model) prior to recruitment. This conditional recruitment was meant to reduce incidences of open defecation, thus reducing disease transmission to the people and animals, especially when the latter leave the forest for human settlements in search for alternative foods. The sanitation conditioning model used by BCFS has now been adopted by other NGOs working in the Budongo landscape, such as Village Enterprise, Hoima Caritas Development Organisation and Jane Goodall Institute, and this has improved primary health care and provided livelihood benefits to communities in the Budongo Forest Reserve landscape.

One of the conservation and development initiatives that has positively impacted on conservation and livelihoods in the last five years is the ex-poachers' alternative livelihoods scheme, which was initiated following the realisation that over 45% of chimpanzees in Budongo Forest were maimed or killed by snares (Amati et al., 2008; Tumusiime et al., 2010). Through this project, ex-poachers in communities surrounding Budongo Forest who denounced poaching were given breeding goats and pigs with regular veterinary treatments. Besides providing alternative livelihoods to ex-poachers, BCFS employs a team composed of some ex-poachers as snare patrol men, who survey the forest compartments daily to recover set traps.

This increased snare removal effort discourages poachers since they lose interest in buying snares only to have them removed before serving their purpose. Consequently, there has been a significant reduction in the encounter rate of snares set by poachers, from five per day in 2011 to less than one per day in 2016 (Figure 6.1).

There has also been improved health of the wildlife, domestic animals and people. For example, there have been a reduced number of cases of respiratory disease outbreaks in the Sonso chimpanzee community, which is in frequent contact with the adjacent local communities (Figure 6.2). We acknowledge that this short time period is not sufficient to draw concrete conclusions regarding pathogen transmission trends since other ecological and biological factors, including climate change and pathogen evolution, could play important roles. However, this trend provides an important insight. Additionally, every year, the veterinary team of BCFS treats over 3,000 domestic animals belonging to forest-edge communities with the goal of minimising trans-species disease transmission and creating a positive attitude among local communities towards conservation.

While BCFS relishes the conservation and development benefits impacted by these interventions, some pitfalls have been encountered. Since the scheme initially targeted poachers, using this as a recruitment strategy could have possibly incentivised individuals who were originally non-poachers to start hunting in order to partake of the benefits from it too (Asiimwe, pers. obs.). Consequently, BCFS modified the beneficiary recruitment requirements to include all vulnerable forest-edge communities (BCFS, 2016).

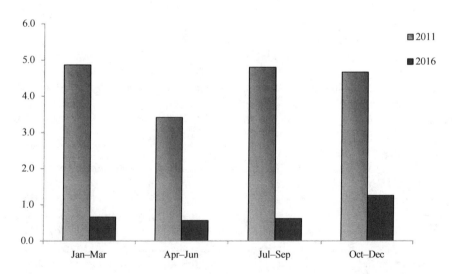

Figure 6.1 Comparison of snares recovered per day in selected compartments of Budongo Forest Reserve before the introduction of the alternative livelihoods scheme (2011) and after (2016).

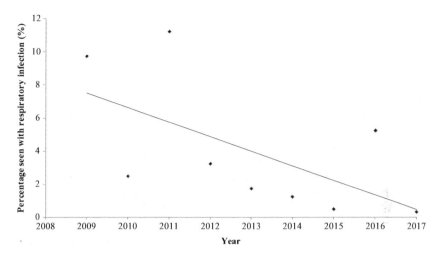

Figure 6.2 Trends of respiratory infections in Sonso chimpanzee community in Budongo Forest Reserve, between 2009 and 2010.

We also acknowledge that the alternatives given to the ex-poachers and other vulnerable forest-edge communities are small compared with the economic benefits from illegal resource harvest. Conservation interventions can thus hardly eliminate illegal resource harvest completely and may need to be complemented by other strategies, notably law enforcement.

Additionally, BCFS, just like other conservation NGOs in the area, relies on donor grants that, unfortunately, are short term. For such initiatives, which require behavioural change for long-term conservation benefits, it is hard to attribute the observed impacts to the initiatives alone. The fact that funding for these initiatives is short-lived and depends for a large part on the priorities of the donors leaves a lot to be desired in terms of the sustainability structures put in place by the recipient implementing agencies. Indeed, recent studies in other parts of the country have reported stagnation of conservation initiatives upon withdrawal of donor financial and technical support, largely due to lack of incentive and sustainability structures (Petursson and Vedeld, 2017).

Collaborative Forest Management

The NFA piloted Collaborative Forest Management (CFM) in Budongo Forest Reserve in 1998 with an aim of curbing illegal activities through regulated access to forest resources and encouraging local community participation in protection of the forest (GoU, 2013). In the CFM arrangement, the state agency (NFA or District Forest Service) enters into co-management arrangements with organised local community groups surrounding forest reserves. The idea is to provide an incentive for the local communities (who are regarded as the main agents of forest resource depletion) to conserve forest resources by participating in forest monitoring activities such as patrols while gaining access to specified forest resources meant to support their livelihoods. Although a 'livelihood' improvement objective prominently features in this co-management arrangement, the interest of NFA is skewed towards protection of forest resources from 'illegal' uncontrolled access by surrounding community members. In Budongo, conservation agreements valid for ten years were signed with the local communities. Within the first decade of implementation of CFM in Budongo, the forest structure had improved in CFM compared with non-CFM compartments in the northern part of Budongo, probably because of controlled extraction (Turyahabwe et al., 2013). In their research, Turyahabwe et al. (2013) revealed that although CFM was ecologically beneficial, about 50% of the respondents in their study were dissatisfied with CFM arrangements, specifically pointing out inequality in distribution of the already insufficient benefits and limited involvement of local communities in making key management decisions. To some local community members, the lack of transparency in CFM activities, especially by the NFA, had bred mistrust among the local participants towards the motives of NFA.

Ecotourism development

The commencement of ecotourism in Budongo was based on the notion that alienating local communities from forest reserves is a recipe for disaster. Whereas the Forest Department (predecessor of National Forestry Authority) focused more on timber production, there was a growing realisation that integrating community conservation into the forest management plan was indeed the optimal way for ensuring sustainable forest management. Thus, two ecotourism sites were established in 1994, one to the north (Kaniyo Pabidi), and the other to south (Busingiro) of the forest reserve (Langoya and Long, 1998). Both sites were established to promote chimpanzee tracking, bird watching and forest walks and the revenue would be used to improve conservation of the endangered chimpanzees. Local communities have directly benefited from ecotourism development in the area through employment and sale of their handicrafts (Kigenyi, 2008) in addition to indirect benefits through support rendered to local primary schools and health centres (Langoya and Long, 1998).

The ecotourism development scheme, though largely beneficial, faced implementation challenges. First, the habituation of chimpanzees for ecotourism is quite expensive and requires skilled personnel. For example, during habituation, chimpanzees exhibit different behavioural responses, for instance, flight, aggression, fight and, sometimes, stealthy retreat (McLennan and Hill, 2010), some of which could aggravate human–wildlife conflicts, especially if the habituated community is close to human settlement. Second, lack of funds to sustain the eco-tourism initiative could lead to its collapse with negative repercussions on both wildlife and neighbouring local communities. Such was the case with the Busingiro eco-tourism site, which could explain the current rampant illegal activities including timber harvesting around the site (Babweteera, pers. obs.). The expectations by the communities of the potential benefits that were to accrue from the ecotourism developments were quite high. Failure to realise the perceived benefits could have compelled the local communities to revert to illegal activities.

Mitigating human–wildlife conflicts

In 2001, Masindi District Local Government in collaboration with BCFS developed and implemented a four-year 'live trap' project to curb the usage of indiscriminate and lethal crop protection methods among the Budongo-Forest-Reserve-edge communities. Through the project, live traps made from locally available materials were constructed and set to allow the identification of crop-raiding animals. From the trapped animals, pest species could be disposed of and threatened species released unharmed (Webber et al., 2007). However, at the time the project was terminated in 2004, none of the traps were functioning, a failure that Webber et al. (2007) attributed to the project's largely top-down design and implementation strategy, and a lack of long-term funding commitment by the conservation agencies. Currently, BCFS is involved in education and awareness promotion, especially among school-going children, who are vulnerable to primate attacks, and farmers at the forest edge. Increased knowledge and awareness of primate behaviour has been effective in reducing the frequency of physical human–wildlife interactions, which can result in fatal situations for both wildlife and humans. In addition, BCFS piloted buffer-zone farming techniques that encouraged farmers to grow crops that are not palatable to crop-raiding wildlife. Vulnerability of buffer crops was studied at the demonstration gardens where various high-economic-value crops such as soya bean and eggplant were found to have potential for use as buffer crops. This led to the production of buffer-zone farming guidelines for the forest-edge communities (BCFS, 2016).

Political economy of conservation and development

Actors involved and their power relations

Budongo Forest Reserve has attracted a number of actors with varied interests at local, national, and international levels. We adopted the actor-centred power approach that examines the social relationship between different actors to identify the different actors and the dominant power elements that they use to alter the behaviour of other actors. The approach helps to provide a clear picture of the various actors' power relations (Maryudi and Sahide, 2017). The common elements of power in the approach are coercion, incentives or disincentives, and trust (Schusser, 2013; Krott et al., 2014; Schusser et al., 2015). Coercion and incentives involve use of 'carrot and stick' to influence the behaviour of other actors. Trust, on the other hand, hinges on the positioning of an actor's reputation to make the other actor(s) accept information without verifying it.

Important actors in the conservation and development of Budongo Forest Reserve include forest-fringe communities, NFA, local politicians, the business community and NGOs. At the international level, the major actors are bi-lateral donors, tourists, researchers and research institutions. Access to the forest by the local communities surrounding the reserve is often regulated by NFA and this is a major cause of conflict between these two key actors. Local politicians, powerful business entities and other state agencies often join the fray in the quest for resource access and control.

There are a number of prominent NGOs that have shaped the conservation rhetoric in and around Budongo Forest (Table 6.1). These NGOs have utilised their commendable conservation profiles to attract funding from international donor agencies to support conservation of primates, promote research and engage in livelihoods development projects with the local communities surrounding the Budongo Forest Reserve. They largely rely on incentives and trust to influence the behaviour of other actors – especially the local community members surrounding the reserve.

The BCFS in particular has been instrumental in the conservation efforts, given the daily presence of its research teams in the forest for data collection, snare removal and maintenance of research grid lines. This has augmented the otherwise inadequate patrol effort of NFA. The station attracts both local and international researchers and students. Indeed, in the last 55 years, large volumes of publications and reports about ecological

Table 6.1 Conservation non-governmental organisations active in and around Budongo Forest

Name	Acronym	Type of NGO
Budongo Conservation Field Station	BCFS	Local
Community Development and Conservation Agency	CODECA	Local
Environmental Conservation Trust of Uganda	ECOTRUST	Local
Hoima Caritas Development Organisation	HOCADEO	Local
Jane Goodall Institute	JGI	International
Village Enterprise	VE	International

and social dimensions of conservation in Budongo Forest Reserve have been produced and their wide readership has produced new research questions that have resulted in renewed efforts to conserve the forest. The presence of BCFS in the area since 1990 and its consistency in promoting conservation activities has cultivated trust among the forest-fringe community members – a power basis that helps it to easily gain acceptance among the local communities. In its alternative livelihoods scheme, BCFS, through the sanitation conditioning model, used incentives/disincentives as a basis to promote forest conservation and improve the health of both humans and wildlife.

The CODECA, with its long-established good relationship with forest-fringe communities, was key at the time of initiating the CFM arrangement. Thus, the CODECA relied on trust to minimise resistance of local community members to the CFM scheme. It played the lead role in sensitisation and formation of parish-level Community Based Organisations (CBOs) to manage parts of the reserve with NFA. The JGI, whose major interest is in chimpanzee conservation, is also engaged in promotion of alternative livelihoods and ecotourism in the Budongo Forest Reserve. The NFA, which lacks adequate technical competence in ecotourism, benefits from the expertise of JGI. Recently, ECOTRUST, through its Payment for Ecosystem Services (PES) project, has also been working with private forest owners and tree planters at the periphery of Budongo Forest Reserve.

Although employing different strategies, these different NGOs all work towards sustainable utilisation of Budongo Forest resources. The inadequate conservation support received from central government coffers makes the supplementary role of international donors invaluable. Thus, the donors play a critical role in determining the foci that conservation agencies embrace. Currently, most conservation donors have shifted their focus to include livelihood benefits alongside biodiversity protection. Thus, the donors provide benefits and can use disincentives, for example, through terminating financial support to recipient actors (conservation NGO or government agency) that fail to stick to their side of the bargain. This has resulted in most of the conservation NGOs in the Budongo Forest landscape focussing a lot on livelihoods improvement projects. Their rationale is that dependence on forest resources will be reduced once the neighbouring communities are empowered to have a large portfolio of alternative means of livelihood.

While conservation NGOs in the area mostly use incentives and trust to influence change in the behaviour of the forest resource users, the NFA uses a combination of coercion and incentives to achieve the same. The authority's source of power is in the statutory and legal documents. Coercion is a dominant strategy, especially during patrols where armed guards have to accompany the forest patrol team to help arrest illegal resource users. This strategy instils fear in those intending to engage in illegal forest use activities. It is common for the patrols to end in running battles between the patrol team and those engaging in illegal activities in the forest. Prior to 2010, NFA patrol teams were unarmed. However, following a string of fatal clashes between NFA staff and illegal timber dealers in which the former lost their lives, the patrols were enhanced with armed guards mainly from the Uganda Police Force and Uganda People's Defence Forces (Babweteera, pers. obs.). Parallel to the coercion approach, NFA has also relied on incentives/ disincentives where Collaborative Forest Management groups that abide by the terms and conditions specified in their ten-year agreements receive incentives. These incentives include continued technical support from NFA, offer of part of the forest reserve land for tree planting, being allowed to legally access specified resources from agreed compartments, and partici- pating in exclusion of unauthorised users from extracting forest resources.

Struggles over access to forest resources

Although violent waves of conflicts resulting from restricted access to forest resources in Budongo Forest have not been documented in the recent past, recent research findings predict an increased struggle for forest resources in the near future due to population pressure and loss of the ungazetted forest cover in the reserve's periphery. However, following Kerkvliet (2009), who defined resistance as 'what people do that shows disgust, anger, indignation or opposition to what they regard as unjust, unfair, illegal claims on them by people in higher, more powerful class and status positions or institutions', covert forms of resistance to conservation initiatives can be identified in the area. In his influential book on 'weapons of the weak' in Malaysia, Scott (1985) identified diverse forms of everyday resistance such as verbal char- acterisation of superiors, dissimulation, pilfering, foot dragging, sabotage, false compliance, feigned ignorance, slander, arson, desertion, and so on. In the Budongo Forest area, the most common strategy used by the local communities is false compliance. At inception, many conservation NGOs in the area attract the attention of local community members, some of whom are recruited as project beneficiaries. They join these conservation projects with overly ambitious expectations from membership but require very close monitoring by the NGOs to make them perform what is required of them. For instance, during the implementation of the ex-poachers alterna- tive livelihood scheme, it was observed that some of the beneficiaries who had publicly denounced hunting to receive support were later found hunting again (Babweteera, pers. obs.).

A remote sensing study by Twongyirwe et al. (2015) showed that Budongo Forest had experienced forest recovery in the interior and minor losses at the forest edges in the past three decades. These forest habitat alter- ations in the interior were attributed to illegal livelihood activities such as pitsawing and charcoal burning. The continuation of these activities amidst the conspicuous presence of many conservation NGOs and NFA can be seen to constitute a covert form of resistance by the perpetrators to existing conservation arrangements (Cavanagh and Benjaminsen, 2015), probably because of the weak law enforcement. While there have been various strategies employed by the state and NGOs to provide alternative livelihoods, these agencies continue to grapple with the challenge of finding alternatives that are economically superior to those obtained from the banned livelihood activities. Moreover, most of these projects target rule-breakers not by taking punitive actions against them but through offers of alternative livelihoods that can be seen as a 'reward' for not abiding by the law.

The booming construction industry, as a result of the increased urbanisation created by the sugar industry and the recent discovery of oil in the Albertine Rift area, are likely to substantially increase the demand for construction materials and fuelwood (mainly charcoal) in the area. This places the Forest Reserve at risk of increased pressure since the area has lost most of the forests outside gazetted areas which would provide part of the timber supplies. The local community members, who are usually hired by timber and charcoal traders to clandestinely extract these resources, use their political and social capital to escape the long arm of the law that criminalises such activities. Politicians at various levels of governance, who have to convince voters to support them after every five years, have increasingly found it rewarding to promise increased access to gazetted forest land and the resources therein for the local communities, especially during election periods. Indeed, throughout the country, most of the serious cases of encroachment and illegal harvesting have been reported to either start or considerably expand during election periods (Nsita, 2005).

It is apparent that at the national level, nature conservation and management is steadily being influenced by a neo-liberal conservation narrative that emphasises green development through ecological capital and advances economic justifications on how markets for tourism are needed to finance conservation (Benjaminsen and Bryceson, 2012). Indeed, non-extractive use of the forest is continuously gaining importance in the recent forest management plans. This new focus, coupled with the national drive to promote plantation forestry development, is expected to reduce the pressure on natural forests for timber. Also, the renewed focus on achieving livelihood improvement objectives alongside conservation of biodiversity, especially among the donor community, is likely to strengthen emphasis on off-forest livelihood improvement initiatives by conservation agencies in the area.

Conclusions and lessons learned

Budongo Forest remains a prime conservation area in Uganda. To the local and distant communities, the forest continues to serve as a major source of timber, non-timber forest products and environmental services. Nonetheless, over the past two decades, there seems to be a growing interest in the non-timber values of the Budongo Forest. In addition, Budongo is envisaged to be a unique platform for scientists to assess the impacts of utilisation and management interventions on forest biodiversity and ecosystem functioning. Regardless of these opportunities, Budongo Forest Reserve is likely to come under increasing utilisation pressure due to the loss of buffer natural forests on private land, growing human population, weak institutions and, most important, the recent oil and gas discoveries in the Albertine Rift region.

In view of these opportunities and threats, the forest sector has evolved its management strategy from a predominantly 'policing' approach that focused on timber production to people-centred collaborative and/or conservation through development approaches that focus on multiple-use forest management. The people-centred approach recognises that demand for natural forest products is likely to increase and, as a result, there is a need to offset such growing demands. To this effect, the forestry sector has promoted plantation forest development as an alternative source of wood products. This might pave the way for limiting or abolishing utilisation of Budongo Forest and other natural forests for timber production. In addition, conservation NGOs have engaged the forest-edge user groups in diverse alternative livelihoods projects aimed at reducing the dependence on forest resources. Conservation and development initiatives in and around Budongo Forest are relatively recent. However, it is evident that, in spite of the actual and potential positive impacts of such schemes, they are undermined by weak institutions, especially the statutory organisations that are mandated to manage forest reserves. Nonetheless, the paradigm shift in conservation strategies that blends 'policing approach' and 'provision of alternatives approach' has made significant contribution to sustainable management of Budongo Forest. Whether these initiatives will ease the pressure on the reserve amidst a society that is economically and culturally changing, is yet to be understood.

References

Amati, S., Babweteera, F. and Wittig, R.M. (2008) 'Snare removal by a chimpanzee of the Sonso community, Budongo Forest (Uganda)', *Pan Africa News*, vol. 15, no. 1, pp. 6–8.

Babweteera, F. (2009) 'Cordia millenii: on the risk of local extinction?', *African Journal of Ecology*, vol. 47, no. 3, pp. 367–373.

Babweteera, F. et al. (2012) 'Environmental and anthropogenic changes in and around Budongo Forest Reserve', in Plumptre, A. (ed.) *The Ecological Impact of Long-Term Changes in Africa's Rift Valley*, NOVA Science Pub Inc, New York, NY, USA, pp. 39–55.

Beattie, J. (1960) *Bunyoro: An African Kingdom*, Holt, Rinehart and Winston, New York, NY, USA.

Benjaminsen, T.A. and Bryceson, I. (2012) 'Conservation, green/blue grabbing and accumulation by dispossession in Tanzania', *Journal of Peasant Studies*, vol. 39, no. 2, pp. 335–355.

Budongo Conservation Field Station (BCFS) (2010) 'Sustainable forest resources offtake in collaboratively managed forests around Masindi and Hoima districts, Western Uganda', unpublished report.

Budongo Conservation Field Station (BCFS) (2016) 'Alternative sustainable livelihood sources for forest edge hunting communities', Final Report to DARWIN
INITIATIVE, unpublished report.

Cavanagh, C.J. and Benjaminsen, T.A. (2015) 'Guerrilla agriculture? A biopolitical guide to illicit cultivation within an IUCN Category II protected area', *The
Journal of Peasant Studies*, vol. 42, nos 3–4, pp. 725–745.

Dawkins, H.C. (1958) *The Management of Tropical High Forest with Special
Reference to Uganda, Imperial Forestry Institute Paper, no. 34*. Imperial Forestry
Institute, University of Oxford, Oxford, UK.

Eggeling, W.J. (1947) 'Observations on the ecology of the Budongo Rain Forest,
Uganda', *Journal of Ecology*, vol. 34, no. 1, pp. 20–87.

Government of Uganda (GoU) (1997) *Nature Conservation Master Plan*, Uganda
Forest Department (FD), Kampala, Uganda.

Government of Uganda (GoU) (2003) *The National Forestry and Tree Planting Act*,
Ministry of Water, Lands and Environment (MWLE), Kampala, Uganda.

Government of Uganda (GoU) (2011) *Forest Management Plan for Budongo Central
Forest Reserve for the period 2011–2021*, Ministry of Water and Environment
(MWE), Kampala, Uganda.

Government of Uganda (GoU) (2013) *The National Forest Plan 2011/12–2021/22*,
Ministry of Water and Environment (MWE), Kampala, Uganda.

Government of Uganda (GoU) (2015) *Second National Development Plan (NDP
II) 2015/16–2019/20*, Ministry of Finance, Planning and Economic Development
(MFPED), Kampala, Uganda.

Hill, C.M. (2000) 'Conflict of interest between people and baboons: crop raiding
in Uganda', *International Journal of Primatology*, vol. 21, no. 2, pp. 299–315.

Howard, P.C. (1991) *Nature Conservation in Uganda's Tropical Forest Reserves*,
IUCN, Gland, Switzerland, and Cambridge, UK.

Jagger, P. (2010) 'Forest sector reform, livelihoods and sustainability in western
Uganda', in L. German, A. Karsenty and A.M. Tiani (eds) *Governing Africa's
Forests in a Globalized World*, Earthscan, London, UK.

Kerkvliet, B.J.T. (2009) 'Everyday politics in peasant societies (and ours)', *The
Journal of Peasant Studies*, vol. 36, no. 1, pp. 227–243.

Kigenyi, F.W. (2008) 'Trends in forest ownership, forest resources tenure and institutional arrangement: are they contributing to better forest management and
poverty reduction? A case study from Uganda', in *Understanding Forest Tenure
in Africa: Opportunities and Challenges for Forest Tenure Diversification*,
unpublished report to Food and Agriculture Organization, Kampala, Uganda.

Krott, M. et al. (2014) 'Actor-centred power: the driving force in decentralised community based forest governance', *Forest Policy and Economics*, vol. 49, pp. 34–42.

Langoya, C.D. and Long, C. (1998) *Local Communities and Ecotourism Development in Budongo Forest Reserve, Uganda, Rural Development Forestry Network
Paper 22e, Winter 1997/98*, Overseas Development Institute, London, UK.

Maryudi, A. and Sahide, M.A.K. (2017) 'Research trend: power analyses in
polycentric and multi-level forest governance', *Forest Policy and Economics*,
vol. 81, pp. 65–68.

McLennan, M.R. (2008) 'Beleaguered chimpanzees in the agricultural district of
Hoima, Western Uganda', *Primate Conservation*, vol. 23, no. 1, pp. 45–54.

McLennan, M.R. and Hill, C.M. (2010) 'Chimpanzee responses to researchers in a
disturbed forest–farm mosaic at Bulindi, western Uganda', *American Journal of
Primatology*, vol. 72, no. 10, pp. 907–918.

McLennan, M.R. et al. (2012) 'Chimpanzees in mantraps: lethal crop protection and conservation in Uganda', *Oryx*, vol. 46, no. 4, pp. 598–603.

Muhereza, F.E. (2005) 'Traditional assitional authorities in Uganda and the management of legislatively decentralised forest resources', in S. Evers, M. Spierrenburg, and H. Wels (eds) *Competing Jurisdictions: settling land claims in Africa*, Koninklijke Brill NV, Leiden, The Netherlands.

Mwavu, E.N. and Witkowski, E.T.F. (2008) 'Land-use and cover changes (1988–2002) around Budongo forest reserve, NW Uganda: implications for forest and woodland sustainability', *Land Degradation & Development*, vol. 19, no. 6, pp. 606–622.

Mwavu, E.N. and Witkowski, E.T.F. (2009) 'Population structure and regeneration of multiple-use tree species in a semi-deciduous African tropical rainforest: implications for primate conservation', *Forest Ecology and Management*, vol. 258, no. 5, pp. 840–849.

Nsita, S.A. (2005) 'Decentralization and forest management in Uganda', in C.J.P. Colfer and D. Capistrano (eds) *The Politics of Decentralization: Forests, Power and People*, EarthScan, London, UK.

Petursson, J.G. and Vedeld, P. (2017) 'Rhetoric and reality in protected area governance: institutional change under different conservation discourses in Mount Elgon National Park, Uganda', *Ecological Economics*, vol. 131, pp. 166–177.

Philip, M.S. (1965) *Working Plan for the Budongo Central Forest Reserve: third revision 1964–1974*, Government Printer, Entebbe, Uganda.

Plumptre, A.J. (1996) 'Changes following 60 years of selective timber harvesting in the Budongo Forest Reserve, Uganda', *Forest Ecology and Management*, vol. 89, no. 1–3, pp. 101–113.

Plumptre, A. and Reynolds, V. (1994) 'The effect of selective logging on the primate populations in the Budongo Forest, Uganda', *International Journal of Applied Ecology*, vol. 31, pp. 631–641.

Reynolds, V. (2005) *The Chimpanzees of the Budongo Forest: Ecology, Behaviour, and Conservation*, Oxford University Press, Oxford, UK.

Schusser, C. (2013) 'Who determines biodiversity? An analysis of actors' power and interests in community forestry in Namibia', *Forest Policy and Economics*, vol. 36, pp. 42–51.

Schusser, C. et al. (2015) 'Powerful stakeholders as drivers of community forestry: results of an international study', *Forest Policy and Economics*, vol. 58, pp. 92–101.

Scott, J. (1985) *Weapons of the Weak. Every day forms of peasant resistance*, Yale University Press, New Haven, CT, USA.

Tacconi, L. (2007) *Illegal Logging: law enforcement, livelihood and the timber trade*, Earthscan, London, UK, p. 301.

Tanna, A. (2012) 'Are the demands for the wood of *Cordia millenii* tree for boat building leading to habitat loss in the Budongo forest reserve for wild chimpanzee populations?', MSc thesis, Roehampton University, London, UK.

Tumusiime, D.M. et al. (2010) 'Wildlife snaring in Budongo Forest Reserve, Uganda', *Human Dimensions of Wildlife*, vol. 15, no. 2, pp. 129–144.

Turyahabwe, N. et al. (2013) 'Impact of collaborative forest management on forest status and local perceptions of contribution to livelihoods in Uganda', *Journal of Sustainable Development*, vol. 6, no. 10, pp. 36–46.

Twongyirwe, R. et al. (2015) 'Three decades of forest cover change in Uganda's Northern Albertine Rift Landscape', *Land Use Policy*, vol. 49, pp. 236–251.

Webber, A.D. (2006) 'Primate crop raiding in Uganda: actual and perceived risks around Budongo Forest Reserve', PhD thesis, Oxford Brookes University, Oxford, UK.

Webber, A.D. and Hill, C.M. (2014) 'Using Participatory Risk Mapping (PRM) to identify and understand people's perceptions of crop loss to animals in Uganda', *PLOS One*, vol. 9, no. 7, p.e102912.

Webber, A.D., Hill, C.M. and Reynolds, V. (2007) 'Assessing the failure of a community-based human-wildlife conflict mitigation project in Budongo Forest Reserve, Uganda', *Oryx*, vol. 41, no. 2, pp. 177–184.

Part III

Conservation and development approaches in policy and practice

7 An environmental justice perspective on the state of carbon forestry in Uganda

Adrian Nel, Kristen Lyons, Janet Fisher, and David Mwayafu

Introduction

Uganda represents an important site for forest protection and the prevention of biodiversity loss for a number of reasons. Foremost amongst these is that Uganda is one of the most biologically diverse countries in Africa, with forests of high biodiversity value found in the Albertine Rift stretching from Masindi to Kisoro. Other biodiverse forests are located in mountainous or hilly ecosystems, while wetland forests are also important for biodiversity conservation in the country (MWE, 2016). These landscapes face profound threats, including a high deforestation rate, driven in part by complicated socio-political and cultural dynamics. In this context, and given the global geographic imaginary that understands forests as the 'lungs of the world', the 'imperatives' for intervention appear all too clear to a variety of actors and stakeholders both within, and outside, the country. Traditional forest protection measures in Uganda revolve around state-centric National Parks and Forest Reserves, and regulation, with later trends moving towards partial decentralisation and community based/joint forest management (Turyahabwe and Banana, 2008). Carbon forestry offsetting represents an innovation from these approaches; by combining a market-based approach to forest protection and avoided deforestation/degradation. Carbon offset has been increasingly central to global strategies to combat climate change, including the UN's Paris Agreement, which describes carbon sinks – including forestry for carbon offset – as an important climate change mitigation strategy. Yet the changes that arise in the context of carbon offset projects have been acknowledged to rework local power relations and territorial access (Nel, 2017), and institute new forms of what Swyngedouw (2005) terms governance 'beyond-the-State'. For these reasons they are worthy of scholarly attention.

Forest and forestry carbon offsets rely on what is widely referred to as a 'politics of calculation' (Lyons and Westoby, 2014a), referring to the measurement and commodification of the volume of carbon dioxide and other greenhouse gases that are stored in trees. This storage, or sequestration, is understood as countering greenhouse gas emissions, often including those that take place in other parts of the world. Carbon offset schemes enable industrial polluters, predominantly in the global north, to pay for avoided deforestation, or afforestation, by 'offsetting' their own carbon emissions. Through these market mechanisms, and often supported via donor-funded initiatives, the protection of forests, in conjunction with planted monoculture forestry, becomes eligible for credits through carbon forestry projects. These projects take various guises, including afforestation/reforestation via the Clean Development Mechanism (A/R CDM), Voluntary Carbon Market (VCM) and Reducing the Emissions from Deforestation and Degradation (REDD) projects. These projects are widely championed, both within and outside Uganda, as able to address the twin challenges of land clearing and forest degradation, alongside ensuring sustainable socio-economic development in the global south. For critics, however, forest carbon offsetting is described as driving the commodification of nature and natural systems (*idem*). Carbon offsetting is also broadly understood as a political process, with metrics and definitions an outcome of highly contested global power relations (Leach and Scoones, 2015), and often delivering outcomes where those with most at stake (including directly impacted communities in Uganda) are rendered voiceless in discussions about the sector.

Uganda has attracted significant donor funding for carbon forestry projects, and is widely perceived to be a stable location for conservation and environmental practitioners, and with a generally low level of forest cover (compared with West African countries), which provides the exigency for intervention on the part of numerous actors. On the basis of these conditions, Goldstein and Ruef (2016) report that Uganda has the fourth largest market share of carbon forestry offset credits globally. At the same time as support for Uganda's carbon offset industry has grown, however, its impacts remain little understood, and a number of incidences stand out as cautionary tales. The country's high deforestation rate, complicated political ecology, and contested forestry and land politics, for instance, render places like the Mount Elgon National Park, '(a) funny place to store carbon' (Lang and Byakola, 2006). The high profile failure of the UWA-FACE project in the area – which collapsed during the period of 2004–2006 – has been well studied (e.g., by Cavanagh and Benjaminsen, 2014; Cavanagh and Himmelfarb, 2015). Instances of outright evictions from projects like New Forests Namwasa reforestation initiative (Nel, 2015a) can also be contrasted with seemingly more benign outcomes (see, for example, studies of the Trees for Global Benefit project, Fisher, 2012, 2013; Peskett et al., 2011). That said, there is scope to take stock of the range of projects in the country, and their impacts.

In this chapter we provide a 'state of the art' overview of forest carbon offsetting programmes of various forms in Uganda, and the varied political–ecological implications of these interventions. We begin by outlining the literature and context of carbon forestry in Uganda, before drawing from our combined experiences to characterise the range of carbon projects therein. In doing so we emphasise the environmental justice dimensions of carbon forestry, and their social, ecological and political implications. We conclude by characterising carbon forestry as an experiment, and evaluate it as such.

Carbon forestry in Uganda

The expansion of the carbon forestry sector in Uganda has been both enabled, and constrained, by an array of political, financial, organisational and other structural factors. Uganda's forest/forestry carbon offset sector has grown alongside the neo-liberalisation and marketisation of development (including environment-related forms of development) (Wiegratz, 2016). This development approach has been actively supported through a range of government policies and other state-led interventions in Uganda. Importantly too, the privatisation of development has occurred in tandem with a growing emphasis on the green economy, including green market-based approaches articulated at Rio+20, with which Uganda has been actively engaged (Lyons and Westoby, 2014a; Bergius et al., 2017).

As importantly, the emergence of carbon forestry has come on the back of a long history of change within the Ugandan forestry sector. The formalisation and gazettement of forest territories was gradual, unsystematic and often violent, with forced re-locations of many, including the Benet peoples at Mount Elgon and the Batwa in the South Western Bwindi and Mgahinga forests (Tumushabe and Musiime, 2006). In this context, 'despite regular reformulations and revisions since the gazettement of forest reserves beginning in the 1930s it remains unclear whether these policies and laws are acceptable to the local people and appropriate to local situation' (Turyahabwe and Banana, 2008, p. 641). The most recent restructuring process came in the form of the forestry sector reforms of the 2000s, which restructured the old Uganda Forest Department, perceived as inefficient and corrupt, into three disjointed institutions (Nel, 2015b). The major aim of the reforms was to facilitate the expansion of monoculture timber plantations so as to build a timber industry, and ostensibly 'save' natural forests from timber harvesting. Carbon forestry extends this change by further entrenching the idea of forests as natural capital, as an attempt to 'make forests pay for themselves' through carbon offsets.

As the timeline below indicates, the development of carbon forestry in Uganda has proceeded at two scales; at the individual project level, and in the development of the country's institutional frameworks. A range of individual afforestation and reforestation projects have emerged over recent decades, beginning with large reforestation projects in the mid-90s and 2000s, alongside community level afforestation projects from 2003 (See Table 7.1). Despite the well-documented failure of the UWA FACE Mt Elgon project in 2003, all other projects eventually coalesced into registered A/R CDM or VCM carbon projects, though fewer were also registered via more rigorous accreditation processes. REDD+ projects and institutional structures that support them also began to emerge from 2008, and Uganda submitted its REDD+ Readiness Preparation Proposal (R-PP) to FCPF in June 2011 (MWE, 2011). The implementation of the R-PP from 2012 has been the responsibility of the underfunded Forest Sector Support Department (FSSD). Implementation of the R-PP stalled alongside a delay in funding from the World Bank Forest Carbon Partnership Facility (FCPF) to support REDD+ Readiness in Uganda. In the context of constrained financial (and other) supports, Uganda continues to grapple with a number

Table 7.1 Timeline of carbon forestry development in Uganda

1994	UWA FACE Foundation Mt Elgon Project initiated, envisaged to exist until 2034.
1995	UWA FACE Foundation Kibaale reforestation project initiated (eventual VCM registration in 2011 after failed A/R CDM registration).
1997	Clean Development Mechanism envisaged to start in Uganda post the Kyoto Protocol.
2002	Kikonda Reforestation Voluntary Carbon Market (VCM) project initiated (not approved for A/R CDM).
2003	After contestation, UWA FACE Foundation Project at Mount Elgon ceases reforestation efforts and closes down.
2004	Green Resources Bukaleba Reforestation Project initiated (VCM after failed A/R CDM registration).
2006	New Forests Namwasa A/R CDM project initiated, but allegations of evictions relating to the plantation between 2006 and 2010.
2008	REDD+ Process in Uganda started in 2008, when Uganda became a Participant of the FCPF after approval of the Forest Carbon Partnership Readiness Plan Idea Note (R-PIN).
2009	The Uganda Nile Basin A/R CDM project implemented by NFA with another community-based organisation, RECPA. World Bank REDD+ Preparation Proposal (R-PP) preparation and consultation funded by the Norwegian Government.
2010	R-PP preparation phase.
2011	2011 R-PP approved in June 2011 with Comments. REDD+ National Steering Committee formed.
2012	2008 R-PP final approval.
2013	2013 Implementation of REDD+ Readiness Phase, funded by the Government of Uganda, the FCPF through the World Bank, UN-REDD, and the Austria Government Forestry Sector Support Department of the MWE takes over the REDD+ Secretariat.
2014	Uganda was admitted into the UN-REDD Programme support and has received technical and financial support since 2015.
2015	Uganda expressed interest in participating in the Climate Investment Funds (CIF) to support the preparation of a detailed Forestry Investment Plan to augment Uganda's REDD+ efforts by 2020.

of issues related to sectoral expansion, including clarification related to ownership of carbon credits, clear guidance on carbon rights, how benefit-sharing distributions will be handled, and the need for a conflict and grievance resolution mechanism.

Despite this extensive activity, and the on-going expansion of carbon forestry tied to global forces – including the now ratified 2015 Paris Agreement, which clearly places carbon offset projects, such as carbon forestry, as a cornerstone in climate mitigation projects – there has been a lack of significant and sustained funding from multilateral mechanisms. There have also been significant crashes in carbon market prices. In this light, Ugandan carbon forestry has been described by Nel (2017) as faltering and stalling. It has also been criticised for privileging commercial forestry and forestry management above indigenous species re/afforestation projects, and exacerbating existing tensions over land (*idem*). However, some funding streams have materialised through transfer-based multi-lateral or bilateral REDD+ schemes. Such initiatives, like Norwegian or Austrian R-PP support, are not necessarily limited or affected by market prices, but rather reflect new forms of results-based aid schemes.

The literature on carbon forestry in Uganda is diverse, and articles and research approaches differ widely, for 'carbon forestry projects are as widely variegated in their form and implementation as the diverse contexts from within which they emerge' (Nel and Hill, 2014, p. 33). With that said, however, it is possible to make some comparisons. The most vociferous critics have gone so far as to characterise carbon forestry in Uganda as forms of carbon colonialism (Lyons and Westoby, 2014a), carbon violence (Lyons and Westoby, 2014b) and 'ecolonisation' (Carmody and Taylor, 2016) – referring to the ways climate change mitigation discourses facilitate the 'continued and deepening domination of ecological space by domestic political elites and transnational investors' (Carmody and Taylor, 2016, p. 100). The aforementioned cases of evictions are symptomatic of such processes (Nel, 2017). Others are still critical, but more circumspect. Carton and Andersson (2017), for example, discuss the 'unintended consequences' of the Trees for Global Benefit project, while Fisher (2012) demonstrates the shortcomings of a time-limited payments approach to a temporally sustainable stewardship ethic for trees and forests.

Other research publications are more positive (most recently see Purdon, 2018), indicating that projects can, in the case of the TFGB, deliver to an extent on environmental and equity criteria (Nakakaawa, 2011, p. 277). The project's expansion and growing participant numbers has, however, strained resources for completing monitoring exercises, leading to a delay in many payments (Mwayafu and Kimbowa, 2011). Namaalwa et al. (2017) argue that key achievements of the Ongo REDD project include formalisation of governance institutions, securing land rights, and forest restoration, but that challenges include the bureaucratic process of gazetting community forests and the ambiguity of the payment scheme. Jayachandran et al. (2017) have promoted a randomised controlled research design for examining the effectiveness and efficiency of PES for carbon forestry, by comparing the cost of the scheme versus the social cost of the carbon benefit. They report that tree cover declined by 4.2% during the study period in treatment villages, compared with 9.1% in control villages, arguing that the intervention on trial was responsible for the lower loss of trees, and reporting no evidence of leakage.

In speaking to the critical literature on carbon forestry, some of the problems that have arisen are uniquely bound within the context of Uganda's socio-political environment, including a regressive history of protected area and forest reserve management (Turyahabwe and Banana, 2008), and the association of commercial forestry with human rights abuses and ecological problems (Lyons and Westoby, 2014a). In this context, there are risks that carbon forestry, and discourses that link deforestation to environmental crime, may lead to the recentralisation of control over forests and the further marginalisation of forest-dwelling populations (Cavanagh et al., 2015). For their part, industrial forestry plantations have been shown to provide certain community benefits in their initial years, but can also deny local communities historically established customary access and user land rights (Byakagaba and Muhiirwe, 2017). Regarding REDD, there are problems of unclear and unstable tenure arrangements, a contested relationship between civil society and the state, unclear mechanisms for allocating and administering REDD payments, and a limited awareness of REDD amongst local stakeholders, alongside unrealistically high expectations (Twongirye et al., 2015). In spite of limited, failing attempts at decentralisation of forest management in the country (Turyahabwe et al., 2006), there is a lingering presumption that local people don't, or should not have, rights to forests or forest management, or related carbon-associated initiatives (Fisher 2013; Fisher et al., 2018).

Hence, problems within carbon forestry must be understood as part and parcel of the sector, occurring within the context of limited environmental governance accountability (creating the context for private sector-led resource development), and in the context of an occasional reluctance to learn the lessons from earlier implemented pilot projects of which Uganda has a number. Because of these shortcomings, there is evident opposition to carbon markets, which has coalesced around climate justice and anti-land grabbing movements in Uganda (Lyons, Westoby, and Nel, 2017). Community resistance and contestation is also evident, with the UWA-FACE Mount Elgon project in particular, where boundary disputes (Lang and Byakola, 2006) and a lack of perceived project benefits by communities in the area whose livelihoods and access were constrained, resulted in the 'spectacular' failure of the project (Cavanagh and Benjaminsen, 2014). Within this context an environmental justice framework of analysis is fitting.

Table 7.2 Environmental justice criteria

	Positive	Weakly positive	Neutral	Weakly negative	Negative
Procedural	Strong evidence of consultation and participation, extending to community ownership of project direction.	Tacit involvement of communities or consultation. May have Free Prior Informed Consent (FPIC) but no substantive input into project direction or implementation.	Lack of effective engagement, yet no negative repercussions.	Lack of effective engagement reinforces existing power structures, inequities, and vulnerabilities.	Communities excluded from project design and implementation.
Distributional	Positive livelihood contributions.	Some benefits, but asymmetrical.	No specific livelihoods benefits.	Some negative livelihood implications and marginalisation.	Direct livelihood implications and/or evictions.
Recognition	Acknowledgement of the collective identities of people, including their values and histories, social and cultural differences, and visions of the environment.	Limited acknowledgement or recognition of communities and/or projects implemented so as to deal with community concerns.	No formal recognition of identities and values, but no adverse impacts to communities' material situation result.	Lack of formal recognition can indirectly lead to the marginalisation or further marginalisation of communities.	Feelings of resentment amongst some communities, including those related to the lack of consultation. Some perverse livelihood outcomes can result.

Environmental justice framework

With an understanding of the history and extant literature on carbon forestry in hand, this chapter now turns to an interpretation and evaluation of carbon forestry. To do this, we set out an environmental justice (EJ) framework for use in our analysis (see Table 7.2).

Environmental justice, as developed by Schlosberg (2007), provides a useful framework to make sense of diverse notions of justice; including the various ways distribution, participation, and recognition can be understood. Starting with distributive justice, Schlosberg describes this as the ability of different actors, for instance, to enjoy the environmental or economic benefits related to resources or, alternatively, their ability to avoid environmental harm. In this light, research on carbon forestry indicates payments can have positive effects on local livelihoods (Grieg-Gran et al., 2005; Jindal et al., 2008), with evidence of increases in land-tenure security and socio-institutional strengthening as a result of payments (e.g., Rosa et al., 2004). Others suggest that while the long-term impact for communities may well be positive, in the short term certain sections of communities can be rendered financially poorer (Asquith et al., 2002). By contrast, participation, or *procedural justice*, makes reference to the ways in which decisions about environmental management are made, including attention to people's roles in decision making, alongside the rules governing these processes. Research in this light shows a number of obstacles for the involvement of the poor in PES (Wunder, 2008), including insecure property rights, a lack of financial resources, limited capacity, poor bargaining power, weak cooperative institutions and high transaction costs (Iftikhar et al., 2007). Accordingly, markets tend to reinforce 'existing power structures, inequities, vulnerabilities' and processes of marginalisation (Corbera et al., 2007a, p. 587) and, as such, PES is 'limited in promoting more legitimate forms of decision-making and a more equitable distribution of outcomes' (p. 587) (see also Pagiola et al., 2005). Finally, *recognition justice* involves acknowledging the collective identities of people, including their values and histories, social and cultural differences, and visions of the environment (Martin et al., 2016). Recognition justice has received the least attention in the literature on carbon forestry, but project reviews show deficiencies in the participation of 'service providers' in the design process, and a centralisation in decision-making and implementation (Corbera et al., 2007b). These can cause feelings of resentment amongst some communities (Asquith et al., 2002), especially in contexts of weak rights, a lack of government services and weak accountability in environmental management (Boyd et al., 2007).

Evaluating carbon forestry in Uganda from an environmental justice perspective

This chapter categorises the 11 projects the authors have collectively studied, and classified these according to scores allocated for each of the three justice criteria, outlined above. Each project is classified by procedural, distributional and recognition justice criteria. The project is also classified on the basis of our analysis of active, weak/passive, and negative (indicating evictions and/or similar injustices) classifications (categorical definitions that will become clear below). These project-level comparisons are combined with our experiences from respective research engagements with the projects[1] to form the basis for discussions on the social, ecological and political implications of carbon forestry in Uganda. In the following section, we detail perspectives on the social, ecological and political implications of carbon forestry in Uganda. This is complemented by project-level snapshots, which are detailed in Table 7.2 (see also Figure 7.1 for locations).

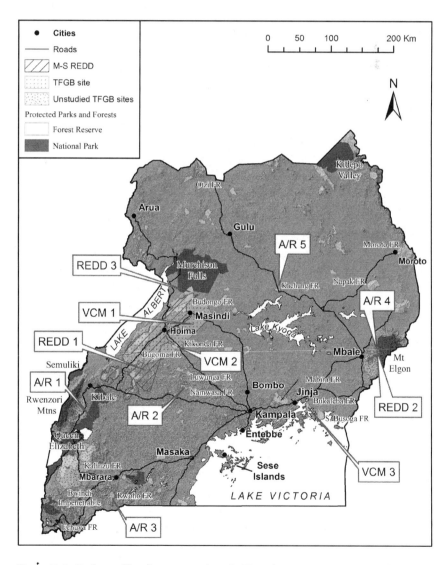

Figure 7.1 Carbon offset forestry projects in Uganda.

Table 7.3 Project evaluations

Project details							Environmental justice criteria		
Project	Title	Project developer	Others involved	How is carbon sequestered/offset	Land tenure (who owns the land)	Certification status and dates	Procedural	Distributional	Recognition
A/R 1	FACE Kibale reforestation project.	FACE and UWA.	Dutch Electricity Generating Board, Nedbank, SGS.	Reforestation and natural regeneration of indigenous species in a 6,200 ha area within the park boundary.	Kibale National Park.	Est. 1994, crediting since 1999. CCBA standard.	Neutral (AN) – top-down structure in which communities only engaged through executive.	Weakly positive (AN) – limited benefit-sharing arrangement in place between FACE, the UWA and local communities that provides for local level projects.	Neutral (AN) – community groups only recognised by ward as an amorphous group.
A/R 2	Namwasa Reforestation Project.	New Forests Company (NFC - UK).	NFA, IFC of the World Bank, HSBC, SPGS (Uganda).	Large-scale monoculture plantation.	Namwasa CFR	Reg. 2013, crediting period 2005 to 2025.	Negative (AN) – community participation only after a settlement through the Ombudsman of the IFC.	Negative (AN) – an estimated 22,000 people from the CFRs (Grainger and Geary, 2011).	Negative (AN) – ex-residents classified as 'illegal aliens' and encroachers.
A/R 3	Nile Basin Reforestation Project.	NFA, BioCarbon Fund (BioCF).	Spanish, French, Japanese companies, RECPA, BECA, KDA and KFD and SWAGEN groups.	Five small monoculture reforestation sub-projects.	Rwoho CFR	Reg. 2009, crediting period 2007 to 2027.	Positive (DM, AN) – Community Based Organisations engaged in project design.	Weakly positive (AN DM) – disappointing benefit-sharing after poor planting performance by parties.	Weakly positive – (DM/AN) Groups recognised but not all the community have a voice.

A/R 4	Mount Elgon FACE project.	Uganda Wildlife Authority (state agency), partnership with Dutch NGO, the 'FACE' Foundation.	UWA	UWA receives payments for carbon sequestered in trees planted within the park.	MENP officially state-owned, but extent of boundary disputed in many areas.	Commenced in 1994 and failed ten years later.	Neutral/Negative (JF) – no aspiration within project design for any kind of procedural or consultative element. (Cavanagh and Benjaminsen, 2014.)	Weakly negative (JF) – no aspiration within project design for any distributional benefits other than employment, which did not ultimately materialise.	Negative (JF) – fundamental lack of recognition of people's property claims to the area or recognition of cultural identity.
A/R 5	Kachung Afforestation Project.	Green Resources (Norway).	NFA, Swedish Energy Agency.	Company receives carbon payments for carbon sequestered from large-scale monoculture plantation.	Kachung CFR.	CDM registered in 2011, crediting period 2006–2026, but funding suspended on the basis of exposure of questions related to social and environmental adverse impacts.	Negative (KL) – limited consultation with some members of community affected by project. Little to no understanding of carbon markets or knowledge that project is a participant in carbon markets.	Weakly positive (KL) – some community development projects delivered (e.g., provision of health clinic, tarmac of roads, etc.), however limited access, and top-down process to decide benefits, rendering them disconnected from vital local needs (e.g., land).	Negative (KL) – sustained denial of recognition of local communities' legitimacy to access land for vital livelihood activities (e.g., food growing, grazing animals, access to water and cultural sites).

(continued)

Table 7.3 (continued)

Project details							Environmental justice criteria		
Project	Title	Project developer	Others involved	How is carbon sequestered/offset	Land tenure (who owns the land)	Certification status and dates	Procedural	Distributional	Recognition
VCM 1	Trees For Global Benefit (TFGB).	ECOTRUST.	Ecotrust organised community groups, Tetra Pak, Future Forests.	Smallholders receive carbon payments for sequestration in indigenous species.	Smallholder land.	Inception in 2003, Plan Vivo registered.	Weak/Limited (JF) – many of the project terms are developed remotely from the communities and the conditionality leads to upwards accountability of participants to implementers, rather than the other way round.	Weakly positive (JF) –skewed to relatively wealthy community members with surplus land. Contestation around costs and share of credit received by participants.	Neutral (JF) – project recognises people's customary claims to land.
VCM 2	Kikonda Reforestation Project.	Global Woods.	NFA.	Large-scale monoculture plantation.	Kikonda CFR.	Project inception in 2002, CarbonFix certification, Gold Standard FSC certified.	Weakly positive (AN) – a ten-year lack of engagement has recently been replaced by a more consultative approach.	Weakly negative (AN) – a failed community tree planting programme. Some marginalisation.	Weakly negative (AN) – communities still referred to as encroachers.
VCM 3	Green Resources Bukaleba Reforestation Projects.	Green Resources (Norway).	NFA.	Large-scale monoculture plantation.	Bukaleba CFR – contested.	Inception 2004. Failed A/R CDM. Verified Carbon Standard (VCM) reg. 2012. FSC certified.	Negative (AN) – no substantive communication with the five villages in the reserve, apart from with groups of employees.	Weakly negative (AN) – limited, predominantly temporary jobs within the plantation, limited development projects, but livelihoods constrained by expansion.	Negative (AN) – communities living within the CFR only recognised as 'encroachers'.

REDD 1	Murchison Semuliiki (M-S) REDD Project.	Northern Albertine Rift Conservation Group (NARCG).	NFA, the Norwegian government and the Waterloo Foundation.	Reforestation initiatives on 'private land' and 'buffer zones' to CFRs in the western Albertine rift.	Reforesting corridors on 'private land' and local forest reserves and Budongo and Bugoma CFRs.	Project stalled in FPIC (Free Prior and Informed Consent) process administered by the WCS.	Neutral/N/A (AN) – project stalled.	Neutral/NA (AN) – project stalled.	Neutral/N/A (AN) – project stalled.
REDD 2	Mount Elgon Regional Ecosystems Conservation Project (MERECP).	Lake Victoria Basin Commission (LVBC).	IUCN, UWA, NFA NEMA NEMA – K KWS KFS Districts, Swedish and Norwegian government. 20 CBOS are involved where by ten in Kenya while ten in Uganda.	Reforestation initiatives on 'private land' and 'buffer zones' along contested boundaries of the Mount Elgon National Park.	Disputed UWA Mount Elgon National Park Boundary.	Co-financed from 2005–2009 four-year grant from Norway and Sweden. Since stalled.	Weakly positive (AN, DM) – community-based organisation engaged in project development. Those who are not members are left out by the project.	Positive (AN, DM) – effectively functioning community revolving funds.	Strong (DM + AN) – recognition of contested boundaries and 'buffer zone' approach to conflict management.
REDD 3	The Ongo Community Forest REDD+ Pilot Project.	ECOTRUST.	IIED (UK), Makerere University, University of Life Science, Norway, CODECA and BUCODO, Ongo and Alimugonza CFAs.	Reforestation of indigenous species on community forest land.	Individual land and two 'local/community forest reserves', Budongo Central Forest Reserve.	Inception in 2009. Funded until 2013 by Norad. Planned Plan Vivo reg. but since stalled.	Neutral – community representation, but some contestation over the community executive.	Weak/neutral(AN) – issues of revenue sharing and disappointed expectations within the communities.	Neutral – project recognises community forests.

Social implications

There is great differentiation in the social outcomes of the 11 carbon offset projects reported on in this chapter. Drawing from the distributional criteria highlighted in Table 7.1, our evaluations demonstrated just one positive outcome; in contrast to five weakly positive, one neutral, three weakly negative, and one negative outcome related to project activities. Overall, these outcomes are indicative of the generalised limited distributional benefits of PES in the literature (Wunder, 2007; 2008). However, many of the documented impacts depend upon how our selected projects were designed. In our analysis of Uganda, REDD+ projects appear more inclined to positive distributional outcomes, with VCM projects more neutral, and A/R CDM balanced between weakly positive and negative distributional outcomes. Such findings may assist to inform sectoral development into the future, a theme we return to further below.

Delving into differentiated project outcomes, the violence associated with the UWA-FACE project does not seem inherent to carbon forestry, but rather reflects the nature of the tensions and challenges associated with that region. Indeed, it is not just project proponents and national actors that have power in determining project outcomes. In this case, local people's perspectives of justices and injustices, alongside their motivations for participation in carbon projects, have implications for the temporal sustainability of PES projects. Demonstrating this, in the case of the UWA-FACE project, community actions were part of what led to the project's collapse, and relative project success (in terms of continuance) in TFGB can be explained by the project mainly being perceived as beneficial, or at least benign, locally (see Fisher et al., in review, for a broader discussion).

Similarly, the TFGB case draws attention to local agency and livelihoods, by recognising that most people use forest resources as inputs to their production activities, and/or as consumption goods that satisfy various livelihood needs. In this light, interventions such as TFGB intend to save forest remnants, by firming the management and control of existing forest due to distributional benefits from carbon payments (Mwayafu and Kimbowa, 2011), even if there is some evidence of a lack of equity in such distribution (Schrekenberg et al., 2013). The prospective Mt Elgon Regional Ecosystems Conservation Programme, as another example, is changing the lives of those who were recipients of the community revolving funds (Nel and Hill, 2013). On the other hand, where land tenure, tree tenure and carbon tenure are not yet formalised, negative outcomes can include communities' loss of a multiple bundle of rights due to REDD+ interventions.

Accordingly, a more critical appraisal can be made of the social implications of carbon forestry that arise to varying degrees in each project, including asymmetric benefits, false promises and expulsions from land that villagers previously relied upon for vital livelihood activities.

According to Nel (2017), a distributional analysis of justice across carbon forestry types shows an asymmetrical form of benefits, including an accumulation of benefits to those most readily able to access forestry resources, including timber plantation companies, or those in communities who are better off. While this does not preclude progressive outcomes, and there are certainly some projects that could be judged to be more or less equitable, with A/R CDM projects in the latter category, some projects can make 'false promises', and directly or indirectly trade off the well-being of poor and marginal communities, including driving evictions and/or constrained access to land.

Similarly, and with a focus on the most pernicious of social outcomes from carbon interventions, in the case of the New Forests or Green Resources projects, there have been incidents of violent and forced removal of people from land (Nel, 2015a; Lyons and Westoby, 2014b); land that is vital to food growing and other livelihood activities (access to water, animal grazing, as well as sites of cultural significance). In the Green Resources Kachung plantation for example, the enclosure of land for industrial plantation forestry is directly tied to the denial of people's access to land, and with no alternative options for land access provided by either the company or the government at this stage (Lyons and Westoby, 2014a). This represents a crisis for those living in proximity to Green Resources' sites, including placing acute pressure in terms of securing food and water. In sum, locally affected communities carry the disproportionate social costs of industrial plantation carbon forestry projects (Lyons and Westoby, 2014a; Lyons, Westoby and Nel, 2017).

Ecological implications

Generally the type of project and choice of species planted in different contexts is fundamental to the ecological implications that stem from it. While the projects undertaking reforestation with indigenous species (such as TFGB) might have stronger ecological credentials, for example, thereby contributing to multifunctional landscapes for a range of human purposes beyond protected areas, we remain cautious and critical in our respective appraisals of industrial-scale plantation carbon forestry. For instance, the establishment of Green Resources plantations – one of the largest privately owned industrial plantation forestry and carbon offset operations on the African continent – has entailed the prior destruction of savannah and grasslands, as well as of the food crops of local communities (see Lyons and Westoby, 2014a, 2014b). This has driven habitat loss and species decline, alongside heightened food insecurity (Lyons and Ssemwogerere, 2017), only to be replaced by large-scale industrial monoculture plantations. These industrial plantations are defined by their reliance upon single species of trees and chemical regimes, especially during the early stages of planting and weed suppression. Monoculture eucalyptus and pine species also adversely impact groundwater, including both depletion as well as chemical runoff into both groundwater and local river and lake systems, including Lake Victoria (*idem*). In this way, and demonstrative of environmental injustice, the impacts of this project can be understood as concentrating the environmental burdens on those in close proximity to the plantation sites. There are also doubts about the ability of these plantations to sequester carbon, with studies demonstrating a general decline in carbon pools in tree plantations by comparison with naturally occurring forests. Indeed, the Kachung industrial plantation forestry operation could be a net polluter in terms of greenhouse gas emissions, when emissions from clearing and habitat destruction, as well as timber transport and processing, alongside consumption and burning, is taken into account (Lyons and Westoby, 2014b).

As previously asserted, the particularities of the case are important in driving local ecological implications. For instance, governance uncertainty surrounding the contested park boundary around the Mount Elgon National Park has affected the implementation of UWA-FACE. Such uncertainty may have led people to exploit the natural resources without legal sanction, and there are reports of park rangers leading processes of degradation in situations where they appear to lack accountability (Sassen and Sheil, 2013; Cavanagh and Benjaminsen, 2015). However, the extent to which UWA-FACE is responsible for this remains moot.

Beyond individual project particularities, the ecological implications of carbon forestry projects can be understood as extending beyond individual projects. In this light, while individual projects, such as the TFGB or TIST models, do reforest indigenous species, the broader governance changes that result from the introduction of carbon offset projects could be said to be driving an uneven shift in the control of forestry resources, including from the management by state actors over defined forest territories to the management of flows of commodified units of carbon and timber (see Nel, 2015b, 2017). The problem with this shift is that many forest resources and territories, especially those outside forest carbon projects – including national parks, CFRs, as well as the majority of forests on so called 'private lands' – are in some respects neglected, as donor funding, institutional support and state capacity is directed elsewhere. An associated danger is that even well-conceived ecological objectives may still be undermined if project design is socially unsustainable (see Fisher, 2012).

Political implications

Beyond the obvious social and ecological implications of carbon forestry, there are more nuanced political implications of carbon offsetting that require some teasing out. To begin with, Table 7.1 highlights procedural and recognition scores of the projects examined. With regards to the former, the projects collectively assessed yielded one positive, two weakly positive, three neutral, three weakly negative, and two negative appraisals. As with the preponderance of less than positive distributional outcomes, these scores do not inspire confidence in the ability of the suite of Ugandan projects to effectively deliver procedural justice.

With regards to recognition criteria, there was one positive, one weakly positive, four neutral, one weakly negative, and four negative appraisals – also demonstrating poor performance regarding recognition criteria. There was also only slightly significant differentiation between project types; with REDD more inclined to neutral/positive and A/R CDM and VCM more inclined towards the neutral/negative.

On the basis of these findings, our perspectives on the viability of carbon offset projects in Uganda range from optimistic, with recognition that carbon offsetting can be used as a tool to promote education about forestry resources, to critical. On the one hand, carbon forestry through REDD+ funding has generated significant interest and dialogue among various actors in the sector, including that related to how forestry might be better managed in the country. This has created awareness and conscientisation among the political class regarding the importance of forestry to both the economy and livelihoods, alongside the implications of rapid loss of forest cover and degradation of forest resources. Contrastingly, and by focussing upon the local level, there is now quite good evidence that PES tend not to strengthen the political power of local people, but instead tends to coexist with, reinforce, or fail to challenge, existing inequalities (Boyd, 2002; Corbera et al., 2007a; Corbera et al., 2007b). Worse still, carbon offsetting programmes may be a trigger for the displacement of people from land.

While the findings presented in this chapter demonstrate that carbon offset projects can garner increased dialogue, they also point to the potential for democratic closures with regards to community engagement. At the same time, too, there are also openings for advocacy and resistance. This is demonstrated, for example, via the local to global advocacy alliances in relation to Green Resources carbon contracts and community impacts, which led the Swedish Energy Agency to withhold payments in 2016 until the company responded to ten specific reforms and actions (Lyons and Ssemwogerere, 2017). These circumstances have increased the scrutiny upon Green Resources activities, as well as driving additional divestment from its major shareholders. This situation not only creates ongoing uncertainty about the future viability of Green Resources in Uganda, but, more broadly, it points to the precarious aspects of environmental injustices entailed by global carbon forestry projects (Lyons and Ssemwogerere, 2017).

Yet advocacy/resistance by local communities, alongside environmental and human rights activists and organisations, and others – including speaking out about international forestry and the frequently associated land grabbing and other social issues – often entails significant risks. This was clearly demonstrated in the case of the Ugandan Land Alliance/Oxfam, each of whom faced threats of having licenses to operate revoked on the basis of their criticism of the activities of the international organisation the New Forest Company (Nel, 2015a). This politically intimidatory climate can be expected to continue to impact the ways in which opposition and resistance movements are able to engage in discussions and dialogue.

Finally, beyond the differentiated distribution of project impacts, including opportunities for (dis)empowerment at the local level, there are questions regarding the extent to which carbon projects and processes, as technocratic interventions, address the broader causes of deforestation. While the carbon unit can enable a technocratic approach to forestry and conservation practice, and thereby connecting producers and consumers economically across the globe, it disconnects them politically. Interventions themselves are 'apolitical', enabling actors to gloss over the complicated local and national political economy of forestry – which includes the expansion of commercial forestry and its sometimes deleterious social outcomes.

Conclusion – carbon experiments in Uganda

In this chapter we have set out the 'state of carbon forestry' in Uganda, including its diverse array of social, political and ecological implications. What we see as common between these projects is that they constitute a series of ongoing experiments in Uganda that continue to unfold. Beyond that, an environmental justice analysis provided further insight. Across all three aspects of distributional, procedural and recognition criteria, the projects do not fare well. Overall, only three projects out of 11 can be said to be positive in any category, with eight weakly positive, eight neutral, seven neutral/negative, and seven out of eleven registering in at least one negative category. In this regard, Ugandan carbon forestry projects are not living up to environmental justice criteria. Distributional outcomes are fairly evenly distributed, but not positive. Likewise, the procedural justice category is quite evenly dispersed, but with little in terms of positive impacts. And, despite one positive score, the recognition category is more negatively skewed.

With regards to project-type differentiation, across all criteria REDD projects tend from neutral to weak, while plantation-related projects tend from the weak to the negative, apart from the Nile Basin Project, which shows more positive alignments. This evaluation of plantation-related projects is in line with work by Nel and Hill (2014), who assert that projects in Africa involving monoculture plantations, and in particular A/R CDM projects, are more likely to have negative social outcomes. The VCM projects are balanced between weak positive and weakly negative, with one negative assessment.

On the basis of the findings presented in this chapter, we conclude that the future for Uganda's carbon forestry remains uncertain. What is clear, however, is the urgent need to take strong action to address both deforestation and climate change, whether these experiments – articulating various attempts at distributive, procedural and recognition justice – will play a significant role remains to be seen.

Note

1 David Mwayafu is a member of the national REDD+ steering committee, and was part of the World Bank FCPF Technical Advisory Panel (TAP) members of Forest Management Team (FMT) that assessed the R-PP for Uganda. David has also completed Masters research on the Trees For Global Benefit project. Kristen Lyons' work over the last five years has been committed to understanding the local-level impacts of one project – the Norwegian owned Green Resources plantation forestry and carbon offset company – which, she argues, has failed to meet the basic social and ecological requirements for participation in carbon forestry and carbon offset markets. Adrian Nel's PhD research fieldwork in 2012 comprised a governance approach, with extensive interviews with forestry actors and stakeholders, and an engagement with nine projects (Nel, 2016, 2017). Finally, Janet Fisher has conducted extensive empirical work over approximately eight months at the aforementioned Trees for Global Benefit (TFGB) site in Bushenyi in 2008–2009; a project considered by many as an exemplar for smallholder carbon forestry projects in Africa. Fisher has also engaged in collaborative research on the UWA-FACE project at Mt Elgon (Fisher et al., 2018).

References

Asquith, N.M., Vargas Ríos, M.T., and Smith, J. (2002) 'Can forest-protection carbon projects improve rural livelihoods? Analysis of the Noel Kempff Mercado climate action project, Bolivia', *Mitigation and Adaptation Strategies for Global Change*, vol. 7, no. 4, pp. 323–337.

Bergius, M., Benjaminsen, T., and Widgren, M. (2017) 'Green economy, Scandinavian investments and agricultural modernisation in Tanzania', *The Journal of Peasant Studies*, vol. 45, no. 4, pp. 1–28, http://dx.doi.org/10.1080/03066150.2016.126 0554.

Boyd, E. (2002) 'The Noel Kempff project in Bolivia: gender, power, and decision-making in climate mitigation', *Gender & Development*, vol. 10, no. 2, pp. 70–77.

Boyd, E., Gutierrez, M., and Chang, M. (2007) 'Small-scale forest carbon projects: adapting CDM to low-income communities', *Global Environmental Change*, vol. 17, no. 2, pp. 250–259.

Byakagaba, P. and Muhiirwe, R. (2017) 'Industrial forest plantations in Uganda: local adjacent community perspectives', *Journal of Sustainable Forestry*, vol. 36, no. 4, pp. 375–387.

Carmody, P. and Taylor, D. (2016) 'Globalization, land grabbing, and the present-day colonial state in Uganda: ecolonization and its impacts', *The Journal of Environment and Development*, vol. 25, no. 1, pp. 100–126.

Carton, W. and Andersson, E. (2017) 'Where forest carbon meets its maker: forestry-based offsetting as the subsumption of nature', *Society and Natural Resources*, vol. 30, no. 7, pp. 1–15.

Cavanagh, C. (2012). *Unready for REDD+? Lessons From Corruption in Ugandan Conservation Areas, Michelsen Institute*, available at: www.u4.no/publications/unready-for-REDD+-lessons-from-corruption-in-ugandan-conservation-areas.

Cavanagh, C. and Benjaminsen, T.A. (2014) 'Virtual nature, violent accumulation: the "spectacular failure" of carbon offsetting at a Ugandan National Park', *Geoforum*, vol. 56, pp. 55–65.

Cavanagh, C.J. and Benjaminsen, T.A. (2015) 'Guerrilla agriculture? A biopolitical guide to illicit cultivation within an IUCN Category II protected area', *Journal of Peasant Studies*, vol. 42, nos 3–4, pp. 725–745.

Cavanagh, C.J. and Himmelfarb, D. (2015) 'Much in blood and money: necropolitical ecology on the margins of the Uganda Protectorate', *Antipode*, vol. 47, no. 1, pp. 55–73.

Cavanagh, C.J., Vedeld, P.O., and Trædal, L.T. (2015) 'Securitising REDD? Problematising the emerging illegal timber trade and forest carbon interface in East Africa', *Geoforum*, vol. 60, pp. 72–82.

Corbera, E., Brown, K., and Adger, W.N. (2007a) 'The equity and legitimacy of markets for ecosystem services', *Development and Change*, vol. 38, no. 4, pp. 587–613.

Corbera, E., Kosoy, N., and Martinez Tuna, M. (2007b) 'Equity implications of marketing ecosystem services in protected areas and rural communities: case studies from Meso-America', *Global Environmental Change*, vol. 17, nos 3–4, pp. 365–380.

Engel, S., Pagiola, S., and Wunder, S. (2008) 'Designing payments for environmental services in theory and practice: an overview of the issues', *Ecological Economics*, vol. 65, no. 4, pp. 663–674.

Fairhead, J., Leach, M., and Scoones, I. (2012) 'Green grabbing: a new appropriation of nature?', *Journal of Peasant Studies*, vol. 39, no. 2, pp. 237–261.

Ferraro, P.J. (2001) 'Global habitat protection: limitations of development interventions and a role for conservation performance payments', *Conservation Biology*, vol. 15, no. 4, pp. 990–1000.

Fisher, J. (2012) 'No pay, no care? A case study exploring motivations for participation in payments for ecosystem services in Uganda', *Oryx*, vol. 46, no. 1, pp. 45–54.

Fisher, J. (2013) 'Justice implications of conditionality in payments for ecosystem services', in T. Sikor (ed.) *The Justices and Injustices of Ecosystem Services*, Earthscan, London, UK, pp. 21–45.

Fisher, J.A., Cavanagh, C.J., Sikor, T., and Mwayafu, D.M. (2018) 'Linking notions of justice and project outcomes in carbon offset forestry projects: insights from a comparative study in Uganda', *Land Use Policy*, vol. 73, pp. 259–268.

Fletcher, R., Dressler, W., Büscher, B., and Anderson, Z.R. (2016) 'Questioning REDD+ and the future of market-based conservation', *Conservation Biology*, vol. 30, no. 3, pp. 673–675.

Goldstein, A. and Ruef, F. (2016) 'View from the understory: state of forest carbon finance 2016', Forest Trends' Ecosystem Marketplace, Washington, DC, USA.

Grainger, M. and Geary, K. (2011) *The New Forests Company and its Uganda Plantations*, OXFAM International, Washington, DC, USA.

Grieg-Gran, M., Porras, I., and Wunder, S. (2005) 'How can market mechanisms for forest environmental services help the poor? Preliminary lessons from Latin America', *World Development*, vol. 33, no. 9, pp. 1511–1527.

Iftikhar, U.A., Kallesoe, M., Duraiappah, A., Sriskanthan, G., Poats S.V., and Swallow, B. (2007) Exploring the Inter-linkages Among and Between Compensation and Rewards for Ecosystem Services (CRES) and Human Well-Being, World Agroforestry Centre Working Paper 36, Nairobi, Kenya, pp. 1–44.

Jack, B.K., Kousky, C., and Sims, K.R.E. (2008) 'Designing payments for ecosystem services: lessons from previous experience with incentive-based mechanisms', *Proceedings of the National Academy of Sciences*, vol. 105, no. 28, pp. 9465–9470.

Jayachandran, S., de Laat, J., Lambin, E.F., Stanton, C.Y., Audy R., and Thomas, N.E. (2017) 'Cash for carbon: a randomized trial of payments for ecosystem services to reduce deforestation', *Science*, vol. 357, no. 6348, pp. 267–273.

Jindal, R., Swallow, B., and Kerr, J. (2008) 'Forestry-based carbon sequestration projects in Africa: potential benefits and challenges', *Natural Resources Forum*, vol. 32, no. 2, pp. 116–130.

Lang, C. (2016) 'REDD is dead. What's next?', *REDD-Monitor*, available at: www.redd-monitor.org/2016/02/04/redd-is-dead-whats-next, accessed 30 June 2017.

Lang, C. and Byakola, T. (2006) *A Funny Place to Store Carbon: UWA-FACE Foundation's Tree Planting Project in Mount Elgon National Park, Uganda (No. 9)*. World Rainforest Movement, Montevideo, Uruguay.

Leach, M. and Scoones, I. (2015) *Political Ecologies of Carbon in Africa. Carbon Conflicts and Forest Landscapes in Africa*, Routledge, Abingdon, UK.

Lund, J.F., Sungusia, E., Mabele, M.B., and Scheba, A. (2017) 'Promising change, delivering continuity: REDD+ as conservation fad', *World Development*, vol. 89, pp. 124–139.

Lyons, K. and Ssemwogerere, D. (2017) *Carbon Colonialism. Failure of Green Resources' Carbon Offset Project in Uganda*, Oakland Institute, Oakland, CA, USA.

Lyons, K. and Westoby, P. (2014a) 'Carbon colonialism and the new land grab: plantation forestry in Uganda and its livelihood impacts', *Journal of Rural Studies*, vol. 36, pp. 13–21.

Lyons, K. and Westoby, P. (2014b) 'Carbon markets and the new "carbon violence": a story from Uganda', *International Journal of African Renaissance Studies, special edition on green grabbing*, vol. 9, no. 2, pp. 77–94.

Lyons, K., Westoby, P., and Nel, A. (2017) 'Movement building to resist carbon violence: opportunities for social justice in international carbon markets?' *Journal of Political Ecology*, special issue, vol. 24, pp. 324–341.

Martin, A., Coolsaet, B., Corbera, E., Dawson, N.M., Fraser, J.A., Lehmann, I., and Rodriguez, I. (2016) 'Justice and conservation: the need to incorporate recognition', *Biological Conservation*, vol. 197, pp. 254–261.

Ministry of Water and Environment (MWE) (2011) *REDD Readiness Preparation Proposal For Uganda*. Ministry of Water and Environment, Kampala, Uganda.

Ministry of Water and Environment (MWE) (2016) *State of Uganda's Forestry 2015*. Ministry of Water and Environment, Kampala, Uganda.

Mwayafu, D. and Kimbowa, R. (2011) 'Benefit sharing in the Trees for Global Benefit (TGB) initiative: Bushenyi District (Uganda)', *REDDnet Case study*, REDDnet, Kampala, Uganda.

Nakakaawa, C.A. (2011) *Forest Carbon Sequestration: contribution of the private, public and civil societies to poverty alleviation and management of forest resources in Uganda*, Norwegian University of Life Sciences, Oslo, Norway.

Namaalwa, J., Nantogo, P., and Nabanoga, G.N. (2017) 'REDD+ readiness phase in Uganda: learning from a carbon offset project implemented in Ongo Community Forest in Mid-Western Uganda', *International Forestry Review*, vol. 19, no. 3, pp. 321–332.

Nel, A. (2015a) '"Zones of awkward engagement" in Ugandan carbon forestry', in M. Leach and I. Scoones (eds) *Carbon Conflicts and Forest Landscapes in Africa*, Earthscan, London, UK.

Nel, A. (2015b) 'The neoliberalisation of forestry governance, market environmentalism and re-territorialisation in Uganda', *Third World Quarterly*, vol. 36, no. 12, pp. 2294–2315.

Nel, A. (2016) 'A critical reflection on social equity in Ugandan carbon forestry', in S. Fiske and S. Paladino (eds) *The Carbon Fix: Forest Carbon, Social Justice, and Environmental Governance*, Routledge, Abingdon, UK, p. 302.

Nel, A. (2017) 'Contested carbon: carbon forestry as a speculatively virtual, falteringly material and disputed territorial assemblage', *Geoforum*, vol. 81, pp. 144–152.

Nel, A. and Hill, D. (2013) 'Constructing walls of carbon – the complexities of community, carbon sequestration and protected areas in Uganda', *Journal of Contemporary African Studies*, vol. 31, no. 3, pp. 421–440.

Nel, A. and Hill, D. (2014) 'Beyond "win–win" narratives: the varieties of eastern and southern African carbon forestry and scope for critique', *Capitalism Nature Socialism*, vol. 25, no. 4, pp. 19–35.

Pagiola, S., Arcenas, A., and Platais, G. (2005) 'Can payments for environmental services help reduce poverty? An exploration of the issues and the evidence to date from Latin America', *World Development*, vol. 33, no. 2, pp. 237–253.

Peskett, L., Schreckenberg, K., and Brown, J. (2011) 'Institutional approaches for carbon financing in the forest sector: learning lessons for REDD+ from forest carbon projects in Uganda', *Environmental Science and Policy*, vol. 14, no. 2, pp. 216–229.

Peters-Stanley, M., Hamilton, K., Marcello, T., Orejas, R., Thiel, A., and Yin, D. (2012) *Developing Dimension: state of the voluntary carbon markets 2012*, Ecosystem Marketplace, Washington, DC, USA.

Peters-Stanley, M., Hamilton, K. and Yin, D. (2012) *Leveraging the Landscape: state of the forest carbon markets 2012*, Ecosystem Marketplace, Washington, DC, USA.

Purdon, M. (2018) 'Finding common ground: a critique of subsumption theory and its application to small-scale forest carbon offsetting in Uganda', *Society and Natural Resources*, online only, doi: 10.1080/08941920.2017.1414908, pp. 1–12.

Rosa, H., Barry, D., Kandel, S., and Dimas, L. (2004) *Compensation for Environmental Services and Rural Communities: Lessons from the Americas*. Political Economy Resource Institute Working Paper Series, Number 96, Political Economy Resource Institute, Amherst, MA, USA.

Sassen, M. and Sheil, D. (2013) 'Human impacts on forest structure and species richness on the edges of a protected mountain forest in Uganda', *Forest Ecology and Management*, 307, pp. 206–218.

Schlosberg, D. (2007) Defining Environmental Justice: theories, movements, and nature, Oxford University Press, Oxford, UK.

Schreckenberg, K., Mwayafu, D., and Nyamutale, R. (2013) *Finding Equity in Carbon Sequestration: a case study of the Trees for Global Benefits project, Uganda*. Uganda Coalition for Sustainable Development, Kampala, Uganda.

Swyngedouw, E. (2005) 'Governance innovation and the citizen: the Janus face of governance-beyond-the-state', *Urban Studies*, vol. 43, no. 11, pp. 1991–2006.

Tumushabe, G. and Musiime, E. (2006) *Living on the Margins of Life: the plight of the Batwa communities of south western Uganda*, Advocates Coalition for Development and Environment, Kampala, Uganda.

Turyahabwe, N. and Banana, A. (2008) 'An overview of history and development of forest policy and legislation in Uganda', *International Forestry Review*, vol. 10, no. 4, pp. 641–656.

Turyahabwe, N., Geldenhuys, C.J., Watts, S., and Banana, A.Y. (2006) 'Technical and institutional capacity in local organisations to manage decentralised forest resources in Uganda', *Southern African Forestry Journal*, vol. 208, no. 1, pp. 63–78.

Twongyirwe, R., Sheil, D., Sandbrook, C.G., and Sandbrook, L.C. (2015) 'REDD at the crossroads? The opportunities and challenges of REDD for conservation and human welfare in South West Uganda', *International Journal of Environment and Sustainable Development*, vol. 14, no. 3, pp. 273–298.

Wiegratz, J. (2016) *Neoliberal Moral Economy: Capitalism, Socio-Cultural Change and Fraud in Uganda*. Rowman and Littlefield, London, UK.

Wunder, S. (2007) 'The efficiency of payments for environmental services in tropical conservation', *Conservation Biology*, vol. 21, no. 1, pp. 48–58.

Wunder, S. (2008) 'Payments for environmental services and the poor: concepts and preliminary evidence', *Environment and Development Economics*, vol. 13, no. 3, pp. 279–297.

8 Parks, people, and partnerships

Experiments in the governance of nature-based tourism in Uganda

Wilber M. Ahebwa, Chris Sandbrook, and Amos Ochieng

Introduction

Among all the approaches deployed around the world in the name of integrated conservation and development, tourism is probably the most high profile (Ashley et al., 2007; Duffy, 2006). Tourism can contribute to development by creating jobs and stimulating improvements in social amenities such as roads, schools, and other related facilities, which can help to transform rural livelihoods (Scheyvens, 2007). Tourism can contribute to conservation directly by generating revenues for conservation activities, and indirectly when benefits for people generate support for biodiversity conservation (Wall, 1998). However, tourism is not free from criticisms. In regions where tourism has been developed, incidences of displacement, cultural distortion, rising land values and land grabbing, drugs, prostitution (Cabezas, 2008), and poor treatment of communities living close to tourism areas have been well documented (Mowforth and Munt, 2015). Others consider tourism-related benefits too insignificant to cause a substantial change in the state of poor people living around protected areas in the developing world (Kiss, 2004), which is worsened by the external control of the sector, leading to leakages and limited impact on local destinations (Sandbrook, 2010; Ahebwa et al., 2012). Laudati (2010) argues that tourism increases the vulnerability of communities, which can worsen already existing wildlife conflicts. Pro-poor tourism is criticised for solely focusing on the 'poor' and alienating key tourism stakeholders such as investors and even tourists (Sofield et al., 2004; Chok et al., 2007). Even where tourism does provide opportunities within the local economy, it can create a scenario of over-dependence, leading to loss of other traditional economic activities like agriculture (Lepp, 2008). Tourism can also have adverse ecological effects, especially when the level of tourist use is greater than the environment's ability to cope with this use within acceptable limits of change (Harrison, 2008; Sunlu, 2003).

In order to circumvent the shortfalls associated with tourism development and to consolidate its gains for conservation and development, a number of governance models have been developed and experimented with in Africa and, in particular, in Uganda. However, few studies have considered the implementation and outcomes of these models. Using four case study sites in Uganda that exemplify different governance arrangements, this chapter contributes to tourism, conservation and development debates by investigating the structure and outcomes of the selected cases. It begins with a brief overview of tourism in Uganda, before describing several tourism governance models in more detail. It then describes and analyses the four case studies, before concluding with lessons to be learned from the Ugandan experience for the future of tourism as a conservation and development tool.

Tourism in Uganda

Tourism is a crucial sector of the Ugandan economy, accounting for 9% (US$ 2.2bn) of the country's GDP (MTWA, 2017). Formal wildlife-based tourism began shortly after the first three national parks (Queen Elizabeth, Murchison Falls and Kidepo) were gazetted in the 1950s. Initially the preserve of colonial settlers and their visitors on hunting expeditions, tourism in Uganda's protected areas has grown and still remains the main revenue generation approach for conservation funding (UWA, 2018). The nature and wildlife tourism segment generates over 80% of the total tourism sector's contribution to GDP, despite being only 18% of Uganda's international tourism market share (1.35 million tourists) as of 2017 (UBOS, 2017). As a result, tourism has been emphatically promoted by government and conservation actors as a market-based mechanism to finance the sustainable conservation of wildlife resources in the country. Primate and game viewing in protected areas (national parks, wildlife reserves, and forest reserves) are the iconic tourism products in the country. Other products hinged on Uganda's natural endowments include bird watching, mountaineering, sport fishing, and adventure tourism (such as boat rides, white water rafting, and bungee jumping) (MTWA, 2015). As such, conservation sites in Uganda are critical tourist attractions that create opportunities for the local economy, as well as contributing over 90% of the current total wildlife conservation budget (UGX 66.4bn; UWA, 2018). More than 50% of the tourism revenues accrue from the sale of gorilla viewing permits at Bwindi Impenetrable National Park (Table 8.1).

Recent studies from Uganda on the links between tourism, conservation, and development do indeed suggest that when local communities are organised and are assured of tourism benefits, they are more willing to conserve the natural resources on which tourism depends (see Van der Duim, 2011; Lepp, 2008; Ahebwa et al., 2012; Ayorekire et al., 2011; Tumusiime and Sjaastad, 2014). However, despite the apparent success of nature-based tourism in Uganda, the degree to which tourism contributes to conservation and development, and whether it should further be encouraged in protected areas, remain contested (e.g., see Tumusiime et al., this volume, Chapter 4).

Table 8.1 Tourism revenue contributions from Ugandan national parks

Protected area	% tourism revenue contribution
Murchison Falls National Park	20.4
Queen Elizabeth National Park	12.1
Mt Elgon National Park	1.1
Kidepo Valley National Park	1.2
Bwindi Impenetrable Forest National Park	50.8
Mgahinga National Park	0.6
Lake Mburo National Park	4.2
Kibale Forest National Park	8.2
Rwenzori Mountain National Park	1.0
Semuliki National Park	0.3
Semuliki Wildlife Reserve	0.2
Katonga Wildlife Reserve	0.0

Source: UWA, 2018.

Opponents agitate for low levels of tourism in protected areas, citing excessive impacts on the natural environment and negative development impacts (Harrison, 2008). In contrast, advocates of tourism push for higher levels of tourist activities in order to generate significant income to finance both conservation and development activities (Kiss, 2004). Amidst all this, the official position of the government of Uganda, as enshrined in the wildlife and tourism policies, is to encourage both non-consumptive as well as consumptive forms of tourism development to address and ameliorate conservation threats and to contribute to poverty reduction in the country (MTWA, 2017; Ochieng, 2011).

Tourism governance models

One possible explanation for the contradictory perspectives on tourism in Uganda is the wide range of different tourism governance models that are in use. Drawing on innovations from elsewhere, a range of different forms of partnership between actors have been implemented as tourism governance models to enable the linkage between conservation and development through tourism in Uganda (Ahebwa et al., 2012; Mitchell and Coles, 2009; Table 8.2). These generally fall into three main categories. First, public–private–community partnerships; a governance engagement involving the public (government or its agency), the private (usually investors) and communities managing and sharing of benefits that accrue from tourism. Second, private–community partnerships (also known as corporate–community or business–community partnerships; Roe, 2001; Ahebwa et al., 2012); an arrangement in which private investors sign an agreement with the local people on the management and sharing of benefits derived from the use of a tourism resource. In most cases, the negotiation between the private actor and communities is mediated and facilitated by third sector players (conservation NGOs) and government or its agencies. Third, public–community partnerships; an arrangement normally initiated by government or its agency to bring communities on board in managing a wildlife resource by directly co-running a tourism venture.

An alternative governance model that does not involve formal partnerships is what we call 'direct community engagement'. This entails communities taking an upper hand in managing tourism business and associated benefits. At the initial stages, the model is typically supported technically and financially by conservation NGOs, with individual volunteers working hand in hand with government or its agencies (Ahebwa and Van der Duim, 2013). After takeoff, the communities take a leading role in running the affairs of the tourism venture. The communities as actors in this arrangement are represented by a board of directors and a technical team that is directly responsible for day-to-day running of the business. The communities, however, wield power in the election of the board members who in turn appoint and manage the technical team. In theory this approach overcomes the exclusive focus on profit in the private sector, creating opportunities for local people such as jobs, markets and skills (ibid).

The categorisation of the governance forms is determined by variables such as the actors involved, who holds power in the arrangement, the type of management, the main sources of investment capital, land and other tourism resource tenure and ownership (Van der Duim, 2011). This chapter provides an analysis of four selected case studies that stand out as exemplars of different governance models for tourism in Uganda (Table 8.2).

Table 8.2 Details of the tourism governance model case studies analysed in this chapter

Tourism governance model	Case study	Natural attractions
Private–Community Partnership	Clouds Mountain Gorilla Lodge	Mountain gorillas and other wildlife in Bwindi Impenetrable National Park.
Public–Community Partnership	Rwenzori Mountaineering Services	Mountaineering in Rwenzori Mountains National Park.
Private–Community– Public Partnership	Various sport hunting concessions	Trophy animals to be hunted.
Direct Community Engagement	Kibale Association for Rural and Environmental Development (KAFRED).	Birds and other wildlife in Bigodi Wetland and cultural exploration along the village trail.

Methods

We adopted a multi-faceted approach for the research presented in this chapter. This centred on an extensive review of documents, interviews with key stakeholders (n=15), and eight Focus Group Discussions (FGDs): two with beneficiary communities in each of the four case study locations. The documents reviewed included, inter alia, agreements of engagement, minutes of implementation meetings, and progress reports (performance monitoring and financial reports). The stakeholders selected for interview included representatives from Uganda Wildlife Authority (n=4), the private sector players (n=4), community leaders directly involved in the implementation of the partnership arrangements (n=4) and third sector players (NGOs) (n=3) who supported and continue to support implementation of these arrangements. Data generated through these approaches were augmented by observations during field visits. Generated data were triangulated, analysed, and summarised in the respective thematic areas, which informed development and structuring of this chapter. Fieldwork and interviews were conducted by Ahebwa and Ochieng from November 2016 to March 2018.

Drawing on the Policy Arrangements Approach (Arts, 2006), this chapter analyses each case study in turn, exploring how actors shape implementation, the accruing benefits, and the politics and power dynamics (Arts and Leroy, 2006). We take actors to be those players in the partnership arrangement who are legitimately involved as stipulated in the 'rules of the game' whose boundaries shape the governance arrangements (Arts and Goverde, 2006).

Results

Private–Community Partnership Model – Clouds Mountain Gorilla Lodge

Clouds Mountain Gorilla Lodge (*hereafter* Clouds lodge) operates as a private–community partnership (PCP) tourism model just outside the southern 'Nkuringo' sector of Bwindi Impenetrable National Park (BINP), Kisoro district. It was started in 2004, and mediated by Uganda Wildlife Authority (UWA) and the International Gorilla Conservation Programme (IGCP) on behalf of the local communities. Initially, 23 community members were guided to form the Nkuringo Conservation and Development Foundation (NCDF), which they later registered as a company, limited by guarantee (Ahebwa et al., 2012). This company had a piece of land they had acquired from financial proceeds attained by offering labour services to clear (of exotic plant species) the buffer area that had just been acquired by UWA to cushion communities from wildlife. They initially planned to set up a community camp ground on their land to engage in tourism business. However, drawing from the tourism development plan for the area, UWA and IGCP interested communities in setting up a high end lodge, which was seen as a superior business opportunity in this area at the time. This proposal attracted a monopoly offer from UWA on the sale of the six daily gorilla permits available at that time for the southern sector. The high end lodge idea led to a capitalisation grant of US$ 250,000 from USAID.

The idea of a partnership arrangement with a private operator was proposed, since communities lacked technical capacity or the top-up finances to set up and run a high end lodge (Ahebwa et al., 2012). The Uganda Safari Company (TUSC), a prominent private sector tourism business in Uganda, was recruited into the partnership through a negotiation that was facilitated by IGCP and UWA. This resulted in a contract of engagement to set up and co-own the high end Clouds Lodge on a private–community partnership arrangement. The contract stipulations involved passing on the six permits monopoly rights and the initial grant funds of US$ 250,000 to the TUSC. In turn the TUSC had to mobilise top-up resources to build the lodge and to operate it on a partnership arrangement that stipulated sharing of financial resources and other benefits (such as employment and supply opportunities with the local communities; Ahebwa et al., 2012).

Although the idea to start a private–community partnership in Nkuringo was intended to promote gorilla conservation and enhance rural livelihoods, it later turned into a messy arena with numerous conflicts involving multiple actors with different interests (Table 8.3). First, the local communities

Table 8.3 Clouds lodge actors and their interests

Actors	Interests
Communities	Economic gains and alternative livelihood options.
Local government	Political and economic oversight and arbitration.
Uganda Wildlife Authority	Community support to conservation and meeting high end visitor requirements at BINP.
International Gorilla Conservation Programme	Community support to conservation in the southern sector.
African Wildlife Foundation	Wildlife conservation.
Kisoro District Tourism Association	Reducing monopoly by one private actor.
United States Agency for International Development	Provide community equity funds to support sustainable rural development.
Association of Uganda Tour Operators	Reducing monopoly by one private actor.
The Uganda Safari Company	Profit making by offering high-end accommodation services.
Inspector General of Government	Resolving escalating conflict.

Source: Ahebwa et al., 2012.

strongly rejected the registration of the Clouds lodge as a limited company by liability arguing that this would make it cease being a community entity. Yet this was necessary to enable formal contract engagement with a private company (IGCP, pers. comm., 2018). Second, the Association of Uganda Tour Operators (AUTO) opposed the monopoly idea of NCDF retaining six gorilla permits, which they saw as limiting fair competition for tourism business on the southern part of BINP. This made some local residents and tourism companies consider NCDF to be using a pretext of helping local people when really it was aimed at achieving the selfish interests of a few individuals (Ahebwa et al., 2012).

As of March 2018, this conflict has eased. Multiple additional gorilla groups have been habituated and opened to tourism, bringing the number of groups to six in the southern sector and 14 overall. Permits for these groups are available on the open market, which has reduced competition and disquiet over the original Clouds lodge monopoly for the Nkuringo group. In fact, UWA is currently grappling with the challenge of unsold gorilla tracking permits. Between 2015 and 2016 less than 50% of permits were sold (Table 8.4). This situation, however, is likely to improve as a result of the recent raising of gorilla tracking permit prices from US$ 750 to US$ 1,500 in the neighbouring Rwanda.

Despite its difficult early days, the Clouds lodge PCP has matured into a successful nature-based tourism business that is distributing significant funds to the local community. On average, US$ 42,541 has been collected annually under this PCP arrangement and channeled to NCDF. Other than in 2015 when there were conflicts in the neighbouring Democratic Republic of Congo that affected tourist arrivals, the community earnings from the Clouds PCP arrangement have consistently increased, pointing to a bright future if proper management structures are put in place (Table 8.5). Indeed, funds from tourism have been invested by NCDF in various local development projects (Table 8.5).

It is evident from the above that, unlike the original financial scarcity situation for community groups before tourism in the southern sector of BINP, there is now some substantial and consistent annual flow of financial

Table 8.4 Trend of gorilla permit sales in Uganda 2012–2016

Year	Available permits	Permits sold	Permits not sold	Percentage sales
2012	26,352	16,756	9,596	64%
2013	29,296	19,867	9,429	67.80%
2014	35,136	19,664	15,472	55.90%
2015	37,960	15,775	22,185	41.50%
2016	37,960	17,783	20,177	46.80%

Source: UWA Reservations Office, 2017.

Table 8.5 Annual earnings from Clouds PCP arrangement and local projects invested in

Year	Community income in USD	Projects invested in
2005	No data	• Buying Clouds land by paying back the loan that topped up the buying of Clouds land.
2006	No data	• Buying Clouds land by paying back the loan that topped up the buying of Clouds land.
2008	13,350	• Purchase of 100 piglets for distribution.
2009	29,850	• Purchase of bulls for distribution to communities. • Extension of water supply to Bikingi village. • Purchase of 260 piglets for distribution to communities.
2010	34,790	• Sponsorship scheme for needy children. • Provision of fuel to repair tourism roads in the areas which were impassable. • Conservation of herons. • Purchase of 130 sheep for distribution.
2011	35,280	• Construction of Buniga Trail to diversify income. • Purchase of land for a cultural centre. • Sponsorship scheme for needy children. • Construction of Nombe teacher's house.
2012	47,960	• Sponsorship scheme. • Construction of Igabiro primary school staff houses. • Construction of Suma primary school staff house. • Purchase of motorcycle for community projects.
2013	55,520	• Repair of water tank for a Batwa settlement. • Purchase of two laptops. • Tea nursery bed. • Sponsorship of needy pupils selected from the community membership. • Trail construction. • Construction of Nyabaremura visitor centre.
2014	61,800	• Investment in tea nursery bed. • Community visitor centre. • Construction of community technical institute classes. • Conservation of herons.
2015	44,440	• Commercial tea plantation in the buffer zone. This will be another income-generating avenue for the community. Have established an MOU with Kigezi Highland Tea CO Limited, leasing the tea plantation, and currently (2018) earns $2,500 per month. • Hamuswamba Health Centre construction. • Construction of Nkuringo Community Vocational Secondary School with about 97 students (45 girls and 52 boys).

(continued)

.

Table 8.5 (continued)

Year	Community income in USD	Projects invested in
2016	59,880	• Payment for tea plantation labour. • Bursaries for the needy (15). • Distributed 27 heifers to community members. • Construction of visitor centre in Nyabaremura. • Installing four water tanks of 30,000 litres in Nombe, Nyabaremura, Kahurire, and Kikobero villages. • Construction of Community Weavers' House (crafts centre) in Ntungamo trading centre.
Total	**382,870**	

Source: NCCDF, 2017.

resources to the communities as a result of this PCP arrangement. This positive outcome is likely to be due to a combination of two factors: the inherent strength of the governance model (where communities capitalise on the business expertise, capacity and network of the private actor) and the nature of the product (gorilla tracking) being sold. However, the prevailing challenge currently is how to transparently and effectively utilise the financial resources emerging from the arrangement. This is made more difficult by the large operational area covered by the arrangement and the large human population (about 30,000 people) with a claim on these resources. As a result, the revenue available per capita is very low – around $2 per person in 2016. Given persistent crop raids by the mountain gorillas and other wild animals from the park, which continue to perpetuate uneasiness in park–community relationships, it is difficult to see how such levels of income can achieve a long term win–win for conservation and development.

Public–community partnership model – Rwenzori Mountaineering Services (RMS)

The public–community partnership model is being implemented in Rwenzori Mountains National Park (RMNP), which was gazetted in 1991. The national park is located in the Albertine Rift Afromontane region of east-central Africa and is rich in biodiversity. The park's uniqueness and conservation importance led to its recognition as a world heritage site in 1994 and as a Ramsar site in 2008. However, it experienced significant threats in the last decades (Muhumuza and Byarugaba, 2009). The threat largely came from the mountain-dwelling communities who relied on the park for their livelihoods, but gained no direct benefits from the park that would motivate them to support its conservation (Senior Warden, Rwenzori National Park, 2018). Partnership with communities was seen as the viable strategy to conserve this crucial biodiversity resource in Uganda (ibid; for further discussion of conservation activities with local stakeholders in the Rwenzori, see Infield and Mugisha, this volume, Chapter 9). Through local leaders and as part of its community conservation policy, Uganda Wildlife Authority encouraged the Rwenzori communities to join in a business partnership arrangement. The communities organised themselves into an entity called Rwenzori Mountaineering Services (RMS), which entered into a formal contract engagement with UWA. The RMS currently has a membership of over 1,600 from 14 parishes around the park. Of these, 450 are females and 1,150 males (RMS Report, 2018).

The contract engagement granted communities, through their entity Rwenzori Mountaineering Services, monopoly rights to co-run the only available route (central circuit) to the highest peak of Rwenzori Mountains. The RMS–Uganda Wildlife Authority partnership arrangement is in the form of a concession to provide trekking tourism services/support on the Central Circuit Trail within the RMNP. Under the concession agreement, RMS, a community entity, offers services to tourists and manages accommodation, catering, and guiding. On the other hand, UWA develops and maintains tourist-trekking trails and oversees the RMS services. This arrangement was guided by the assumption that partnering with communities through tourism can conserve natural resources as well as improve the livelihoods of the neighbouring local people. Revenue from the venture goes to RMS, which then pays UWA the entry fees for every tourist who enters the park.

Although RMS started as a monopoly in providing tourism-trekking services in RMNP, service provision gaps and value for money complaints emerging from the tour operators and tourists forced UWA to rethink the monopoly arrangement. Whereas the RMS contract is still running, UWA brought new actors on board to streamline service provision on the mountain (Senior Warden, RMNP, pers. comm., 2018). Rwenzori Ranges Guides and Escorts Association (RRGEA) and Rwenzori Trekking Services (RTS), as private players, were granted concessions to offer services to clients climbing the mountain by service choices and alternative route segments. From UWA's perspective, this was intended to create competition and hence improve service provision, but also to reduce congestion and degradation in the central route, and to increase the volume of visitor arrivals.

According to UWA, despite the strategic location of the Rwenzoris along Uganda's main tourism circuit (the Western Uganda route), the park receives few visitors compared with other parks along the circuit. For instance, in 2016, RMNP received only 23% of the visitor traffic to Kibale Forest National Park and just 3.7% of the visitor traffic to Queen Elizabeth National Park. Tourism in Rwenzori is still limited to climbing peaks, yet the park has potential for other products based on resource endowment such as chimpanzee tracking, water-based activities on water bodies in the mountain ranges, short nature walks, birding based on rich bird species endowment as well as cable cars and zip-lining that cannot easily be exploited through the RMS arrangement. At a regional level, although comparable with Mount Kilimanjaro in altitude, toughness and attractiveness, Rwenzori, a World Heritage Site, receives just 3.1% of the tourist traffic to the Tanzanian mountain. Kilimanjaro remains number two in generation of tourism traffic and revenue in Tanzania. The poor performance of Rwenzori National Park has for a long time been attributed to the inadequacies in service provision caused by the monopoly arrangement with RMS (AUTO, 2018) and limited product range despite the wide array of potential tourism resources the park is endowed with.

Although UWA's decision to open up operational space did not go well with RMS, since it led to what they called 'unfair' competition, leading to ongoing conflict, the concession agreement allows UWA to engage new players and, as such, RTS and RRGEA are legitimately engaged. Conversely, the conflict is bound to further escalate since UWA has published a new map and developed a new business plan for RMNP that gives information on more business opportunities for private investors in the mountains. These plans include alternative routes to the peak including the 61 km Bukurungu Trail, which the World Wide Fund for Nature (WWF) is developing for UWA, short circuits, and lower range tourism business opportunities.

Nevertheless, from the meager tourism volume handled by RMS, the community group still continues to generate substantial amounts of revenue, which is ploughed back into community livelihood projects (RMS CEO, pers. comm., 2018; Table 8.6). Currently, 40 job opportunities have accrued to the communities. Currently, 23 males and 17 females are directly employed by RMS as guides, porters, Chief Executive Officer, cooks (RMS CEO, pers. comm., 2018). However, considering that RMS membership is over 1,600, this is a drop in the ocean considering the potential for the park to provide more opportunities.

Besides employment opportunities and conservation of the mountain resources, residents have also built social networks with international donor organisations like United States Agency for International Development (USAID) and US Forest Service (USFS). As of now, efforts are underway to enable the model to deliver more results amidst the strong competition. A team of experts from the USFS International Program is training both

Table 8.6 RMS tourism revenues

Year	Amount UGX (millions)	Amount US$
2012	880	241,294
2013	638	174,938
2015	492	134,905
2016	657	180,148
2017	593	162,599

Source: RMS, 2018.

the UWA and RMS rangers and guides in trail planning, construction, maintenance, and handling of mountain accidents. For example, in 2012, UWA on behalf of RMS received mountain rescue equipment from USAID's Sustainable Tourism in the Albertine Rift Project through the US Forest Service International Program. The United States Agency for International Development has also supported RMS with over UGX 600 million (US$ 166,806) to construct high-end tourist camps.

Considering that Kilimanjaro Mountain National Park is the second highest revenue-earning park in Tanzania after Serengeti, and that it is comparable with Rwenzori in tourism potential, it is clear that, despite these improvements, the public-community partnership governance model has not maximised benefits accruing from Rwenzori. This under-performance has been attributed to lack of private sector engagement and its associated benefits, such as market linkages, business management skills, capacity to enhance service provision; limited marketing; blurred and uninformative brand, to mention but a few (Ahebwa and Van der Duim, 2013; WWF/UTB, 2018).

Private–community–public partnership model – sport hunting around Lake Mburo National Park

The sport hunting model was reintroduced by UWA on private land around Lake Mburo National Park in 2001. This was in response to the persistent complaints by the local communities of increased wildlife numbers on private land that had become a nuisance (Ochieng et al., 2017; Infield and Mugisha, this volume, Chapter 9). In response, the local communities started to take their revenge by poisoning wildlife and inviting poachers to kill wildlife in the hope of reducing wildlife numbers. According to UWA estimates, over 65% of wildlife in the Lake Mburo National Park region was found on community land (UWA, 2004). In order to save the remaining wildlife outside Lake Mburo and to enable the local communities to realise benefits from wildlife, the government through UWA piloted sport hunting in Rurambiira, Nyakahiita, and Rwakanombe parishes (a parish is the lowest administrative unit in Uganda) around Lake Mburo. The reintroduction was guided by the following objectives: to provide incentives for local people to protect wildlife outside protected areas; to reduce human–wildlife conflicts among the people; to provide lessons to guide management decisions on sport hunting as a wildlife conservation tool, and to positively change the residents' attitude towards wildlife conservation (UWA, 2001).

To implement the model, UWA collaborated and granted a hunting license to a private company (Game Trails Uganda Limited). The local communities were represented by local associations (Community Wildlife Associations, registered as community-based organisations to manage hunting benefits on behalf of the communities). Other stakeholders that UWA collaborated with included the District Local Government and the Community Protected Areas

Institutions, formed by the government in 1997 to harmonise community-protected area interactions in Uganda (see Twinamatsiko et al., this volume, Chapter 3). These stakeholders performed different roles (see Table 8.7).

Generally, the Lake Mburo sport hunting is guided by strict rules: for example, the company follows set and approved annual animal quotas, hunting is only conducted on privately owned land which is at least 5 km away from the park boundary, only old male animals are hunted and the hunting company is supposed to record the animals hunted by showing a GPS location of where it was hunted, and hunting is strictly conducted during the day and in the company of UWA rangers. Some of the commonly listed species for hunting around Lake Mburo and also in the other hunting areas in Uganda include: buffalo *Syncerus caffer*, impala *Aepyceros melampus*, waterbuck *Kobus ellipsiprymnus*, zebra *Equus quagga*, and red hartebeest *Alcelaphus buselaphus caama*.

Table 8.7 Stakeholders involved in sport hunting around Lake Mburo National Park

Stakeholder	Roles and responsibilities
UWA	• Grant use-rights and licenses to professional hunting companies. • Monitor the hunting activities and advise companies. • Determine the animal and area booking fees in consultation with the hunting company and the CWA. • Conduct wildlife management training for CWA members together with the hunting company. • Control illegal hunting in the project area. • Build capacity among stakeholders to monitor and evaluate project operations.
Local government (local councils and sub-county administration)	• Facilitate registration and legalisation of CWAs. • Provide guidance and support to the project to ensure sustainable utilisation of wildlife. • Assist in policing and monitoring illegal activities in the project area.
Community Wildlife Associations (CWAs) and landowners	• Ensure protection of wildlife within the hunting blocks against illegal hunting through participating in policing and monitoring of project activities. • Report instances of poaching, ensure land-use practices are consistent with promotion of wildlife conservation. • Secure protection of sport hunters and employees of professional hunting companies while within their hunting block. • Work together with local authorities, keep proper books and accounts and granting UWA access thereto. • Provide information to the hunting company and UWA on the status and distribution of wildlife within the hunting blocks.

Community Protected Area Institutions (CPIs)	• Ensure project activities are integrated into local government development plans. • Facilitate dialogue and conflict resolution. • Represent local community interests and concerns with regard to wildlife conservation. • Mobilise local people to support project implementation.
Game Trails Uganda Limited	• Carry out professional hunting in the project area. • Record hunting activities on daily basis and submit the data to UWA for quarterly analysis. • Provide quarterly operational reports, enforce wildlife laws among clients and ensure personnel abides by the law. • Ensure that animals wounded by clients are humanely handled and accounted for. • Maintain appropriate camping facilities for clients in the hunting blocks, where necessary.

Source: Ochieng et al., 2015

Based on the previous evaluation reports (UWA, 2005; Muhimbura and Namara, 2009) and recent studies (Ayorekire et al., 2011; Ochieng et al., 2015; 2017; 2018), sport hunting around Lake Mburo has made significant contributions towards enhancing rural livelihoods, reducing human–wildlife conflicts, and improving communities' attitudes towards wildlife. For example, around Lake Mburo, sport hunting contributed an estimated US$ 993,616 between 2001–2016 (Ochieng et al., 2018). Accordingly, the stakeholders first shared the hunting benefits in the following agreed percentage: CWA received 65% of the fee, UWA 25%, CPI 5% and the sub-county 5% (see Ochieng et al., 2017). However, following continuous battles over the benefits, the benefit-sharing percentages around Lake Mburo changed over time. Currently, benefits are shared as follows: landowners received 50%, the association 40%, and UWA 10% (Ochieng et al., 2017). The association used the money to provide different livelihoods projects such as to support tree planting, beekeeping, goat rearing and construction of classroom blocks, health facilities, roads and dams etc., while individual landowners use their share to meet household needs (cf. Ochieng et al., 2018). Consequently, some local communities neighbouring Lake Mburo have confirmed protection of wildlife in and outside PAs encouraged by realised or hoped-for benefits from sport hunting (Ochieng et al., 2017).

Following the 2002 internal (UWA, 2005) and the 2008 external positive evaluations (Muhimbura and Namara 2009), UWA decided to replicate sport hunting in and outside other protected areas in Uganda. For example, UWA introduced sport hunting in Kabwoya Wildlife Reserve in 2006 with the main aim of deriving money to finance the conservation of the area. This followed a prolonged period of poaching in the area due to the absence of UWA rangers. It was later extended to include Kaiso-Tonya Community

Wildlife Area in 2008, with the aim to protect the remaining wildlife on community land. Kabwoya Wildlife Reserve and Kaiso-Tonya Community Wildlife Area together form Kabwoya and Kaiso-Tonya Game Management Area. Other protected areas in Uganda where hunting is conducted include: Katongo Wildlife Reserve, Bokora-Matheniko wildlife reserve, Karenga and Iriri community wildlife area, Ajai wildlife reserve, Pian-Upe wildlife reserve and Amudati community wildlife area (see Ochieng et al., 2015). These hunting areas are managed under different hunting concessions and revenue-sharing agreements.

Despite over a decade of sport hunting implementation in Uganda, there are concerns that struggles, politics and elite capture dominate its implementation. Around Lake Mburo for example, Ochieng et al. (2017) demonstrated how the battles over the benefits flawed the sport hunting implementation and debates. Furthermore, in the Aswa-Lolim game reserve and Kilak controlled hunting areas, sport hunting has been interpreted as a way of grabbing land from the poor and vulnerable residents by the elites – consequently spurring conflicts between the local residents and local leaders in the districts of Gulu and Amuru. The residents accuse the private operator in both Kabwoya and Kaiso-Tonya Game Management Area and East Madi Wildlife Reserve of land grabbing. Such sentiments work to weaken the potential of sport hunting to enhance local livelihoods. Similar scenarios were reported in the Kabwoya area, where the local residents of Buseruka sub-county, Hoima district, opposed the initial implementation of sport hunting, 'arguing that the government wanted to grab land and would eventually restrict subsistence hunting' (Ochieng et al., 2017, p. 6). As such, in some areas the local residents have opposed hunting even amidst the benefits. Ochieng et al. (2018), for example, report that the communities around LMNP exhibit an ambivalent perception of the policy impact. While some are positive about the benefits they received, others mention that they accept the benefits because they lack alternatives.

Direct community engagement model – Kibale Association for Rural and Environmental Development (KAFRED)

The Kibale Association for Rural and Environmental Development (KAFRED) was started in 1992 with support from a US Peace Corps Volunteer, Mark Noonan. He mobilised six community members to start conserving the Bigodi wetland sanctuary. Although the wetland is legally owned by the government of Uganda, the local farming community in Bigodi acquired rights to conserve and use it for conservation and community development under the Local Government Act 1997. The wetland is located adjacent to Kibale Forest National Park (KFNP) in Kamwenge district, western Uganda. The national park is rich in biodiversity and is home to eight species of primates and over 200 species of birds. Prior to the 1990s, the wetland experienced degradation amidst increasing demand for farming land and settlement. However, following the successful chimpanzee habituation at KFNP and the opening of tourism at the nearby Kanyanchu tourism centre in 1991 by UWA, the six-member committee together with Mark Noonan started a small-scale ecotourism activity at the Bigodi wetland. This took advantage of the swampy vegetation of the wetland – dominated by the papyrus grasses – which enabled ecotourism activities such as bird watching, primate viewing and nature walks.

From the six founders in 1992, KAFRED has grown to a membership of over 150 individuals and other affiliate and KAFRED-supported groups, and is supporting multiple beneficiaries (Table 8.8). Some of the prominent women's groups in KAFRED include: the Bigodi Women's Group (BWG) with 40 members, the Kiyoima Women's Group with 30 members, the Bigodi peanut butter group, and the Enyange dramactors (singers and actors group) (UNDP, 2012). Through KAFRED, over 300 households directly and indirectly benefit by using the wetland resources in a regulated manner instead of completely degrading it through subsistence agriculture. Furthermore, KAFRED provides direct employment to over 33 members of the Bigodi village as tour guides, managers, medical staff, teachers, and other support staff. Also the Bigodi Women's Group provides social support to local women through training in making fine handicrafts and artisanal goods for sale to tourists (UNDP, 2012). The KAFRED has also registered significant progress in reducing wetland degradation through campaigns aimed at discouraging illegal use (small-scale logging) and resource extraction, land clearance, and settlement, especially within a radius of five kilometers from the park. Moreover, the local residents have gained indirect

Table 8.8 KAFRED stakeholders and beneficiaries

KAFRED beneficiaries	
Type	*Number*
Voting members	117
Non-voting members	37
Employees	33
Secondary school children and parents	500
Members of the women's groups	110
Wetland resource users	2,400 people from about 300 households estimated at an average of 8 people
Tourists	About 4,000/year
Local tour operators	20+ tour companies
Local service providers (lodging, food, and catering)	225 people from 15 service providers
Mothers helped by midwives/year	100+

Source: UNDP, 2012; www.Bigoditourism.com, accessed 19 July 2017.

economic benefits through the support of the Bigodi Women's Group and the revolving loan scheme for farming residents (UNDP, 2012).

The KAFRED is currently considered a model community-based organisation (CBO), founded and managed by the local communities and promoting direct community engagement in conservation of the wetland – as opposed to state-led conservation (Lepp and Holland, 2006). The initial primary objective of KAFRED was to use ecotourism as a tool for promoting conservation of the wetland. However, over the years, KAFRED has evolved from using ecotourism for conservation to using tourism income to finance community development projects (UNDP, 2012) – especially following the launch of a loaning scheme – the revolving fund. A fund of US$ 2,000 was offered to representatives from 120 families in 2005 that owned land adjacent to the wetland, with the objective of creating entrepreneurial opportunities for local residents to improve their household income. Under the KAFRED constitution, the businesses are supposed to be eco-friendly. Some of the entrepreneurial projects being trialled around Bigodi wetland include aquaculture (fish-keeping), bee-farming, goat-rearing, piggery, tree planting (agro-forestry) and growing of vegetables (Bigodi Tourism, n.d.). The families are empowered to elect their own representatives who manage the lending process and ensure that the borrowed money is returned with interest.

The KAFRED has managed to avert wetland degradation in Bigodi for more than two decades now – amidst increasing demand for agricultural land. However, although KAFRED is portrayed as having positively contributed to conservation and development, there exists a thin line distinguishing the organisation from some of its individual leaders. Informal talks with some of the community members revealed that, without KAFRED's first and very long-serving national secretary, the future of KAFRED may be bleak. It emerged that he has monopolised KAFRED undertakings to date and has built inadequate capacity in other community members to undertake his role. Because of the failure to separate the organisation from individuals, a few local residents resist subscribing to KAFRED membership. They claim ignorance of KAFRED's accountability process. They also criticise the manner in which KAFRED was registered as company limited by liability (implying some individuals could be shareholders in the organisation) – an act contrary to the principles of CBO operations (Nyakaana and Ahebwa, 2011). As such, although leading to a number of livelihood and conservation benefits, KAFRED as a governance arrangement has not been spared by the 'scourge' of elite capture that is inherent in most tourism initiatives in the developing world.

Summary and conclusions

Drawing on the Policy Arrangements Approach (Arts, 2006), this chapter analysed four case studies in which different tourism governance models have been implemented to achieve conservation and livelihoods enhancement. We explored how actors in the different case studies shaped implementation, the accrued benefits, and the politics and power dynamics. Overall, different narratives, benefits and challenges emerge from the different case studies in relation to the tourism governance models that they represent (Table 8.9).

Table 8.9 Describing different governance models, benefits, costs and challenges

Governance model	Benefits	Costs/limitations	Challenges
Clouds Lodge Private–community–partnership	• Revenue US$ 382,870. • Employment. • Market for local produce. • Provision of social goods.	• Dependence on gorilla tourism. • Limited local entrepreneurial development due to the monopoly of NCDF. • Potential congestion and degradation of vegetation by the high numbers of gorilla trackers.	• Governance issues. • Lack of technical capacity at local levels. • Mistrust. • High unsold gorilla permits. • Minimal tourism impact due to the large area coverage by NCDF. • Competing land uses.
Rwenzori Mountaineering Services. Public–community–partnership.	• Revenue US$ 41,800. • Employment.	• Dependence on mountain tourism. • Congestion and degradation. • Opened doors to competition.	• Competition for clients. • Inadequate skills by mountain guides. • Elite capture.
Sport hunting. Private–community–public partnership.	• Revenue. • Provision of social goods. • Reduced poaching and wildlife conserved.	• Increased wildlife numbers that became a nuisance.	• Elite capture. • Governance issues (e.g., lack of accountability and transparency. • Mistrust.
KAFRED. Direct community–private partnership.	• Jobs. • Revolving loan scheme. • Provision of social goods.	• Dependence on tourism.	• Failure to separate individuals from organisation. • Governance issues. • Mistrust. • Elite capture.

A striking feature of the highly diverse tourism governance arrangements analysed in this chapter is the level of overlap between them in terms of the benefits, challenges and limitations they have experienced. On the benefit side, all our case studies have delivered some form of revenue to the local economy and three of the four have provided funding for social development projects. On the cost side, mistrust and elite capture both feature in three of the four case studies. While we acknowledge that our sample of one case study for each model does not allow for generalised conclusions, it would seem that certain features are common to wildlife-based tourism models that include community actors, irrespective of the other partners involved.

Despite certain features appearing across our case studies, one important feature of governance design did seem to play an important role. This was whether or not the partnership involved a private sector partner. The presence of such partners seems to ensure better performance of the business side of a tourism partnership involving local communities. This is clearly evident looking at the operational challenges that RMS is experiencing in the Rwenzori. They will either have to benchmark private sector best practices, or engage a private sector partner if they are to effectively survive in business. Nonetheless, partnership with private sector businesses does come with the risk that they will have the power to steer a partnership in a way that may not be in the interests of local beneficiaries, as seemed to happen in the early years of the Clouds Lodge case study.

Tourism has played a crucial role in the history of conservation and development in Uganda, and looks set to continue to do so into the future. The challenge has always been how to deliver benefits to local communities while achieving commercial success in a ruthlessly competitive industry, and all without placing excessive stress on the wildlife assets upon which tourism depends. Uganda's experiments with various partnership models provide some useful insights into how such a balance might be struck. However, these innovations cannot in themselves address the consistent challenges of elite capture, mistrust and a lack of revenue for communities at a sufficient scale to make a real difference to local livelihoods.

Acknowledgements

Special thanks to the ALBORADA Research Fund and the Cambridge–Africa Partnership and Research Exchange (CAPREX) for funding the research presented in this chapter.

References

Ahebwa, M.W. and Van der Duim, R. (2013) 'Conservation, livelihoods, and tourism: a case study of the Buhoma-Mukono Community-Based Tourism Project in Uganda', *Journal of Park and Recreation Administration*, vol. 31, no. 3, pp. 96–114.

Ahebwa, M.W., Van der Duim, R., and Sandbrook, C.G. (2012) 'Private–community partnerships: investigating a new intervention to conservation and development in Uganda', *Journal of Conservation and Society*, vol. 10, no. 4, pp. 305–317.

Anderson, W. (2012) 'Analysis of "all-inclusive" tourism model in the Balearic Islands', *Tourismos*, vol. 7, no. 1, pp. 309–323.

Anyango-Van Zwieten, N., Van Der Duim, R., and Visseren-Hamakers, I.J. (2015) 'Compensating for livestock killed by lions: payment for environmental services as a policy arrangement', *Environmental Conservation*, vol. 1, no. 4, pp. 363–372.

Arts, B. (2006) *Forests, Institutions, Discourses: A discursive institutional analysis of global forest politics*, inaugural address, Wageningen University, Wageningen, The Netherlands.

Arts, B. and Goverde, H. (2006) 'The governance capacity of (new) policy arrangements: a reflexive approach', in B. Arts and P. Leroy (eds) *Institutional Dynamics in Environmental Governance*, Springer, Dordrecht, The Netherlands.

Arts, B. and Leroy, P. (2006) *Institutional Processes in Environmental Governance*, Springer, Dordrecht, The Netherlands.

Ashley, C., De Brine, P., Lehr, A., Wilde, H., and Rt, O. (2007) *The Role of the Tourism Sector in Expanding Economic Opportunity*, Corporate Social Responsibility Initiative Report no. 23, Kennedy School of Government, Harvard University, Cambridge, MA, USA.

Association of Uganda Tour Operators (AUTO) (2018) *Official Communication from the CEO of the Association of Uganda Tour Operators*, Association of Uganda Tour Operators, Kampala, Uganda.

Ayorekire, J., Ahebwa, M.W., and Ochieng, A. (2011) 'Managing conservation and development on private land: an assessment of sport hunting around Lake Mburo National Park, Uganda', in R. van der Duim, D. Meyer, J. Saarinen and K. Zellmer (eds) *New Alliances for Tourism, Conservation and Development in Eastern and Southern Africa*, Eburon, Delft, The Netherlands, pp. 185–201.

Bigodi Tourism (n.d.) [website], www.bigoditourism.com, accessed 19 July 2017.

Büscher, B., Sullivan, S., Neves, K., Igoe, J., and Brockington, D. (2012) 'Towards a synthesized critique of neoliberal biodiversity conservation', *Capitalism Nature Socialism*, vol. 23, no. 2, pp. 4–30.

Cabezas, A.L. (2008) 'Tropical blues: tourism and social exclusion in the Dominican Republic', *Latin American Perspectives*, vol. 35, no. 160, pp. 21–36.

Chok, S., Macbeth, J., and Warren, C. (2007) 'Tourism as a tool for poverty alleviation: a critical analysis of "pro-poor tourism" and implications for sustainability', *Current Issues in Tourism*, vol. 10, nos 2–3, pp. 144–165.

Deguignet, M., Juffe-Bignoli, D., Harrison, J., MacSharry, B., Burgess, N., and Kingston, N. (2014) *United Nations List of Protected Areas*, UNEP-WCMC, Cambridge, UK.

Duffy, R. (2006) 'Global environmental governance and the politics of ecotourism in Madagascar', *Journal of Ecotourism*, vol. 5, nos 1–2, pp. 128–144.

Elliott, J. and Sumba, D. (2011) *Conservation Enterprise: what works, where and for whom?*, International Institute for Environment and Development, London, UK.

Font, A.R. (2000) 'Mass tourism and the demand for protected natural areas: a travel cost approach', *Journal of Environmental Economics and Management*, vol. 39, no. 1, pp. 97–116.

Harrison, D. (2008) 'Pro-poor tourism: a critique', *Third World Quarterly*, vol. 29, no. 5, pp. 851–868, doi: 10.1080/01436590802105983.

Kiss, A. (2004) 'Is community-based ecotourism a good use of biodiversity conservation funds?', *Trends in Ecology & Evolution*, vol. 19, no. 5, pp. 232–237.

Lamers, M., Nthiga, R., van der Duim, R., and van Wijk, J. (2014) 'Tourism–conservation enterprises as a land-use strategy in Kenya', *Tourism Geographies*, vol. 16, no. 3, pp. 474–489.

Laudati, A. (2010) 'Ecotourism: the modern predator? Implications of gorilla tourism on local livelihoods in Bwindi Impenetrable National Park, Uganda', *Environment and Planning D: Society and Space*, vol. 28, no. 4, pp. 726–743.

Lepp, A. (2008) 'Tourism and dependency: an analysis of Bigodi village, Uganda', *Tourism Management*, vol. 29, no. 6, pp. 1206–1214.

Lepp, A. and Holland, S. (2006) 'A comparison of attitudes toward state-led conservation and community-based conservation in the village of Bigodi, Uganda', *Society & Natural Resources*, vol. 19, no. 7, pp. 609–623.

Manyara, G. and Jones, E. (2007) 'Community-based tourism enterprises development in Kenya: an exploration of their potential as avenues of poverty reduction', *Journal of Sustainable Tourism*, vol. 15, no. 6, pp. 628–644, doi: 10.2167/jost723.0.

Ministry of Tourism, Wildlife and Antiquities (MTWA) (2015) 'Tourism products and potentials of Uganda', Ministerial Operational Report, unpublished, Ministry of Tourism, Wildlife and Antiquities, Kampala, Uganda.

Ministry of Tourism, Wildlife and Antiquities (MTWA) (2017) *Annual Tourism Sector Performance Report, Financial Year 2016/2017: "Accelerating tourism growth to attain middle income status by 2020"*, Ministry of Tourism, Wildlife and Antiquities, Kampala, Uganda.

Mitchell, J. and Coles, C. (2009) *Enhancing Private Sector and Community Engagement in Tourism Services in Ethiopia*, Overseas Development Institute, London, UK.

Mowforth, M. and Munt, I. (2015) *Tourism and Sustainability: development, globalisation and new tourism in the third world*, fourth edition, Routledge, Abingdon, UK.

Muhimbura, A. and Namara, A. (2009) 'The pilot sport hunting program in the ranches surrounding Lake Mburo National Park', project evaluation report, draft 2.

Muhumuza, M. and Byarugaba, D. (2009) 'Impact of land use on the ecology of uncultivated plant species in the Rwenzori mountain range, mid-western Uganda', *African Journal of Ecology*, vol. 47, no. 4, pp. 614–621, doi:10.1111/j.1365-2028.2009.01033.x.

Nyakaana, J.B. and Ahebwa, W.M. (2011) 'Governance of community-based tourism in Uganda: an analysis of the Kibale Association for Rural and Environmental Development (KAFRED)', in R. van der Duim, D. Meyer, J. Saarinen and K. Zellmer (eds) *New Alliances for Tourism, Conservation and Development in Eastern and Southern Africa*, Eburon, Delft, The Netherlands, pp. 185–201.

Nzinjah, J. (2002) 'Rwenzoris merge', *New Vision*, 1 November. Available at: www.newvision.co.ug/new_vision/news/1045803/rwenzoris-merge, accessed 19 July 2017.

Ochieng, A. (2011) 'Linking tourism, conservation and livelihoods: an analysis of sport hunting around Lake Mburo National Park, Uganda', MSc thesis, Wageningen University, Wageningen, The Netherlands.

Ochieng, A., Ahebwa, W.M., and Visseren-Hamakers, I.J. (2015) 'Hunting for conservation? The re-introduction of sport hunting in Uganda examined', in R. Van der Duim, M. Lamers, and J. Van Wijk (eds) *Institutional Arrangements for Conservation, Development and Tourism in Eastern and Southern Africa*, Springer, Dordrecht, The Netherlands, pp. 139–155.

Ochieng, A., Visseren-Hamakers, I.J., and Van der Duim, R. (2017) 'The battle over the benefits: analysing the two sport hunting policy arrangements in Uganda', *Oryx*, vol. 52, no. 2, pp. 359–368, doi:10.1017/S0030605316000909.

Ochieng, A., Visseren-Hamakers, I.J. and Van der Duim, R. (2018) 'Hunting or poaching? The social and ecological impacts of sport hunting in Uganda', *Oryx*, forthcoming.

Roe, D. (2001) *Getting the Lion's Share from Tourism: Private Sector–Community Partnerships in Namibia* (Vol. 3 of 3 volumes), International Institute for Environment and Development, London, UK.

Rwenzori Mountaineering Services (RMS) (2018) 'Rwenzori Mountaineering Services operational report', unpublished, Kasese, Uganda.

Sandbrook, C.G. (2010) 'Putting leakage in its place: the significance of retained tourism revenue in the local context in rural Uganda', *Journal of International Development*, vol. 22, no. 1, pp. 124–136.

Scheyvens, R. (2007) 'Exploring the tourism poverty nexus' in C. Michael Hall (ed.) *Pro-poor Tourism: Who Benefits?* Cromwell Press, Trowbridge, UK, pp. 121–141.

Sofield, T., Bauer, J., De Lacy, T., Lipman, G., and Daugherty, S. (2004) *Sustainable Tourism-Eliminating Poverty (ST-EP): an overview, CRC for sustainable tourism*, CRC for Sustainable Tourism Pty Ltd, Queensland, Australia.

Sunlu, U. (2003) 'Environmental impacts of tourism', in D. Camarda and L. Grassini (eds) *Local Resources and Global Trades: environments and agriculture in the Mediterranean region*, International Center for Advanced Mediterranean Agronomic Studies, Bari, Italy, pp. 263–270.

Tumusiime, D.M. and Sjaastad, E. (2014) 'Conservation and development: justice, inequality, and attitudes around Bwindi Impenetrable National Park', *Journal of Development Studies*, vol. 50, no. 2, pp. 204–225.

Uganda Bureau of Statistics (UBOS) (2017) 'Uganda's tourism statistical abstract', unpublished, Uganda Bureau of Statistics, Kampala, Uganda.

Uganda Wildlife Authority (UWA) (2001) *Professional Hunting Agreement in the Former Ankole Ranching Scheme Between Uganda Wildlife Authority and Rurambiira Wildlife Association and Game Trails (U) Limited*, Uganda Wildlife Authority, Kampala, Uganda.

Uganda Wildlife Authority (UWA) (2004) *Uganda Wildlife Policy*, Uganda Wildlife Authority, Kampala, Uganda.

Uganda Wildlife Authority (UWA) (2005) 'The implementation of sport hunting project on the ranches outside LMNP: report on sport hunting with proposals for change', July 2005, unpublished policy document, Uganda Wildlife Authority, Kampala, Uganda.

Uganda Wildlife Authority (UWA) (2018) 'Revenue generation in protected areas', Uganda Wildlife Authority operational report, unpublished, Uganda Wildlife Authority, Kampala, Uganda.

United Nations Development Programme (UNDP) (2012) *Kibale Association for Rural and Environmental Development (KAFRED), Uganda*, Equator Initiative Case Study Series, United Nations Development Programme, New York, NY, USA.

Van der Duim, V.R. (2011) *Safari. A journey through tourism, conservation and development*, inaugural lecture, Wageningen University, Wageningen, The Netherlands.

Van Wijk, J., Van der Duim, R., Lamers, M., and Sumba, D. (2015) 'The emergence of institutional innovations in tourism: the evolution of the African Wildlife Foundation's tourism conservation enterprises', *Journal of Sustainable Tourism*, vol. 23, no. 1, pp. 104–125.

Wall, G. (1998) 'Implications of global climate change for tourism and recreation in wetland areas', *Climatic Change*, 40(2), 371–38

Weaver, D.B. (2000) 'A broad context model of destination development scenarios', *Tourism Management*, vol. 21, no. 3, pp. 217–224.

World Wide Fund for Nature/Uganda Tourism Board (WWF/UTB) (2018) 'Rwenzori product review and marketing strategy report', unpublished.

9 Cultural values and conservation
An innovative approach to community engagement

Mark Infield and Arthur Mugisha

Introduction

This chapter discusses a cultural values approach to conservation developed and implemented in Uganda. Cultural values are understood here as the knowledge, practices and institutions that connect people to their natural world and their place in it. We argue that the potential of cultural connections to nature to strengthen conservation practice is great, creating opportunities to build relations with communities based on their values, and providing ways to analyse, understand and address conflicts that exist between protected areas and communities. Cultural approaches to conservation are, therefore, interventions that seek to recognise, validate and build on cultural connections to nature, rather than undermining them as exclusionary protected areas do, in order to strengthen nature conservation as well as to help retain cultural connections to nature within society.

In this chapter we use the gazettment and management of Lake Mburo National Park as a case study to demonstrate linkages between politics and conservation, and to examine the community-based approaches designed to address problems resulting from this, their limitations, and how they led to the development of a cultural values approach. We also describe a number of other interventions carried out in partnership with the Uganda Wildlife Authority and assess their strengths and weaknesses. We conclude with a discussion of the implications of these experiences for the wider adoption of cultural values approaches to conservation.

Failure to consider culture in integrated conservation and development thinking

Protected areas are considered by many within the conservation community to be the crown jewels of modern conservation, and their global spread as one of the most significant achievements of the 20th century. Though they make important contributions to the conservation of biodiversity (Gray et al., 2016), the establishment and management of exclusionary areas such as national parks is hotly contested by parties both within and outside the world of nature conservation. From their beginnings, protected areas were gazetted with scant regard for the rights of communities living in or around them, and with little concern for the dependencies and attachments of these peoples on lands and resources. Many communities have been displaced from their lands and alienated from their resources in the process of establishing protected areas (Manspiezer, 2004; West et al., 2006). Regard for local rights within protected area design and management continues in many cases to be more rhetorical than actual (e.g., Dowie, 2009). Concerns over the morality and sustainability of the 'fortress conservation' model and its 'fines and fences' approaches stimulated the rise of community-based approaches and initiatives to link conservation to poverty alleviation (Adams and McShane, 1992; Adams et al., 2004). These sought to share the benefits of conservation and create a set of common values between conservation authorities and communities living in and around protected areas. Community approaches to conservation became part of the economic development programme (Hulme and Murphree, 2001) and reached their apogee in large and complex integrated conservation and development programmes in the 1980s and 1990s (Wells et al., 1992).

Integrated conservation and development focused on building partnerships with communities, usually based on sharing the economic values of protected areas and natural resources. Cultural values, the intangible values of nature for people, were largely ignored. The IUCN's World Parks Congress in 1981, a key event in the development of community-based conservation, made frequent references to the links between culture and nature and the relevance of these to conservation (McNeely and Miller, 1985) but there was little adoption of these ideas (Infield, 2002). Studies in ethnobotany led Posey to suggest that nature and culture were inextricably linked (Posey, 1999), a proposition strengthened by analysis showing overlaps in the distribution of linguistic and biological diversity (Loh and Harmon, 2005; Gorenflo et al., 2012). This opened the potential to identify synergies in the conservation of culture and nature and led to the development of the concept of 'biocultural diversity' (Maffi and Woodley, 2010).

Practical explorations of conservation through a cultural lens began to emerge, in some quarters at least, in the 2000s (Infield et al., 2017). These were a by-product of the mainstreaming of community-based conservation that was taking place in Uganda and elsewhere in the 1990s (Hulme and Murphree, 2001) rather than inherent in these interventions. Critiques of the failure of formal protected areas to recognise the rights of indigenous peoples, including their right to enjoy their own culture, also grew louder. The Convention on Biodiversity and other international agreements placed an onus on governments to recognise these rights and include local communities in the management of protected areas. The need to respond to these pressures was complemented by recognition that traditional knowledge could strengthen conservation actions (Berkes et al., 2000), and by the evolution of multi-dimensional frameworks that accepted cultural values and institutions as critical to improving livelihoods and achieving economic development (Ashley and Carney, 1999). The consideration of culture and local values in nature began to be seen as a way of deepening and strengthening community-based approaches that had hitherto focused on economic links between people and nature (Infield, 2001).

Academic interest over the last decade or two in critically analysing conservation practice in general and protected areas in particular has demonstrated that the dispossession of communities in the name of conservation was not only material in nature. The exclusion of communities from cultural resources on which social identity, cohesion and resilience depended could be as damaging to communities as their exclusion from resources of food, medicines and income (Jax et al., 2013), while strong cultural institutions have been identified as relevant to successful social and economic development, supporting communities' capacity to respond to rapid change, opportunities and challenges (Sen, 2004).

More recently, the description of ecosystem services to explain nature's values and provide justification for its conservation has, perhaps inadvertently, focused attention on cultural services provided by nature, the need to describe them, and the value of integrating them into decision-making processes (Church et al., 2011; Chan et al., 2012; Chan et al., 2016). It is worth noting that describing the benefits of nature as services gave strength to market-based mechanisms for conserving nature, but also helped areas of interest in connection to and dependence on nature to be recognised by decision makers, and acceptance that they could not be reasonably described or measured in economic terms, but could be best understood in cultural terms. However, despite these developments and its apparent potential, the development and implementation of cultural approaches to conservation remains in its infancy.

The emergence of a cultural values programme within the Uganda Wildlife Authority: from Lake Mburo to the national scale

The establishment of formal protected areas in Uganda, which started in the 1930s under colonial rule, was characterised by the displacement of local communities who were denied access to both cultural and natural resources (see also Banana et al., this volume, Chapter 2). This inevitably led to resentment and the start of conflict between protected areas and neighbouring communities that persists to this day. This process is exemplified by the case of Lake Mburo, which was historically associated with Ankole long-horned cows, the traditional breed of the Bahima people, grazing in a wildlife-rich landscape. In the 1930s, the colonial government gazetted the area as a controlled hunting area, which allowed the grazing of cattle to continue. In 1963 the area became a game reserve, which also allowed cattle to graze. This arrangement enabled wildlife to thrive within a pastoral landscape, despite occasional conflicts that would generally be resolved through informal financial exchanges between game rangers and cattle owners. Through the 1970s, however, conflicts worsened as the Game Department, fearing that the conservation status of the reserve was eroding, strengthened efforts to exclude pastoralists and their herds.

Relations between conservation authorities and communities deteriorated further during the 15 years of political, economic and social turmoil of Idi Amin (1971 to 1979) and Milton Obote's (1980 to 1985) regimes. The state inspired, condoned or was the source of unregulated hunting and encroachment of many protected areas, while communities passively or actively participated in the destruction of wildlife and habitats. During this period large mammals declined greatly (Douglas-Hamilton et al., 1980), while both white and black rhinos became locally extinct.

At Mburo, relations also deteriorated, but in this case because, following the disputed 1980 presidential elections, the government of Milton Obote declared Lake Mburo a National Park. It is widely held that this was designed to punish the pastoral community who had not voted for Obote. The pastoralists were forcefully evicted, denying them not just access to water and grazing but also to the cultural landscape where they had bred and managed their 'Beautiful Cows' for centuries. The evicted families provided good recruits for the rebel National Resistance Army (NRA) that waged a bush war against the Obote government. The injustice of the establishment of the National Park was included in the political programme of the NRA.

In 1986 the NRA dislodged the Obote government. The park was invaded and a campaign to systematically kill the wildlife began, while the new government made it a priority to address the injustices meted out to the pastoral community. A commission was established and recommended that 60% of the park be degazetted to settle those made landless by the park and the war. Despite this, negative attitudes continued to challenge efforts to manage the area that remained national park. Responding to this, the government and its partners initiated integrated conservation and development approaches, and projects were established to support several national parks including Lake Mburo. These focused on economic perspectives, either working to strengthen economic links by formalising access to resources and sharing tourism revenues, or working to reduce dependence on natural resources in the parks by providing alternatives.

The Lake Mburo Community Conservation project, funded by the Swedish International Development Agency and implemented by the African Wildlife Foundation, ran from 1991 to 1998 and was designed to strengthen the conservation status of Lake Mburo National Park in the face of serious resistance. The 260 km² that retained National Park status was left without political or financial support and was fast being lost as farming and fishing villages grew rapidly. Over 20,000 head of cattle were being grazed in the park, more than double the recommended stocking rate for commercial ranching, with negative impacts on the park's wildlife (Guard, 1991).

The project employed a range of measures to support the park by helping community development. On the one hand it rebuilt park infrastructure and staff capacity to strengthen protection and supported tourism to generate income; on the other it helped communities negotiate access to park resources, supported the sharing of park revenues, and delivered micro-development projects. The project established Uganda's first Community Conservation Unit, trained rangers in community engagement, supported community–park interactions, and delivered conservation outreach and education programmes. These interventions helped the park recover its conservation function while improving relations with communities and their leaders. However, relations with the pastoral community were more negative than with other groups (Infield et al., 1993) and remained so even after five years of the community conservation programme. Though 57% of farming households were assessed as positive towards the park, just a quarter of pastoralist households were (Infield and Namara, 2001).

Efforts to build positive relations with the pastoralists by employing economic incentives were undermined by the strength of conflicting values and cultural world-views of pastoralists and park managers. The cultural lives of Bahima pastoralists revolved around the breeding of long-horned Ankole cows for beauty – rather than production – which was indelibly linked to their ancestors, their lands and their identity. These values were identified as the drivers of the on-going conflict, offering an alternative understanding of a conflict attributed to economic competition over land and resources (Infield, 2002). Infield investigated the values of the pastoralists in park lands and concluded that both the 'protectionist' and 'community' approaches had failed to engage the pastoralists because their scientific and economic prescriptions failed to engage with the pastoralists' cultural attachments to nature and the park. He proposed that the park be managed to recognise these different sets of values, to seek synergies in them, and opportunities to employ them to increase interest in the park amongst the pastoralists.

Building on the Lake Mburo study, a pilot project was funded by the MacArthur Foundation and implemented by Fauna & Flora International and the Uganda Wildlife Authority (UWA) (Infield et al., 2017). Starting in 2005, this project designed and implemented cultural values approaches to protected area management in Lake Mburo and Rwenzori Mountains national parks. The project also began the process of mainstreaming cultural values approaches across the UWA institution. After three years, a second phase extended activities to Semuliki National Park and a community conserved area, Musambwa Islands in Lake Victoria, which, though not gazetted, were protected by local institutions for their sacred values. At the request of UWA, cultural values approaches were also applied to improve relations with Batwa communities living around Bwindi Impenetrable and

Mgahinga national parks. Extending the work on Musambwa Island, cultural values approaches were applied to support the protection of other community-conserved areas lying within the Lake Victoria basin, funded by the Darwin Initiative and the MacArthur Foundation between 2015 and 2018. From 2005 to 2015, the cultural values approach spread from two to nine sites, including half of Uganda's national parks.

Despite changes in senior staff and the general outlook at the top of UWA, the cultural values and conservation programme continued to work with the institution and with park level staff to establish organisational norms and frameworks for integrating cultural values into protected area design and management. The concluding step in this process was support for park managers to draft best practice guidelines for cultural values approaches within UWA. These guidelines have yet to be adopted and promulgated across all national parks and wildlife areas, but cultural values assessments are now integrated into UWA's formal park planning process.

Implementing the Culture, Values and Conservation Project

The intention behind the Culture, Values and Conservation Project was to

> demonstrate through a pilot project the theory and practice of building local support for protected areas by creating values for parks, based on landscape and cultural values of local communities and to use these lessons to strengthen protected area status.
>
> (FFI, 2005)

The conclusion of Infield's research (2002), that integrating local cultural values in and connections to nature and place would create support for protected areas, underpinned the design and implementation of the project. Activities focused on developing a practical means of identifying relevant local values connected to a particular site, facilitating agreement between communities and managers on which to prioritise, and supporting measures that would, in direct and mutually acceptable ways, make local values park values too. Building awareness and acceptance of cultural perspectives within the management culture and philosophy of the parks, and influencing day-to-day management actions to respond to cultural perspectives, were also key objectives pursued at an institutional level.

Examples of interventions made are discussed below to suggest the degree to which this approach was accepted by communities and park officials, the level to which practical actions were undertaken by park officials and community champions, and the extent to which local values were actually integrated into the day-to-day management of the parks, all as evidence of the degree to which a cultural values approach was perceived to be valuable by the Uganda Wildlife Authority in delivering positive conservation and community outcomes.

Integrating cultural cows into Lake Mburo National Park – 2005 to 2015

Actions to strengthen relations with the pastoral community focused on integrating the cultural values associated with their long-horned Ankole cows into the management of the park. This was proposed following discussions with the pastoralists and park managers and reflected the findings of Infield (2002). A new institution – the Ankole Cow Conservation Association (ACCA) – was established to champion this concept, its members comprising individuals wishing to conserve the breed and the knowledge and practices connected to it, as well as parties keen to help resolve the ongoing conflict between the park and the pastoralists, including the authors. A range of collaborative activities were developed and a mechanism to establish a conservation herd of 'cultural cows' to be owned by ACCA but grazed within the park was put forward.

The park management and ACCA developed an education and cultural centre to conserve the Ankole cow, its cultural values, and its links to the conservation of the park. The ACCA established a 50-strong herd of 'pure' Ankole cows, and a dam for them was constructed within the park. Though the animals graze within the park much of the time, and despite accepting the construction of the education centre within the park, primarily perceived as a tourism attraction, the Uganda Wildlife Authority refused to formally approve this or accept the cultural cows and their values as part of the park as originally agreed with park managers, arguing that the Wildlife Act prohibited it. The same Act, however, was the basis for developing multiple-use zones and other forms of access to parks, and empowers park management to allow activities otherwise defined as illegal if they support conservation objectives. The ACCA has continued to argue for the original agreement to be implemented, but without success. However, the process of engagement between pastoralists, civil society and the authorities, has helped create a platform for ongoing negotiations and maintained a meaningful dialogue over the management of this highly contested park. This has contributed to the retention of the park's natural values and continues to support its cultural meaning and potential.

Infield's (2002) research into the cultural basis of the conflicts between pastoralists and park managers at Lake Mburo was a response to shortcomings observed in the community-based conservation approaches applied there. That the presence of domestic animals within a park was anathema to conservationists, African and international, meant that support for an investigation of the cultural values of Lake Mburo to the pastoralists needed strong institutional backing. Without this, the research could never have begun and the cultural values programme would likely have never come about. The then Director of UWA, Dr Eric Edroma, agreed to consider the concept of 'cultural cows', allowing research into this potentially controversial approach to park management. High-level support continued under the next Director, Arthur Mugisha (an author of this chapter), and the next, Moses Mapesa, who oversaw the first phase of the project and supported its continuation and expansion. In more recent years, however, support for the cultural values approach has weakened despite its achievements and local interest. It is unlikely that the original research into the cultural nature of conflicts at Lake Mburo would be allowed today, or that UWA would partner a project to integrate culture into park management, demonstrating the critical role of institutional champions if new ideas are to be entertained and sustained.

A concern over the cultural values approach is the apparently unavoidable link between cultural identity and the politics of ethnicity. When the cultural box is opened, even though with constrained and specific intentions, politics springs out and its impact on activities can be hard to contain. Efforts that focused on Ankole cows were considered by some to indicate that the project supported the return of the Ankole kingship, creating difficulties for the project's local relationships and how it was perceived. The return of the king was strongly resisted by most of the local population.

The sacred values of the Rwenzori Mountains National Park – 2005 to 2015

The processes to establish the Rwenzori Mountains National Park in 1992, and to inscribe it as a World Heritage Site in 1994, made no reference to the mountains' sacredness for the Banyarwenzururu people despite this being well known, both locally and internationally. A process to negotiate access by local communities to various natural resources was undertaken in the mid-1990s and these continue today. Access to cultural and sacred sites, however, was not included in these negotiations and local communities remained indifferent to the implementation of these agreements (Masereka, 1996). A cultural analysis carried out by a project and park team identified the mountains' sacred values and park authorities quickly agreed to recognise these in the park's operational plans and to negotiate access to specific sacred and cultural sites. The grave of Isaya Mukirania, the first king of the Banyarwenzururu, selected by the clan elders in 1963 as an act of defiance against the Ugandan government and a statement of intent to form a nation has, since his death in 1966, been an important site for the Banyarwenzururu. King Isaya is remembered as the founder of the nation and his grave was visited clandestinely despite the dissolution of the kingship and following the establishment of the park within which it lies. The king's shrine was rehabilitated with project support and a museum constructed outside the park in 2010. An annual pilgrimage and festival to commemorate the king was formally agreed, allowing celebrations to be made openly rather than stealthily. Plans for access to other sites were negotiated over the next five years with local guardians of the sites and their communities, a process that still continues.

Building on the positive relations established by these activities and the growing trust between park staff and the leadership of the *Obusinga Bwa Rwenzururu* (the court of the king), Ridge Leaders (the guardians of sacred sites associated with ridge communities) work together with park staff to manage access to spiritual zones within the park that loosely conform to different ecological zones, control the harvesting of natural resources by employing traditional rules, and regulate access to sacred sites (Infield and Mugisha, 2013). The meaningful engagement between communities, cultural institutions and the park authorities has been one of the most successful interventions of the programme.

Political dimensions of cultural approaches were also evident in the Rwenzori initiative. Government dismantled the Banyarwenzururu kingship in 1996 and blocked the king's return until 2008. The king was the head of the system of cultural governance of the mountains. Starting in 2006 the project worked with local leaders to establish an association to champion integration of cultural values into the park. This, however, was perceived as undermining efforts to secure the return of the kingship, and when government recognised King Charles Wesley and the royal institutions in 2009, the project came under considerable pressure to abandon its partner and work only through the institutions of the kingship. Though initially strained, this partnership proved effective and the project was able to broker a relationship between the kingship and the park authorities. It remains to be seen how this success will be affected by the fighting that broke out between followers of the king and the government in 2016, which led to over 150 deaths.

Batwa values, cultural access and tourist experiences – 2010 to 2015

The UWA recognised that relationships with Batwa communities living on the periphery of Bwindi, Mgahinga and Semuliki national parks were problematic, with park managers wrongly blaming them for poaching in the parks (Twinamatsiko et al., 2014). Little if any progress had been made on meeting international expectations on the rights and roles of indigenous peoples in the management of parks, and there was broad acceptance outside UWA that Batwa communities had been wrongly treated by protected area management interventions, and that these wrongs and their impacts had not been properly addressed. Activities were designed following consultations with Batwa communities, their civil society supporters and park managers, and an assessment of the impact of numerous interventions to improve the wellbeing of the Batwa. The Batwa Forest Values Project was funded in 2012 by the Darwin Initiative to strengthen Batwa communications with the park and local government authorities, to identify skills and knowledge the Batwa could bring to park management and other local enterprises, and to negotiate access for Batwa to cultural sites and park resources.

Access was considered central for Batwa to retain cultural values and practices that represented critical connections to the forest. Despite expressing interest in validating the special relationship between Batwa and the forests, progress on agreeing access to sites for specified cultural purposes was limited. The park authorities found it difficult to grant Batwa access to the parks, continuing to adhere to the principle backed by legislation of excluding the people's presence and activities within the parks. Walking trails have been designed in three parks in which tourists are guided into the parks by Batwa who interpret the forest and their traditional practices, demonstrate hunting and gathering skills, and perform their songs and dances. In all three cases these enterprises are controlled by park management, Batwa benefit materially and culturally to only a limited extent, and the guides are largely relegated to the role of entertainers. Regrettably, UWA has also misidentified these trails as providing Batwa access to their cultural sites within the parks, and there has been limited progress in agreeing access for Batwa to enjoy their cultural practices. Continued negotiations are required to give meaningful recognition to the value of Batwa knowledge of the parks and their forests, their traditional practices, or the importance of strengthening and retaining these values and integrating them into the management of the parks.

Musambwa, the Spirit Island – 2010 to 2015

Musambwa, an island of no more than ten hectares located on the western edge of Lake Victoria, is sacred to the inhabitants of the nearby mainland who recognise numerous sites of spiritual importance on the mainland as well as sites on Musambwa and within the lake. Musambwa is a key part of this sacred network, falling under the authority of members of the Leopard Clan. A cave on the island is the site of rituals and offerings, but the entire island is considered sacred and governed by denizen spirits through spiritual leaders under a set of rules and prohibitions. Perhaps the most important rule is that no living creature on the island should be harmed, which extends to birds, snakes and even flies. The protection of living creatures did not prevent, however, the collection of bird eggs, though rules did regulate the level of collection. Nor did it protect fish as the island functions as a fish-landing site, though rules did relate to fishing activities and offerings were made to the gods of the lake. The other key prohibition prevented women from overnighting on the island, though the intention was to prevent sexual intercourse happening on the island.

Musambwa is Africa's most important breeding site for grey-headed gulls (*Larus cirrocephalus*) (http://natureuganda.org/MusambwaIslands ConservationProjectNatureUganda.html) and supports 16% of the species' global population (https://rsis.ramsar.org/ris/1641). Previously, however, traditional control over egg harvesting had failed, and the breeding population fell to less than 100 pairs by 1990 (Bakamwesiga, 1999). In 2000, *Nature*Uganda, a national conservation organisation, partnered with a local community organisation, the Musambwa Island Joint Conservation Organisation (MIJCO), to protect the island's bird colonies. In return for developing basic sanitation facilities on the crowded island, *Nature*Uganda negotiated the re-imposition of traditional controls on egg collection; successfully arguing that failure of cultural institutions not only threatened the birds, but also the community. Cultural leaders enforced a total ban on egg collection and, within a decade, the island's gulls had increased to over 100,000 with large numbers of other water birds also present (Rakai District, 2013).

Ongoing activities on the island focus attention on the role of the guardians of the island's sacred values. They were assisted to develop a plan for the island that focused on regulating the behaviour of fishermen under cultural institutions. Project support to improve livelihoods and social infrastructure empowers the guardians of the islands' cultural values, allowing them to insist on respect for cultural values and norms, even from the many fishermen from other ethnic groups.

An important difference between activities on Musambwa to those at other sites under the cultural values programme was that the island was a community-conserved site, even if traditional institutions were failing, rather than a formal protected area. This helped external interests in conservation to define and describe synergies with local interests. That the island was administered by local government, rather than by UWA, provided a more open operating environment, less constrained by legislation and more open to recognising cultural interests and the concept of local management. This chapter has focused largely on UWA-controlled areas. The UWA has found it difficult to compromise its institutional culture of control to achieve strengthened relations with communities based on new forms of partnership. Other government bodies responsible for natural resources and lands, including the National Forest Authority and the Wetlands Management Department, show similar inflexibility, do not have strong community programmes, and have not engaged with cultural approaches. This contrasts strongly with the flexibility of the Rakai District government and their acceptance of a cultural perspective on conservation.

Discussion and conclusions

The Culture, Values and Conservation Project that began in 2005 was largely without precedent within African conservation in terms of its dedicated focus on cultural values approaches. As such, it had few examples to refer to, scant lessons and experience to draw on for design or implementation, and little to compare its successes or failures with. This suggests, however, that the lessons from the 12-year initiative may be of interest to other initiatives setting out to cover the same or similar ground.

Early successes of the project were not institutionalised within UWA and community institutions established to champion cultural values have weakened. If meaningful dialogues cannot be maintained, and without for-malised support, the primary achievements made at park level may not be sustained. The guidelines prepared together with park managers describing best practice in cultural values approaches and proposals for policy and practice have yet to be endorsed by the UWA, and there is little indication of an institutional widening out of the approach to other parks and protected areas or other areas of policy. In retrospect it seems that this critical require-ment for sustainability of cultural values interventions received insufficient attention. The interest and commitment of individuals who worked with the project has, however, seen cultural values approaches carried between parks as staff are transferred. The project's primary achievements, however, have been made at park level, but without formalised and documented support these are not secure.

A key objective of the pilot project, carried across the subsequent phases of the programme, was to facilitate the modification of both general and operational park management plans to integrate cultural as well as biodi-versity and economic values. This was considered important to re-defining the values of the parks and, therefore, justifications for protecting them, as well as for building practical activities into the day-to-day actions of park staff. That this has been largely successful, with management plans revised in all the project-supported parks, provides some evidence of institutional buy-in to the concept that parks can and should reflect multiple value sets. However, support has remained largely rhetorical and, outside the project context, few practical actions to reflect cultural values have been designed or implemented.

Adopting a cultural values approach is especially effective at the local level because it necessitates engaging with the specifics of local culture. Local leaders tended to be strongly interested in and excited by the cul-tural approach. Despite the trend in Uganda, as elsewhere, to marginalise traditional culture and beliefs, especially in the context of growing religi-osity centred on Christianity and Islam, there was broad recognition of the difference between a cultural values approach and integrated conservation and development approaches to which they had been exposed. As noted by one community member living in the Rwenzori Mountains, 'Finally you are talking to us about things that really matter to us!' A depth of inter-est in traditional relations to place and nature exists, and many members of communities who participated in project activities saw opportunities for the cultural approach to give recognition to these. Staff of the parks and members of local communities recognised that new opportunities for working together had been generated by the cultural values approach. Establishing dialogues over cultural values and traditional interests in a place, resource or practice, promoted a genuine two-way engagement that had not been apparent in earlier discussions and processes for man-aging resource access. The previous establishment of resource access zones allowed park authorities to remain dominant in discussions as the recognised and empowered technocrats charged with resource management. Discussing the values of local communities required a more level playing field and led to a more balanced and open process. Positive changes in attitudes and relationships resulted.

Not all values can be easily integrated into conservation initiatives and protected areas. Some difficulties relate to the actual interference between cultural interests and conservation needs. For example, high levels of unregulated human presence threaten the health of mountain gorillas as a result of disease transmission. Most difficulties, however, result from cultural conflicts and differences in worldviews that could, in theory, be accommodated. They can, however, be hard to resolve in practice. The refusal of UWA to agree to the grazing of 'cultural cows' in Lake Mburo is a good example of a cultural conflict. The anathema of the institution and individual wardens to cows in parks is based on UWA's institutional culture, which informs unfounded beliefs about the negative impacts of cattle grazing on biodiversity and conceptions of 'naturalness' and prevents a more synergistic approach (Infield, 2002). Where cultural demands of communities were *considered* to conflict with conservation objectives, conservation objectives trumped cultural interests. This was as much the case where there was no real conflict, for example in allowing Batwa to access the forest for ceremonies of dance and song, as it was at Lake Mburo where grazing of cattle might be seen to compromise biodiversity conservation, despite data to the contrary (Infield, 2002). Where practices that communities might consider to be cultural, hunting primates for example, were clearly going to conflict with UWA management perspectives and culture, these were not even tabled for discussion. It was preferable and pragmatic to make progress on integrating cultural practices and values where compromises were possible, than to block the possibility of progress by demanding things that would not be accepted by the authorities.

Despite the potential for synergies between different cultural interests in retaining protected sites or species, and for protected areas to reflect a number of values simultaneously with a degree of compromise, this would require a more open attitude than currently exists within UWA. Despite its willingness to share resources and revenues, there has long been resistance to sharing power. This has made progress in park governance difficult and also, therefore, the mainstreaming of a cultural values approach. The impact has been less acute for community conservation initiatives based on sharing economic resources, as it is easier for UWA to retain control over these and to remain the sole authority over its parks. Sharing the determination of the meaning of its parks would be a much greater and therefore threatening concession requiring true sharing of power over the parks.

The cases presented above referenced cultural links between communities and nature mediated through traditional practices and institutions, histories of occupation and use of lands, historical and mythical associations with places, sites and natural resources, community and individual identity, and rituals, ceremonies and sacredness. These and others provide the potential for integration into conservation initiatives. Notwithstanding the difficulties encountered by the Culture, Values and Conservation Programme, its success in improving relations at park level by identifying and defusing cultural conflicts, the level of engagement promoted between park staff and local communities on issues of particular significance and meaning to communities, and the revision of management plans and the planning process to pay attention to local cultural values were important achievements that offer lessons for conservation elsewhere.

References

Adams, S.J. and McShane, O.T. (1992) *The Myth of Wild Africa: conservation without illusion*, University of California Press, Berkeley and Los Angeles, CA, USA.

Adams, W.K., Aveling, R., Brockington, D., Dickson, B., Elliot, J., Hutton, J., Roe, D., Vira, B. and Wolmer W. (2004) 'Biodiversity conservation and the eradication of poverty', *Science*, vol. 306, no. 5699, pp. 1146–1148.

Ashley, C. and Carney, D. (1999) *Sustainable Livelihoods: lessons from early experience*, Department for International Development, London, UK.

Bakamwesiga, H. (1999) 'The distribution, diversity and status of species in Sango Bay area', unpublished MSc thesis in Environment Management, Makerere University, Kampala, Uganda.

Berkes, F., Colding, J. and Folke, C. (2000) 'Rediscovery of traditional ecological knowledge as adaptive management', *Ecological Applications*, vol. 10, no. 5, pp. 1251–1262.

Chan, K.M.A., Guerry, A.D., Balvanera, P., Klain, S., Satterfield, T., Basurto, X., Bostrom, A., Chuenpagdee, R., Gould, R., Halpern, B.S., Levine, J., Norton, B., Ruckelshaus, M., Russell, R. and Tam, J. (2012) 'Where are cultural and social in ecosystem services? A framework for constructive engagement', *Bioscience*, vol. 62, no. 8, pp. 744–756.

Chan, K.M.A., Balvanera, P., Benessaiah, K., Chapman, M., Díaz, S., Gómez-Baggethun, E., Gould, R., Hannahs, N., Jax, K., Klain, S., Luck, G.W., Martín-López, B., Muraca, B., Norton, B., Ott, K., Pascual, U., Satterfield, T., Tadaki, M., Taggart, J. and Turner, N. (2016) 'Opinion: why protect nature? Rethinking values and the environment', *Proceedings of the National Academy of Sciences of the United States of America*, vol. 113, no. 6, pp. 1462–1465, doi:10.1073/pnas.1525002113.

Church, A., Burgess, J. and Ravenscroft, N. (2011) 'Chapter 16 – Cultural Services', in *The UK National Ecosystem Assessment Technical Report*, UK National Ecosystem Assessment, UNEP-WCMC, Cambridge, UK, http://uknea.unep-wcmc.org.

Douglas-Hamilton, I.R., Malpas, E., Edroma, P., Holt, G., Ajok, L. and Weyerhaeuser, R. (1980) *Elephant and Wildlife Survey, Uganda*, Report to WWF, Uganda Institute of Ecology, Uganda.

Dowie, M. (2009) *Conservation Refugees*, MIT Press, Cambridge, USA.

Fauna & Flora International (FFI) (2005) *Culture, Values and Conservation: using local cultural values to build support for protected areas in Uganda*, a proposal from the Africa Programme of Fauna & Flora International, Cambridge, UK.

Gorenflo, L.J., Romaine, S., Mittermeier, R.A. and Walker-Painemilla, K. (2012) 'Co-occurrence of linguistic and biological diversity in biodiversity hotspots and high biodiversity wilderness areas', *Proceedings of the National Academy of Sciences of the United States of America*, vol. 109, no. 21, pp. 8032–8037.

Gray, C.L., Hill, S.L.L., Newbold, T., Hudson, L.N., Börger, L., Contu, S., Hoskins, A.J., Ferrier, S., Purvis, A. and Scharlemann, J.P.W. (2016) 'Local biodiversity is higher inside than outside terrestrial protected areas worldwide', *Nature Communications*, vol. 7, no. 12306, doi:10.1038/ncomms12306.

Guard, M. (1991) 'The interactions between domestic animals and wild ungulates in Lake Mburo National Park, Uganda: a question of competition or complementarity?', MSc thesis, Makerere University, Kampala, Uganda.

Hulme, D. and Murphree, M. (2001) *African Wildlife and Livelihoods; the promise and performance of community conservation*, James Currey, Oxford, UK, p. 336.

Infield, M. (2001) 'Cultural values: a forgotten strategy for building community support for protected areas in Africa', *Conservation Biology*, vol. 15, no. 3, pp. 800–802.

Infield, M. (2002) 'The culture of conservation: exclusive landscapes, beautiful cows and conflict over Lake Mburo National Park, Uganda', PhD thesis, University of East Anglia, Norwich, UK.

Infield, M., Entwistle, A., Anthem, H., Mugisha, A. and Phillips, K. (2017) 'Reflections on cultural values approaches to conservation: lessons from 20 years of implementation', *Oryx*, vol. 52, no. 2, pp. 1–11, doi: 10.1017/S0030605317000928.

Infield, M. and Mugisha, A. (2013) 'Sacred sites and conservation of the Rwenzori Mountains in Uganda', *Oryx*, vol. 47, no. 1, pp. 13–18.

Infield, M. and Namara, A. (2001) 'Community attitudes and behaviour towards conservation: an assessment of a community conservation program around Lake Mburo National Park, Uganda', *Oryx*, vol. 35, no. 1, pp. 48–60.

Infield, M., Namara, A. and Marquardt, M. (1993) *The Socio Economy, Natural Resource Use, and Attitudes Towards the Park of Communities Living In and Around Lake Mburo National Park: Report of a Rapid Rural Appraisal*. Research Paper 2, Access to Land and other Natural Resources in Uganda, Research and Policy Development Project, Wisconsin Land Tenure Centre/Makerere Institute of Social Research, Kampala, Uganda.

Jax, K., Barton, D.N., Chan, K.M.A., de Groot, R., Doyle, U., Eser, U., Görg, C., Gómez-Baggethun, E., Griewald, Y., Haber, W., Haines-Young, R., Heink, U., Jahn, T., Joosten, H., Kerschbaumer, L., Korn, H., Luck, G.W., Matzdorf, B., Muraca, B., Neßhöver, C., Norton, B., Ott, K., Potschin, M., Rauschmayer, F., von Haaren, C. and Wichmann, S. (2013) 'Ecosystem services and ethics', *Ecological Economics*, vol. 93, pp. 168–260.

Loh, J. and Harmon, D. (2005) 'A global index of biocultural diversity', *Ecological Indicators*, vol 5, no. 3, pp. 231–241.

Maffi, L. and Woodley, E. (2010) *Biocultural Diversity Conservation: a Global Sourcebook*, Earthscan, London, UK.

Manspeizer, I. (2004) 'Ideas, history and continuity in the practice of power: the case of wildlife management in Zambia', *Policy Matters: History, Culture & Conservation*, Issue 13, IUCN, pp. 116–125.

Masereka, A.J. (1996) 'The role of traditional knowledge in the conservation of the Rwenzori mountains' in H. Osmaston, J. Tukahirwa, C. Basalirwa and J. Nyakana (eds) *The Rwenzori Mountains National Park*, Department of Geography, Makerere University, Kampala, Uganda.

McNeely, J.A. and Miller, K.R. (1985) 'National parks, conservation, and development: the role of protected areas in sustaining society', Proceedings of the World Congress on National Parks, Bali, Indonesia, 11–12 October 1982. IUCN, Gland, Switzerland, p. 825.

Posey, D.A. (1999) *Cultural and Spiritual Values of Biodiversity*, UNEP, Intermediate Technology Publications, London, UK.

Rakai District (2013) *Musambwa Islands General Management Plan: 2013–2018*, Rakai District, Uganda.

Sen, A. (2004) 'How does culture matter?' in V. Rao and M. Walton (eds) *Culture and Public Action*, Stanford University Press, Stanford, CA, USA.

Twinamatsiko, M., Baker, J., Harrison, M., Shirkhorshidi, M., Bitariho, R., Wieland, M., Asuma, S., Milner-Gulland, E.J., Franks, P. and Roe, D. (2014) *Linking Conservation, Equity and Poverty Alleviation: understanding profiles and motivations of resource users and local perceptions of governance at Bwindi Impenetrable National Park, Uganda*, IIED Research Report, International Institute of Environment and Development, London, UK, http://pubs.iied.org/14630IIED, p.103.

Wells, M., Brandon, K. and Hannah, L. (1992) *People and Parks: linking protected area management with local communities*, World Bank/WWF/USAID, Washington, DC, USA.

West, P., Igoe, J. and Brockington, D. (2006) 'Parks and peoples: the social impact of protected areas', *Annual Review of Anthropology*, vol. 35, pp. 251–277, doi: 10.1146/annurev.anthro.35.081705.123308.

Part IV

Cross-sectoral dynamics and their links to conservation and development

10 Conservation and agriculture

Finding an optimal balance?

Katy Jeary, Matt Kandel, Giuliano Martiniello, and Ronald Twongyirwe

Introduction

Agriculture, conservation and development have a complex, interdependent relationship. Moreover, poverty, food insecurity and a history of violent intra-state and inter-communal conflict (the latter often being rooted in attempts to control land and resources) pose critical threats to sustainable development. The vast majority of people in the country base their livelihoods around agriculture. Approximately a quarter of Uganda's GDP comes from agriculture while some 70% of households obtain their livelihoods from small-scale farming (Deloitte, 2016). Agriculture as an industry is dominated by smallholder subsistence farmers, with around 75% of all agricultural production originating on small-scale farms (UNDP, 2013). Given the outsized significance of agriculture to livelihoods in Uganda, increasing agricultural productivity, and, as a result, incomes, could provide a significant development opportunity (UBOS, 2014).

Commercial agricultural expansion threatens small-scale farming; additionally, it poses a risk to the conservation of biodiversity and natural habitats, resources upon which virtually all rural communities are reliant. Yet both government and global institutions recommend, in seeking inclusive growth, a shift from subsistence farming to commercial agriculture. How to pursue the goal of a thriving agricultural sector without damaging valuable natural resources or the wealth of biodiversity found in Uganda is the challenge at the heart of this chapter. We make the case that the current strategy for agricultural modernisation – specifically, the commercialisation of agricultural production – will not only continue to threaten conservation efforts and overall productivity, but will also make it harder for small-scale farmers to create sustainable livelihoods.

The chapter begins by discussing the highly dynamic interrelationship between agriculture and the environment. The second section investigates reasons for considering these competing land uses jointly. In the final section we highlight the approaches, along with their associated theories of change, which aim to minimise the trade-offs between agriculture and conservation. In doing so we ask the question: how can the government design and enact policies that integrate the need for increasing agricultural productivity (and raising smallholder incomes) while not undermining conservation demands?

The impact of agriculture on the environment

Agriculture is a well-known driver of the conversion of natural habitats, but it also impacts biodiversity and the provision of ecosystem services on-farm and in the wider landscape (Power, 2010; Cardinale et al., 2012). So while initial disturbance may set in motion a cascade of extinctions and co-extinctions along the trophic chain, the impacts of farming on conservation go beyond those at the point of production. Converting uncultivated land into land for farming can fragment or isolate habitats; change connectivity patterns, biotic and abiotic environment; and stimulate gene flow from domesticated varieties to wild species (Perrings et al., 2006; Fischer and Lindenmayer, 2007). Changes to hydrological and biogeochemical cycles, which lead to nutrient runoff, soil leaching, and the sedimentation of waterways, may result in changes to species compositions in more distant locations (Pimentel, 1995; Farella et al., 2001; Diaz and Rosenberg, 2008).

In Uganda the influence agriculture has had on the landscape goes back some 3,000 years when palynological research suggests crops were first introduced (Hamilton et al., 2016). When farming communities began practicing slash and burn agriculture, the floristic composition of landscapes was considerably altered. In particular, certain valued species of plants were encouraged while areas cleared for agriculture allowed species adapted to fast establishment to flourish.

Agriculture continues to exert an impact on the environment in contemporary Uganda. For example, the Lake Mburo–Lake Nakivale wetland system, which supports such threatened species of birds as the papyrus yellow warbler (*Chloropeta gracilirastris*), red faced barbet (*Lybius rubrifacecies*), papyrus gondlek (*Laniarus mufumbiri*) and shoebill (*Balaeniceps rex*), has been rapidly altered due to the shift over the past two decades from semi-nomadic pastoralism to permanent subsistence crop farming (Kaggwa et al., 2009; Mugisha, 2011; Kamukasa and Bintoora, 2014). The clearing of vegetation and opening up of land for agriculture has exposed the soils and led to degradation and siltation of the wetlands. Apart from the associated loss of wildlife as the wetlands are converted to agriculture, important local resources such as fish, medicinal herbs, and handcraft and building materials are being lost alongside vital ecosystem services. Complex factors have driven the establishment of these cropping systems, which includes increased human settlement by Tutsi pastoralists who were driven from Rwanda due to tribal and ethnic conflict. This also includes crop growing by Hutu and other refugees, all of whom were encouraged by the Ugandan government to become reliant on their own farming as opposed to food relief (Mundia and Murayama, 2009). A number of regions in Uganda have also seen the replacement of nomadic forms of farming with settled crop farmers. In Teso farming systems in eastern Uganda, for example, land under cultivation between 1960 and 2001 increased from 6% to 78% and communal grazing lands have all but been replaced with static cropping systems (Ebanyat et al., 2010).

The intensification of agriculture can cause declines in crop genetic diversity, farm birds, natural enemies and soil biota from farm environments. These are all critical for soil fertility, pollination and natural pest control, and for the ongoing resilience of production (Perrings et al., 2006; Barthel et al., 2013). Home gardens, where traditionally a diversity of indigenous, medicinal and food crops are grown, were found to be declining in diversity in a commercial monoculture sugarcane cultivation land matrix in eastern Uganda (Mwavu et al., 2016). In particular, crops such as cowpeas, soya beans, bambara groundnuts, finger millet, cotton, aerial yams and oysternut were being lost. This shift is thought to be being driven by the reduction in number and size of home gardens as commercial agriculture and cash cropping expands.

Today forest and wetland habitats in Uganda as well as on-farm agricultural biodiversity are under threat from settlement and changing farming practices. This latter point pertains to both small-scale and commercial agricultural farming (van Soesbergen et al., 2017). Many biodiverse areas in Uganda are landscapes characterised by protected areas that are surrounded by farms, and, as such, conserving habitats and biodiversity can no longer be carried out effectively without considering the impact of farming (Wittemyer et al., 2008). Indeed much of Uganda's forest has been replaced with intensive agriculture. During the period 1990 to 2005, 26.3% of the remaining forest cover was cleared (1.3 million ha per year) (Nabanoga et al., 2010). The Joint Water and Environment Sector's 2017 report put forest coverage in Uganda at 9%, a 2% drop from 2015 (MoWE, 2017). Analysed at a smaller scale around Budongo Forest Reserve, the link between commercial agricultural expansion and forest clearance is evident (Box 10.1).

Box 10.1   Sugarcane and forest cover in Budongo

Analysis of multi-spectral Landsat imagery over the Budongo area (in western Uganda) for the period 1985 to 2014 shows that the protection of Budongo forest has remained remarkably successful, while virtually all forests located outside the protected estate were cleared in this period (Twongyirwe et al., 2015). The rate of forest loss was very high (approximately 3.3% per annum), and was more rapid after 1995 following the reopening of Kinyara Sugar Works, before which production had ceased during the rule of Idi Amin. The data further indicate that natural forest erosion outside the protected estate has been mostly driven by the aggressive expansion of commercial sugarcane

(continued)

192   *Katy Jeary et al.*

(continued)

production. This started around an initial nucleus near Kibwona and continued to spread outwards, resulting in the covering of nearly the entire southern section of the Budongo region (Figure 10.1). There is spatial evidence of commercial farm expansion over small-scale farmlands (which may have implications for food security in the region).

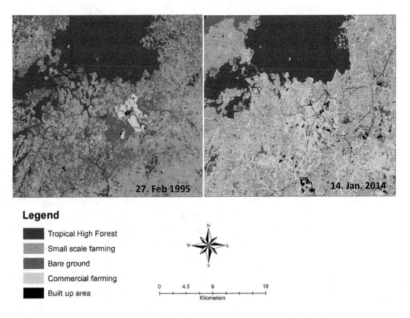

Figure 10.1 Spatial patterns of land uses/vegetation in the Budongo region.

The expansion of sugarcane is mostly driven by a large sugar company in the region, Kinyara Sugar Works Limited, which has reached a franchise-based arrangement with outgrowers. The company owns a core sugar estate that is seen as insufficient to produce adequate raw material for the factory. The company seeks outgrowers (signing five- to six-year supplier agreements with them) and provides them with inputs. These associated costs are later recovered after the sale of sugarcane to the company.

Aside from direct impacts on the environment such as forest clearance, the thriving sugar industry has contributed to the growth of small towns around Budongo. The sugar industry has also facilitated increased migration into the area for casual jobs in the industry, both of which have an implication for the supply and availability of natural resources (Mwavu and Witkowski, 2008; Twongyirwe, 2015; Twongyirwe et al., 2017).

The effects of the sugar bonanza in some parts of the country are evident in the region of Busoga where the exponential expansion of sugarcane mono-cropping has developed to the detriment of other indigenous forms of resources and land use. The region, which was previously known as the bread basket of the country (it even used to export its maize surplus to countries such as Somalia and Sudan [Sorensen, 1996]), has now been turned into a veritable sugar belt where various contracts are signed between millers (new and old) and a rapidly increasing number of socially stratified outgrowers. Fuelled by sugarcane's fungibility – i.e., the possibility of using cane for multiple end products (beside refined sugar) such as ethanol and green electricity – the region is undergoing a significant landscape and eco-systemic transformation, which has been driven by intensified capitalist agro-extractive logics. This has resulted in widespread deforestation, soil fertility deterioration, the pollution of existing streams, and the degradation of water sources from Lake Victoria, all of which have made pre-existing livelihood strategies untenable (Martiniello, 2017).

Expansion in sugar production in Uganda also has links to one of the most politically challenging and globally publicised issues across Africa over the last decade: large-scale land acquisitions. Schoneveld's (2014) study analyses the vast amount of land that countries in sub-Saharan Africa have made available for agricultural investment between 2005 and 2013, although it should be noted that methodologies of data gathering in this regard are highly contested (Edelman, 2013; Oya, 2013). However, while countries such as Ethiopia, Mozambique, and Ghana lead the way with respect to land alienation for agricultural investment (over 2,000,000 hectares each), Uganda ranks low relative to other countries in Africa (less than 200,000 hectares).

Large-scale land acquisitions in Uganda have been facilitated by processes of agricultural restructuring over the last couple of decades through the Poverty Eradication Programmes (1997/98–2008/09) and the Plan for Modernisation of Agriculture (2001–2009), which supported enterprise development, agricultural zoning, and large-scale agriculture (Martiniello, 2015a). In 2007, for example, Yoweri Museveni allocated one third of Mabira rainforest to the Sugar Corporation of Uganda Limited (SCOUL) to turn it into a large-scale sugarcane plantation. Yet the Mabira Forest Crusade mobilised environmental advocacy groups, civil society institutions, and community-based organisations, which eventually succeeded in paralysing the implementation of the proposed project by questioning its environmental viability and social desirability despite some opportunistic interests hidden behind the protests (Honig, 2014). If their efforts had failed, the conversion of such a large portion of rainforest to intensive cash cropping would have directly reduced biodiversity and no doubt had indirect effects on the wider environment. The particularly vigorous push for sugarcane cultivation by the Ugandan government in the last years was meant to capture the market opportunities of mounting global sugar prices. This was fuelled by the idea – often expressed by the President himself in various public speeches – that 'every sugar plantation is an oil field' (Child, 2009).

Conservation agencies such as the National Forestry Authority (NFA) have also been linked to attempts to sell or lease out land for commercial agricultural development. For instance, land in the Pian-Upe reserve was offered up in 2002 to Libyan investors (Rugadya and Kamusiime, 2013). The Libyan investment team sought to utilise the land for a commercial agricultural venture, although this was ultimately dropped in the face of fierce resistance by local political leaders and communities. In September of 2017, the Kibale District chairperson accused the NFA of attempting to lease out plots of forest land to individual investors interested in commercial tree farming (*Daily Monitor*, 2017). The NFA has also allowed for natural resource extraction in conservation areas, including in Karamoja where Tororo Cement Company harvests limestone that is then processed further south in Tororo (Rugadya and Kamusiime, 2013).

These examples show that the agricultural industry and its focus on production is a major threat to forest and other habitats. However, the relationship between agriculture and conservation is not one-sided; conservation has also posed a threat to the livelihoods of small-scale farmers, both in the past and more recently. We explore the implications of this development in the following section.

The impact of conservation on agriculture

The 1900 Buganda Agreement, which allocated 9,000 square miles to 'tribal' chiefs, was instrumental in shaping the landscape and favouring certain agricultural systems. Peasants of Buganda and eastern provinces were mobilised, and in some cases coerced, to increase coffee and cotton production as a means to pay colonial taxes and other duties and expand the exports towards European markets (van Zwanenberg and King, 1975, p. 60). Yet the Buganda agreement also instituted a system of protected areas which brought 1,500 square miles of forests under the control of the British Uganda Administration (Himmelfarb, 2006; see also Banana et al., this volume, Chapter 2). This agreement was accompanied by various Orders-in-Council that applied to East Africa as a whole and later to the Uganda Protectorate.

Throughout subsequent agreements in the Toro, Ankole and Bunyoro regions the colonial government assumed control of 'all forest and waste and uncultivated land' encompassing many thousands of square miles (Webster and Osmaston, 2003, p. 125). Colonial land laws reclassified native land as colonial land. Enclosures were justified on the assumption that the absence of individualised and private forms of land tenure were synonymous with vacancy, despite long histories of articulated systems of land management, access and use by African populations (Martiniello, 2015b). Officials throughout British colonial territories enforced highly protectionist and exclusionary policies based on eco-centric views of human change. They considered traditional patterns of land use to be detrimental to protected ecosystems, erroneously assuming that areas designated for conservation existed in isolation from human activities rather than being produced by them, i.e., anthropogenic (Himmelfarb, 2006).

Neumann (1998) argues that the creation of national parks was one component of the wider process of colonial appropriation of land and natural resources as well as a symbolic legitimisation of that process. Forest conservation was imposed through legal and physical violence, effectively divorcing the local population from their means of production and curtailing indigenous use of forest resources (Cavanagh and Himmelfarb, 2015). As Cavanagh and Himmelfarb have argued in the case of Mount Elgon, the enclosure of common resources was strictly tied to mutually reinforcing processes of colonial state formation and primitive accumulation to ensure the sustainability of the region's water-dependent coffee industry and curtail non-taxable autonomous livelihood strategies (2015, pp. 69–70).

Such control over land has led to numerous violent conflicts, many of which have significantly impacted the agricultural sector. These conflicts, which include multiple insurgencies and large-scale cattle raiding, have particularly impacted northern Uganda. One of the most important agrarian questions in northern Uganda pertains to the central government's initiative to convert the historically transhumant pastoralist Karamojong into small-scale farmers (Gray et al., 2002; Caravani, 2016) (Box 10.2).

Box 10.2   Karamoja

The conversion – or 'sedentarisation' – plan in Karamjoa came on the heels of the largely successful state-led disarmament programme in the mid to late-2000s. The programme has been central to state efforts to assert territorial control over Karamoja; it also formed the basis for more substantive economic incorporation of the sub-region into Uganda (Kandel, 2018). While almost all of the Karamojong sub-groups historically practiced a degree of small-scale cultivation (sorghum has long served as the primary cereal crop), this was combined with livestock husbandry and non-static cropping systems. Not only is Karamoja the most arid region in Uganda (Matete and BakamaNume, 2011), but the 2015/2016 drought has highlighted the risks of the sedentarisation policy. Food insecurity remains a major problem in Karamoja and it has been exacerbated by poor harvests. This is why the government policy of preventing Karamojong from farming in the Pian-Upe Game Reserve and Bokora Wildlife Reserve (ostensibly for conservation purposes) appears highly contradictory to local residents.

As Rugadya and Kamusiime (2013) underscore, the processes of 'gazetting' and 'degazetting' – or the incorporation and release of land as protected areas for conservation – in Karamoja has a very long history.

(continued)

196   *Katy Jeary et al.*

(continued)

It is also complicated by the fact that much of the land protected for conservation consists of some of the most fertile areas of Karamoja. This includes the Bokora and Pian-Upe reserves in southern Karamoja, but also parts of Kidepo Valley National Park in the north. While wildlife authorities long permitted pastoralists to graze animals on reserve land in Karamoja, the authorities consider agricultural activities to pose a direct threat to the ecosystem (Rugayda and Kamusiime, 2013). Napak District Chairperson, Lomonyang Robert, underlined the significance of this point in 2013 when he noted that one of the most fertile stretches of land in Napak – locally known as the 'green belt' – overlaps with the Bokora Wildlife Reserve, making cultivation there illegal (Interview 2012). Teso residents from sub-counties bordering Karamoja, also seeking to access the green belt for cultivation purposes, similarly accuse the Uganda Wildlife Authority (UWA) of evicting them from land on the grounds that it was reserve land (Kandel, 2016).

Rugadya and Kamusiime (2013) note that in Karamoja any knowledge of degazettement often remains exclusive to 'a small elite, a number of whom have used it for political ends and self-aggrandizement' (59). It is not uncommon for elites with direct access to government resources to exploit their networks in order to acquire large landholdings and develop commercial agricultural ventures. Conservation, therefore, does not purely fall under the scope of policy; on the contrary, it is inherently political, and the ways in which some well-connected elites abuse their positions sows distrust amongst small-scale farmers towards government conservation efforts. Their logic is simple: smallholders also seek their just desserts, and if elites are allowed to bend or circumnavigate conservation laws, then what about them – especially since they are not seeking to become rich but to simply support sustainable livelihoods?

Rural farmers have to bear the costs of conservation measures, such as exclusion from land and resources as well as the costs from commercial agricultural expansion, when they are unable to take advantage of market opportunities (Fairhead, Leach, and Scoones, 2012). Even where collaborative management agreements exist between local communities surrounding protected areas and management authorities they do not always reimburse those who are most disadvantaged and can be used as a bargaining chip in seeking compliance (Vedeld et al., 2016). Where small-scale farming is promoted as a livelihood alternative to pastoralism, encroachment onto conservation land seems virtually inevitable. While certain political and economic dynamics in Karamoja are particular to the sub-region, tensions between conservation and agriculture are increasingly surfacing across Uganda. This holds true in both UWA- and NFA-protected areas. Recent resistance by cultivators to NFA authority over forests has occurred in Kibaale in western Uganda, in Amuru in northern Uganda (Martiniello, 2015b) and along the slopes of Mt Elgon in the east. In the case of the latter, Cavanagh and Benjaminsen (2015) document 'the range of tactics that rural communities use to circumvent laws and regulation that criminalize agricultural production, and to ensure their own food security' (p. 735). They refer to resistance through cultivation as 'guerrilla agriculture', a tribute to the risks that residents take in their efforts to circumvent state authority and attempt to create viable agrarian livelihoods.

The tensions conservation activities and agricultural development can incite, particularly when carried out in isolation, are evident in Uganda and, despite agriculture's long history of shaping the national landscape, the growth of commercial farming we are seeing today poses a direct threat to valuable biodiversity, habitats, food production, and livelihoods. We argue that conservation and agriculture should be considered jointly in order to minimise the trade-offs between the two. They should be managed in concert because land is scarce and landscapes must serve multiple purposes. But to what extent have they been considered jointly, in Uganda and more broadly?

Theories of change: minimising the trade-offs between agriculture and conservation

Few examples of on-the-ground projects exist with regard to trying to meet both conservation and agricultural objectives in Uganda. This is perhaps because these sectors have typically been separate in both government ministries and in the agendas of non-governmental organisations. The Albertine Rift Conservation Programme, a consortium of organisations working in this biodiverse region located in western Uganda and neighbouring countries, is one example of a partnership working across a broad landscape with diverse uses. It has helped to re-establish a forest corridor 6.4 km long, one of several corridors identified in 2009, from Bugoma to Wambabya forest. Since this riparian corridor cuts through community land, the Programme engaged with local stakeholders to re-establish a 15 m buffer on either side of the forest. The buffer reached then down to the water's edge, an area previously completely cleared of trees. As part of the project, those people farming up to the river's edge were required to give part of their land to the buffer. In exchange they were provided with improved varieties of staple crops – peanuts, cassava, and rice – and trained on basic agricultural practices. As a result yields increased significantly, allowing farmers to re-purpose a portion of their land for the buffer (pers. comm. Peter Apell, JGI, 28 January 2015).

The project incentivised the corridor rehabilitation further, using both natural regeneration of trees but also buffer planting – fast growing species that can be used for firewood and livestock fodder. They trained local people to start nurseries and raise seedlings. Some of these seedlings were sold, giving immediate revenue, some planted in the buffer. Once planted the trees also became a source of poles to sell as well as selectively logged. Due to the double benefit mechanism (increased yields and revenue from the forest, as well as a nearby water supply) community engagement was significant, and over three years the buffer has been established and the river is rehabilitated. The group, who self-report these successes, are now looking to rehabilitate the 34 km corridor between Wambabya and Budongo forests, linking the Budongo and Bugoma forest corridor (BBC) (JGI, n.d.; Tumwine and Anewa, 2015).

Despite this apparent success, there are few other examples of agencies combining agriculture and conservation goals in practice. However, the two are being united in 'theories of change' and new framings that will likely impact future conservation and development activities. These include sustainable agricultural intensification, which is defined as 'producing more output from the same area of land while reducing the negative environmental impacts and at the same time increasing contributions to natural capital and the flow of environmental services' (Pretty et al., 2011), landscape approaches, which aim to reconcile multiple social, economic and environmental objectives across different stakeholders (Sayer et al., 2013), and the land sharing/sparing framework (Box 10.3).

Box 10.3   Land sparing and land sharing

The land sparing/land sharing framework is a proposed method for assessing the trade-offs between agriculture and biodiversity conservation in order to optimise the efficiency of landscapes in terms of these two objectives. Under land sparing, it is hoped that increasing yields on existing farmland can reduce pressure on natural habitats. In contrast, under land sharing, conservation and food production are integrated on farms, adapting them to mimic natural habitats more closely by reducing synthetic inputs and maintaining wild areas as reservoirs for biodiversity (Balmford et al., 2012).

Land sparing is more consistent with a traditional protectionist approach to conservation, effectively separating conservation and farming and advocating that large undisturbed areas of habitat are more effective at protecting biodiversity (Grau et al., 2013; Hulme et al., 2013). In contrast, land sharing proposes a more holistic integrated approach, creating multi-functional agricultural landscapes or mosaics that generate and utilise natural ecological processes within a social and cultural context (Knoke et al., 2009; Chappell and LaValle, 2011).

Empirical evidence for land sparing has largely been based on models of yield-density curves for bird, tree and insect species in tropical landscapes, measures that are themselves the subject of some debate (Robbins et al., 2015). Since the majority of species in the world can't survive in farming systems of even the lowest management intensity, land sparing is argued to be the best strategy for conserving most biodiversity (Phalan et al., 2011; Balmford et al., 2012). In Uganda's banana–coffee growing arc to the south, yield-density curves found bird species diversity to be greater, at a set level of agricultural output, under a land sparing philosophy (Hulme et al., 2013). Evidence on the ground of the ability of agricultural intensification to spare land is scarce, however, and intensification may actually hamper efforts to conserve the wider environment and promote expansion of farmland (Grau and Aide, 2008; Barretto et al., 2013; Cohn et al., 2014). The (in)effectiveness of protected areas and the growing importance of human-modified landscapes shape the arguments for land sharing (Hannah et al., 2007; Dawson et al., 2011; Andersson et al., 2012). For example, a time series between 1970 and 2005 for 69 species of large mammals in 78 African protected areas revealed a 59% decline in population abundance (Craigie et al., 2010). Land sharing will be hard to institute or maintain, however, if yield penalties ensue and the composition of species residing in human-modified landscapes may largely be made up of generalist or common species (Grau et al., 2013). European programmes to conserve farmland biodiversity have had only a small effect on the population sizes of vascular plants, birds and arthropods, and had no impact whatsoever on conserving endangered species (Kleijn et al., 2006).

Overall, land-sparing and land-sharing approaches reflect a critical difference in thinking between two camps. More specifically, land sparing is rooted in a conservation biology perspective, as it seeks to conserve endangered species; land sharing, on the other hand, stems from a human development perspective, as it aims to increase the quantity and quality of ecosystem services received by local people. While the land sparing/land sharing framework fails to account for other ecosystem services or the value placed on habitats and services by local people, it is unique in relating agriculture directly to biodiversity.

Interventions that reflect these emerging theories of change for combining agricultural development and conservation have thus far been few and far between, perhaps because cross-sectoral work is uncommon in the public sector. There is little communication between state or NGO actors, and little consideration of the needs of people living in the landscape – farmers included. Approaches have generally considered only a small geographical area, ignoring the wider landscape impacts. Furthermore, the development and implementation of agricultural and conservation projects have often been poor. Uganda must overcome various hurdles if it is to safeguard its food production for current and future generations. This includes building a diverse and thriving agricultural sector, as well as protecting and sustaining its natural environment.

Conclusion

Beyond new rhetoric, projects on the ground will, more and more, have to consider multiple objectives as global and local threats to Uganda's food production and environment intensify. In an assessment of a set of plausible socio-economic and climate scenarios for agricultural production and biodiversity in Uganda, Rwanda and Burundi between 2005 and 2050, all scenarios predicted agricultural development at the expense of habitat and biodiversity loss (van Soesbergen et al., 2017). The growth of agriculture may isolate habitats and change connectivity patterns. It can also alter biotic and abiotic environments. Large-scale land acquisitions for commercial farming are also altering social patterns. Moreover, this has led to unrest, tension over land tenure security and, in some cases, displacement. Yet agriculture is a sector central to Uganda's economy, development and to people's livelihoods. A main objective of this chapter has been to discuss the need to reconcile agriculture development and conservation, as well as to point to several theoretical approaches that aim to achieve this goal.

One of the most important underlying questions in this chapter pertains to the role of the state in Uganda. While commercial agricultural development remains a key pillar of the government's development goals, it remains relatively underinvested in comparison to other sectors such as oil and infrastructure. One of the major flaws to the government's agricultural policies over the last 15 years is the lack of sustained commitment and strategic focus. This is an ongoing issue but it reflects the continuing lack of strategic agricultural planning and poor project implementation by the government. Furthermore, it greatly weakens any trust that farmers have in the government as a development actor. Without a doubt, Uganda will have to grapple with these politically sensitive challenges moving forward if a more integrated vision of agricultural development and conservation is to be achieved.

References

Andersson, J.A., de Garine-Wichatitsky, M., Cumming, D.H.M., Dzingirai, V., and Giller, K.E. (eds) (2012) *Transfrontier Conservation Areas: People living on the edge*, Routledge, London, UK.
Balmford, A., Green, R., and Phalan, B. (2012) 'What conservationists need to know about farming', *Proceedings of the Royal Society B: Biological Sciences*, vol. 279, no. 1739, pp. 2714–2724.
Barretto, A.G., Göran Berndes, O.P., Sparovek, G., and Wirsenius, S. (2013) 'Agricultural intensification in Brazil and its effects on land-use patterns: an analysis of the 1975–2006 period', *Global Change Biology*, vol. 19, no. 6, pp. 1804–1815.
Barthel, S., Crumley, C., and Svedin, U. (2013) 'Bio-cultural refugia: safeguarding diversity of practices for food security and biodiversity', *Global Environmental Change*, vol. 23, no. 5, pp. 1142–1152.

Caravani, M. (2016) 'Transforming livelihoods at the margins: understanding class dynamics in Karamoja, Uganda', unpublished PhD dissertation, University of Sussex, Sussex, UK.

Cardinale, B.J., Duffy, J.E., Gonzalez, A., Hooper, D.U., Perrings, C., Venail, P., Narwani, A., Mace, G.M., Tilman, D., Wardle, D.A., Kinzig, A.P., Daily, G.C., Loreau, M., Grace, J.B., Larigauderie, A., Srivastava, D.S., and Naeem, S. (2012) 'Biodiversity loss and its impact on humanity', *Nature*, vol. 486, no. 7401, pp. 59–67.

Cavanagh, C.J. and Benjaminsen, T.A. (2015) 'Guerilla agriculture? A biopolitical guide to illicit cultivation within an IUCN category II protected area', *The Journal of Peasant Studies*, vol. 42, nos 3–4, pp. 725–745.

Cavanagh, C.J. and Himmelfarb, D. (2015) 'Much blood and money. necropolitical ecology on the margins of the Uganda Protectorate', *Antipode*, vol. 47, no. 1, pp. 55–73.

Chappell, M.J. and LaValle, L.A. (2011) 'Food security and biodiversity: can we have both? An agroecological analysis', *Agriculture and Human Values*, vol. 28, no. 1, pp. 3–26.

Child, K. (2009) 'Civil society in Uganda and the struggle to save the Mabira Forest', *Journal of Eastern African Studies*, vol. 3, no. 2, pp. 240–258.

Cohn, A.S., Mosnier, A., Havlik, P., Valin, H., Herrero, M., Schmid, E., O'Hare, M., and Obersteiner, M. (2014) 'Cattle ranching intensification in Brazil can reduce global greenhouse gas emissions by sparing land from deforestation', *Proceedings of the National Academy of Sciences*, vol. 111, no. 20, pp. 7236–7241.

Craigie, I.D., Baillie, J.E.M., Balmford, A., Carbone, C., Collen, B., Green, R.E., and Hutton, J.M. (2010) 'Large mammal population declines in Africa's protected areas', *Biological Conservation*, vol. 143, no. 9, pp. 2221–2228.

Daily Monitor (2017) 'NFA in the spotlight over forest reserve giveaways', *Daily Monitor*, 28 September (online), www.monitor.co.ug/News/National/NFA-in-the-spotlight-over-forest-reserve-giveaways/688334-4114986-7b2vxlz/index.html.

Dawson, T.P., Jackson, S.T., House, J.I., Prentice, I.C., and Mace, G.M. (2011) 'Beyond predictions: biodiversity conservation in a changing climate', *Science*, vol. 332, no. 6025, pp. 53–58.

Deloitte (2016). 'Uganda Economic Outlook 2016. The story behind the numbers', Deloitte, www2.deloitte.com/content/dam/Deloitte/ug/Documents/tax/Economic%20Outlook%202016%20UG.pdf.

Diaz, R.J. and Rosenberg, R. (2008) 'Spreading dead zones and consequences for marine ecosystems', *Science*, vol. 321, no. 5891, pp. 926–929.

Ebanyat, P., De Ridder, N., de Jager, A., Delve, R.J., Bekunda, M.A., and Giller, K.E. (2010) 'Drivers of land use change and household determinants of sustainability in smallholder farming systems of Eastern Uganda', *Population and Environment*, vol. 31, no. 6, pp. 474–506.

Edelman, M., Oya, C., and Barros, Jr, S.M. (2013) 'Global land grabs: historical processes, theoretical and methodological implications and current trajectories', *Third World Quarterly*, vol. 34, no. 9, pp. 1517–1531.

Fairhead, J., Leach, M., and Scoones, I. (2012) 'Green grabbing: a new appropriation of nature?', *The Journal of Peasant Studies*, vol. 39, no. 2, pp. 237–261.

Farella, N., Lucotte, M., Louchouarn, P., and Roulet, M. (2001) 'Deforestation modifying terrestrial organic transport in the Rio Tapajós, Brazilian Amazon', *Organic Geochemistry*, vol. 32, no. 12, pp. 1443–1458.

Fischer, J. and Lindenmayer, D.B. (2007) 'Landscape modification and habitat fragmentation: a synthesis', *Global Ecology and Biogeography*, vol. 16, no. 3, pp. 265–280.

Grau, H.R. and Aide, M. (2008) 'Globalization and land-use transitions in Latin America', *Ecology and Society*, vol. 13, no. 2, pp. 1–12.

Grau, R., Kuemmerle, T., and Macchil, L. (2013) 'Beyond "land sparing versus land sharing": environmental heterogeneity, globalization and the balance between agricultural production and nature conservation', *Current Opinion in Environmental Sustainability*, vol. 5, no. 5, pp. 477–483.

Gray, S., Leslie, P., and Akol, H. (2002) 'Uncertain disaster: environmental instability, colonial policy, and resilience of East African pastoral systems', in W.R. Leonard and M.H. Crawford (eds) *Human Biology of Pastoral Systems*. Cambridge University Press, Cambridge, UK.

Hamilton, A.C., Karamura, D., and Kakudid, E. (2016) 'History and conservation of wild and cultivated plant diversity in Uganda: forest species and banana varieties as case studies', *Plant Diversity*, vol. 38, no. 1, pp. 23–44.

Hannah, L., Midgley, G., Andelman, S., Araújo, M., Hughes, G., Martinez-Meyer, E., Pearson, R., and Williams, P. (2007) 'Protected area needs in a changing climate', *Frontiers in Ecology and the Environment*, vol. 5, no. 3, pp. 131–138.

Himmelfarb, D. (2006) 'Moving people, moving boundaries. The socio-economic effects of protectionist conservation, involuntary resettlement and tenure insecurity on the edge of Mt. Elgon national park, Uganda', *Agroforestry in Landscape Mosaics* Working Paper Series. World Tropical Agroforestry Centre, Nairobi, Kenya.

Honig, P. (2014) 'Civil society and land use policy in Uganda: the Mabira Forest case', *Africa Spectrum*, vol. 2, pp. 53–77.

Hulme, M.F., Vickery, J.A., Green, R.E., Phalan, B., Chamberlain, D.E., Pomeroy, D.E., Nalwanga, D., Mushabe, D., Katebaka, R., Bolwig, S., and Atkinson, P.W. (2013) 'Conserving the birds of Uganda's banana-coffee arc: land sparing and land sharing compared', *PLoS One*, vol. 8, no. 2, ppe54597.

Interview (2012) conducted by Matt Kandel with Napak District Chairperson, Lomonyang Robert, Napak District, 20 December 2012.

Jane Goodall Institute (JGI) (n.d.) 'Community centered conservation project', Jane Goodall Institute, janegoodallug.org/wp/cause-view/community-centered-conservation-project.

Kaggwa, R., Hogan, R., and Hall, B. (2009) 'Enhancing wetlands' contribution to growth, employment and prosperity', UNDP.NEMA/UNEP Poverty Environment Initiative Project, Kampala, Uganda, www.unpei.org/sites/default/files/e_library_documents/uganda-enhancing-wetlands-contribution-prosperity-final.pdf.

Kamukasa, A. and Bintoora, K. (2014) 'Assessment of the effects of changing land use from pastoralism to crop farming on Lake Nakivale wetland system in Isingiro District Uganda', *Journal of African Studies and Development*, vol. 6, no. 4, pp. 56–66.

Kandel, M. (2016) 'Struggling over land in post-conflict Uganda', *African Affairs*, vol. 115, no. 459, pp. 274–295.

Kandel, M. (2018) 'State formation and the politics of land in north-eastern Uganda', *African Affairs*, vol. 117, no. 467, pp. 261–285.

Kleijn, D., Baquero, R.A., Clough, Y., Díaz, M., De Esteban, J., Fernández, F., Gabriel, D., Herzog, F., Holzschuh, A., Jöhl, R., Knop, E., Kreuss, A., Marshall,

E.J.P., Steffan-Dewenter, I., Tscharntke, T., Verhulst, J., West, T.M., and Yela, J.L. (2006). 'Mixed biodiversity benefits of agri-environment schemes in five European countries', *Ecology Letters*, vol. 9, no. 3, pp. 243–254.

Knoke, T., Calvas, B., Aguirre, N., Román-Cuesta, R.M., Günter, S., Stimm, B., Weber, M., and Mosandl, R. (2009) 'Can tropical farmers reconcile subsistence needs with forest conservation?', *Frontiers in Ecology and the Environment*, vol. 7, no. 10, pp. 548–554.

Martiniello, G. (2015a) 'Food sovereignty as a praxis? Rethinking the food question in Uganda', *Third World Quarterly*, vol. 36, no. 3, pp. 508–525.

Martiniello, G. (2015b) 'Social struggles in Uganda's Acholiland: understanding responses and resistance to Amuru sugar works', *Journal of Peasant Studies*, vol. 42, nos 3–4, pp. 653–669.

Martiniello, G. (2017) 'Bitter sugarification: agro-extractivism, outgrower schemes and social differentiation in Busoga', paper presented at the International Conference on Agro-Extractivism, Peasantries and Social Dynamics organised by BRICS Initiative in Critical Agrarian Studies, Moscow, 13–17 October.

Matete, N. and BakamaNume, B. (2011) 'Climate of Uganda' in B.B. BakamaNume (ed.), *Geography of Uganda*, Mkuki na Nyota Publishers, Tanzania.

Ministry of Water and Environment (MoWE) (2017) *Water and Environment Sector Performance Report 2017*, www.mwe.go.ug/sites/default/files/library/SPR%20 2017%20Final.pdf.

Mugisha, A.H. (2011) 'Wetlands for forests: twenty years of wetlands conservation in Uganda. Have Uganda's wetlands become wastelands again?', A public talk on the World Wetland Day held at Uganda Museum. National Environmental Management Authority, Kampala, Uganda.

Mundia, C.N. and Murayama, Y. (2009) 'Analysis of land use/cover change and animal population dynamics in a wildlife sanctuary in East Africa', *Remote Sensing*, vol. 1, pp. 952–970.

Mwavu, E.N., Ariango, E., Ssegawa, P., Kalema, V.N., Baleganya, F., Waiswa, D., and Byakagaba, P. (2016) 'Agrobiodiversity of homegardens in a commercial sugarcane cultivation land matrix in Uganda', *International Journal of Biodiversity Science, Ecosystem Services and Management*, vol. 12, no. 3, pp. 191–201.

Mwavu, E.N. and Witkowski, E.T.F. (2008) 'Land-use and cover changes (1988–2002) around Budongo forest reserve, NW Uganda: implications for forest and woodland sustainability', *Land Degradation and Development*, vol. 19, no. 6, pp. 606–622.

Nabanoga, G., Namaalwa, J., and Ssenyonjo, E. (2010) 'REDD working papers: REDD and sustainable development – perspective from Uganda', International Institute for Environment and Development, London, UK.

Neumann, R.P. (1998). *Imposing Wilderness: Struggles over livelihood and nature preservation in Africa*. University of California Press, Berkeley, USA.

Oya, C. (2013) 'Methodological reflections on "land grab" databases and the "land grab" literature "rush"', *The Journal of Peasant Studies*, vol. 40, no. 3, pp. 503–520.

Perrings, C., Jackson, L., Bawa, K., Brussaard, L., Brush, S., Gavin, T., Papa, R., Pascual, U., and De Ruiter, P. (2006) 'Biodiversity in agricultural landscapes: saving natural capital without losing interest', *Conservation Biology*, vol. 20, no. 2, pp. 263–264.

Phalan, B., Balmford, A., Green, R.E., and Scharlemann, J.P.W. (2011) 'Minimising the harm to biodiversity of producing more food globally', *Food Policy*, vol. 36, pp. S62–S71.

Pimentel, D. (1995) 'Amounts of pesticides reaching target pests: environmental impacts and ethics', *Journal of Agricultural and Environmental Ethics*, vol. 8, no. 1, pp. 17–29.

Power, A.G. (2010) 'Ecosystem services and agriculture: trade-offs and synergies', *Philosophical Transactions of the Royal Society B: Biological Sciences*, vol. 365, no. 1554, pp. 2959–2971.

Pretty, J., Toulmin, C., and Williams, S. (2011) 'Sustainable intensification in African agriculture', *International Journal of Agricultural Sustainability*, vol. 9, no. 1, pp. 1–241.

Robbins, P., Chhatre, A., and Karanth, K. (2015) 'Political ecology of commodity agroforests and tropical biodiversity', *Conservation Letters*, vol. 8, no. 2, pp. 77–85.

Rugadya, M.A. and Kamusiime, H. (2013) 'Tenure in mystery: the status of land under wildlife, forestry and mining concessions in Karamoja region', *Nomadic Peoples*, vol. 17, no. 1, pp. 33–65.

Sayer, J.A., Sunderland, T.C.H., Ghazoul, J., Pfund, J.L., Sheil, D., Meijard, E., Venter, M., Boedhihartono, A.K., Day, M., García, C., Van Oosten, C., and Buck, L.E. (2013) 'Ten principles for a landscape approach to reconciling agriculture, conservation, and other competing land uses', *Proceedings of the National Academy of Sciences*, vol. 110, no. 21, pp. 8349–8356.

Schoneveld, G.C. (2014) 'The geographic and sectoral patterns of large-scale farmland investments in sub-Saharan Africa', *Food Policy*, vol. 38, pp. 34–50.

Sorensen, P. (1996) 'Commercialization of food crops in Busoga, Uganda, and the renegotiation of gender', *Gender and Society*, vol. 10, no. 5, pp. 608–628.

Tumwine, U. and Anewa, O.A. (2015) *Forest Corridor Project Implemented by the Jane Goodall Institute – Uganda. Final Report*, The Jane Goodall Institute, www.janegoodall.at/wp-content/uploads/2013/03/Forest-Corridor-Project-FINAL-REPORT2.pdf.

Twongyirwe, R. (2015) 'Forests under threat? Changes in land use and forest cover in rural western Uganda', PhD thesis, University of Cambridge, Cambridge, UK, www.repository.cam.ac.uk/handle/1810/252713.

Twongyirwe, R., Bithell, M., Richards, K.S., and Rees, W.G. (2015) 'Three decades of forest cover change in Uganda's Northern Albertine Rift Landscape', *Land Use Policy*, vol. 49, pp. 236–251.

Twongyirwe, R., Bithell, M., Richards, K.S., and Rees, W.G. (2017) 'Do livelihood typologies influence local perceptions of forest cover change? Evidence from a tropical forested and non-forested rural landscape in western Uganda', *Journal of Rural Studies*, vol. 50, pp. 12–29.

Uganda Bureau of Statistics (UBOS) (2014) *National Population and Housing Census, 2014*, www.ubos.org/onlinefiles/uploads/ubos/NPHC/2014%20National%20Census%20Main%20Report.pdf.

United Nations Development Programme (UNDP) (2013) *Uganda: HDI values and rank changes in the 2013 Human Development Report*, UNDP, New York, NY, USA.

Van Soesbergen, A., Arnell, A.P., Sassen, M., Stuch, B., Schaldach, R., Göpel, J., Vervoort, J., Mason-D'Cros, D., Islam, S., and Palazzo, A. (2017) 'Exploring future agricultural development and biodiversity in Uganda, Rwanda and Burundi: a spatially explicit scenario-based assessment', *Regional Environmental Change*: 1–12, CGIAR, Montpellier, France.

Van Zwanenberg, R.M.A and King, A. (1975) *An Economic History of Kenya and Uganda 1800–1970*, Macmillan Press, London, UK.

Vedeld, P., Cavanagh, C., Petursson, J.G., Nakakaawa, C., Moll, R., and Sjaastad, E. (2016) 'The political economy of conservation at Mount Elgon, Uganda: between local deprivation, regional sustainability and global public goods', *Conservation and Society*, vol. 14, no. 3, pp. 183–194.

Webster, G. and Osmaston, H.A. (2003) *A History of the Uganda Forest Department 1951–1965*, Commonwealth Secretariat, London, UK.

Wittemyer, G., Elsen, P., Bean, W.T., Burton, A.C.O., and Brashares, J.S. (2008) 'Accelerated human population growth at protected area edges', *Science*, vol. 321, no. 5885, pp. 123–125.

11 Lost in the woods?

A political economy of the 1998 forest sector reform in Uganda

Jon Geir Petursson and Paul Vedeld

Introduction

Uganda is endowed with substantial forest resources of high production and biodiversity values important for livelihoods and commercial forestry. Apart from such provisioning services, they also form important origins for ecosystem services of other kinds, such as supporting and regulating services and various cultural and traditional services of great importance for actors at multiple levels.

Over the last decades, Uganda has experienced major deforestation and degradation processes driving the forest cover from 24% in 1990 to around 9% in 2015 (MWE, 2015). The current forest cover is very low relative to the natural growing conditions, the remaining productive forests are scarce and most tropical high forest areas are now confined to protected areas. The Ugandan forests are characterised by a great diversity of uses and users with different powers, rights and interests. Forest governance structure and performance is a principal issue for understanding the politics of conservation and development in Uganda.

The historical process of political and institutional development in the forest sector is well described by Turyahabwe and Banana (2004) and Banana et al., this volume, Chapter 2).

In line with more general structural adjustment reforms, Uganda entered a major reform of its forest sector in the period from 1998–2004. The reform dismantled the 100-years-old Forestry Department, which had been overseeing all forestry functions in the country. This implied an establishment of new institutional structures and organisations with new roles and responsibilities, a strategic forest action plan, and the enactment of a new forestry law, supposed to be guiding the forest sector development in the country (Kiyingi, 2010).

Donors were important contributors to and actors in this 'reconstruction' process, partly driving the reform and shaping its design and content, both politically and economically. The restructured Ugandan forestry sector was supposed to be up and running after the enactment of the legislation and the establishment of the National Forest Authority (NFA) in 2003.

Uganda has now almost two decades of experiences with the reforms in the forest sector. This provides a basis for a critical assessment of its viability and capacity to cope with emerging conservation and sustainable development challenges.

Accordingly, the reformed forest sector is reported, by some, to have had some good years after its inauguration, but only a few years later skies started to cloud over its canopy. A growing number of studies criticise the implementation and delivery of the reformed forest sector, claiming that it has neither been successful for conservation nor for development in Uganda (e.g., Kiyingi, 2010; LTS, 2010).

This is not surprising as forest governance in many African countries is characterised by an obvious gap between official policy ambitions and actual implementation, or between rhetoric and reality (Nel, 2015; Petursson and Vedeld, 2017). This calls for a better understanding of agendas, motivations and agency in the political and institutional contexts that the ambitious forest reforms enter. This is not least because most of these reforms in African countries have emerged and been implemented under strong support and 'supervision' by donor and development elites with their own often strong agendas.

The emerging outcomes of the forest reforms have been noted by senior policy-makers and politicians in Uganda. In a speech in 2010, the late Hon. Maria Mutagamba, the then Minister for Water and Environment, stated the importance of coming up with a strategy for action. There are good laws, good policies and the question therefore is, 'why is the [forest] sector still a disgrace to the country?' the Minister asked (Kiyingi, 2010).

Our objective in this chapter is to describe, analyse and understand why the forest sector reforms in Uganda apparently have delivered such 'disgraceful' outcomes. We aim to examine the different political and institutional factors that can help explain the policy reform delivery in the forestry sector. The common explanation – 'bad governance' – as the cause, or 'lack of funding', may not bring the understanding of forest management or reform in Uganda further forward and our endeavour is to look into underlying political and institutional factors. The key research questions we ask are:

1   What was the rationale behind the reform, how was it designed and what were important driving forces and motivations behind the planning stages?
2   How have the forest reform structures and processes played out?
3   What are the key results and outcomes of the reforms and what explains these?

We base our analysis on data and information drawn from our long engagement with the environment and natural resources sector in Uganda through multiple projects (e.g., Baatvik et al., 2002; Petursson et al., 2013; Petursson and Vedeld, 2015, 2017).

A conceptual institutional and political framework for analysing sectoral reforms

We use a political economy lens for our analysis of Ugandan forest sector reforms, with a key focus on political and institutional factors that explain the dynamics and trajectories of change. The forest sector encompasses a nation's forest resources and all the environmental services they deliver, as well as the many and multilevel institutions and organisations necessary for their governance. We draw upon institutional and political theory to understand how political, economic and social actors and structures, institutions and processes influence each other and shape outcomes.

First, we focus on the institutional aspects of the reforms. Institutions are seen, in our context, as the bundles of rules, norms, and conventions that guide, and are being guided by, social and socio-ecological interactions (Scott, 1995). Organisations can be seen as actors with resources, authority and directions in terms of policies and a home to many institutions (Peters, 2005). Thus, we see the Ugandan forest sector reform as a comprehensive process configuring and re-configuring the sector's organisational setup, power relations and institutional structures related to the governance of forest resources. Institutional change is strongly guided by the legacies of the past, as well as by the existing institutional arrangements that shape current decision-making path dependency (Young, 2002; Petursson et al., 2013). In this sense, institutional formation and reform constitutes a historical process of successive decisions and evolving policies that continue to shape current arrangements and reform ambitions (Thelen, 2003). Therefore, the capacity that actors actually have in changing their circumstances is constrained by the complex interplay within the institutional landscape in which changes take place (Young, 2002). Although organisations do have the power to develop and shape policy discourses, allocate funding, and influence the political agenda, the existing power relations and the more general institutional contexts will impact both their institution-building and rule-making abilities and activities (Arts, 2003).

Second, we focus on the political contexts and motivation of the reforms and their implementation trajectories. We especially draw upon the literature on neo-patrimonialism, the mixture of two co-existing, partly interwoven types of domination, namely patrimonial and legal–rational bureaucratic domination (Erdmann and Engel, 2007). The concept of neo-patrimonialism, but with an added historical–institutional understanding, is useful in understanding the Ugandan state, the political context of the reform processes and linking the political and institutional forces driving the reform processes and shaping their outcomes (Khisa, 2013). We will try to avoid the 'history by analogy' trap and seek to understand the Ugandan state and how it operates, based on its own legacies, historic and cultural specifications and, in particular, the state governance foundations brought in during the colonial rule (Mamdani, 1996).

We use these perspectives for the study of the political economy of the Ugandan forest sector reform, following broadly a frame suggested by Robinson (2006). He conducted a study on challenges of governance reforms in selected sectors in Uganda and identified some important common features shaping the outcomes for the reform processes.

The background and drivers of the forest reform

The Amin coup in 1971 was a perilous factor for political development in independent Uganda, accompanied by a dismantling of the state and of rights-based and legitimate governance, also strongly affecting forest governance. During his reign until 1979 and the following political upheavals from 1979–1986 under his immediate successors, we saw a breakdown in law and order, leaving the state apparatus and resources in shambles.

Following a guerrilla war, relative stability was achieved in Uganda with the takeover of the President Museveni and his National Resistance Movement (NRM) regime in 1986, still ruling today. The state reconstruction under the Museveni regime attracted large-scale development assistance and he became acknowledged as a 'donor darling', praised for his work of restoring stability and launching an ambitious development agenda. The government has thus been able to rely on aid for large parts of its budget, with donors accounting for an astonishing 42% of the state budget in 2006. Although this ratio has decreased in recent years, the government still relies heavily on aid to fund their bills.

The forest sector reform came as a part of the overall reform involving most of Uganda's state governance sectors and it was therefore informed by the general ideology behind the larger agenda. The reform, theoretically speaking, followed a change from a more Weberian-influenced old public administration model based on a comprehensive state-driven administrative rationality with a focus on public interests, over to a state contraction approach. This latter approach implied a type of new public management model, still influential, which was based on economic rationality and efficiency of governance (Denhart and Denhart, 2000).

This does put reform processes in Uganda in a special light or context. As Harrison (2005) phrases it, 'government reforms (in Uganda) have been as much concerned with constructing the state as they have with reforming it'. This is important when analysing the forest reforms and their outcomes. The bad performance of the Uganda state apparatus in initiating the reforms was not necessarily or only due to a 'wrong' and/or 'inadequate' governance design, or structural or institutional aspects of it, but also, to a large degree, as an outcome of the 15 years of lawlessness and tyranny that no governance institutions could endure.

The governance reforms did enjoy strong political support from the (at the onset) highly popular Museveni NRM regime and were leveraged by major financial and technical support from multiple development agencies, who had a positive view of the Museveni government regime in the 1980s and early 1990s. The hegemonic actors behind the overall reform were the World Bank and IMF forming the structural reforms, while multiple bilateral and multi-lateral donor agencies supported individual components or sectors of the reforms.

The institutional and organisational design of the forest reform

The establishment of a multi-donor unit, the Forest Sector Umbrella Programme (FSUP) was a lead step by the Ugandan government in implementing the forest sector reforms. It was mandated to spearhead the reforms, running from 1999–2003 (Harrison, 2004). This was led by the Ministry of Water, Lands and Environment (MWLE), and coordinated by the Forest Sector Coordination Secretariat (Jagger, 2009). The FSUP commissioned a Forest Sector Review (FSR), running from 1999–2001, and providing a comprehensive overview of Uganda's forestry sector and informing the policy changes that followed. The lead donors, partly funding the reform process and driving the FSUP, included GTZ, DFID, NORAD, UNDP, FAO and the European Union. The NORAD later became the lead donor. The forest reform was comprehensive and implied a major overhaul of all organisational and institutional frameworks related to forestry.

The reform had ambitious objectives for mainstream forestry linking into several government-wide processes, with the central focus being to highlight the important contribution forests make to rural livelihoods countrywide, emphasising the potential role for forestry in the context of Uganda's wider poverty reduction strategies (Jagger, 2009).

The forest policy reform was based on three key formal policy and institutional pillars, the National Forest Policy in 2001, the National Forest Plan in 2002 and the National Forestry and Tree Planting Act in 2003.

The 2001 National Forestry Policy suggested new approaches and political directions for the development of the forest sector. The vision for the policy was: 'An integrated forest sector that achieves sustainable increases in the economic, social and environmental benefits from forests and trees by all the people of Uganda, especially the poor and vulnerable' (MWLE, 2001). The major guiding principles had an explicit ambition of combining an economic development of the sector with poverty alleviation and a livelihood improvement focus also involving gender, culture, and biodiversity management values.

The National Forest Policy paved the way for a more detailed and operational National Forest Plan finalised in 2002. The objectives of the National Forest Plan thus had a focus on poverty eradication, economic development, and sustainable forest resource management, and were to contribute directly to the national poverty reduction objectives. The National Forest Plan developed programmes that outlined the restructuring of the Forest Department and the establishment and roles of new lead actors to operationalise the policy.

The reform removed the Forest Department (FD), which has been operating continuously since its colonial establishment in 1898, obviously under varying political and institutional conditions. The FD was replaced with three bodies; the District Forestry Services (DFS), the National Forestry Authority (NFA); and the Forestry Inspection Division (FID), each with different statuses. In addition, the Uganda Wildlife Authority was mandated to govern forests in national parks and game reserves.

While there was a general political understanding of a need for a reform in the forest sector, there was a significant political debate around the organisational structure of the reform. Powerful actors within the FD, as an example, suggested a major reform of the sector but still maintaining the FD in charge of the Central Forest reserves (CFR). This was not acceptable to DFID (Jagger, 2009). The donors actually did take an active part in the reform of the sector and funded different elements of the reform process, but they primarily supported the NFA establishment and its first years of operation (Jagger, 2009). The NFA establishment was disputed in the Ugandan Parliament, not least the split up of the regulatory and implementation wings into separate organisations, but the current set-up was accepted in the end (Nel, 2015).

The role of overall coordination of forest resource management was put in the hands of the Forest Inspection Division (FID) in the Ministry for Water, Lands and Environment. It was established to provide a body for oversight of sector policies and regulatory functions. It was meant to have a 'lean outfit' and was established with only seven staff. The FID has in recent organisational changes been renamed the Forest Sector Support Department in the Ministry for Water and Environment, however it has a similar role as outlined in the initial policy. The key difference is, however, that the former Division was a semi-autonomous entity within the Ministry, while the Department is now embedded in the Ministry, under its political leadership, and it has around 40 staff. Its primary functions are responsibility for policy, standards and legislation, co-ordination, provide support to local districts, to monitor the activities of the NFA and DFA, and to mobilise funding to realise the National Forest Plan.

The National Forest Authority was a new government forest organisation, the lead agency in forest management and in charge of the CFRs. As a parastatal organisation, it was established to be semi-autonomous, with some political authority, and to service the state indirectly. The NFA was planned to have considerable autonomy in its own forestry operations, and to generate and manage its own human and financial resources. As a parastatal, it was supposed to be financially viable, operating in a business-like manner, but leaving the forest sector policy, planning, and legislation to the Ministry division. The NFA was set to have two principal functions;

sustainable management of the CFRs, and promotion and development of private forestry. It has a wide authority to lease out CFRs for privatised commercial plantations, with a mandate to strengthen private sector involvement in the forest sector.

The District Local Governments and their forest services (DFS) were mandated to govern Local Forest Reserves (LFRs), and the provision of advisory services to and regulatory oversight of forests on private and customary land.

One important political and institutional issue in this process was to define what should become Central, and what Local, Forestry Reserves, hence under the responsibility of NFA or under that of the Local District Governments. The outcome was that extremely small areas were defined as LFRs, or less than 1% of the total reserved forests.

The third part of the reserved forest estate was put under the responsibility of Uganda Wildlife Authority (UWA) and with a much stricter conservation regime. The UWA is a parastatal organisation similar to the NFA with the mandate to manage national parks, wildlife and game reserves. This part of the reform came after a major tug of war within the central administration. After major pressures from donor agencies, especially USAID, it was decided to convert some major forest reserves like Elgon, Bwindi, and Rwenzori to national parks and therefore their administration moved from forestry to the conservation-orientated UWA (USAID, 2003) (Figure 11.1).

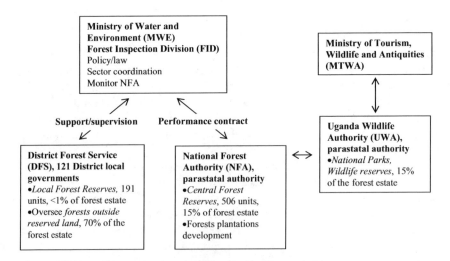

Figure 11.1 Key organisations, institutional arrangements and mandates over the forest estate of the Ugandan forest reform.

Political and institutional forces shaping the forest reform processes and outcomes

A promising start?

During the initial phase of the reforms, the three forest organisations, NFA, DFS, and FID, were established and mandated. This process was reviewed by, among others, Hobley (2004). She stated that the initial planning and implementation stages had reportedly good processes, with a 'progressive forest policy, strong and clear legislation and a National Forest Plan describing the necessary activities'. She further states that all 'the major building blocks have been in place, with its launch of the NFA and the agreed separation of roles between regulator (FID), manager (NFA) of central forest reserves and manager/advisor at local level (the DFS), enshrined in legislation'.

However, she stressed that, at that stage, no actor had agreed to finance any other element of the reform than NFA, thus leaving the policy and the institutional regulatory environment, and a 'virtually non-existent' service provision at local levels, without funding. The government did not step up to this either (LTS, 2010). The implementation stage of the process thus threatened the overall success and political and institutional sustainability of the sector reform. From a conservation and development point of view, Hobley (2004) further claimed that the focus on the more business-like NFA would easily crowd out the 'poverty and livelihood objectives' among the potential funders. She also pointed out that the CFR management hinged on an operational DFS that would cater for outreach and collaborative management schemes in cooperation with NFA field staff, to prevent an 'incomplete and unsupported reform' that 'can lead to the destabilization of other parts of the reform process'.

This all came true. The NFA did receive considerable attention from the donors and was leveraged with a great political commitment and sizable funds to implement its operations from the first years. By contrast, the DFS and the FID never became operational to the extent intended by the policy ambition. The NFA 'emergence' has, however, also been bumpy and has found its operations gradually undermined, losing momentum and actually reversing its initial objectives.

The NFA was financially well-endowed with a start-up fund and technical support funded by Norway, the UK, and the EU. The donors also requested the recruitment of an expatriate executive director, a Norwegian ('from a very distant tribe'![1]). The NFA establishment and implementation was seen by many as successful during the first years. It came with significant reduction in staff compared with the old FD and recruited few from the old FD. The NFA staff morale and confidence was high in the beginning. They had been selected out of a large pool of forestry professionals, considering themselves superior to the former FD staff that had been sacked under allegations of being dysfunctional and corrupt. In addition, the NFA could also, due to its semi-autonomous status, pay higher salaries than the government.

In the first years, NFA was capable of extracting revenues from mature forest plantations, and to lease out land in Central Forests Reserves to private actors engaging in commercial plantation forestry, adding internally generated revenue to a sizable donor support (Bjella, 2007).

The perceived initial success of NFA seems to have dominated the direction of the donor funding. But the NFA only had a mandate over a limited part of the Ugandan forest estate (*c*.15%) as most of the forest land was mandated and managed under other bodies. The FID was too weak and not capable of handling its coordination role and DFS was hardly established by the local governments and hadn't been given any funding. Both issues were of particular concern for the overall forest reform as DFS would have the responsibility for the bulk of Ugandan forest areas.

The real political power and interests surface

After NFA's first operative years, things started to deteriorate, and a series of political interventions and events of mismanagement gradually undermined the organisation, its operations, and reputation (Nsita and Kiyingi, 2010).

For an understanding of the political context, some general trends of the present Ugandan political environment should be noted. In the beginning of its reign, the Museveni government created a broad alliance in the society and made real commitments to democratic and transparent rule. However, the government has not been willing or able to retain these initial structures and has gradually consolidated power around a narrow group of loyal followers of Museveni (Tangri and Mwenda, 2001; Robinson, 2006). An increasing personalised political style has developed, including widespread corruption/cronyism in the powerful actor circles and a culture of political interventions. The concentration of political powers has evolved gradually, the democratic space for political opposition has been reduced and corruption increasingly institutionalised, not least at high levels.

Museveni has further had hard times in securing victory in the recent presidential elections and in 2016 he was accused of rigging elections to secure his continued power. The contemporary political landscape may thus, in general terms, be seen as gradually resembling a neo-patrimonial regime, where politics and the state are understood to operate through a mix of rent-seeking, patronage, clientelism, and personal rule.

The forest sector has also been subject to this Ugandan neo-patrimonial politics and the reformed institutional structures have not been able to counter this. In fact, in one sense, it seems to have been conducive to that type of behaviour. The forest sector has several attributes that make it vulnerable to neo-patrimonial politics, such as clandestine, informal, and illegal forms of access to land and forest resources. Observing this in relation to NFA, towards the Presidential elections in 2006 the NFA started to experience major high-level political interventions. Let us look into this.

The legacy of human settlements within the CFRs, partly from the Amin period, quickly appeared on the NFA agenda. Although the reserves were originally gazetted as governmental land for forest purposes, the conflicts, corruption and poor governance of these areas during the Amin and post-Amin period led to significant human encroachment (Cavanagh and Benjaminsen, 2014). A nation-wide NFA survey in 2005 found around 150,000 people living in the forest reserves (ACODE, 2005). This became a highly contested issue for NFA, when using high-handed methods to evict people. Local people often claimed that their residency was fully legitimate and approved by the predecessors of NFA or other official bodies (ACODE, 2005). They could often even document this. This issue seemed to have surprised the commercially oriented parastatal, which did not have the capacity nor the understanding to mediate and resolve these issues in legal or civilised ways. This escalated into violence and sabotage in many forest reserves and this also rightfully gained much public attention. It resulted in a direct intervention by the President in 2005 with a ban on evicting encroachers, a ban that is still in force. This proved and still proves to be difficult for NFA to handle.

The President also intervened directly with give-away strategies of Central Forest Reserves for agricultural development, an issue to which the first NFA senior management strongly objected. The most controversial political give-away interventions that the President accomplished were on the Bugala Island in Kalangala Forest Reserves, resulting in the conversion of thousands of hectares of native forests to oil palm plantations by the company BIDCO. There was also a case in the Mabira Forest Reserve where the President tried to give away the forest to the Madvani Group for sugarcane plantations. This was halted after a massive civil society campaign and international environmental pressures. However, this still led to a major collision between the NFA director and the politically elected board and led to the resignation of both in 2006. Explaining what happened, the Norwegian expatriate executive director said that the President had simply advised them to choose between giving a license to BIDCO or resigning.[2] This led to the recruitment of a new and more politically disciplined board and executive director, that again led to a weakened organisation, more susceptible to political pressures.

The NFA has also suffered from gross corruption and rent-seeking behaviour. The most notorious was the 'suitcase under the bed' scandal in 2009 where the then executive director was found to have hidden around US$ 450,000 in cash in a suitcase under his bed at home. He was not able to reasonably explain its origin. This led to his resignation and a major crisis and loss of legitimacy of the organisation, donors delaying and withdrawing their payments, and a long delay to install a new functional executive director.

The institutional framework for the semi-autonomous NFA has not at all been insulated from becoming a venue of political interference and corruption. On the contrary, it has become a fertile ground for both. This conflicts with the rationale for the conversion of public administration organisations to parastatal semi-autonomous organisations, as the reforms precisely aimed to distance the bureaucracy from political and private economic interests. The reform and establishment of a forestry parastatal organisation has thus been inefficient in protecting the sector from corruption. Instead, it has become a venue for grand corruption. It is difficult to see if or how the NFA can be revitalised under the current institutional structure.

Institutional aspects: failure by design?

The reforms restructured important institutional attributes of the forest sector. When seeking explanations for the weak performance and outcomes, it is therefore essential to scrutinise the institutional design, organisational structure and the role of different units, moving beyond the more simplistic explanations of lack of capacity, resources, or dishonest agency. There are 'failure by design' elements that should be scrutinised (Bivens, 2011).

The three heterogeneous organisations created by the reform got different mandates, splitting up the rather unitary Forest Department. Central to this idea was the role of FID as a coordination device and with NFA and DFS as operational units for state and communal forest areas. That has, however, proven to be a bureaucratic impasse.

The NFA is a parastatal organisation with great autonomy, more resources, better paid employees and it can simply find its own way regardless of the FID. The DFS, on the other hand, was placed within the relatively independent and now quite numerous and economically weak District Local Governments (111 units) that constitutes a coordination and capacity challenge in its own right. The FID (now FSSD) itself is an annex within the Ministry and lacks financial resources to direct the operations of the other two organisations with a support or performance contract, as initially outlined in the forest policy (Figure 11.1). The FSSD is now running its own donor-funded tree planting projects in some local districts, desperately trying to fund its own existence. Its coordination function has proven not to be effective.

This mix of semi-autonomous state bodies and traditional bureaucracies operating under scarce resources has resulted in a structurally weak, scattered and un-coordinated forest sector governance, unfit to meet the demanding forest conservation and development challenges. There are also internal and confusing mismatches in the design. For example, the Local Forest Reserves are supposed to be governed by public administration while the Central Forest Reserves belong to the semi-autonomous NFA. And the vast and diminishing areas of private and customary forests are supposed to be governed by the DFS that, in most districts, has very limited resources.

The decentralisation aspect of the reform was therefore not wholeheart-edly followed up by the government, nor by any of the donor agencies, and was structurally much more in line with the observations by Muhereza (2003), stating: 'while reforms in Uganda are invariably termed "decentrali-zation", they actually involve a combination of processes such as delegation, de-concentration, privatization – and devolution'. The agenda to split up the districts, creating small and weak units, has substantially perverted the decentralisation process and led to strengthened central powers, in line with Ribot et al.'s (2006) observation of recentralisation even if claiming that there is a decentralising agenda.

Further, the funding of the forest organisations has been problematic and based on unrealistic assumptions. The financial models behind the NFA and the DFS have proven not to be sustainable. The initial ideas of the NFA becoming a self-financing viable unit seems to be illusionary. In the first years, it could extract revenues from mature plantations and by renting out land, in addition to donor and governmental support. These funding types are now much depleted and, in the coming years, the organisation is quite far from being financially self-sustaining. This came in addition to the organisation being seen as a venue for corruption, making it so toxic that donors are now reluctant to provide forest-related support. It is a paradox that the NFA, which was supposed to be financially autonomous from the government according to the forest policy, is now totally dependent on state funding for its operations. It is therefore a pertinent question to ask if there is any rationale to keep NFA as a parastatal organisation.

The establishment of the DFS never fully took off and it was based on unrealistic financial models and assumptions (see also LTS, 2010). The reserved forest resources that were left for the districts were meagre, with tiny and heavily encroached Local Forest Reserves and a substantial privately/customary-owned forest mass (70%) with little room for public management and control and with heavy rates of deforestation. Some of the underfunded District Local Governments have actually engaged in the deple-tion of the local forest resources, desperate to fund their own operations.

Few of the synergies planned between the DFS and NFA were realised. Donors were not directed to and would not support the DFS. At the same time, the Local Government reform itself, with a non-sustainable expan-sion in numbers of Districts, led to a situation where most of the Districts were left without personnel or competence in forest management, and leaving much open to 'private enterprise' and bad, incompetent govern-ance. According to Nsita and Kiyingi (2010), it has 'almost become normal for District Forestry Officers to do what the [local government] political masters demand, regardless of the negative implications for responsible forest management'.

This has further produced an incentive to develop the private good ele-ments of the forest estate, but fallen short on enhancing the public goods of the forests.

The NFA initially capitalised on logging or leasing out plantations and land for plantation development, while simultaneously distancing itself from other public agencies. This has led to some private plantations on state land doing relatively well, however with low rates of land rents and very long-term land leases, currently attracting subsidised funding from schemes like the EU-funded Sawlog Production Grant Scheme.[3] The plantation forestry sector has also been accelerated with access to global carbon funding and the entry of large plantation companies like the Green Resources with concessions from NFA. This arrangement has been subject to heavy political economic criticism as it is mainly generating benefits to the foreign investors and grabbing land, adversely impacting local people's livelihoods and interests (Lyons and Westoby, 2014; Nel, 2015). This has resulted in expansion of forest plantations in the CFR from around 18,000 ha in 1990 to around 65,000 ha in 2015, in addition to around 30,000 ha established on private/communal lands (MWE, 2015). This is, in reality, a privatisation process of state and public assets. In addition comes the fact that this focus on plantation production implies a narrowing of the scope of NFA and not of its broader social mandate for livelihoods, poverty and biodiversity concerns. What is further striking in the NFA's performance is that the pro-poor development components have hardly delivered at all.

It is notable how forest on private/customary land was somehow left out in the reform, being the largest share of the forest estate with important functions in providing public good services and multiple environmental incomes to local people. It was assumed that the District Local Governments would be responsible for those areas. However, they were given vague mandates and no resources. And there was no meaningful attempt or interest, either from the ministry or from the NFA, to build community, participatory, or co-management forest management institutions to govern these forests. This has had dramatic consequences, as these forests are disappearing fast. Donors here also have great responsibility for the lack of support for following up the reform.

Lastly, in an attempt to counter the deteriorating of the forest sector, the Ugandan government updated the National Forest Plan in 2012, the work carried out by the Forestry Sector Support Department with some financial support from FAO (MWE, 2013). The updated policy has, however, not become any vehicle for change and is not a carrier of innovative or radical changes in the current structure.

The fate of the forest estate: transitions 1990–2015

Let us finally look at the physical effects of the reform on the forest estate over time, using forest cover, hence woodlands, tropical high forest, and plantations, as an indicator, and relating it to the responsibilities of different forestry actors. We see rather dramatic overall forest losses, from *c.*24% forest cover in 1990 down to only *c.*9% in 2015 (Table 11.1). From 1990,

Table 11.1 Trends in forest cover in Uganda from 1990–2015 and different forest regimes

Management responsibility	Area (ha) and year					Loss of forest area (ha)	% loss of forest area	% of the remaining forest estate
	1990*	2000	2005	2010	2015			
NFA	751,986	658,140	744,940	522,568	462,023	289,963	39%	25.2%
DFS	1,634	1,074	1,634	122	976	658	40%	0.1%
UWA	794,642	734,076	676,945	549,624	621,743	172,899	22%	33.9%
UWA & NFA	37,620	38,599	37,510	39,346	36,229	1,391	4%	2.0%
Private	3,347.390	2,479.806	2,141.336	1,200.862	714.176	2,633.214	79%	38.9%
Total forest	4,933.272	3,911.695	3,602.365	2,312.522	1,835.147	3,098.125		100.0%
Forest cover % of total land	24%	20%	18%	12%	9%			

*The current management responsibilities were defined in the reforms after 2000. The 1990 data is therefore based on that categorisation.

Source: NFA, 2017.

Uganda has thus lost more than half of its forest cover and, according to this data, there is no sign of reduction in the deforestation rate since the forest reforms were initiated. The largest deforestation has been on private and communal land, where around 80% of the forests are lost.

Areas under NFA have also suffered great losses of around 40% from 1990–2015. For the relatively small and heavily degraded LFRs, under the mandate of the District Local Governments, a similar share of *c.*40% is lost. Forests are even lost in the strictly protected national parks and wildlife reserves under UWA (22%).

The remaining Ugandan forests are thus becoming more and more defined within reserved enclosures, hence national parks and central forest reserves (almost two-thirds) with weak and often lack of institutional provisions for local people and their rights of access to vital forest environmental incomes. This matters greatly for the conservation and development context.

These figures also underline the weak performance of lead actors of the forest sector reform, especially the DFS and the NFA, as discussed in preceding sections.

Conclusions

Major governance reforms were undertaken in sub-Saharan Africa in the 1990s. These were driven by hegemonic global actors such as the World Bank and IMF and then funded and kept running by multiple donors under diverse conditionalities. This treated countries with a set of prescribed neoliberal policy packages that, however, entered diverse political and institutional landscapes with weak democratic traditions and regimes operating according to neo-patrimonial practices (Cammack, 2007). The process and outcomes of these reforms have been a mixed success, as in the case of Uganda (Fjeldstad, 2005; Robinson, 2006). Our interest here has been to study this within the natural resource sector in Uganda, and that has been dominated by this reform agenda.

We have examined processes and outcomes of the Ugandan forest sector reform initiated in 1998. We find the sector 'lost in the woods', two decades after it went through the audacious, donor-influenced reform process. The reform has not been capable of addressing the real issues pertinent for the forest sector performance. The lead Ugandan organisations are not delivering well, especially on public goods essential for conservation, development, and important for local livelihoods. The sector performance is even described as disgraceful by lead politicians. It is a disaster in that more than half of the forest cover has been lost, and its lead organisation, the NFA, is currently unable to receive donor support due to mismanagement and the DFS being, modestly expressed, dysfunctional. The most vital elements are the private-sector plantations that still attract both private and donor support, especially under the Sawlog scheme. These are, however, relatively small in scale and with limited and perhaps pervasive negative spin-off effects for poor local people. The forest sector reform in Uganda has thus not proven able to address its most pressing policy objectives. In its current position, it is fragile and rather badly unfit to cope with the contemporary conservation and development challenges.

Both political agency and institutional and organisational factors can help explain these outcomes. The neo-patrimonial Ugandan political system has entered the forest sector with many interventions in recent years and that has placed the sector in some kind of a deadlock. We argue that the problems are partly rooted in the institutional design of the reform and the neo-patrimonial nature of Ugandan politics. Actually, the structure of the reformed forest sector has proven to be well-designed to exercise neo-patrimonial politics as we have shown, and provided venues for major political interventions and corruption.

The Ugandan government did not act alone in this. Donors are also responsible for the forest reform saga, both as key drivers and as designers of the reform, and being major supporters with strong conditionalities attached.

Are there any reasons to believe that a different structural form could have been better? There is no clear answer to that, but it is obvious that the current structure is not operating well. The organisations are unfit, there is lack of coordination and the sector is not delivering properly to local people, as also observed by Jagger (2009). This can be explained by different factors.

First, the policy makers and donors were strangely naïve about the reality of implementation dynamics of the sector reform and the policies were far too ambitious in relation to the on-the-ground financial and capacity realities.

Second, the largest share of the forest estate, held under customary tenure, was only vaguely assigned as the responsibility of the District Local Governments, which openly had limited capacity and mandate to govern these areas. This has resulted in large-scale erasure of these forests. This is a result of the reform design and structure. It should have been made a central pillar in the reform. And especially if it had been combined with attempts to design functional community or participatory forest management institutions to govern and secure provisions of public goods from these areas. Donors also have great responsibilities here, by not directing funds or interests towards this part of the forest sector. And how to govern these forests is still an unsettled issue for the Ugandan forest sector management.

Third, the reforms needed to acknowledge the neo-patrimonial political reality, the agency of powerful actors, and should have been able to understand what is implied to govern under such conditions. A radical economic reform seemed to be bogged down relatively quickly in the neo-patrimonial political landscape and, actually, the focus on private goods prioritised and produced by the reform became a tempting target for the powerful actors operating under the neo-patrimonial rule.

Last, the organisational structure is far too complex, mixing private and public roles, decentralising some while re-centralising others. This structure should be revisited. It is especially difficult to see the NFA move forward under its current structure and there are few arguments for seeing it continuing as a semi-autonomous organisation. Greater coordination or even merger of the three forest organisations seems like a more sensible suggestion.

It needs, however, to be noted that the problems within the reformed forest sector are in no way unique. Most of the World Bank-driven reforms in Uganda after the Museveni takeover are struggling, meeting many of the same obstacles as the forest sector (Robinson, 2006).

It is now timely and urgent, 20 years after the initiation of forest reform in Uganda, to realise that the sector is not delivering well and that its current institutional attributes are not fit to cope with the current governance, conservation, and development challenges. There is a great need to revisit the reforms open-mindedly and with a far more radical approach than the 2012 update of the Forest Policy.

We have highlighted issues such as the institutional attributes with a much stronger focus on the contribution to local livelihoods and a revisit of the mandate of the forest organisations. Further, one could consider re-establishing a system for more holistic public administration of the forest estate and more accountability to the Parliament, facilitating internal and sector coordination. Last, one should reconsider the NFA as parastatal unit, establish realistic and sustainable funding models, develop community-based forest institutions, especially on customary land, and seek other more socially inclusive models of forest governance.

This will not eliminate the risk of political interventions by a neo-patrimonial state, but it might reduce and spread the risks and, further, give the forest sector new confidence and a breathing-space it now desperately needs. Otherwise there might be few Ugandan forests left 'to get lost in' within a few decades.

Acknowledgements

This study was supported by the University of Iceland Research Fund (Rannsoknasjodur Haskola Islands). We would like to thank the reviewers for their valuable comments and suggestions to improve the quality of the chapter.

Notes

1 As Museveni stated for a Swedish woman recruited to the head of the URA position (Fjeldstad, 2005).
2 See more at: www.newvision.co.ug/new_vision/news/1135192/forestry-chief-resigns-bugala#sthash.eAEjJY96.dpuf.
3 See: https://ec.europa.eu/europeaid/action-document-sawlog-production-grant-scheme-iii-uganda_en.

References

Advocates Coalition for Development and Environment (ACODE) (2005) *Balancing Nature Conservation and Livelihoods. A Legal Analysis of Forestry Evictions by the National Forestry Authority*, Advocates Coalition for Development and Environment, Kampala, Uganda.

Arts, B. (2003) 'Non-state actors in global governance. A power analysis', paper presented at the 2003 ECPR Joint Sessions, Workshop 11: The Governance of Global Issues – Effectiveness, Accountability and Constitutionalization, 28 March–2 April, Edinburgh, Scotland.

Baatvik, S.T., Kaboggoza, J.R.S., Kabutha, C., and Vedeld, P. (2002) *Mt. Elgon Regional Ecosystem Conservation Programme (MERECP) Appraisal Report*, Noragric Report no. 25, Agricultural University of Norway, Noragric, Ås, Norway.

Bivens, J. (2011) *Failure by Design. The story behind America's broken economy*, Cornell University Press, Ithaca, NY, USA.

Bjella, O. (2007) 'Erfaringer etter tre ar some Statskogsjef i Uganda. Institusjons-byggning, plantasjeinvesteringer og politisk maktkamp'. *Presentation at UMB*, 9 May, Ås, Norway.

Cammack, D. (2007) 'The logic of African neopatrimonialism: what role for donors?', *Development Policy Review*, vol. 25, no. 5, pp. 599–614.

Cavanagh, C. and Benjaminsen, T.A. (2014) 'Virtual nature, violent accumulation: the 'spectacular failure' of carbon offsetting at a Ugandan National Park', *Geoforum*, vol. 56, pp. 55–65.

Denhardt, R.B. and Denhardt, J.V. (2000) 'The new public service: serving rather than steering', *Public Administration Review*, vol. 60, no. 6, pp. 549–559.

Department for International Development (DFID) (1999) *Uganda Forest Sector Policy and Strategy Project*, Project Memorandum, Department for International Development, London, UK.

Erdman, G. and Engel, U. (2007) 'Neopatrimonialism reconsidered: critical review and elaboration of an elusive concept', *Commonwealth and Comparative Politics*, vol. 45, no. 1, pp. 95–119.

Fjeldstad, O. (2005) 'Corruption in tax administration: lessons from institutional reforms in Uganda', *CMI Working Papers 2005:10*, Bergen, Norway, p. 23.

Harrison, G. (2004) 'Why economic globalization is no enough', *Development and Change*, vol. 35, no. 5, pp. 1037–1047.

Harrison, G. (2005) 'The World Bank, governance and theories of political action in Africa', *The British Journal of Politics and International Relations*, vol. 7, no. 2, pp. 240–260.

Hobley, M. (2004) *Uganda Forest Sector Policy and Strategy Project. End of Project Review*, Department for International Development, London, UK.

Jagger, P. (2009) 'Can forest sector devolution improve rural livelihoods? An analysis of forest income and institutions in western Uganda', PhD Public Policy, Indiana University Dissertation, Indianapolis, IN, USA.

Khisa, M. (2013) 'The making of the "informal state" in Uganda', *Africa Development*, vol. 38, no. 1–2, pp. 191–226.

Kiiza, J. (2005) 'Understanding economic and institutional reforms in Uganda', paper presented at GDN workshop, Delhi, 2004. Submitted under the Understanding Reform Project, Kampala, Uganda.

Kiyingi, G. (2010) 'Report on the workshop on forest governance', organised by MWE and WB, Kampala, 15–16 June, Kampala, Uganda.

LTS International (2010) 'Review of the forestry sector in Uganda', in S. White and P. Byakagaba (eds) *Main Report*, LTS, Edinburgh, UK.

Lyons, K. and Westoby, P. (2014) 'Carbon colonialism and the new land grab: plantation forestry in Uganda and its livelihood impacts', *Journal of Rural Studies*, vol. 36, nos 3–4, pp. 13–21.

Mamdani, M. (1996) *Citizen and Subject: contemporary Africa and the legacy of late colonialism*, Princeton University Press, Princeton, NJ, USA.

Ministry of Water and Environment (MWE) (2013) *The National Forest Plan 2012–2022*, Ministry of Water and Environment, Kampala, Uganda.

Ministry of Water and Environment (MWE) (2015) *State of Uganda Forests 2016*, Ministry of Water and Environment, Kampala, Uganda.

Ministry of Water, Lands, and Environment (MWLE) (2001) *Uganda Forest Policy*, Ministry of Water, Lands, and Environment, Kampala, Uganda.

Ministry of Water, Lands, and Environment (MWLE) (2002) *The National Forest Plan*, Ministry of Water, Lands, and Environment, Kampala, Uganda.

Muhereza, F.E. (2003) 'Commerce, kings and local government in Uganda. Decentralizing natural resources to consolidate the Central State', Working Paper Series, World Resources Institute, Washington, DC, USA.

National Forestry Authority (NFA) (2017) 'Draft national biomass report', National Forestry Authority, Kampala, Uganda.

Nel, A. (2015) 'The neoliberalisation of forestry governance, market environmentalism and re-territorialisation in Uganda', *Third World Quarterly*, vol. 36, no. 12, pp. 2294–2315.

Nsita, S.A. (2005) 'Decentralization and forest management in Uganda', Chapter 10 in C.J.P. Colfer and D. Capistrano (eds) *The Politics of Decentralization. Forests, Power and People*, Earthscan, London, UK.

Nsita, S.A. and Kiyingi, G. (2010) 'Forest governance reform: a draft strategy note for Uganda', Annex 1, Ministry of Water and Environment and World Bank, Kampala, Uganda.

Peters, B.G. (2005) *Institutional Theory in Political Science: the new institutionalism. The roots of the new institutionalism-normative institutionalism*, Continuum, London, UK, pp. 25–45.

Petursson, J.G. and Vedeld, P. (2015) 'Nine lives of protected areas: a historical–institutional analysis from the transboundary Mt Elgon, Uganda and Kenya', *Land Use Policy*, vol. 42, pp. 251–263.

Petursson J.G. and Vedeld, P. (2017) 'Rhetoric and reality in protected area governance: discourses, actors and institutional change in Mount Elgon National Park, Uganda', *Ecological Economics*, vol. 131, pp. 166–177.

Petursson, J.G., Vedeld, P., and Sassen, M. (2013) 'An institutional analysis of deforestation processes in protected areas: the case of the transboundary Mt. Elgon, Uganda and Kenya', *Forest Policy and Economics*, vol. 26, no. 1, pp. 22–33.

Ribot, J., Agrawal, A., and Larson, A. (2006). 'Recentralizing while decentralizing: how national governments reappropriate forest resources', *World Development*, vol. 34, no. 11, pp. 1864–1886.

Robinson, M. (2006) 'The political economy of governance reforms in Uganda', Discussion Paper 386, Institute of Development Studies, Sussex, UK, p. 35.

Scott, W.R. (1995) *Institutions and Organizations*, Sage, London, UK.

Statistics Uganda (2015) 'Statistical abstract', Uganda Bureau of Statistics, Kampala, Uganda.

Tangri, R. and Mwenda, A. (2001) 'Corruption and cronyism in Uganda's Privatization in the 1990s', *African Affairs*, vol. 100, no. 398, pp. 117–133.

Tenywa, G. (2006) 'Forestry Chief Resigns over Bugala', *New Vision*, 10 December, Kampala, Uganda.

Thelen, K. (2003) 'How institutions evolve', in J. Mahoney and D. Rueschemeyer (eds) *Comparative Historical Analyses in Social Sciences*, Cambridge University Press, New York, NY, USA.

Turyahabwe, N. and Banana A.Y. (2004) 'An overview of history and development of forest policy and legislation in Uganda', *International Forest Review*, vol. 10, no. 4, pp. 641–656.

United States Agency for International Development (USAID) (2003) *USAID's Enduring Legacy in Natural Forests: livelihoods, landscapes and governance*, ed. R. Clausen, Volume 3, Focus Country profiles, Chemonics Int., United States Agency for International Development, Washington, DC, USA.

Young, O.R. (2002) *The Institutional Dimensions of Environmental Change: Fit, Interplay, and Scale*, MIT Press, Cambridge, MA, USA.

12 Dialectics of conservation, extractives, and Uganda's 'land rush'

Patrick Byakagaba, Bashir Twesigye, and Leslie E. Ruyle

Introduction

Land is an important resource because it provides identity and enables flow of benefits such as food, income and employment, thus constituting a major asset for the rural poor (Zoomers, 2011; German et al., 2013). Land rush is occurring at a very large scale in areas where extractives have been discovered (Cotula, 2012), and where energy demand has increased (Scheidel and Sorman, 2012), severely affecting the socio-ecological system of these areas in many cases (Balehegn, 2015). Most studies that have investigated impacts of land rush have focused on impacts on environment, rights, sovereignty, livelihoods, development and conflict (Collins et al., 2011).

The systemic effects of land rush on socio-ecological systems have not been widely studied (Messerli et al., 2013). This is in spite of increasing evidence that understanding the resilience, vulnerability, and adaptability of social-ecological systems is crucial (Young et al., 2006; Collins et al., 2011; Liu et al., 2007a). Even more so, land rush is often accompanied by negative impacts especially to the poor who own land customarily where tenure rights are not well-defined (Zoomers, 2011). It is estimated that approximately 90% of all the land in Africa is customarily owned (Chimhowu and Woodhouse, 2006). Land under customary tenure is vulnerable to involuntary loss (Wily, 2011a). This can result in irreversible natural resource degradation, livelihood shortfalls for smallholder farmers, and potential suffering from the natural resource curse (Robertson and Pinstrup-Andersen, 2010).

In this chapter we examine land rights abuses linked to the prevailing land rush in the Albertine Graben of Uganda, and further seek to investigate their consequences for the socio-ecological system in this region and the implications for biodiversity conservation in the Murchison Falls conservation area in western Uganda. Studies elsewhere have shown that extractive sector projects usually involve the acquisition of land for subsoil resources and auxiliary infrastructure, and therefore can exacerbate pressures on land due to the economic appreciation of land, which inevitably may become a recipe for increased incidents of land conflicts, land rights abuses and land rush (André and Platteau, 1998; Cotula, 2012). The direct and indirect impacts of the extractives sector on local communities in resource-bearing sites, particularly at the early stages of resource extraction projects, are still understudied (Luning, 2012; Bybee and Johannes, 2014).

We postulate that as the nascent oil and gas industry develops in Uganda, land rush will be persistent, thus precipitating more consequences on the socio-ecological system (Messerli et al., 2013) of the Albertine region, which may jeopardise biodiversity conservation efforts. This is because humans depend on ecological systems found on land for a variety of ecosystem services (Liu et al., 2007a) and therefore changes in access to land due to land rush may change land use patterns and consequently the socio-ecological system of the region. Feedback loops in which humans both influence and are affected by natural patterns and processes are a common phenomenon because there are very few ecosystems that are free from human influence (Liu et al., 2007b; Monticino et al., 2007).

Land rush due to various socio-economic and political reasons may contribute to increased conversion of natural ecosystems and consequently affect the robustness of the socio-ecological system of the landscapes in this region. This may threaten biodiversity in the region, cause degradation of natural ecosystems, and subsequently loss of livelihood opportunities. Conversion of natural ecosystems may be for oil exploration and development projects such as drilling of exploration and production wells and associated infrastructure such as new roads, brine pits and pipelines (Kharaka and Dorsey, 2005).

We use the definition of land rush as cited by Scheidel and Sorman (2012), denoting processes of large-scale and long-term land acquisitions through private and governmental actors that are associated with large and drastic changes in land use patterns and land use rights. We first present an overview on oil and gas exploration and biodiversity status in the Ugandan Albertine Graben and an empirical case study on land rights abuses, scale and actors in the Albertine region of Uganda. Through literature review and applying a socio-ecological lens, we demonstrate the potential consequences of land rights abuses on the socio-ecological system and biodiversity of the Albertine region in Uganda.

Overview on oil and gas exploration and biodiversity status in the Ugandan Albertine Graben

The Ugandan Albertine Graben extends along the western part of the country, from the South Sudan border to the northern end of Lake Edward and to the border with the Democratic Republic of Congo (Figure 12.1).

The discovery of oil reserves in this region was first formally reported by geologists who worked for the British colonial administrators in the 1920s when natural oil seeps were first identified in the area (Anderson and

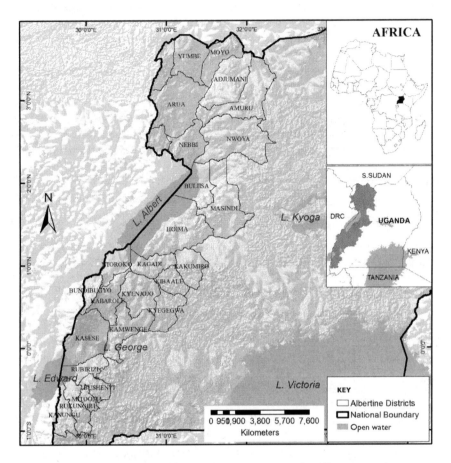

Figure 12.1 Map of Uganda showing districts covering the Albertine Graben.

Browne, 2011). The first well was drilled in 1938 but it was not until 2006 that commercial development began (ibid.). It was estimated as of June 2016 that Uganda had about 6.5 billion barrels of oil equivalent in place with about 1.4 to 1.7 billion barrels of these resources recoverable, i.e., that can be technically and economically extracted. It is worthy to note that these oil reserves were confirmed from an area covering less than 40% of the Albertine Graben, thus suggesting that there is potential for additional oil reserves to be discovered in this region (MEMD, 2017b). Considering the current confirmed reserves, Uganda has a potential to produce 220,000 barrels (1 barrel is equivalent to 159 litres) per day (ibid). This is about 48 times lower than Russia, which is currently the largest oil producer in the world (10,551,497 barrels per day), and would make it the 8th largest producer in Africa next to Equatorial Guinea, which produces 227,000 barrels per day (EIA, 2017). Currently, three companies have been granted exploration and production licenses and they include Tullow Operations Pty Ltd (from Ireland), Total E&P (from France) and China National Offshore Oil Corporation from China (ibid).

The Albertine Graben is a global biodiversity hotspot with many endemic vertebrates and plant species. The region contains more vertebrate species than any other region on the continent and contains more endemic species of vertebrate than any other region on mainland Africa (Plumptre et al., 2007; WCS, 2016). It hosts seven of Uganda's ten national parks and 20 forest reserves that are critical in the provision of ecosystem services such as climate, water and hydrological regulation, erosion control, provision of raw materials, recreation, pollinators and biodiversity conservation. Estimates by the Wildlife Conservation Society suggest that the Albertine Graben contains 39% of Africa's mammal species, 52% of its bird species, and 19% of its amphibian species, along with 14% of the plant and reptile species (Plumptre et al., 2003).

There are over 20 central and local forest reserves and internationally recognised wetland systems in the Albertine Graben such as Murchison Falls–Albert Delta Wetland System, which is a Ramsar site (Plumptre, 2002; GoU, 2016). The Government of Uganda acknowledged the biodiversity value of this region and ensured that the *National Oil and Gas Policy 2008* provides for the protection of the environment and conservation of biodiversity (GoU, 2008).

One of the key components of the purpose of the Petroleum (Exploration, Development and Production) Act 2013 (GoU, 2013) is protection of the environment in petroleum activities. The process of reviewing the *National Environment Management Policy 1995* and the National Environment Act 1995, which is still on-going, was partly triggered by the envisaged environmental challenges associated with oil and gas discovery in a region that is rich in biodiversity (GoU, 1995a; GoU, 1995b). The responsibility to protect the environment is placed on licensed companies in areas in which they are operating, while government is expected to legislate, regulate and monitor compliance through relevant agencies and ministries (GoU, 2014; GoU, 2017). The Petroleum (Exploration, Development and Production) Act 2013 (GoU, 2013) further entrenches environment protection in the oil and gas sector and requires oil companies to adhere to existing environmental legislation.

Uganda is currently implementing oil-related activities in the exploration and development phases. The Ugandan government has confirmed plans to build a refinery at Kabaale in Buseruka sub-county, Hoima district, and is currently soliciting for a company to construct it under public–private sector partnership (Magona and Angom, 2017). It is envisaged that the Government of Uganda will contribute 40% of the project equity while the Lead Investor will contribute the other 60% (MEMD, 2017a). It is anticipated that the refinery will have a capacity of 60,000 barrels per day (ibid).

In addition to the refinery in Kabaale area, there will be an international airport built and the project is expected to start in 2018 and be completed by 2020 (Mbanga, 2017). The airport is expected to ease the transportation of heavy materials needed for exploration and development of oil resources (ibid).

On 26 May 2017 the Governments of Uganda and of the United Republic of Tanzania signed the *Inter-Governmental Agreement for the East African Crude Oil Pipeline (EACOP) Project* (MEMD, 2017b). The proposed pipeline will be approximately 1,445 kilometres and worth $3.55b with a capacity to transport 216,000 barrels of oil per day, making it the world's longest electrically heated crude oil pipeline (Musisi, 2017; Kamoga, 2017; MEMD, 2017b). The pipeline works will be undertaken by Total Exploration and Production (E&P), China National Offshore Oil Corporation (CNOOC) and Tullow Oil plc, together with the two governments of Uganda and Tanzania (MEMD, 2017b). Two feeder pipelines, i.e., the northern feeder line from Buliisa district to the refinery in Kabaale, Hoima district, and the southern feeder line from Kingfisher oil well to Kabaale, will also be constructed. A pipeline for refined products will be constructed from Kabaale to Buloba in Wakiso district near Kampala and this will be coupled with power transmission lines covering 213 kilometres (Lyatuu, 2016; Muhumuza, 2016; Kwesiga, 2016). The construction of new roads and upgrading of existing ones is on-going and more have been planned and budgeted for to ensure reliable transport infrastructure for the oil and gas industry from the Albertine region to Kampala and the neighbouring countries (Agaba, 2017).

Case study

Land rights abuses, scale, and actors in the Albertine region

The case study was conducted in the districts of Buliisa (02 11N, 31 24E), Hoima (01 24N, 31 18E) and Nebbi (02 28 45N, 31 05 24E). The 2014 Uganda National Population Census report (UBOS, 2016) indicates that Hoima district has a population of 572,986, while Buliisa has 113,161 and Nebbi 396,794 people respectively. Most of the population in these districts is rural and majorly derive their livelihood through crop cultivation, while others are involved in fishing and livestock production (Byakagaba and Twesigye, 2015). The population traditionally is divided into clans, sub-clans or lineages. Each clan or lineage traditionally has leaders who would arbitrate in conflicts and allocate rights to the use of land because land was communally owned and held in trust by the clan leaders (Howes, 1997).

Most of the land in the Albertine region of Uganda is customarily owned through communal rights arrangements (Byakagaba and Twesigye, 2015), but these remain 'informal' because they are not formally registered as provided in the Land Act 1998 (Tumusiime et al., 2016). The Land Act 1998 (GoU, 1998) recognises communal customary land, whether registered or not, but that the de facto interpretation of unregistered communal land is that it is informally owned.

The population is dominated by peasants who have been reported elsewhere (Zalik, 2009) to be discriminated against and deprived of their right to access productive resources on land due to oil and gas activities. The objective of this case study was to determine the nature of land rights abuses, their scale and actors involved in the Albertine region of Uganda.

Methodology

A multi-level sampling procedure was applied. Two sub-counties were purposively selected from each district, depending on intensity of oil and gas activities, and one parish purposively chosen from the selected sub-counties, depending on the proximity to oil and gas activity. One village that is nearest to an oil and gas activity was purposively selected from the parish and 30 respondents randomly selected from a local council register of each village. Panyimur and Pakwach sub-counties were selected in Nebbi, while Buliisa and Ngwedo were selected in Buliisa district. Buseruka and Kabwoya were selected in Hoima district. A total of 21 key informants were selected, depending on the ascertained knowledge on objectives of the study. These included local politicians, area members of parliament, bureaucrats in land administration, opinion and cultural leaders, and members of civil society organisations operating in the region.

Quantitative data were collected using a questionnaire at household level, while qualitative data were collected using key informant interviews, focus group discussions and village meetings, which were all guided by predetermined questions. All data were collected in 2014.

At least two focus group discussions (FGDs) and one village meeting were held in each sampled site. Each FGD included on average 4–8 participants. The focus groups included women, youth, men, fisher folks, cultivators, and traders. Key informants were interviewed individually to triangulate information obtained from the households. Focus group discussions and village meetings were applied to have more detailed collective narration of views related to the objective of the study by the different social groups. They were useful because they enabled peer reviewing and checks of information shared by participants, and this became the first step of validating the data but they were also useful in identifying views that may be unique to a particular social group.

Data from the household surveys were edited, coded and entered for analysis using the SPSS package. Logistic regression was used to determine the relationship between binary responses and socio-demographic characteristics of the respondents. Descriptive statistics of selected parameters for each study objective were generated. We followed the approach of Svarstad (2010) of manual coding of the key messages from the FGDs and key informant interviews to identify perceptions on the themes of study.

Findings from case study

Nature of land rights abuses, scale and actors

About 92% of the respondents were aware of land rights abuses, while 7% had not heard of any land rights abuses and 1% did not provide a response on this issue. Various types of land rights abuses were reported (Figure 12.2).

Knowledge of the existence of land rights abuses significantly improved with the length of residence within the Albertine region of Uganda ($p<0.017$). Respondents who had lived in the area for a long time were more likely to respond in affirmative when asked the question on whether there were land rights abuses. The most mentioned abuse was unfair compensation of residents whose land was taken over by government for oil exploration and refinery activities. This was mentioned in nearly all sites visited and was particularly prevalent in Kabaale parish (Hoima district), the proposed location of the oil refinery. Within the FGDs, unfair compensation was mostly mentioned by crop farmers compared with those involved in fishing.

One participant in the women FGDs in Kabaale parish (a site the government of Uganda secured for constructing an oil refinery), Hoima district, said:

> These people from government promised us that they would compensate us based on the market value of our crops, but they instead pay us less than what one [would] get in the market. For our fruit trees, it seems they only count fruits on the tree and then pay for that yet this tree can potentially continue supplying me with fruits [in perpetuity]. This is very unfair and unacceptable.

(Interview, 2014)

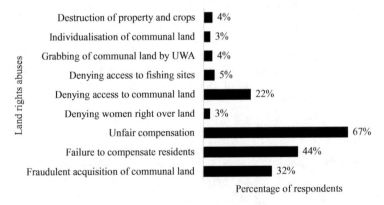

Figure 12.2 Land rights abuses in the Albertine Graben.

A key informant from Buliisa who worked for a local community-based organisation said:

> We as local people find the compensation rates very low for our crops. Imagine these people do not look at the tubers under each cassava shrub, but instead just fix a price depending on the area planted with cassava. We don't participate at all in determining the rates yet we are the ones losing our crops to create space for oil activities.
>
> (Interview, 2014)

Another key informant who worked for the District Local Government of Buliisa indicated that compensation rates prepared by districts are often revised downwards by the Chief Government Valuer from the Ministry of Lands, Housing and Urban Development without any justifiable explanation, and this has often created acrimony between those who have lost their property and district officials. He further said: 'It is very common for the compensation rates to be way below the market value and our hands are tied because the Chief Government Valuer has the final say on compensation rates that government agencies apply' (Interview, 2014).

The rates were perceived to be unfair in all the FGDs and key informant interviews held. For instance, one key informant who was a local leader in Kabaale, Hoima district, said:

> One acre of land is valued at UGX 4.5 million shillings by government ($1,250) yet the market price of equivalent land in neighbouring areas is 7–8 million shillings ($1,944–2,222). I wonder who provides government with information on market rates of land in this area? It is impossible for us to buy land in neighbouring areas because what we have been compensated with is not sufficient.
>
> (Interview, 2014)

The FGDs of men in Nebbi district revealed that the compensation for their land to create roads for oil activities was very low. One of them was quoted to have said: 'Government pays very little for our land claiming that we don't have land titles. This is one way of cheating us because most people in Nebbi live on customary land which has never had land titles' (Interview, 2014).

The practice of fraudulent acquisition of communal land by the elite within the community (commonly referred to as land grabbing in Uganda's media) was mentioned by relatively many respondents as one of the other most frequent land rights abuses. Key informant interviews revealed that communal land was fraudulently registered as freehold by financially and politically connected individuals with support from some bureaucrats in agencies responsible for land administration and control, especially the Area Land Committees and District Land Boards in all the three districts that were sampled for the study. A local opinion leader in Buliisa said:

These land grabbers are so rich, cunning, sophisticated and are powerful and some of them are our sons. They work with all government agencies to grab our land. This has left our people landless yet land is our most important resource for our livelihood considering that we keep livestock.

(Interview, 2014)

Causes of land rights abuses

One of the major causes of the land rights abuses was residents' lack of awareness of their rights (59%), as shown in Figure 12.3.

Key informant interviews and focus group discussions revealed that there are no interventions focusing on raising civic consciousness and knowledge of the policy and legal framework governing land in Uganda. The women groups showed that they were totally unaware of the legal provisions that protect family land. One of the participants in the women FGD said: 'Those issues of laws on land are known by men who attend meetings that non-governmental organisations organise. For us women, we are always busy taking care of our homes' (Interview, 2014).

One of the key informants who worked with Buliisa local government indicated that some sub-counties within the district did not have Area Land Committees that would have raised awareness on laws relevant to land among the local population. He said:

Some of the areas in the district do not have land committees. To make matters worse, the laws and policies are in English and most local people are illiterate. This keeps them in the dark as far as land matters in the law are concerned.

(Interview, 2014)

The FGD that included members of a civil society organisation indicated that they have a challenge in raising awareness on land across the region or

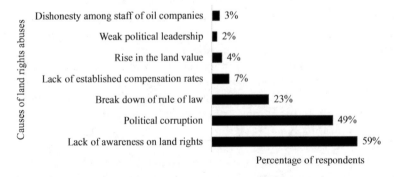

Figure 12.3 Causes of land rights abuses in the Albertine Graben.

district because their operating licenses do not provide for covering other areas outside the jurisdiction that their licenses indicate. This has affected their activities in areas where they are not expected to operate.

One of the participants observed that a:

> Lack of NGOs in some of the areas in the region is partly the reason why people are very ignorant on land policies and laws. They do not know what rights and privileges the law provides for them on land. This ignorance is what the land grabbers are taking advantage of and this is really absurd.
>
> (Interview, 2014)

Political corruption and breakdown of the rule of law were the other major causes of land rights abuses in the region. All the FGDs and most key informant interviews indicated that duty bearers in land offices were using their authority to facilitate fraudulent acquisition of communal land. One key informant mentioned that:

> These officers in lands are bribed by rich people to facilitate fraudulent acquisition of communal land. Many of them are untouchable even when you attempt to use the law. It seems they are now bigger than the laws of Uganda.
>
> (Interview, 2014)

The men's FGD in Buliisa revealed that members of the Area Land Committees are often bribed to facilitate fraudulent acquisition of communal land, which is consequently registered as freeholds and privately owned. One member said:

> These land committees use their authority to clear land grabbers once they have paid them. Remember they don't have a salary and only survive on land transactions. This makes them very vulnerable to being bribed thus promoting illegal land acquisitions.
>
> (Interview, 2014)

Perpetrators of land rights abuses

Approximately 57% of respondents mentioned that local political leaders were the most common category of perpetrators of land rights abuses. Other actors are shown in Figure 12.4.

Local political leaders, bureaucrats, together with the 'rich and politically connected people' were the main perpetrators of land rights abuses. Most land rights abuses, especially where communal land was fraudulently converted into freeholds, involved all the three categories. Local politicians and bureaucrats benefited financially by facilitating such illegal dealings while the rich and powerful speculators benefited by acquiring land. This was

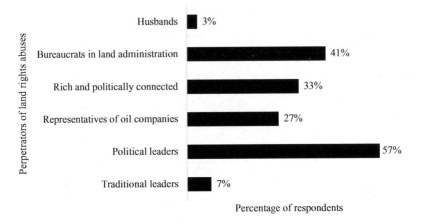

Figure 12.4 Perpetrators of land rights abuses.

mainly due to citizens' lack of awareness of their land rights, and the complexity and high costs of accessing justice through the formal legal systems. The FGDs showed that the motivation to fraudulently acquire land in this region by the rich and politically connected was the speculation that there were oil and gas deposits. One member of the FGD involving members of a civil society organisation in Buliisa said:

> Local politicians and government bureaucrats benefit financially from such dealings while the rich and powerful acquire land which they speculate will give them high returns because of the potential economic growth that may come with the oil industry in the area.
>
> (Interview, 2014)

When respondents were asked about the main activities undertaken by local leadership leading to land rights abuses, about 82% mentioned that some traditional leaders such as clan heads connived with land grabbers to register their customary land into freeholds, while 18% stated that traditional leaders abdicate their role of sensitising the community on their land rights, thus rendering them susceptible to land rights abuses. Approximately 74% mentioned that political leaders promote or sustain land rights abuses by conniving with land speculators to grab land. One key informant in Hoima district who worked with a local community-based organisation said:

> Our biggest challenge in this place is that our political leaders whom we would expect to protect the rights of the people they serve are instead in bed with land grabbers. The local communities do not have anywhere to run to for any meaningful redress.
>
> (Interview, 2014)

According to respondents, companies and firms responsible for preparing Resettlement Action Plans and similar compensation packages contribute to land rights abuse by undervaluing the property of the people for compensation in areas where oil activities were being implemented. This problem was mentioned by 79% of the respondents. Apparently, the organisations responsible for valuing land did not put into consideration the inherent variation of the value of property in 'villages' and trading centres and, in some cases, they were inconsistent in the valuation procedure applied to households in the same vicinity. The FGDs and key informant interviews revealed that the individuals involved in valuation for compensation were corrupt and often valued the property of those who bribed them highly, and undervalued property of those who did not. It was common to find two adjacent affected people being paid different rates for similar properties, as was observed by one of the women in an FGD in Hoima district who said:

> Can you imagine, I and my neighbour with the same type of house and a distance of 10 metres separating us had a disparity in compensation that was nearly 10 times. I wondered whether his bricks had something special that justified the high value compared to mine.
>
> (Interview, 2014)

Surely he must have spoken the language those who compensate understand. A key respondent in Hoima who worked with the sub-county local government also mentioned that the organisation responsible for valuing land did not put into consideration the inherent variation of the value of property in 'villages' and trading centres. A uniform rate was given to all claimants irrespective of the location of the property, yet there are differences in value based on existing economic activities.

The companies involved in compensation were also faulted for failing to register all legitimate claimants for compensation. Some of the FGDs and key informants showed that the companies involved in registering claims focused only on what they considered to be valuable property. One participant in a women's FGD in Nebbi district said:

> Government never compensated me for the termite mounds on my land that offer us white ants every year. When we asked they told us that the district authorities did not have a compensation rate for them and therefore they could not pay for termite mounds.
>
> (Interview, 2014)

Failure to inform communities on their rights over land by companies responsible for preparing resettlement action plans and compensation was mentioned by 11% of the respondents. Similar observations were made by key informants and in FGDs. One key informant in Buliisa said: 'None of those companies ever tell you what you should expect in terms of rights before they take your land or property. We are simply at their mercy' (Interview, 2014).

Synthesis of the case study

Increasing value of land in the Albertine region due to speculation of positive externalities from oil and gas development has led wealthy and politically connected elites to acquire land, whether vacant or inhabited, through fraudulently purchasing and registering communally owned lands into individual freeholds, where they can exclude communities that hitherto had rights over the land. This has been made possible due to their access to finances and relevant political connections to influence the formal registration process of the fraudulently acquired land.

This is in spite of unregistered communal land ownership being recognised under the customary tenure system, which is provided for in Section 3 of the Land Act 1998 (GoU, 1998). Section 23 of the Land Act 1998 (GoU, 1998) provides for registration of such land through communal land associations for the purpose of grazing and watering of livestock, hunting, gathering of wood fuel and building materials, gathering of honey and other forest resources for food and medicinal purposes, and such other purposes as may be traditional among the community using the land communally. Registration of communal land is, however, not mandatory and failure to register it does not in any way remove ownership rights (GoU, 1998).

Some of the key informants interviewed revealed that communal land that is not occupied is perceived by the duty bearers of land administration as land that is not owned by anybody and therefore is at risk of being fraudulently acquired. This is exacerbated by the fact that Section 59 (1) (a) of the Land Act 1998 gives authority to the District Land Boards to hold and allocate land in the district that is not owned by any person or authority. It is therefore not surprising that bureaucrats in land administration were identified as the second most common perpetrators of land rights abusers after political leaders. The District Land Boards seem to be taking advantage of that specific provision since the Act does not provide an interpretation of 'land not owned by any person'.

Local communities are finding it hard to protect and defend their customary claims due to inadequate knowledge of their legal rights, corruption among local leaders and duty bearers in land administration and eroding rule of law in the Albertine region. The process of registering customary land to acquire certificates of customary ownership or certificates of communal land ownership through communal land associations that is provided for in the Land Act 1998 is still relatively expensive and bureaucratic for the local people in the Albertine region. This further confirms Wily (2011b) who posits that customary land in Africa – especially land that has not been settled on or farmed – is vulnerable to involuntary loss.

Local leaders mandated to protect local land rights and to enforce the legal regime are not performing their duties diligently, considering the rate at which fraudulent land acquisition is occurring in the region. The legal safeguards in the *Land Policy 2013* (GoU, 2013) and Land Act 1998

(GoU, 1998), intended to prevent land rights abuses, do not seem to be effectively preventing misconduct, thus local communities find themselves in increasing risk of dispossession of land as oil sector development spurs land rush in the region.

There seems to be no visible political will at national and local level to provide redress or prevent the current fraudulent acquisition of communal land in the region. The Ministry of Lands, Housing and Urban Development has not prioritised this region in terms of registering customary land in this area, despite the threats of loss of land that the local communities face. One of the key informants noted:

> The Ministry of Lands, Housing and Urban Development is not interested in the oil districts because the current fraudulent acquisition of communal land and sometimes private customary land is by politically connected people who act as surrogates of very powerful people in this country with influence in central government including controlling where the Ministry can implement their pilot projects for registering customary land.
>
> (Interview, 2014)

The FGDs of men and some key informant interviews indicated that the land that is usually targeted is that suspected to have oil reserves, suggesting that the local elites have information on which sites are targeted for exploration. One of the participants claimed that:

> Rich people get information from government officials on which land has oil and then acquire it fraudulently so that they get all the compensation that government pays on exploration sites. It cannot be a coincidence that the land that is fraudulently acquired is usually the one where there is exploration or oil has been confirmed. We shall continue to lose our land as long as there is oil in this area because of the connections with powerful people in government that these land grabbers have.
>
> (Interview, 2014)

The current case study shows that, in spite of having a legal provision for customary communal land tenure system in Uganda, communal land that has not been registered as the law suggests remains susceptible to being fraudulently acquired in areas where there is oil and gas activities.

The involvement of politicians, local elites, and bureaucrats in land administration in fraudulent acquisition of communal land in this region suggests that this issue can be best understood with a political-economy lens. The current case study corroborates Wily (2011b), who contends that legal weaknesses and political-economic interests of state-level actors are the underlying reasons for land grabbing in Africa. At the local level, fraudulent acquisition of land is being driven by the anticipation of increase in value of land due to oil and gas development while, at national level, it is driven by the desire of powerful politicians and elites who have control over state agencies to be compensated with colossal sums of money in case there are oil deposits on the acquired land.

Land rush in the Albertine region is orchestrated by local and national elites who act as surrogates of national and international companies that envision economic opportunities of the nascent oil and gas industry. As Uganda moves into mid-stream oil and gas activities, there are more economic opportunities, thus attracting more local and international investors. In their study, CRED (2015) reported numerous scenarios of fraudulent land acquisitions that were partly inspired by inflow of finances from local and international companies that are targeting investing in infrastructure relevant to the oil and gas industry such as waste facilities. This will leave the local communities worse off amidst oil and gas reserves. This is because land rush denies local communities the most important asset for any community whose livelihood is nature-based.

Potential consequences of land rights abuses on the socio-ecological system of the Albertine region

Large-scale land acquisition often targets communal land that is not farmed, forests and rangelands Wily (2011b), yet these natural ecosystems are important for human livelihoods (Liu et al., 2007b). We used the framework developed by Ostrom (2009) to delineate the components of the socio-ecological system with its subsystems that may be affected by land rush in the Albertine region of Uganda. This is because human beings shape ecosystem dynamics and rely on ecosystems services and support and there is feedback (Folke, 2006).

In his review on the social and environmental impacts of land rush in Africa, Richards (2013) observed that land degradation, depletion of water resources, biodiversity loss, soil erosion, and carbon emissions were a common occurrence in countries that had experienced land rush. Similarly, Schoneveld (2017), in his synthesis of lessons from 38 case studies in Ethiopia, Ghana, Nigeria, and Zambia, showed that land rush is analogous to displacement, dispossession, and environmental degradation. He observed that local people lose pastureland and forestland, and this may result in negative impacts on livelihoods, reduced capacity to cope, and increased pressure on the remaining community resources.

Land rush can result in conversion of natural habitats such as forests and hitherto uncultivated or uncultivable communal rangelands (Balehegn, 2015). It increases pressure on existing forests and rangelands (De Schutter, 2011).

Deforestation can threaten biodiversity, climate, and livelihoods (Bala et al., 2007). In their study of forest cover change in the Albertine region of Uganda in the last three decades, Twongyirwe et al. (2015) found that annual forest loss in areas outside protected land in the Albertine Graben was 3.3%, which was higher than the national average (1–2%) as indicated in the State of Forest report (GoU, 2016). They observed that protected areas in the Albertine region of Uganda had been under more threat in the recent years than 20 years ago. This may be attributed to the current land rush that leaves many people landless and thus encroaching on protected areas as a result. This may have severe social and ecological consequences both within and outside protected areas (Twongyirwe et al., 2015), including increased carbon emissions, thus contributing to global environmental and climatic change. If this is not addressed, Uganda may not be able to achieve the targets made in the Nationally Determined Contributions of the 2015 Paris Agreement under the United Nations Framework Convention on Climate Change.

Land rush due to oil and gas activities has resulted in a breakdown of the governance system, especially on customary land, thus increasing land tenure insecurity through fraudulent acquisition of land by powerful elites in the region. Other authors (Hall, 2011; Borras and Franco, 2011; Davis et al., 2014) found that it causes displacement of the local communities, negation of existing land rights, social polarisation, political instability, food insecurity, and decline in income and employment. This may result in expansion of settlements into reserved land for socio-ecological benefits, such as forests and rangelands, thus accelerating environmental damage (Borras and Franco, 2011).

Studies done elsewhere in Uganda by Banana and Gombya-Ssembajjwe (2000) found that the ecological forest conditions of sites where tenure rights were insecure were poor compared with where there was security of tenure.

This therefore suggests that local communities may resort to unsustainable practices in the use of the remaining common resources such as forests, wetlands, and rangelands. This, if not addressed, may result in degradation and/or depletion of the resource system. Considering the fact that most communities in the Albertine region derive their livelihood through use of natural ecosystems, their degradation will reduce their social and ecological resilience.

Conclusion

Land rush in the Albertine Graben is majorly perpetuated by weaknesses in the land laws of Uganda, in regard to customary communal land and political–economic interests of state-level actors that operate with local actors either as direct or indirect surrogates.

The motivation is to acquire ownership of land that may potentially have oil deposits so as to gain from compensation by government or is suitable for supporting the oil and gas industry. This has led to loss of customary land rights of especially the marginalised communities who do not have the capacity to seek legal redress. This has caused displacement of these communities and potentially will lead to settlements expanding into marginal and protected areas in the region. This will not only deepen economic disparities but also increase social division, which may be a recipe for instability in this region. Loss of customary land rights will cause more pressure on existing protected areas as local communities try to eke out a living under the current conditions of lack of the most productive asset in agrarian economies. This will negatively affect the socio-ecological balance, since it is no longer plausible to implement traditional landuse systems such as rotational grazing and other adaptive land-use practices that the local communities have always practiced because of the new land-tenure arrangements that promote land fragmentation.

There is a high chance that natural ecosystems that are still available on land that has not been acquired by speculators will be over-utilised beyond their natural rates of recovery. This will not only cause land degradation but may eventually result in biodiversity loss in areas that are not protected. This potentially can negatively affect the livelihoods of the local communities due to decline in the flow of ecosystem services that they depend on and, eventually, the socio-ecological system may collapse, thus further threatening the biodiversity in the protected areas such as Murchison Falls conservation area, which is one of Uganda's iconic biodiversity landscapes.

Acknowledgements

Data collection was funded by Democratic Governance Facility. The authors thank all the communities and organisations that participated in the study. Research assistants that were involved in the data collection are equally acknowledged. The staff at CRED (Civic Response on Environment and Development) are acknowledged for all the logistical arrangements for the field work.

References

Agaba, J. (2017) 'Government prioritizes 10 oil roads', *Sunday Vision*, Kampala, Uganda.

Anderson, D.M. and Browne, A.J. (2011) 'The politics of oil in Eastern Africa', *Journal of Eastern African Studies*, vol. 5, no. 2, pp. 369–410.

André, C. and Platteau, J.P. (1998) 'Land relations under unbearable stress: Rwanda caught in the Malthusian trap', *Journal of Economic Behavior and Organization*, vol. 34, no. 1, pp. 1–47.

Bala, G., Caldeira, K., Wickett, M., Phillips, T.J., Lobell, D.B., Delire, C., and Mirin, A. (2007) 'Combined climate and carbon-cycle effects of large-scale deforestation', *Proceedings of the National Academy of Sciences*, vol. 104, no. 16, pp. 6550–6555.

Balehegn, M. (2015) 'Unintended consequences: the ecological repercussions of land grabbing in Sub-Saharan Africa', *Environment: Science and Policy for Sustainable Development*, vol. 57, no. 2, pp. 4–21.

Banana, A.Y. and Gombya-Ssembajjwe, W. (2000) 'Successful forest management: the importance of security of tenure and rule enforcement in Ugandan forests', in C. C. Gibson, M. A. McKean and E. Ostrom (eds), *People and Forests: communities, institutions, and governance*, MIT Press, Cambridge, MA, USA, pp. 87–98.

Borras, S. and Franco, J. (2011) *Political Dynamics of Land-grabbing in Southeast Asia*. Transnational Institute, Amsterdam, The Netherlands.

Byakagaba, P. and Twesigye, B. (2015) *Securing Communal Land and Resource Rights in the Albertine region of Uganda: the case of Hoima and Buliisa districts*, Civic Response on Environment and Development (CRED), Kampala, Uganda.

Bybee, A.N. and Johannes, E.M. (2014) 'Neglected but affected: voices from the oil-producing regions of Ghana and Uganda', *African Security Review*, vol. 23, no. 2, pp. 132–144.

Chimhowu, A. and Woodhouse, P. (2006) 'Customary vs private property rights? Dynamics and trajectories of vernacular land markets in Sub-Saharan Africa', *Journal of Agrarian Change*, vol. 6, no. 3, pp. 346–371.

Civic Response on Environment and Development (CRED) (2015) *'Up Against Giants'. Oil-influenced land injustices in the Albertine Graben in Uganda*. Case study research findings presented by CRED in partnership with TIU and DGF, Kampala, Uganda, p. 44.

Collins, S.L., Carpenter, S.R., Swinton, S.M., Orenstein, D.E., Childers, D.L., Gragson, T.L., Knapp, A.K., et al. (2011) 'An integrated conceptual framework for long-term social–ecological research', *Frontiers in Ecology and the Environment*, vol. 9, no. 6, pp. 351–357.

Cotula, L. (2012) 'The international political economy of the global land rush: a critical appraisal of trends, scale, geography and drivers', *Journal of Peasant Studies*, vol. 39, nos 3–4, pp. 649–680.

Davis, K.F., D'Odorico, P., and Rulli, M.C. (2014) 'Land grabbing: a preliminary quantification of economic impacts on rural livelihoods', *Population and Environment*, vol. 36, no. 2, pp. 180–192.

De Schutter, O. (2011) 'How not to think of land-grabbing: three critiques of large-scale investments in farmland', *Journal of Peasant Studies*, vol. 38, no. 2, pp. 249–279.

Energy Information Administration (EIA) (2017) *Monthly Energy Review, May 2017*. Energy Information Administration, Washington, DC, USA.

Folke, C. (2006) 'Resilience: the emergence of a perspective for social–ecological systems analyses', *Global Environmental Change*, vol. 16, no. 3, pp. 253–267.

German, L., Schoneveld, G., and Mwangi, E. (2013) 'Contemporary processes of large-scale land acquisition in sub-Saharan Africa: legal deficiency or elite capture of the rule of law?', *World Development*, vol. 48, August, pp. 1–18. Available at: http://dx.doi.org/10.1016/j.worlddev.2013.03.006.

Government of Uganda (GoU) (1995a) *The National Environment Act*. Government of Uganda, Kampala, Uganda.

Government of Uganda (GoU) (1995b) *The National Environment Management Policy*. Government of Uganda, Kampala, Uganda.

Government of Uganda (GoU) (1998) *The Land Act*. Government of Uganda, Kampala, Uganda.

Government of Uganda (GoU) (2008) *National Oil and Gas Policy for Uganda*. Government of Uganda, Kampala, Uganda.

Government of Uganda (GoU) (2013) *Petroleum (Exploration, Development and Production) Act*. Government of Uganda, Kampala, Uganda.

Government of Uganda (GoU) (2014) *The Draft National Environment Management policy for Uganda*. Government of Uganda, Kampala, Uganda.

Government of Uganda (GoU) (2016) *Uganda Wetland Atlas (Volume 2)*. Government of Uganda, Kampala, Uganda.

Government of Uganda (GoU) (2017) *The National Environment Bill*. Government of Uganda, Kampala, Uganda.

Hall, R. (2011) 'Land grabbing in Southern Africa: the many faces of the investor rush', *Review of African Political Economy*, vol. 38, no. 128, pp. 193–214.

Howes, M. (1997) 'NGOs and the development of local institutions: a Ugandan case-study', *The Journal of Modern African Studies*, vol. 35, no. 1, pp. 17–35.

Kamoga, J. (2017) 'Construction of Uganda's oil pipeline flagged off in Tanzania', *The Observer*, 5 August, Kampala, Uganda.

Kharaka, Y.K. and Dorsey, N.S. (2005) 'Environmental issues of petroleum exploration and production: introduction', *Environmental Geosciences*, vol. 12, no. 2, pp. 61–63.

Kwesiga, P. (2016) 'Building oil pipeline: evaluation of firms starts', *Sunday Vision*, 2 January, Kampala, Uganda.

Liu, J., Dietz, T., Carpenter, S.R., Alberti, M., Folke, C., Moran, E., Ostrom, E., et al. (2007a) 'Complexity of coupled human and natural systems', *Science*, vol. 317, no. 5844, pp. 1513–1516.

Liu, J., Dietz, T., Carpenter, S.R., Folke, C., Alberti, M., Redman, C. L., and Taylor, W.W. (2007b) 'Coupled human and natural systems', *AMBIO: A Journal of the Human Environment*, vol. 36, no. 8, pp. 639–649.

Luning, S. (2012) 'Corporate Social Responsibility (CSR) for exploration: consultants, companies and communities in processes of engagements', *Resources Policy*, vol. 37, no. 2, pp. 205–211.

Lyatuu, J. (2016) 'Oil-rich Bunyoro seeks answers over pipeline', *The Observer*, 30 December, Kampala, Uganda.

Magona, F. and Angom, M. (2017) *State of Oil and Gas in Uganda – 2017*, MMAK Advocates, Kampala, Uganda.

Mbanga, J. (2017) 'MPs approve Shs 1.3 tn loan for Hoima airport', *The Observer*, 17 December, Kampala, Uganda.

Messerli, P. et al. (2013) 'From "land grabbing" to sustainable investments in land: potential contributions by land change science', *Current Opinion in Environmental Sustainability*, vol. 5, no. 5, pp. 528–534.

Ministry of Energy and Mineral Development (MEMD) (2017a) *The Oil and Gas sector in Uganda: frequently asked questions*. Ministry of Energy and Mineral Development, Kampala, Uganda.

Ministry of Energy and Mineral Development (MEMD) (2017b) *Uganda and Tanzania Sign Inter Governmental Agreement for Crude Oil Pipeline*, press statement, Ministry of Energy and Mineral Development, Kampala, Uganda.

Monticino, M., Acevedo, M., Callicott, B., Cogdill, T., and Lindquist, C. (2007) 'Coupled human and natural systems: a multi-agent-based approach', *Environmental Modelling and Software*, vol. 22, no. 5, pp. 656–663.

Muhumuza, M.K. (2016) 'Government starts resettlement study on Hoima-Buloba oil pipeline', *Daily Monitor*, 5 May, Kampala, Uganda.

Musisi, F. (2017) 'Uganda, Tanzania sign off Hoima–Tanga oil pipeline construction', *Daily Monitor*, 23 May, Kampala, Uganda.

Ostrom, E. (2009) 'A general framework for analyzing sustainability of social-ecological systems', *Science*, vol. 325, no. 5939, pp. 419–422.

Plumptre, A.J. (2002) *Extent and Status of the Forests in the Ugandan Albertine Rift*, Wildlife Conservation Society, Kampala, Uganda.

Plumptre, A.J., Behangana, M., Ndomba, E., Davenport, T., Kahindo, C., Kityo, R. Ssegawa, P., Eilu, G., Nkuutu, D., and Owiunji, I. (2003) *The Biodiversity of the Albertine Rift*, Albertine rift technical reports No. 3, Wildlife Conservation Society, Kampala, Uganda.

Plumptre, A.J. et al. (2007) 'The biodiversity of the Albertine Rift', *Biological Conservation*, vol. 134, no. 2, pp. 178–194.

Richards, M. (2013) *Social and Environmental Impacts of Agricultural Large-Scale Land Acquisitions in Africa: with a focus on West and Central Africa*. Rights and Resources Initiative, Washington, DC, USA.

Robertson, B. and Pinstrup-Andersen, P. (2010) 'Global land acquisition: neo-colonialism or development opportunity?', *Food Security*, vol. 2, no. 3, pp. 271–283.

Scheidel, A. and Sorman, A.H. (2012) 'Energy transitions and the global land rush: ultimate drivers and persistent consequences', *Global Environmental Change*, vol. 22, no. 3, pp. 588–595.

Schoneveld, G.C. (2017) 'Host country governance and the African land rush: 7 reasons why large-scale farmland investments fail to contribute to sustainable development', *Geoforum*, vol. 83, pp. 119–132.

Svarstad, H. (2010) 'Why hiking? Rationality and reflexivity within three categories of meaning construction', *Journal of Leisure Research*, vol. 42, no. 1, pp. 91–110.

Tumusiime, D.M., Mawejje, J., and Byakagaba, P. (2016) 'Discovery of oil: community perceptions and expectations in Uganda's Albertine region', *Journal of Sustainable Development*, vol. 9, no. 6, pp. 1–14.

Twongyirwe, R., Bithell, M., Richards, K.S., and Rees, W.G. (2015) 'Three decades of forest cover change in Uganda's northern Albertine Rift landscape', *Land Use Policy*, vol. 49, pp. 236–251.

Uganda Bureau of Statistics (UBOS) (2016) *National Population and Housing Census 2014. Main Report*, Uganda Bureau of Statistics, Kampala, Uganda.

Wildlife Conservation Society (WCS) (2016) *Nationally Threatened Species for Uganda. National: Red List for Uganda for the following Taxa: Mammals, Birds, Reptiles, Amphibians, Butterflies, Dragonflies and Vascular Plants*, Wildlife Conservation Society, Kampala, Uganda.

Wily, L. (2011a) *The Tragedy of Public Lands: Understanding the Fate of the Commons under Global Commercial Pressure*, International Land Coalition, Rome, Italy.

Wily, L.A. (2011b) '"The law is to blame": the vulnerable status of common property rights in sub-Saharan Africa', *Development and Change*, vol. 42, no. 3, pp. 733–757.

Young, O.R., Berkhout, F., Gallopin, G.C., Janssen, M.A., Ostrom, E., and Van der Leeuw, S. (2006) 'The globalization of socio-ecological systems: an agenda for scientific research', *Global Environmental Change*, vol. 16, no. 3, pp. 304–316.

Zalik, A. (2009) 'Zones of exclusion: offshore extraction, the contestation of space and physical displacement in the Nigerian Delta and the Mexican Gulf', *Antipode*, vol. 41, no. 3, pp. 557–582.

Zoomers, A. (2011) 'Introduction: rushing for land: equitable and sustainable development in Africa, Asia and Latin America', *Development*, vol. 52, no. 1, pp. 12–20.

Part V
Conclusion

13 Conservation, development, and the politics of ecological knowledge in Uganda

Connor Joseph Cavanagh, Chris Sandbrook, and David Mwesigye Tumusiime

Introduction

In the introductory chapter to this volume we highlighted both the dynamism and the fundamentally *uneven* character of conservation and development processes in Uganda. In many respects, the contributions to this book have illuminated precisely how such unevenness at times produces tensions, trade-offs, and potential contradictions between conservation and development objectives. In turn, efforts to implement related programmes despite these tensions have given rise to material outcomes for both human livelihoods and biodiversity that are highly unequal in their distribution across communities and landscapes.

Perhaps as a result, these outcomes are also fraught with contestation from both 'above' and 'below', involving the often-contending views of a diverse range of actors primarily based within Uganda as well as far beyond the country's borders. These opposing perspectives illuminate how what we might call a 'politics of ecological knowledge' is often at work in the representation of conservation and development outcomes. Here, particular ways and means of 'knowing' the environment (e.g., natural science or quantitative analyses) have historically often been privileged over others (e.g., 'traditional' ecological knowledge, local testimonies, and perhaps also qualitative research). In this sense, determinations about which views or sources of information 'count' for inclusion in decision-making processes are inherently political, reflecting the preferences – and perhaps also the biases – of the powerful in adjudicating between divergent claims, experiences, and narratives of conservation, development, and their consequences. In short, the chapters that comprise this volume confirm that, in practice, the tensions between conservation and development aims – as well as representations of their effects – in Uganda remain enduringly controversial.

Notwithstanding the *empirical* context above, the Ugandan state is now squarely engaged in a new round of policymaking – with the assistance of a variety of bilateral and multilateral organisations – that once again seeks to reframe conservation and development as mutually complementary rather than mutually exclusive pursuits. Here, the old concerns of sustainability and sustainable development have notably been complemented by a number of new policies and concepts. Chief among these are notions of 'green growth' or a 'green economy' transition (Republic of Uganda, 2017), as well as a shift towards a 'low carbon, climate resilient development' pathway in the country (Republic of Uganda, 2013). These efforts mirror a similar shift in global environment and development policy more broadly, especially following the UN Environment Programme's (2011) promotion of 'green economy' transition in advance of the Rio+20 conference on sustainable development in 2012, as well as the World Bank's (2012) related advocacy for a global development model of 'inclusive green growth'.

There is nothing especially 'new' about such endeavours to align conservation and development goals. As Adams (2009) reminds us, various efforts to 'green' development in East Africa are nearly as old as the states that constitute the region's contemporary political geography. This is not to say, however, that the futures of nature, conservation, and 'sustainable' or green development in Uganda will be defined by precisely the same difficulties that characterised their pasts (Adams, 2003; Doak et al., 2015). While familiar challenges such as antagonistic park–community relations, uneven cost–benefit distributions, crop raiding by protected wildlife, and other well-known concerns certainly persist, an increasingly diverse range of actors, concepts, discourses, and institutions continuously seem to enter this field of research and practice. As a result, the challenges of the past are in many ways *recombinant* with these novel dynamics, resulting in a conservation and development milieu that is continuously evolving.

In this concluding chapter, we offer a review of such recombinant interactions between longstanding and emerging dynamics by synthesising key lessons and insights from the preceding contributions to this volume. In what follows, we proceed by considering each substantive or empirical section of this book in turn, beginning with the individual case studies of specific protected areas explored in Part II. Second, as discussed in Part III, we consider both promising results and unfortunate pitfalls encountered in the performance of specific conservation and development tools adopted in Uganda to date. Third, we reflect on the broader implications of Part IV and its engagement with cross-sectoral dynamics influencing conservation and development outcomes. Finally, we conclude with a consideration of key questions for further research, which remain somewhat underexplored both in this volume and the extant literature on conservation and development in Uganda.

Celebrity sites? Experimentation and dissensus in place-based conservation governance

In Part II, individual chapters explored legacies of varying approaches to conservation and development at Bwindi Impenetrable National Park (Tumusiime *et al.* in Chapter 4), Mount Elgon National Park (Himmelfarb and Cavanagh in Chapter 5), and Budongo Central Forest Reserve (Babwe-teera et al. in Chapter 6). Each of these chapters has illuminated in considerable detail that the contemporary challenges faced by these and other protected areas in the country have deep roots. Indeed, as pointed out in a framing historical chapter by Banana et al. (Chapter 2), in particular, many of the latter challenges date to the adoption of certain conserva-tion policies and institutions in the British colonial era (1894–1963), as well as how these institutions fared within the tumultuous period of authoritarian rule that characterised the aftermath of Uganda's political independence (1962–1986). Rather than simple 'events' whose significance has faded over time, then, these processes have decidedly structured – but certainly not determined – both opportunities and constraints for the forms of conservation and development programmes that have followed in subsequent decades.

Considered over the longer sweep of Uganda's colonial and post-colonial histories, for instance, it is clear that protected areas at Bwindi, Mount Elgon, and Budongo have been the site of considerable experimentation with different approaches to conservation and development over time. Not least, such experimentation began with the colonial importation of the exclusionary protected area model itself to East Africa in the early twentieth century. Though the genealogy of modern protected areas can be traced to institutions like Yellowstone National Park (established in 1872) and Yosemite National Park (established in 1890) in the United States, the ear-liest protected areas in Uganda were notably created at a time when such measures were almost entirely unprecedented in eastern Africa.[1] Certainly, regulations on hunting and resource extraction were implemented under British rule from the late nineteenth century onward; for instance, in the form of the Land and Game Regulations issued by royal orders-in-council in 1897 and 1899 respectively (Johnston, 1902). Yet most of Uganda's first game and forest reserves did not begin to be demarcated until the 1930s (Webster and Osmaston, 2003), alongside early African protected areas like Albert National Park (now Virunga National Park) in the Belgian Congo in 1925, and Kruger National Park in South Africa in 1926 (see also Adams, 2004). The creation of these areas is thus perhaps best conceived as a tenuous kind of experiment in its own right rather than an extension of an already well-honed and easily adaptable blueprint for universally successful conservation.

At both Bwindi and Mount Elgon, for example, the creation of increas-ingly strict protected areas ushered in both a conceptual and a spatial distinction between human 'society' and nonhuman 'nature' amongst com-munities that had not previously drawn such a categorical division between the two. In particular, both the Batwa of contemporary Bwindi Impenetrable National Park and the Benet of Mount Elgon had previously resided *within* forests or upland forest glades, and had developed systems of social, politi-cal, and economic organisation that were well-adapted to these landscapes (e.g., Blomley, 2003; Himmelfarb, 2012). Pre-colonial communities of agri-culturalists and agro-pastoralists also evinced rich connections with forests both for cultural and practical reasons, and had developed pre-colonial institutions to regulate the use of natural resources as a result (Scott, 1998; Turyahabwe and Banana, 2008).

Hence, if modern conservation's 'first experiment' in Uganda was the demarcation of the early game and forest reserves, subsequent forms of trial and error would hinge upon managing the consequences of separat-ing rural communities from the ecosystems to which they had previously enjoyed more substantial access. As Himmelfarb and Cavanagh (Chapter 5) suggest, protected areas that appeared as legal, neatly gazetted, and fully documented from the vantage of the (colonial) state have thus often been unevenly territorialised on the ground. In short, numerous communi-ties have simply ignored newly demarcated boundaries and continued to practice their longstanding customary livelihoods within protected areas. In turn, this inconvenient empirical fact of the inconclusive separation of human communities from protected ecosystems has given rise to a sustained preoccupation with 'encroachment' and 'boundary conflicts' that lingers in discourses about conservation governance in Uganda to date (e.g., National Forestry Authority, 2011).

Indeed, in each of the three cases of Bwindi, Mount Elgon, and Budongo, recurring evictions or arrests of 'encroachers' or apparently 'illegal' resource users has been an enduring feature of protected area management over time. Uganda's *New Vision* newspaper, for instance, recently declared that '493 out of 506 central forest reserves in the country [or more than 97%] are under heavy encroachment, especially in the central region, south west and northern areas' (Lumu, 2017). Though certainly under pressure from grow-ing local communities, it is also the case that many of these reserves were perhaps never fully or conclusively territorialised in the first instance. In other words: the concept of 'encroachment' presumes that these areas were once comparatively free of human influence.

The question of how to ameliorate such conflicts whilst maintaining boundaries between communities and protected areas has therefore been a mainstay of both research and conservation practice in these areas. As Tumusiime et al. (Chapter 4) discuss, attempts to pilot many related 'community-based' conservation and benefit sharing schemes at Bwindi Impenetrable National Park in particular have arguably led to the park's emergence as something of a 'celebrity site' in international conserva-tion and development discourses. The park does indeed feature heavily in 'spectacular' (e.g., Igoe, 2017) NGO, donor, and media representations of conservation in both Uganda and sub-Saharan Africa more generally. Simultaneously, however, there has been considerable dissensus concern-ing both conservation effectiveness at Bwindi and the park's impacts on local communities. Whereas conservationists and donors have often high-lighted Bwindi's successes at both raising tourism revenue and preserving certain 'charismatic megafauna' – such as the area's precious community of mountain gorillas – critical social scientists have frequently stressed the ways in which the park has engendered conflicts with local residents, precipitated forceful evictions, and facilitated the elite capture of shared benefits from conservation. In many ways, such dissensus is also a common feature of both scholarly and popular discourses on conservation across the three sites of Bwindi, Mount Elgon, and Budongo, in which divergent conclusions often reflect the varying disciplinary backgrounds and interests of individual commentators. A lesson is perhaps that narratives of conservation's (in)effectiveness on either ecological or socio-economic grounds should always be taken with 'a grain of salt', given that the performance of these institutions can precipitate stridently normative as well as straightforwardly empirical debates.

The evolution and performance of conservation and development tools

Just as the effectiveness of many of Uganda's protected areas has been the source of considerable debate, so too has the performance of particular conservation and development 'tools' or approaches (see also Twinamatsiko et al. in Chapter 3). Part III of this volume explores some of the most salient of these, including carbon forestry and associated payment for ecosystem services (PES) initiatives (Nel et al. in Chapter 7), eco-tourism and related benefit-sharing mechanisms (Ahebwa et al. in Chapter 8), and the 'cultural values' approach to integrating conservation and development objectives (Infield and Mugisha in Chapter 9). Here again, the metaphor of 'experimentation' is salient, as Uganda has often been at the global forefront of early attempts to implement or test many of these approaches, if not constituting an important site of their 'invention' outright. Indeed, although Murphree (2000, p.12) once nicely quipped that community-based conservation in Africa had 'to date not been tried and found wanting; it has been found difficult and rarely tried', the last two decades have yielded a considerable amount of evidence precisely about diverse and sometimes contending efforts to 'try' the latter.

As Nel et al. (Chapter 7) note in their review of the literature on carbon forestry in Uganda, for instance, the country hosted one of the world's first carbon offsetting projects in the forestry sector. This was in the form of a partnership between a Dutch NGO – the Forests Absorbing Carbon Emissions (FACE) Foundation – and the Uganda Wildlife Authority (UWA) at Mount Elgon in the early 1990s (Cavanagh and Benjaminsen, 2014). Although the project largely collapsed due to local contestation nearly a decade after its implementation, Nel et al. (Chapter 7) point out that the project model adopted by UWA-FACE was only one of a range of possible institutional designs (see also Fisher et al., 2018). Since the inception of UWA-FACE in 1992, the carbon forestry sector in Uganda has grown to such an extent that it has recently been estimated to account for the fourth largest market share of carbon credits globally (Goldstein and Ruef, 2016). The latter emerge from dozens of projects trading either under the Clean Development Mechanism's (CDM) afforestation and reforestation framework, or over voluntary markets following certification from a range of third-party NGOs and private firms. Though controversies have certainly emerged about several of the latter on social and environmental justice grounds (e.g., Nel and Hill, 2013; Lyons and Westoby, 2014), project models integrating carbon forestry into smallholder farms and properties – rather than into exclusionary protected areas at the latter's expense – appear to have in some cases received a more welcome reception from certain rural communities (Cavanagh and Freeman, 2017; Fisher et al., 2018). Learning from these vastly divergent experiences will be especially critical as national-level plans for Reducing Emissions from Deforestation and Forest Degradation (REDD+) proceed apace, and with the potential to reproduce either the successes or the failures of past initiatives.

Similar to the manner in which a diversity of carbon offsetting project models have been tested in Uganda, Ahebwa et al. (Chapter 8) illuminate how a similar process of diversification has characterised the interface between conservation and the ecotourism sector. Tourism is a critical part of conservation and development efforts in the country, given that the sector contributes approximately 9% of Uganda's Gross Domestic Product (GDP). Both within and adjacent to protected areas, therefore, tourism promises to contribute to development by creating 'environmentally friendly' employment opportunities and generating finances that can be redistributed to nearby communities. Yet these efforts are likewise also not without their own controversies. Although ecotourism does indeed create employment, contribute to economic growth, and generate funds that may support local communities, questions of proportionality and distribution remain salient. Indeed, protected area-adjacent residence often entails a variety of costs for local households, for instance in the form of damage from crop-raiding wildlife or restrictions on access to natural resources. Benefits from tourism may therefore in some cases not be proportional to the scale of these costs, or – in other words – may insufficiently compensate for them. Likewise, redistributed funds and other benefits are often marginal relative to demand, and may therefore sometimes be used to strategically support or reward favoured constituencies at the expense of others, or may simply be captured by elites. Though certainly challenging, Ahebwa et al. (Chapter 8) note that efforts to resolve issues such as the latter are important, given that they are critical for securing the levels of local participation and support upon which successful ecotourism initiatives depend.

Seeking to identify means of achieving precisely such synergies between the interests of communities and conservationists, Infield and Mugisha (Chapter 9) review experiences in Uganda to date with what they term the 'cultural values approach' to conservation. In short, the cultural values approach seeks to 'recognise, validate, and build on [existing] cultural connections to nature' (ibid), rather than to undermine these with conservation models and institutions that erode the latter, even if unintentionally. Over the last two decades, this approach has been experimented with even inside state conservation agencies such as the Uganda Wildlife Authority, conceived as a prospective means of ameliorating persistent boundary conflicts throughout the protected area estate. As of 2015, for instance, UWA had explicitly incorporated cultural values programming into the management of at least half of Uganda's national parks. Despite early willingness to pilot cultural values initiatives, however, Infield and Mugisha (Chapter 9) note waning interest in the approach over time, and failures or refusals to fully institutionalise related best practices within the management frameworks of individual protected areas. In many ways, this reflects a longstanding politics of ecological knowledge *within* Uganda's conservation institutions. Here, modern 'scientific' language and methods for understanding the environment have often been privileged over local or vernacular conceptions of wildlife, ecosystem functions, and the symbolic importance of both. Though frequently conceived as a means of adjudicating impartially between conflicting rights claims or narratives of human–environment interactions, methods rooted in natural science and quantitative analysis are themselves also partial in the sense that they may exclude local communities and other constituencies who might lack the requisite training to effectively participate in these discussions or decision-making processes. Accordingly, such divergent understandings of the environment often contribute to tensions between local communities and various protected areas throughout the country.

Looking at the approaches reviewed in this section of the book as a whole, two points stand out. First, the approaches have tended to be developed and implemented as highly technical interventions that are developed by (often external) experts to achieve 'optimal' outcomes. Concepts like carbon forestry, tourism and even the cultural values approach have been introduced 'from above' rather than emerging 'from below'. In this respect, the Ugandan experience is similar to many conservation and/or development interventions from around the world that 'render technical' (Murray Li, 2007) processes that perhaps ought to be subject to a more deliberative and participatory political process. Second, there are constant shifts in the approaches to conservation and development that are to some degree 'trendy', or especially in favour at any given moment in time (see also Redford et al., 2013). New approaches emerge, and old ones fall out of favour (or are reinvented). Had this book been written ten years ago, the list in this section would be very different (only tourism would feature from the current set) and, likewise, if the book were written ten years from now, things would have changed again. For example, one new approach that did not quite make it into this book is biodiversity offsetting, which is now being practiced for the first time in Uganda around Mabira Forest Reserve.

Uneven conservation and development: cross-sectoral dynamics and Uganda's protected area estate

Although the above contributions have yielded a number of important insights about the available 'tools' for governing interactions between communities and protected areas, Part III of this volume has further enhanced our understanding by highlighting the salience of cross-sectoral dynamics in influencing conservation and development outcomes. Here, Jeary et al. (Chapter 10) focused on interactions between conservation and agriculture, whereas Petursson and Vedeld (Chapter 11) examined the influence of international donors on both commercial and conservationist forestry, and Byakagaba et al. (Chapter 12) interrogated the controversial prevalence of other extractive industry activities within and around Ugandan protected areas. In short – and albeit in different ways – each of these chapters illuminates the fundamentally *uneven* character of conservation and development throughout Uganda, as well as the dynamic processes that influence the governance of the latter at multiple scales. In other words, these contributions highlight the manner in which decisions about the intensity of conservation and other environmental regulations are increasingly made in the context of formal, informal, and continuously shifting calculations about the fiscality or profitability – and thus the desirability – of conservation relative to a variety of alternative land uses and across a range of ecologically distinct landscapes.

As Jeary et al. (Chapter 10) demonstrate, perhaps the most pressing alternative valuations and appraisals of conservation areas stem from the competing uses to which such lands and resources might be put within the agricultural sector. In Uganda, agriculture accounts for almost 25% of GDP and 70% of employment, with an estimated 75% of production occurring on small-scale or household farms (Deloitte, 2016). Agricultural products also comprise more than 65% of export values (ibid.). In such a context, massive pressure understandably exists to convert protected areas to agricultural use, given that this might result in considerable profits for agribusinesses or substantial employment and short-term livelihood security for smallholding farmers. In addition, corporate and agribusiness interests are increasingly successful at lobbying local governments and state agencies to make concessions in favour of agriculture – perhaps also at the expense of conservation (see, inter alia, Child, 2009; Kandel, 2015; Martiniello, 2015).

Despite these challenges, trade-offs between conservation and agriculture are not *inevitable*, however, as proposals for integrating conservation and sustainable food production through either 'land sharing' or 'land sparing' schemes increasingly indicate (Jeary et al., Chapter 10). Conversely, these authors also emphasise the crucial role of the state – or certain networks embedded within the state – in supporting integrative conservation and agricultural schemes rather than either strict exclusionary conservation (at the expensive of smallholder agriculture) or large agribusiness concessions (at the expense of both conservation and smallholders). In other words, although evidence is mounting for how both land-sharing and land-sparing approaches to sustainable agriculture might be effectively pursued, they still require political will and investment in order to be successful.

The role of the political economy of particular state agencies in the context of international donor support is a theme also squarely addressed by Petursson and Vedeld's (Chapter 11) analysis of reforms in Uganda's forest sector. Of particular interest to these authors is the set of processes put in place in the late 1990s with support from Germany, the United Kingdom, United States, Norway, and a variety of other donors to increase the efficiency and effectiveness of Ugandan forest management. This led to the transformation of the former Forest Department into the contemporary National Forestry Authority (NFA), as well as the devolution of responsibility over certain forests to the newly-established District Forestry Services (DFS).

Although this reorganisation was intended to correct many of the types of corruption and mismanagement of forest resources prevalent during the regimes of former presidents Milton Obote and Idi Amin, Petursson and Vedeld note that similar processes quickly resurfaced as President Yoweri Museveni's government sought to consolidate its hold on political power throughout the early 2000s. Such dynamics are crucial in accounting for the inconvenient fact – to take but one example – that unprecedented donor investment in Ugandan forestry authorities has been paralleled with a loss of almost 40% of forest cover under NFA control since 1990 (ibid.) This predicament in many respects cannot be explained without considering the often informal or neo-patrimonial mechanisms through which government officials either concede forest resources to private interests – such as via the agribusiness enterprises mentioned above (e.g., Child, 2009) – or allow local encroachment into forest reserves in exchange for political support.

Since the early 2000s in particular, a new range of powerful actors and interests have also begun to exert considerable influence over certain Ugandan protected areas: namely, oil companies and other extractive industry firms. Such is the focus of Byakagaba et al.'s (Chapter 12) contribution, which examines how these processes are unfolding in the context of both western Uganda's Albertine Graben generally, as well as the region surrounding Murchison Falls National Park more specifically. Their analysis is interesting in particular as it illuminates quite clearly the both direct and indirect implications of shifting valuations of land, natural resources, and ecosystems. Indeed, following the discovery of oil and surging potential ground rents, both communities and conservationists *alike* may find themselves displaced from protected areas. The influence of these dynamics is not limited to national parks and reserves, moreover, as speculation throughout entire geological regions such as the Albertine Graben may lead to rising land prices and the displacement of communities who lack clear titles to land and property. In turn, newly dispossessed populations may find themselves with little choice but to encroach upon protected areas or other sensitive environments to find shelter and extract at least a subsistence livelihood from the resource base. Hence, whilst extractive activities within protected areas of course entail direct environmental impacts, the second-order economic consequences of extractive industry also threaten to produce much more far-reaching consequences for land markets, investment patterns, and rural communities' relationships with ecosystems and the resource base.

Key questions and priorities for future research and policy

Despite the at times explicitly synthetic and comprehensive nature of many of the contributions to this volume, a number of conceptual or empirical 'gaps' admittedly remain both within this book and the literature on conservation and development in Uganda more broadly. In what follows, we thus conclude this work with a discussion of the prospects and potential advantages of directing future research and policymaking efforts toward a consideration of the latter.

- *Neglected communities, landscapes, and protected areas.* The research literature on conservation and development in Uganda is to some degree also characterised by its own element of unevenness. Whilst 'celebrity sites' such as Bwindi Impenetrable National Park and its mountain gorillas have attracted considerable attention from academics, scientists, and activists, other protected areas have been quite understudied by comparison. Even Mount Elgon National Park, which receives comparatively few tourist visitors, has precipitated a relatively large body of scholarship on prevailing approaches to conservation governance and their effects. By contrast, protected areas such as the majestic Kidepo Valley National Park in the far north-eastern corner of Uganda appear much less frequently in the literature. This is despite considerable biodiversity values and a fascinating socio-ecological milieu populated by some of Uganda's most historically marginalised communities. A better understanding of the perhaps idiosyncratic consequences and effects of conservation in such areas will therefore arguably be important in producing future rounds of conservation and development policy that are as equitable as possible across the whole Ugandan protected area estate.
- *Empirical consequences of eviction and resettlement for livelihoods and biodiversity.* All of the case studies discussed in this volume and several of the other chapters' foreground issues related to eviction, resettlement, and resource access restrictions for conservation. Whilst the fact and scale of such evictions is often discussed in the scholarly literature in Uganda and elsewhere in East Africa, it is much less common for scholars to engage in fine-grained empirical analyses of the consequences of such evictions for both communities and biodiversity (see, for instance,

Brockington, 2002). A more robust understanding of the activities of evicted persons is crucial, however, for evaluating the *effectiveness* of evictions and other hard-line law enforcement approaches to conservation. If evictions in fact erode community perceptions of conservation whilst simultaneously failing to curb de facto access to protected areas, for instance, efforts to rethink the nature of conservation law enforcement may very much be in order.

- *Decentralisation and its implications.* Since the middle of the twentieth century, the number of district administrative units in Uganda has increased from a mere 16 towards the end of the British colonial era in 1959 to more than 121 as of 2018 (Ministry of Local Government, 2018). Each of these districts in turn harbours its own local politicians and administrative officials, leading to a proliferation of government bureaucracies at increasingly smaller scales. By implication, protected areas across Uganda increasingly find themselves neighbouring an apparently steadily growing number of districts, whose politicians occasionally seek to garner local support with anti-conservationist rhetoric or policies. Whilst some contributions to the literature have examined the implications of decentralisation for the forest sector generally (e.g., Banana et al., 2003), efforts to do so explicitly in relation to conservation and protected areas have been rarer to date. Nonetheless, given the ongoing proliferation of local administrative units, such an initiative may be more pressing than ever.

- *Informality, patronage, and corruption.* The above relations between district administrative units, other branches of government, and various constituencies in Uganda often evince a range of both formal and informal dynamics (e.g., Khisa, 2013). As a consequence, practices of governance cannot always be assumed to proceed in precisely the same way that is stipulated by formal laws, policies, and other political institutions. Moreover, in the natural resource sector, past investigations and audits commissioned by the World Bank and the Ugandan parliament have unearthed considerable evidence of corruption and misappropriation of public funds in multilateral initiatives such as the $36 million 'Protected Areas, Management, and Sustainable Use' programme financed by the World Bank (Cavanagh, 2012). Despite these and related scandals, however, corruption, patronage, and various other kinds of informal governance strategies in practice remain somewhat under-studied in the empirical literature on conservation and development in the country. Given that the latter entail a number of challenges for conservation law enforcement from both 'above' as well as 'below', however, an enhanced empirical knowledge base on these issues is important.

- *Securitisation, militarisation, and their consequences.* A growing body of literature in geography, anthropology, and political ecology examines tendencies towards the increasing securitisation and militarisation of conservation and protected area management (e.g., Duffy, 2014; Lunstrum, 2014; Cavanagh et al., 2015). Given considerable issues with several local or regional insurgencies and domestic terrorism in Uganda, as well as extra-territorial military engagements in the Democratic Republic of Congo, South Sudan, and Somalia, it might admittedly be assumed that much of this 'green militarisation' or 'green violence' (Büscher and Ramutsindela, 2015) literature already maintains a focus on Uganda. Yet this has generally not been the case despite heavy government and donor investment in both the Ugandan military and paramilitary conservation agencies. As pointed out by Sandbrook (2015) regarding the adoption of military technologies such as surveillance drones in conservation governance, however, these strategies may in fact have unintended negative consequences, particularly with regard to the risk of polarising local attitudes against conservation efforts.

- *Interdisciplinarity and epistemological reflection.* In recent decades, the literature on conservation and development in Uganda has grown to encompass contributions from authors and researchers working in an increasingly wide range of academic disciplines. This is generally quite positive, as many of these recent perspectives have brought issues to light that were arguably neglected within mid-twentieth century writings on conservation in Uganda authored primarily by biologists, zoologists, foresters, and other natural scientists. Most pressing here, perhaps, are the human rights, equity, and livelihood concerns raised by social scientists in increasing volumes from the late 1980s onward. Yet this growing range of perspectives also raises methodological issues that warrant discussion. Even within this volume, for instance, social justice concerns and explicitly political dynamics have been more squarely addressed by authors with training in the critical social sciences than those who primarily have a background in the natural sciences, and vice versa. This suggests the need for heightened interdisciplinary collaboration between natural and social scientists in ways that are able to better integrate different forms and sources of data, analytical methods, and research foci. In turn, however, such integration also raises its own issues about 'disciplinary capture' (Brister, 2016) and the *epistemologies* that prevail – or do not – when interdisciplinary collaborations are launched. In other words, interdisciplinarity does not preclude the need for explicit considerations of epistemology, or the forms of data, methods, and knowledge that are thought to 'count' for the purposes of scientific analysis.
- *Heightened institutional collaboration and the 'decolonisation' of research.* Across sub-Saharan Africa, numerous scholars are increasingly highlighting the ways in which many institutions of higher education and research on the continent were forged within the very same histories and (colonial) power relations that have also shaped the legacies of

conservation and development explored in this volume (e.g., Zeleza, 2009). Accordingly, there are growing calls to 'decolonise' both universities and research practices in Africa (Mbembe, 2016; Ndlovu-Gatsheni and Zondi, 2016), as well as to reflect critically but constructively upon the role of foreign academics and institutions in research throughout the developing world (see also Robbins, 2006). At a minimum, evolving best practices might seek far greater levels of collaboration with both academics and research institutions in host countries. In this volume, for instance, six of eleven substantive chapters have been lead-authored by Ugandan scholars, and most have involved collaborations between Ugandan and international scholars (where relevant).[2] Yet much more could be done in conservation and development research to nurture such collaborations over the longer term, thus fostering a greater diversity of both Ugandan and non-Ugandan perspectives in the literature on these issues.

- *Hybrid knowledges and forms of science.* Lastly, arguably one of the most pressing imperatives for future generations of research and policy on conservation and development in Uganda is to rework the ways in which both researchers and conservation professionals engage with local communities. Since the late 1980s, much emphasis has admittedly been placed on the 'participation' of local people in conservation and development efforts. However, researchers in particular have tended to approach local communities as *objects* of scientific inquiry – that is, as populations to be studied – rather than as active *subjects* that retain the potential to meaningfully contribute to research programmes in their own right. To some degree, the forms of literacy and numeracy demanded by conservation science work as barriers to entry in this regard, often limiting meaningful participation of rural communities simply because they have been historically marginalised from relevant forms of education and training. At the same time, however, the distinction between 'scientific' and 'traditional' or indigenous ecological knowledge can sometimes be in danger of overstatement (Agrawal, 1995). Rather than simply the extension of scientific training, what is also needed is a willingness on the part of researchers to engage in the work of *translation*, or to more seriously consider the 'hybrid' ways in which local forms of knowledge and authorial voice might be incorporated into conservation science itself (see also Batterbury et al., 1997; West, 2016). Efforts to do so may break much needed ground in undoing the often uncomfortably colonial legacies of both conservation research and conservation practice by valorising the knowledge and experiences of local people within science itself in unprecedented ways. Indeed, doing so may constitute one amongst other promising inroads towards redressing many of the tensions between conservation and development objectives identified throughout this volume.

Notes

1 With the exception of the North Game Reserve and South Game Reserve in the East Africa Protectorate (later Kenya Colony), which began to be demarcated in the late nineteenth century (Chongwa, 2012) – though incrementally and with uneven success.
2 While we are pleased with the balance of Ugandan and international authors in this volume, we are disappointed with the final gender balance in the author team. Unfortunately several chapters with lead or contributing female authors fell through during the writing and editing process.

References

Adams, W.M. (2003) *Future Nature: a vision for conservation*, revised edition, Routledge/Earthscan, London, UK, and New York, USA.

Adams, W.M. (2004) *Against Extinction: the story of conservation*, Earthscan, London, UK.

Adams, W.M. (2009) *Green Development: environment and sustainability in a developing world*, third edition, Routledge, London, UK, and New York, USA.

Agrawal, A. (1995) 'Dismantling the divide between indigenous and scientific knowledge', *Development and Change*, vol. 26, no. 3, pp. 413–439.

Banana, A.Y., Gombya-Ssembajjwe, W. and Bahati, J. (2003) *Decentralization of Forestry Resources in Uganda: realities or rhetoric?*, Faculty of Forestry and Nature Conservation Working Paper, Makerere University, Kampala, Uganda.

Batterbury, S., Forsyth, T. and Thomson, K. (1997) 'Environmental transformations in developing countries: hybrid research and democratic policy', *Geographical Journal*, vol. 163, no. 2, pp. 126–132.

Blomley, T. (2003) 'Natural resource conflict management: the case of Bwindi Impenetrable and Mgahinga Gorilla National Parks, southwestern Uganda' in A. P. Castro and E. Nielsen (eds) *Natural Resource Conflict Management Case Studies: an analysis of power, participation and protected areas*, Food and Agriculture Organization of the United Nations, Rome, Italy, pp. 231–250.

Brister, E. (2016) 'Disciplinary capture and epistemological obstacles to interdisciplinary research: lessons from central African conservation disputes', *Studies in History and Philosophy of Science Part C: Studies in History and Philosophy of Biological and Biomedical Sciences*, vol. 56, pp. 82–91.

Brockington, D. (2002) *Fortress Conservation: the preservation of the Mkomzi game reserve, Tanzania*, James Currey, Oxford, UK.

Büscher, B. and Ramutsindela, M. (2015) 'Green violence: rhino poaching and the war to save Southern Africa's peace parks', *African Affairs*, vol. 115, no. 458, pp. 1–22.

Cavanagh, C.J. (2012) *Unready for REDD+? Lessons from corruption in Ugandan conservation areas*, U4 Anti-Corruption Resource Centre Policy Brief. Chr. Michelsen Institute, Bergen, Norway.

Cavanagh, C.J. and Benjaminsen, T.A. (2014) 'Virtual nature, violent accumulation: the 'spectacular failure' of carbon offsetting at a Ugandan National Park', *Geoforum*, vol. 56, pp. 55–65.

Cavanagh, C.J. and Freeman, O. (2017) 'Paying for carbon at Mount Elgon: two contrasting approaches at a transboundary park in East Africa', in S. Namirembe,

B. Leimona, M. van Noordwijk and P. Minang (eds) *Co-Investment in Ecosystem Services: global lessons from payment and incentive schemes*, World Agroforestry Centre (ICRAF), Nairobi, Kenya.

Cavanagh, C., Vedeld, P. and Traedal, L.T. (2015) 'Securitizing REDD+? Problematizing the emerging illegal timber trade and forest carbon interface in East Africa', *Geoforum*, vol. 60, pp. 72–82.

Child, K. (2009) 'Civil society in Uganda: the struggle to save the Mabira Forest Reserve', *Journal of Eastern African Studies*, vol. 3, no. 2, pp. 240–258.

Chongwa, M.B. (2012) 'The history and evolution of national parks in Kenya', *The George Wright Forum*, vol. 29, no. 1, pp. 39–42.

Deloitte (2016) 'Uganda Economic Outlook 2016. The story behind the numbers', www2.deloitte.com/content/dam/Deloitte/ug/Documents/tax/Economic%20 Outlook%202016%20UG.pdf, accessed 1 April 2018.

Doak, D.F., Bakker, V.J., Goldstein, B.E. and Benjamin, H. (2015) 'What is the future of conservation?', in G. Wuerthner, E. Crist and T. Butler (eds) *Protecting the Wild: parks and wilderness, the foundation for conservation*, Island Press, Washington, DC.

Duffy, R. (2014) 'Waging a war to save biodiversity: the rise of militarized conservation', *International Affairs*, vol. 90, no. 4, pp. 819–834.

Fisher, J.A., Cavanagh, C.J., Sikor, T. and Mwayafu, D.M. (2018) 'Linking notions of justice and project outcomes in carbon offset forestry projects: insights from a comparative study in Uganda', *Land Use Policy*, vol. 73, pp. 259–268.

Goldstein, A. and Ruef, F. (2016) *View from the Understory: State of Forest Carbon Finance 2016*, Forest Trends' Ecosystem Marketplace, Washington, DC.

Himmelfarb, D.K. (2012) 'In the aftermath of displacement: a political ecology of dispossession, transformation, and conflict on Mt. Elgon, Uganda', Doctoral dissertation, University of Georgia, Athens, GA, USA.

Igoe, J. (2017) *The Nature of Spectacle: on images, money, and conserving capitalism*, University of Arizona Press, Tucson, USA.

Johnston, H.H. (1902) *The Uganda Protectorate*, Hutchinson, London, UK.

Kandel, M. (2015) 'Politics from below? Small-, mid-and large-scale land dispossession in Teso, Uganda, and the relevance of scale', *Journal of Peasant Studies*, vol. 42, nos (3–4), pp. 635–652.

Khisa, M. (2013) 'The making of the "informal state" in Uganda', *Africa Development*, vol. 38, nos 1&2, pp. 191–226.

Lumu, D. (2017) 'Over 400 forest reserves in Uganda encroached on', *New Vision* (22 March), www.newvision.co.ug/new_vision/news/1449205/400-forest-reserves-uganda-encroached, accessed 29 March 2018.

Lunstrum, E. (2014) 'Green militarization: anti-poaching efforts and the spatial contours of Kruger National Park', *Annals of the Association of American Geographers*, vol. 104, no. 4, pp. 816–832.

Lyons, K. and Westoby, P. (2014) 'Carbon colonialism and the new land grab: plantation forestry in Uganda and its livelihood impacts', *Journal of Rural Studies*, vol. 36, pp. 13–21.

Martiniello, G. (2015) 'Social struggles in Uganda's Acholiland: understanding responses and resistance to Amuru sugar works', *Journal of Peasant Studies*, vol. 42, nos (3–4), pp. 653–669.

Mbembe, A. (2016) 'Decolonizing the university: new directions', *Arts and Humanities in Higher Education*, vol. 15, no. 1, pp. 29–45.

Ministry of Local Government (2018) 'Ministry of Local Government fact sheet', http://molg.go.ug/sites/default/files/MoLG%20-%20%20Fact%20Sheet.pdf, accessed 30 March 2018.

Murphree, M. (2000) 'Community-based conservation: old ways, new myths and enduring challenges', in R.D. Baldus and L.S. Siege (eds) *Tanzania Wildlife Discussion Paper*, No. 29, Deutsche Gesellschaft für Technische Zusammenarbeit, Dar er Salaam, Tanzania.

Murray Li, T. (2007) *The Will to Improve: governmentality, development and the practice of politics*, Duke University Press, Durham, NC, USA.

National Forestry Authority (NFA) (2011) *Assessment of Trends of Evictions From Protected Areas During the Period 2005–2010 and their Implications for REDD+*, NFA, Kampala, Uganda.

Ndlovu-Gatsheni, S. and Zondi, S. (2016) 'Introduction – the coloniality of knowledge: between troubled histories and uncertain futures', in S. Ndlovu-Gatsheni and S. Zondi (eds) *Decolonizing the University, Knowledge Systems and Disciplines in Africa*, Carolina Academic Press, Durham, NC, USA, pp. 3–26.

Nel, A. and Hill, D. (2013) 'Constructing walls of carbon – the complexities of community, carbon sequestration and protected areas in Uganda', *Journal of Contemporary African Studies*, vol. 31, no. 3, pp. 421–440.

Redford, K.H., Padoch, C. and Sunderland, T. (2013) 'Fads, funding, and forgetting in three decades of conservation', *Conservation Biology*, vol. 27, no. 3, pp. 437–438.

Republic of Uganda (2013) *National Strategy and Action Plan to Strengthen Human Resources and Skills to Advance Green, Low-Emission and Climate Resilient Development in Uganda 2013–2022: Uganda national climate change learning strategy*, Ministry of Water and Environment Climate Change Unit, Kampala, Uganda.

Republic of Uganda (2017) *The Uganda Green Growth Development Strategy 2017/18–2030/31*, National Planning Authority, Kampala, Uganda.

Robbins, P. (2006) 'Research is theft: environmental inquiry in a postcolonial world', in S. Aitken and G. Valentine (eds), *Approaches to Human Geography*, SAGE, London, UK, pp. 311–324.

Sandbrook, C. (2015) 'The social implications of using drones for biodiversity conservation', *Ambio*, vol. 44, no. 4, pp. 636–647.

Scott, P. (1998) *From Conflict to Collaboration: people and forests at Mount Elgon, Uganda*, IUCN, Gland, Switzerland.

Turyahabwe, N. and Banana, A.Y. (2008) 'An overview of history and development of forest policy and legislation in Uganda', *International Forestry Review*, vol. 10, no. 4, pp. 641–656.

UN Environment Programme (2011) *Towards a Green Economy: pathways to sustainable development and poverty alleviation*, UN Environment Programme, Nairobi, Kenya.

Webster, G. and Osmaston, H. (2003) *A History of the Uganda Forest Department, 1951–1965*, Commonwealth Secretariat, London, UK.

West, P. (2016) '*Dispossession and the Environment: rhetoric and inequality in Papua New Guinea*', Columbia University Press, New York, USA.

World Bank (2012) *Inclusive Green Growth: the pathway to sustainable development*, World Bank, Washington, DC.

Zeleza, P.T. (2009). 'African studies and universities since independence: the challenges of epistemic and institutional decolonization', *Transition*, vol. 101, no. 1, pp. 110–135.

Index

ACCA *see* Ankole Cow Conservation
	Association
accountability 40, 52, 130, 140, 222
ACHPR *see* African Commission on
	Human and Peoples' Rights
actor-centred power approach 113–114
afforestation 17, 126, 127, 129,
	135, 254
African Commission on Human and
	Peoples' Rights (ACHPR) 96
African Wildlife Foundation 153, 174
agriculture 4, 5–6, 11–12, 189–205,
	256–257; Albertine region 230;
	Budongo Forest Reserve 105,
	106–107, 113; Bwindi Impenetrable
	National Park 62, 63, 66, 69,
	76; Central Forest Reserves 215;
	colonial period 22; deforestation
	38; future scenarios 200; impact of
	conservation on 194–197; impact
	of tourism on 148; impact on the
	environment 190–194; integrated
	conservation and development 48;
	Kibale Forest National Park
	162–163, 164; minimisation
	of trade-offs with conservation
	197–199; Mount Elgon 87, 88,
	89, 90–93; National Development
	Plans 106; pre-colonial period 23;
	weakness in governance 108
agro-forestry 96–97
Albertine Graben 226–242, 257–258
Albertine Rift 12, 34, 38, 118;
	biodiversity 125; carbon forestry
	137; Conservation Programme
	197–198; Rwenzori Mountains
	National Park 156; tourism 159
alternative livelihoods schemes
	109–111, 115, 116, 117, 118

Amin, Idi 5, 28–29, 63, 174, 209;
	forestry reforms 215, 257; Mount
	Elgon 91, 93, 95; sugarcane
	production 191
animal management 66, 69
Ankole Cow Conservation Association
	(ACCA) 177
Association of Uganda Tour Operators
	(AUTO) 73, 153, 154

Bafumbira-Hutu 62, 63
Bagisu 87–88, 91, 96
Bakiga 62, 63, 75–76
Banyarwenzururu 178–179
Banyoro 105
Batwa 47, 62, 65, 127, 251–252;
	critical narrative 77; cultural values
	175–176, 179–180, 183; social
	relations 63, 75–76
BCFS *see* Budongo Conservation Field
	Station
benefit sharing 46, 172; integrated
	conservation and development 53;
	Mount Elgon National Park 92,
	97–98; sport hunting 161, 162;
	tourism 254; *see also* revenue sharing
Benet 23, 37, 92, 93, 95–96, 127,
	251–252
Benet Resettlement Area 92, 93, 95–96
Bigodi wetland sanctuary 151, 162–164
BINP *see* Bwindi Impenetrable
	National Park
biocultural diversity 172
biodiversity 5, 6, 125; agriculture
	189, 190, 191, 197, 198, 200;
	Albertine Graben 229; Budongo
	Forest Reserve 109, 115, 117–118;
	Bwindi Impenetrable National
	Park 65; contemporary dynamics

and challenges 35–37, 40; cultural values 183; deforestation 240; early post-colonial period 29, 40; forestry reforms 210; impact of evictions 258–259; impact of land rush 227, 240, 242; integrated conservation and development 45, 46; inventories 39; Kibale Forest National Park 162; Kidepo National Park 258; land sparing/land sharing 198–199; Mount Elgon National Park 87; Murchison Falls 242; offsetting 255; reserved tree species 26; Rwenzori Mountains National Park 156–157; species diversity 199; tourism 148; uneven conservation and development 249

birds 5, 112; Albertine Graben 229; impact of agriculture 190, 191; Kibale Forest National Park 162–163; Musambwa Island 180–181; tourism 149, 151, 157

boundaries 252, 255; colonial period 19, 22, 24, 25–26; contemporary dynamics and challenges 30, 38–39, 40; early post-colonial period 28; Mount Elgon National Park 37, 86, 91–92, 94–98, 100n2

Budongo Conservation Field Station (BCFS) 109–111, 113, 114–115

Budongo Forest Reserve 9, 10, 25, 104–121, 251–253; alternative livelihoods scheme 109–111, 115, 116, 117, 118; Collaborative Forest Management 111–112; conservation and development challenges 105–108; ecotourism 112–113; overview 104–105; political economy of conservation and development 113–117; sugarcane production 191–192

buffalo 3, 4

buffer zones 30, 46; Albertine Rift 197–198; Budongo Forest Reserve 105–106, 113

Bugala Island 215

Buganda 22–23, 25

Buganda Agreement (1900) 18, 194

Bugisu 89

Bugungu Game Reserve 105

Bukaleba Reforestation Project 136

Burundi 200

Busoga 193

Bwindi Impenetrable National Park (BINP) 9, 10, 31, 61–84, 127, 251–253; Collaborative Resource Management 51; corruption 54; cultural values 175–176, 179–180; history of 62–65; integrated conservation and development 47, 48, 49, 53, 54, 66–70; narratives 76–78, 79; research 258; as site of contestation 71–76; tourism 50, 51, 149, 150, 151, 152–156; UWA administration 212

Byakagaba, Patrick 12, 226–246, 256, 257

capacity building 23, 35, 51

carbon emissions 240, 241

carbon forestry 11, 34, 38, 125–147, 253–254, 255; development of 127–130; ecological implications 139–140; environmental justice perspective 132–142; Mount Elgon National Park 92, 97; political implications 140–142; social implications 138–139

carbon sequestration 11, 34, 125–126, 140

carbon sinks 125

CARE International 30, 47, 54, 70

cattle 3, 173, 174–175, 177, 183; *see also* grazing

Cavanagh, Connor Joseph 3–15, 85–103, 195, 197, 249–264

CBC *see* community-based conservation

CBOs *see* community-based organisations

CDM *see* Clean Development Mechanism

Central Forest Reserves (CFRs) 211–212; forestry reforms 213, 214, 215, 216; historical developments 21, 24, 32–33, 35–36, 37–39; lack of access rights 220; Mount Elgon National Park 89–90, 91; plantations 218

CFM *see* Collaborative Forest Management

chimpanzees 109, 110, 111, 112–113, 157, 163

CIF *see* Climate Investment Funds

civil society organisations (CSOs) 6, 34, 38; *see also* non-governmental organisations

civil war 5, 6, 28

Clean Development Mechanism (CDM) 11, 126, 127–128, 138–139, 141, 142, 254

climate change 7, 110; carbon forestry 125, 129, 142; impact of land rush 241; research 34

Climate Investment Funds (CIF) 128

climate justice 130

Clouds Mountain Gorilla Lodge 73, 79, 151, 152–156, 165, 166

co-management 37, 38, 51, 53, 54, 85, 111–112

CODECA *see* Community Development and Conservation Agency

coercion 89–94, 99, 114, 115–116

coffee 89, 194, 195

Collaborative Forest Management (CFM) 32–33, 35, 36, 38, 39, 111–112, 116

Collaborative Resource Management (CRM) 51–53

Collaborative Resource Management Agreements (CRMAs) 92, 94–95, 96, 97

colonial period 17, 18–27, 39, 194–195, 251; Bwindi Impenetrable National Park 62, 63; district administrative units 259; Lake Mburo 173; Mount Elgon 85, 86, 88–89, 90–93, 100n2; oil extraction 227–228

communal land 230–231, 232, 233, 235, 238–239, 241

'communitarian rhetoric' 85, 96–98, 99

community-based conservation (CBC) 10–11, 172, 252, 253; cultural values 173, 177, 181, 183; Mount Elgon National Park 85, 92, 96–98

community-based management 46, 125, 222

community-based organisations (CBOs) 115, 164, 193

Community Conservation Units 175

Community Development and Conservation Agency (CODECA) 35, 114, 115

community engagement 151, 162–164, 165, 175, 179, 182, 184, 198

community forests 32–33

Community-Park Institutions/ Community Protected Areas Institutions (CPIs) 52–53, 159–160, 161

Community Revolving Funds 92, 97

Community Wildlife Associations (CWAs) 159, 160, 161

compensation: integrated conservation and development 46; land rights abuses in the Albertine region 232–233, 234, 237

conflict: agriculture 195; Budongo Forest Reserve 10, 107, 113, 116; Bwindi Impenetrable National Park 61, 63, 64, 71–76, 77, 78, 253; cultural values 175, 177, 178, 183, 184, 255; human-wildlife 50, 51, 53; integrated conservation and development 54; Lake Mburo 173–174; land 226–227; Mount Elgon National Park 37, 86, 91, 94–96, 97; Rwanda 190; sport hunting 159, 161; as threat to sustainable development 189; tourism 153–154, 158; *see also* contestation; resistance; violence

conservation 4–5; agriculture 11–12, 189, 194–199, 200, 256–257; Budongo Forest Reserve 108–118; Bwindi Impenetrable National Park 61, 64–72, 77–78, 79, 252–253; changing policy 85; colonial period 18–27, 251; contemporary dynamics and challenges 30–39, 40; cross-sectoral dynamics 256–258; cultural values 171, 172–173, 176, 183–184, 254–255; early post-colonial period 27–30, 39–40; evolution and performance of conservation tools 253–255; financial burden of 98; forestry reforms 207; future research and policy 258–261; historical developments 8, 16–44; integrated conservation and development 8–9, 11, 45–55, 66–70, 172; KAFRED 164; Lake Mburo National Park 174, 175; Mount Elgon National Park 85–86, 87, 88–89, 90, 92, 96–98, 99; narratives 253; neo-liberal conservation narrative 117; pre-colonial period 16–18; Rwenzori Mountains National Park 156–157; tourism 149–150, 166, 254; unevenness of 4, 11, 249, 256; *see also* protected areas

Constitution of Uganda 31, 39–40

construction industry 117

contestation 171–172, 249; Bwindi Impenetrable National Park 61, 71–76, 78; carbon forestry 130; Mount Elgon National Park 85, 99; *see also* conflict; resistance
Convention on Biodiversity 172
corridors 197–198
corruption 36, 40, 54, 259; Bwindi Impenetrable National Park 69; early post-colonial period 29; forestry reforms 221, 257; land rights abuses in the Albertine region 234, 235, 237, 238; National Forestry Authority 215–216; political 214, 234, 235
CPIs *see* Community-Park Institutions
CRM *see* Collaborative Resource Management
CRMAs *see* Collaborative Resource Management Agreements
crop raiding 37, 250; Budongo Forest Reserve 113; Bwindi Impenetrable National Park 65, 66, 69, 72, 78; gorillas 156; Mount Elgon National Park 97; tourism 254
CSOs *see* civil society organisations
'cultural cows' 177–178, 183
cultural rites 88
cultural values 11, 171–186, 254–255
Culture, Values and Conservation Project 176–184
customary law 88, 90, 226, 238, 241–242
CWAs *see* Community Wildlife Associations

Darwin Initiative 176, 179
decentralisation 6, 125, 259; colonial period 24, 39; contemporary dynamics and challenges 31, 36, 40; early post-colonial period 28; failures 130; forestry reforms 217, 222
decision making: Bwindi Impenetrable National Park 70, 75, 77–78, 79; carbon forestry 132; Collaborative Forest Management 112; cultural values 173; environmental justice 132; institutional change 208; integrated conservation and development 51–52; 'politics of ecological knowledge' 249; understanding the environment 255
decolonisation 90, 260–261

deforestation 5, 7, 16, 206, 218–220, 257; Budongo Forest Reserve 106–107; Bwindi Impenetrable National Park 62; carbon forestry 125, 126, 130, 142; contemporary dynamics and challenges 32, 36, 40; early post-colonial period 40; impact of agriculture 38, 191–192, 193; impact of land rush 240–241; lack of harvesting regulations 27; local government 217; Mount Elgon 92, 93, 97, 126
degazettement 196
development: agriculture 189, 200; Budongo Forest Reserve 108–118; Bwindi Impenetrable National Park 61, 66–70, 71–72, 78, 79; cross-sectoral dynamics 256–258; evolution and performance of development tools 253–255; future research and policy 258–261; integrated conservation and development 8–9, 11, 45–55, 66–70, 172; KAFRED 164; land sharing 199; Mount Elgon National Park 97, 99; Museveni regime 209; neo-liberalisation of 127; tourism 148, 149–150, 166; unevenness of 4, 11, 249, 256
Development Through Conservation (DTC) 47, 48, 49, 54, 70
DFS *see* District Forestry Services
direct community engagement 151, 162–164, 165
displacement 172, 173; agriculture 200; carbon forestry 141; colonial period 22–23; land rush 240, 241, 242, 257–258; Mount Elgon 93, 95–96; *see also* evictions
dispossession 89, 173, 238–239, 240, 257–258; *see also* evictions
distributive justice 131, 132, 134–137, 138–139, 142
District Forestry Services (DFS): CFM agreements 32–33; deforestation 219; forestry reforms 31–32, 35–36, 211–214, 216–217, 220, 257; limited success 35, 37; policy discord 108
donors: Budongo Forest Reserve 111, 114, 115, 117; Bwindi Impenetrable National Park 68–70; forestry reforms 12, 206–207, 210–211, 215, 217, 218, 220–221, 257; integrated

conservation and development 51, 54; market-based conservation 126; Mount Elgon National Park 93, 94, 98; national parks 66; Rwenzori Mountaineering Services 158; state reliance on 209; tourism 158
DTC *see* Development Through Conservation

ecological capital 117
ecological knowledge 249, 255, 261
'ecology without nature' 88
economic development: community-based conservation 172; cultural values 172–173; forestry reforms 210; 'green growth' 7; Mount Elgon National Park 89, 98
economic growth 3, 4, 254
economic value 3, 4
ecosystem degradation 227
ecosystem services 11, 34, 47, 173, 206; agriculture 190; Albertine Graben 229; impact of land rush 227, 242; land sharing 199; *see also* payments for ecosystem services
ecotourism 4, 98, 254; Budongo Forest Reserve 108–109, 112–113; Bwindi Impenetrable National Park 10; KAFRED 163–164; *see also* tourism
ECOTRUST *see* Environmental Conservation Trust of Uganda
education 7, 48, 113
elections 98, 117, 214, 215
elephants 3, 17
elite capture 53, 196; Bwindi Impenetrable National Park 253; tourism 162, 164, 165, 166, 254
employment: agriculture 6, 256; Budongo Forest Reserve 105, 112; Bwindi Impenetrable National Park 77; early post-colonial period 30; 'green growth' 7; impact of land rush 241; informal harvesting 37; integrated conservation and development 45; Mount Elgon National Park 97; tourism 148, 151, 158, 163, 165, 254; *see also* livelihoods
encroachment, concept of 252
endangered species 5, 199
Environmental Conservation Trust of Uganda (ECOTRUST) 35, 114, 115, 136, 137

environmental justice 131, 132–142, 254
epidemics 18, 19
equity 46, 53, 55, 260
European Union (EU) 30, 35, 210; forestry reforms 213; Sawlog Production Grant Scheme 33, 36, 218
evictions 3, 36, 37, 94, 215, 252; Bwindi Impenetrable National Park 47, 76, 253; carbon forestry 139; future research and policy 258–259; Karamoja 196; Lake Mburo 174; Mount Elgon 86, 92, 93, 95–96, 97, 98; reforestation initiatives 126; *see also* displacement; dispossession
extractive industry 226–227, 257–258; *see also* oil

FACE Foundation 95, 97, 126, 128, 130, 134–135, 138, 140, 143n1, 253
FFI *see* Flora & Fauna International
FID *see* Forest Inspection Division
fires 17, 38, 64
fishing 180, 181, 230, 232
Flora & Fauna International (FFI) 175, 176
food insecurity 139, 189, 195, 241
food security 69, 192, 197
Forest Inspection Division (FID) 211, 212, 213, 214, 216
Forest Policy (1929) 19–20
Forest Policy (1948) 20, 21, 24, 26, 27–28
Forest Policy (1988) 92
Forest Policy (2001) 31, 210
forest reserves 5, 125, 127, 215, 252; Albertine Graben 229; colonial period 18–19, 21–22, 23, 24–25, 26, 251; elevation to national park status 31, 37, 212; encroachment 252; integrated conservation and development 47–48; Mount Elgon 85, 89–90, 91; tourism 149; *see also* Central Forest Reserves; Local Forest Reserves; protected areas
Forest Sector Umbrella Programme (FSUP) 210
Forest Stewardship Council (FSC) 35
forestry: Budongo Forest Reserve 118; carbon offsetting 11, 34, 38, 92, 97, 125–147, 253–254, 255; colonial period 24, 26, 39; contemporary

dynamics and challenges 30–39, 40;
early post-colonial period 39–40;
reforms 12, 31–32, 35–36, 127,
206–225, 257; research 34–35;
training 29, 35; weakness
in governance 108; *see also*
deforestation; forest reserves;
plantations
Forestry Rehabilitation Project (FRP)
30, 35, 37
Forestry Sector Support Department
(FSSD) 31–32, 38, 216, 218
Forests Absorbing Carbon-dioxide
Emissions (FACE) Foundation 95,
97, 126, 128, 130, 134–135, 138,
140, 143n1, 253
Forests Act (1947) 20, 21
Forests Act (1964) 28
'fortress conservation' model 172
FRP *see* Forestry Rehabilitation Project
fruit 107
FSC *see* Forest Stewardship Council
FSSD *see* Forestry Sector Support
Department
FSUP *see* Forest Sector Umbrella
Programme
fuelwood 26, 38, 48; Budongo Forest
Reserve 106, 107, 117; colonial
period 17; communal land ownership
238; pre-colonial period 23

Game Act (1964) 63
game reserves 18–19, 23, 173–174,
251, 252
Game Trails Uganda Limited 159, 161
gas 118, 229, 231, 236, 238,
239–240, 241
gazettement 47–48, 172, 196, 215, 252;
Bwindi Impenetrable National Park
63, 64; colonial period 19, 20, 24;
see also national parks
GDP *see* gross domestic product
Gombya-Ssembajjwe, W.S. 241
gorillas 3, 4, 5, 48; Bwindi
Impenetrable National Park 10, 61,
63–65, 67, 68, 71–73, 74, 78–79,
252–253; Collaborative Resource
Management 51; cultural values 183;
habituation of 71–72; tourism 149,
151, 152–156, 165
governance 6, 53, 85; Bwindi
Impenetrable National Park 71,
79; carbon forestry 129, 140;
forestry 36, 40, 206–207, 208,
216, 220–222; impact of land

rush 241; informal 259; integrated
conservation and development 55;
Mount Elgon National Park 86; new
public management 209; tourism 11,
150–151, 156, 164–166; weaknesses
108; *see also* institutions; local
government
grazing 173–175; Bwindi Impenetrable
National Park 62; carbon forestry
135, 139; communal land
registration 238; cultural values
177, 183; Karamoja 196; loss of
customary land rights 242; Mount
Elgon 87, 89; pre-colonial period 23;
replacement with cropping systems
191; *see also* pastoralism
green economy 127, 250
'green growth' 7, 13, 117, 250
Green Resources 128, 135, 136, 139,
141, 143n1, 218
greenhouse gases 140
gross domestic product (GDP) 3–4;
agriculture 5–6, 11–12, 189, 256;
tourism 4, 11, 149, 254
'guerrilla agriculture' 197

habituation 71–72, 112–113, 163
Harrison, G. 209
health care 109
Hoima Caritas Development
Organisation (HOCADEO) 109, 114
home gardens 191
Human Development Index 7
human rights 6, 95, 98, 130, 260; *see
also* rights
human-wildlife interactions 6, 37, 50,
51, 53; Budongo Forest Reserve 107,
113; Bwindi Impenetrable National
Park 77; sport hunting 159, 161
hunter-gatherers 62, 75
hunting: Bwindi Impenetrable National
Park 62, 63, 64; colonial regulation
17, 251; communal land ownership
238; cultural values 183; Mount
Elgon 90; pre-colonial period
23; tourism 151, 159–162, 165;
unregulated 174; *see also* poaching
hybrid knowledge 261

ICDPs *see* integrated conservation and
development projects
identity: cultural 178; land and 226;
recognition justice 131, 132
IGCP *see* International Gorilla
Conservation Programme

illegal activities 6, 29, 36, 39, 48; boundary maintenance 25–26; Budongo Forest Reserve 10, 105, 106, 107–108, 113, 115–117; Bwindi Impenetrable National Park 65; fraudulent land acquisitions 232, 233–234, 235–236, 238–240, 241; integrated conservation and development 53; neo-patrimonialism in the forest sector 214–215; *see also* corruption; poaching
IMF *see* International Monetary Fund
incentives 115–116
independence 23, 28
indigenous knowledge 172, 261
indigenous people 16–17, 18, 39, 47; Budongo Forest Reserve 105; cultural values 179–180; Mount Elgon National Park 37; rights 23, 172
inequalities 65, 77, 141
informality 259
infrastructure 23, 51, 65, 175, 227
institutional theory 208
institutions 8, 10, 16–44; Budongo Forest Reserve 118; Bwindi Impenetrable National Park 70, 79; carbon forestry 129; colonial period 18–27, 39; contemporary dynamics and challenges 30–39, 40; cultural 173; early post-colonial period 27–30, 39–40; forestry reforms 208, 216–218, 221, 222; integrated conservation and development 46; Mount Elgon National Park 88, 90–92; pre-colonial period 16–18, 252
integrated conservation and development projects (ICDPs) 8–9, 11, 45–55, 64, 66–70, 172
interdisciplinarity 260
International Gorilla Conservation Programme (IGCP) 49, 152–153
International Monetary Fund (IMF) 210, 220
International Union for Conservation of Nature (IUCN) 5, 35, 50; CRMAs 96; Mount Elgon National Park 92, 94–95; World Parks Congress 172

Jane Goodall Institute (JGI) 35, 109, 114, 115
JGI *see* Jane Goodall Institute

Kabwoya Wildlife Reserve 161–162
Kachung Afforestation Project 135, 139, 140

KAFRED *see* Kibale Association for Rural and Environmental Development
Kaiso-Tonya Community Wildlife Area 161–162
Kalangala Forest Reserves 215
Kamusiime, H. 196
Karamoja 195–196
Katonga Wildlife Reserve 150
Kenya 6, 17
Kibale Association for Rural and Environmental Development (KAFRED) 162–164, 165
Kibale Forest National Park 9, 31; carbon forestry 134; Collaborative Resource Management 51; integrated conservation and development 48, 49; tourism 150, 151, 157, 162–164, 165
Kidepo Valley National Park 25, 149, 150, 258
Kikonda Reforestation Project 136
Kinyara Sugar Works 105, 106, 192

Lake Mburo National Park 9; Collaborative Resource Management 51; cultural values 173–176, 177–178, 183; integrated conservation and development 49–50, 54; tourism 50, 150, 159–162
land acquisitions 227; agriculture 12, 193, 200; fraudulent 232, 233–234, 235–236, 238–240, 241
Land Act (1998) 31, 230–231, 238–239
land grabbing 141, 218; Albertine region 232, 233–234, 235, 236, 239; tourism 148, 162
land rights: carbon forestry 129; land rights abuses in the Albertine region 226–227, 230–242; Mount Elgon 96, 98; plantations 130
land rush 226–227, 238–242, 257–258
land sparing/land sharing 198–199, 256–257
land use change 106–107
land valuation 237, 257
law enforcement 26, 38–39, 40, 259; Budongo Forest Reserve 107–108, 115–116; Bwindi Impenetrable National Park 66, 68; Mount Elgon National Park 94; *see also* evictions
lawsuits 96, 99
legislation: constitutional provisions 31; Forests Act (1947) 20, 21; Forests Act (1964) 28; Game Act (1964)

63; Land Act (1998) 31, 230–231, 238–239; National Forestry and Tree Planting Act (2003) 31, 32, 34, 38, 108, 210; oil and gas policy 229; Wildlife Act (1996) 31, 74, 177; Wildlife Act (2000) 96

livelihoods 7; agriculture 189, 197, 200; Budongo Forest Reserve 109–111, 112, 115, 116, 117, 118; Bwindi Impenetrable National Park 67; carbon forestry 132, 139; Collaborative Forest Management 112; contemporary dynamics and challenges 37–38; cultural values 172–173; customary 252; deforestation 240; early post-colonial period 29–30, 40; environmental justice 131, 132; forestry reforms 210, 213, 220; impact of evictions 258–259; impact of land rush 227, 240, 242; integrated conservation and development 45, 55; interdisciplinary research 260; KAFRED 164; land rights 226; Mount Elgon 90–93, 99, 130; pre-colonial period 23; tourism 148; uneven conservation and development 249; *see also* employment

Local Forest Reserves (LFRs): forestry reforms 212, 216, 217, 220; historical developments 21, 24, 26–28, 32, 36

local government: colonial period 23, 24, 27, 39; contemporary dynamics and challenges 32; CPIs 52; decentralisation 259; deforestation 220; early post-colonial period 28; forestry reforms 212, 217, 218, 221; land rights abuses in the Albertine region 235–236; Musambwa Island 181; revenue collection 107; revenue sharing 53–54; sport hunting 160; tourism 153–154

Local Government Act (1995) 31

local knowledge 261

Mabira Forest Reserve 193, 215, 255

MacArthur Foundation 175, 176

market-based approaches 11, 117, 173; carbon forestry 125–126; green 127; power relations 132

MERECP *see* Mount Elgon Regional Ecosystem Conservation Programme

Mgahinga National Park 31, 127; Collaborative Resource Management 51; cultural values 175–176, 179–180; integrated conservation and development 47, 48, 49; tourism 50, 150

militarisation 75, 259–260

mining 62, 63

monocultures 127, 139–140, 142, 191

Mount Elgon National Park 9, 10, 31, 85–103, 127, 195, 251–253; agriculture and conservation 197; boundary conflicts 37, 94–98; carbon forestry 38, 126, 128, 130, 135, 137, 138, 140, 143n1, 253; colonial conservation and development 88–89; community-based conservation 96–98; institutions 90–92; integrated conservation and development 49; physical geography 87–88; research 258; tourism 50, 150; UWA administration 212

Mount Elgon Regional Ecosystem Conservation Programme (MERECP) 92, 97, 137, 138

Mount Kilimanjaro 158, 159

multiple use programmes 49–50, 177; Budongo Forest Reserve 118; Bwindi Impenetrable National Park 64, 66, 68; Mount Elgon National Park 92

Murchison Falls National Park 9, 18, 25, 105; carbon forestry 137; impact of land rush 242; oil extraction 4, 12, 257; tourism 50, 149, 150

Musambwa Island 175, 176, 180–181

Museveni, Yoweri 5, 30, 92, 214; agriculture 193, 194; forestry reforms 209–210, 257; Mount Elgon National Park 98; World Bank-driven reforms 222

Namwasa Reforestation Project 126, 128, 134

narratives 61–62, 76–78, 79, 253

National Development Plans (NDPs) 106

National Environment Act (1995) 31

National Environmental Management Agency 6

National Forest Plan (2002) 31, 210–211

National Forest Plan (2012) 218, 222
National Forestry and Tree Planting
  Act (2003) 31, 32, 34, 38, 108, 210
National Forestry Authority (NFA)
  5, 31–32, 36; agriculture 194;
  agriculture and conservation 196–197;
  Budongo Forest Reserve 106, 107,
  114, 115–116; CFM agreements
  32–33, 38, 39, 112; cultural values
  181; deforestation 219, 220; financial
  burden of conservation 98; forestry
  reforms 12, 206, 211–214, 217–218,
  220, 222, 257; funding 217; limited
  success 35, 37; policy discord 108;
  political interventions 215–216
National Forestry Plan (2001) 39
National Forestry Policy (2001) 210
national parks 3, 5, 37, 125, 171–172,
  174, 251; Albertine Graben 229;
  cultural values 175–176, 179–180,
  181–182, 255; deforestation 220;
  elevation of forest reserves to 31,
  37, 212; establishment of 24–25,
  195; governance 53; key sites 9; oil
  extraction 4; tourism 54, 149, 150;
  see also protected areas
National Resistance Army
  (NRA) 174
National Tree Fund 108
natural capital 7, 127
natural resources: agriculture 12,
  189, 192; Budongo Forest Reserve
  105–106; Bwindi Impenetrable
  National Park 66, 77, 78; dependence
  on 6, 7; integrated conservation and
  development 45, 46, 48, 49–50;
  Mount Elgon 88, 90, 97; natural
  resource curse 226; pre-colonial
  institutions 252
*Nature*Uganda 180–181
NCDF *see* Nkuringo Conservation and
  Development Foundation
NDPs *see* National
  Development Plans
neo-liberalism 117, 127, 220
neo-patrimonialism 208, 214–215, 220,
  221, 222, 257
New Forest Company 126, 128, 134,
  139, 141–142
new public management 209
NFA *see* National Forestry Authority
NGOs *see* non-governmental
  organisations

Nile Basin Reforestation Project 128,
  134, 142
Nkuringo Conservation and
  Development Foundation (NCDF)
  152, 154, 165
non-governmental organisations
  (NGOs) 38, 72; Budongo Forest
  Reserve 109, 111, 114–115, 116,
  118; Bwindi Impenetrable National
  Park 78, 79; capacity building 35;
  carbon forestry 254; land rights
  abuses in the Albertine region 235;
  tourism 151, 152
Norwegian Agency for Development
  Cooperation (NORAD) 30, 92, 94,
  137, 210
NRA *see* National Resistance Army

oil 4, 12, 118, 227–230, 257; impact of
  land rush 241; land rights abuses in
  the Albertine region 231–234, 236,
  238–240
Ongo Community Forest 137
Oxfam 141–142

Paris Agreement 125, 129, 241
park environmental income (PEI) 97
Park Management Advisory
  Committees (PMACs) 51–52, 53
participatory forest management 221
partnership models 11, 150–166
PAs *see* protected areas
pastoralism 4, 16, 252; Karamoja 195,
  196; Lake Mburo National Park
  174, 175, 177; Mount Elgon 87–88,
  93; shift to permanent farming 190;
  see also grazing
patronage 259
payments for ecosystem services (PES)
  11, 34, 38; Budongo Forest Reserve
  115; effectiveness and efficiency
  129–130; environmental justice 132,
  138; inequalities 141
PEI *see* park environmental income
permits 72–73, 74, 78, 154
PES *see* payments for ecosystem services
plant resource extraction 62, 63
plantations: benefits and problems
  130; Budongo Forest Reserve 118;
  carbon forestry 134, 135, 139–140,
  142; Central Forest Reserves 212;
  colonial period 20, 24, 25, 26,
  39; contemporary dynamics and

challenges 30, 32, 36, 40; early post-colonial period 28, 29; expansion of 127; forestry reforms 214, 218, 220; neo-liberal conservation narrative 117; oil palm 215; Sawlog Production Grant Scheme 33–34, 218; sugarcane 193–194, 215
PMACs *see* Park Management Advisory Committees
poaching 6; alternative livelihoods scheme 109–111, 116; Bwindi Impenetrable National Park 63, 65; sport hunting 159, 160; *see also* hunting
policy 6, 85; agriculture 200; Budongo Forest Reserve 108; colonial period 19–20; forestry reforms 31–32, 206–225; Mount Elgon 91, 92, 93, 94; oil and gas 229; *see also* Forest Policy; legislation
Policy Arrangements Approach 164–165
politics: agriculture and conservation 196; Budongo Forest Reserve 117; carbon forestry 126, 140–142; forestry reforms 208, 214–216, 221, 257; land rights abuses in the Albertine region 234, 235–236, 239–240; Mount Elgon National Park 85, 98
'politics of calculation' 125
'politics of ecological knowledge' 249, 255
pollution 126, 140, 193
population growth 6, 7, 28, 62, 118
poverty 3–4, 7, 35, 47, 189; Budongo Forest Reserve 105; Bwindi Impenetrable National Park 65; conservation linked to poverty alleviation 172; forestry reforms 210, 213; integrated conservation and development 46
power relations 76, 132; Budongo Forest Reserve 113–116; carbon offsetting 125, 126; institutional theory 208; power sharing 46, 183; research 260–261
pre-colonial period 16–18, 23, 62–63, 88, 252
private-community partnerships 150–151, 152–156, 159–162, 165, 166
privatisation 218

procedural justice 131, 132, 134–137, 140–141, 142
property rights 89, 93, 132; *see also* land rights
protected areas (PAs) 5, 171–172; agriculture 191, 256; Albertine region 241; colonial period 18–19, 194–195, 251; CPIs 52; cultural values 176, 183, 255; encroachment 252; institutional structure 85; integrated conservation and development 45, 46, 49, 54; Lake Mburo 173; land sharing 199; local participation 67; loss of customary land rights 242; Mount Elgon 93, 94; tourism 149–150, 254; *see also* conservation; forest reserves; national parks; wildlife reserves
protectionist model 45, 85, 90, 99, 175, 198
public-community partnerships 151, 156–159, 165
public-private-community partnerships 150, 151, 165

Queen Elizabeth National Park 3, 18, 25; integrated conservation and development 48–49; oil extraction 4; tourism 50, 149, 150, 157

rangelands 240, 241
rangers 25, 140; Bwindi Impenetrable National Park 63, 64, 68; Lake Mburo National Park 175; Mount Elgon National Park 94
recognition justice 131, 132, 134–137, 140–141, 142
Reducing Emissions from Deforestation and Degradation (REDD) 11, 34, 126, 128–129, 137, 142; national-level plans 254; payments for ecosystem services 38; political implications 141; problems 130; social implications 138
reforestation 126, 254; carbon forestry 126, 127, 129, 134, 136–137, 139; Mount Elgon National Park 95, 96–97
regeneration 104, 106, 107
religion 182
research 34–35, 258–261
resilience 173, 226, 241
resistance 99, 116; carbon forestry 130, 141; 'guerrilla agriculture' 197;

Mount Elgon National Park 85–86; *see also* conflict; contestation
revenue sharing 49, 50–51, 52, 53–54; Bwindi Impenetrable National Park 64, 66, 69, 73–75, 77; Lake Mburo National Park 175; Mount Elgon National Park 96–98; *see also* benefit sharing
rhetoric 172, 207; anti-conservationist 259; Budongo Forest Reserve 114; 'communitarian' 85, 96–98, 99; cultural values 182
rhinos 174
rights: carbon forestry 130; colonial period 21; forest resources 33; lack of access rights 220; Mount Elgon National Park 86, 89, 93, 95–96, 98, 99; pre-colonial period 23; protected areas 172; *see also* human rights; land rights
RMNP *see* Rwenzori Mountains National Park
roads 65
Rwanda 190, 200
Rwenzori Mountains National Park (RMNP) 9, 31; cultural values 175, 178–179, 182; integrated conservation and development 49; tourism 150, 151, 156–159, 165, 166; UWA administration 212

Sabiny 87–88, 91
sacred sites 16–17, 178–179, 180
Sawlog Production Grant Scheme (SPGS) 33–34, 36, 38, 218, 220
security issues 71, 75, 259–260
sedentarisation policy 195
selective harvesting 106
Semuliki National Park 18–19, 31; carbon forestry 137; Collaborative Resource Management 51; cultural values 175, 179–180; integrated conservation and development 48; tourism 150
Semuliki Wildlife Reserve 150
social justice 46, 260
socio-ecological systems 227, 240, 242
soil erosion 17, 240
soil fertility 191, 193
SPGS *see* Sawlog Production Grant Scheme

sport hunting 151, 159–162, 165
substitution: Bwindi Impenetrable National Park 66, 70; integrated conservation and development 46, 48–49, 51, 54
sugarcane 105, 106–107, 191–192, 193–194, 215
sustainable development 7, 13, 189, 249–250

taxes 90, 194
tenure insecurity 241
TFGB *see* Trees For Global Benefit
The Uganda Safari Company (TUSC) 153
timber: biodiversity loss 29; Budongo Forest Reserve 104–105, 106, 108, 117; Bwindi Impenetrable National Park 62, 63, 64; colonial period 17, 24; demand for 27, 38; illegal harvesting 48; informal harvesting 37; inventories 30; Mount Elgon National Park 89; plantations 25, 26; Queen Elizabeth National Park 48–49; wood industries 29
tourism 4, 6, 11, 37, 148–170, 254, 255; Budongo Forest Reserve 108–109, 112–113; Bwindi Impenetrable National Park 10, 64–65, 68–69, 71–75, 77, 78–79, 252–253; case studies 152–166; governance models 150–151, 164–166; Mount Elgon National Park 96–97; neo-liberal conservation narrative 117; overview of 149–150; revenue sharing 49, 50–51, 54
training 25, 27, 29, 35; Collaborative Resource Management 51; Lake Mburo National Park 175; SPGS 38; sport hunting 160; tourism 158–159
trees 17, 20; Budongo Forest Reserve 104–105, 107; integrated conservation and development 49; National Tree Fund 108; research 34–35; reserved tree species 26
Trees For Global Benefit (TFGB) 126, 129, 136, 138, 139, 140, 143n1
TUSC *see* The Uganda Safari Company

Uganda Land Commission 28
The Uganda Safari Company (TUSC) 153
Uganda Wildlife Authority (UWA) 3, 5, 37; agriculture and conservation

196–197; Bwindi Impenetrable
National Park 66, 68, 69, 77, 78,
79; carbon forestry 130, 135, 138,
140, 253; cultural values 175–176,
177, 178, 179–180, 181–182,
183, 255; deforestation 219, 220;
financial burden of conservation 98;
forestry reforms 211, 212; gorilla
tourism 71, 72, 73, 74, 78, 152–153,
154; integrated conservation and
development 49, 53; Karamoja
196; mandate 108; Mount Elgon
National Park 95, 96, 97, 99, 126;
revenue sharing 52; Rwenzori
Mountaineering Services 157,
158–159; sport hunting 159,
161–162; tourism revenue
sharing 51
Ugandan Land Alliance 141–142
United Nations Development
Programme (UNDP) 7, 30, 210
United Nations Environment
Programme 250
United States Agency for International
Development (USAID) 50, 68–70,
94, 153, 158–159, 212
UWA *see* Uganda Wildlife Authority

valuation of land 237, 257
VCM *see* voluntary carbon markets
Village Enterprise (VE) 109, 114
village forests 21–22, 27
violence 99, 189, 195, 215; Budongo
Forest Reserve 116; carbon forestry
138, 139; forest conservation 195;
'green' 260; Mount Elgon National
Park 95; *see also* conflict

voluntary carbon markets (VCM) 11,
34, 38, 95, 126, 127–128, 136, 138,
141, 142

walking trails 180
water: impact of agriculture 190, 193;
impact of land rush 240; Mount
Elgon National Park 87, 89
WCS *see* Wildlife Conservation Society
wetlands 162–164, 190, 229, 241
Wetlands Management
Department 181
wilderness 71–72
Wildlife Act (1996) 31, 74, 177
Wildlife Act (2000) 96
Wildlife Conservation Society (WCS)
25, 229
wildlife management 17–18
wildlife reserves 5; deforestation
220; Karamoja 196; sport hunting
161–162; tourism 149, 150; *see also*
forest reserves; protected areas
women: Bwindi Impenetrable National
Park 65; land rights abuses 232, 234;
sexual relations 76, 180; women's
groups 163–164
wood industries 29
World Bank 30, 34, 50, 222; carbon
forestry 128; corruption 259;
forestry reforms 210, 220; 'green
growth' 250
World Parks Congress 66, 172
World Wide Fund for Nature/World
Wildlife Fund (WWF) 35, 47,
77, 158

zoning 92, 105–106, 193